第2版

面向数据科学家的实用统计学（影印版）

Practical Statistics for Data Scientists

Peter Bruce　Andrew Bruce
Peter Gedeck 著

Beijing • Boston • Farnham • Sebastopol • Tokyo　O'REILLY®
O'Reilly Media, Inc.授权东南大学出版社出版

南京　东南大学出版社

图书在版编目(CIP)数据

面向数据科学家的实用统计学：第2版：英文/(美)彼得·布鲁斯(Peter Brue),(美)安德鲁·布鲁斯(Andrew Bruce),(德)彼得·格德克(Peter Gedeck)著.—影印本.—南京：东南大学出版社,2021.7

书名原文：Practical Statistics for Data Scientists, 2nd Edition

ISBN 978-7-5641-9515-1

Ⅰ.①面… Ⅱ.①彼… ②安… ③彼… Ⅲ.①统计学—英文 Ⅳ.①C8

中国版本图书馆CIP数据核字(2021)第093375号

图字：10-2020-380号

面向数据科学家的实用统计学 第2版(影印版)

出版发行：东南大学出版社
地　　址：南京四牌楼2号　　邮编：210096
出 版 人：江建中
网　　址：http://www.seupress.com
电子邮件：press@seupress.com
印　　刷：常州市武进第三印刷有限公司
开　　本：787毫米×980毫米　16开本
印　　张：22.75
字　　数：446千字
版　　次：2021年7月第1版
印　　次：2021年7月第1次印刷
书　　号：ISBN 978-7-5641-9515-1
定　　价：129.00元

本社图书若有印装质量问题，请直接与营销部联系。电话(传真)：025-83791830

Peter Bruce and Andrew Bruce would like to dedicate this book to the memories of our parents, Victor G. Bruce and Nancy C. Bruce, who cultivated a passion for math and science; and to our early mentors John W. Tukey and Julian Simon and our lifelong friend Geoff Watson, who helped inspire us to pursue a career in statistics.

Peter Gedeck would like to dedicate this book to Tim Clark and Christian Kramer, with deep thanks for their scientific collaboration and friendship.

Table of Contents

Preface

This book is aimed at the data scientist with some familiarity with the *R* and/or *Python* programming languages, and with some prior (perhaps spotty or ephemeral) exposure to statistics. Two of the authors came to the world of data science from the world of statistics, and have some appreciation of the contribution that statistics can make to the art of data science. At the same time, we are well aware of the limitations of traditional statistics instruction: statistics as a discipline is a century and a half old, and most statistics textbooks and courses are laden with the momentum and inertia of an ocean liner. All the methods in this book have some connection—historical or methodological—to the discipline of statistics. Methods that evolved mainly out of computer science, such as neural nets, are not included.

Two goals underlie this book:

- To lay out, in digestible, navigable, and easily referenced form, key concepts from statistics that are relevant to data science.
- To explain which concepts are important and useful from a data science perspective, which are less so, and why.

Conventions Used in This Book

The following typographical conventions are used in this book:

Italic
: Indicates new terms, URLs, email addresses, filenames, and file extensions.

`Constant width`
: Used for program listings, as well as within paragraphs to refer to program elements such as variable or function names, databases, data types, environment variables, statements, and keywords.

`**Constant width bold**`
: Shows commands or other text that should be typed literally by the user.

> **Key Terms**
>
> Data science is a fusion of multiple disciplines, including statistics, computer science, information technology, and domain-specific fields. As a result, several different terms could be used to reference a given concept. Key terms and their synonyms will be highlighted throughout the book in a sidebar such as this.

This element signifies a tip or suggestion.

This element signifies a general note.

This element indicates a warning or caution.

Using Code Examples

In all cases, this book gives code examples first in *R* and then in *Python*. In order to avoid unnecessary repetition, we generally show only output and plots created by the *R* code. We also skip the code required to load the required packages and data sets. You can find the complete code as well as the data sets for download at *https://github.com/gedeck/practical-statistics-for-data-scientists*.

This book is here to help you get your job done. In general, if example code is offered with this book, you may use it in your programs and documentation. You do not need to contact us for permission unless you're reproducing a significant portion of the code. For example, writing a program that uses several chunks of code from this book does not require permission. Selling or distributing examples from O'Reilly books does require permission. Answering a question by citing this book and quoting example code does not require permission. Incorporating a significant amount of example code from this book into your product's documentation does require permission.

We appreciate, but do not require, attribution. An attribution usually includes the title, author, publisher, and ISBN. For example: "*Practical Statistics for Data Scientists* by Peter Bruce, Andrew Bruce, and Peter Gedeck (O'Reilly). Copyright 2020 Peter Bruce, Andrew Bruce, and Peter Gedeck, 978-1-492-07294-2."

If you feel your use of code examples falls outside fair use or the permission given above, feel free to contact us at *permissions@oreilly.com*.

O'Reilly Online Learning

O'REILLY® For more than 40 years, *O'Reilly Media* has provided technology and business training, knowledge, and insight to help companies succeed.

Our unique network of experts and innovators share their knowledge and expertise through books, articles, and our online learning platform. O'Reilly's online learning platform gives you on-demand access to live training courses, in-depth learning paths, interactive coding environments, and a vast collection of text and video from O'Reilly and 200+ other publishers. For more information, visit *http://oreilly.com*.

How to Contact Us

Please address comments and questions concerning this book to the publisher:

O'Reilly Media, Inc.
1005 Gravenstein Highway North
Sebastopol, CA 95472
800-998-9938 (in the United States or Canada)
707-829-0515 (international or local)
707-829-0104 (fax)

We have a web page for this book, where we list errata, examples, and any additional information. You can access this page at *https://oreil.ly/practicalStats_dataSci_2e*.

Email *bookquestions@oreilly.com* to comment or ask technical questions about this book.

For news and more information about our books and courses, see our website at *http://oreilly.com*.

Find us on Facebook: *http://facebook.com/oreilly*

Follow us on Twitter: *http://twitter.com/oreillymedia*

Watch us on YouTube: *http://www.youtube.com/oreillymedia*

Acknowledgments

The authors acknowledge the many people who helped make this book a reality.

Gerhard Pilcher, CEO of the data mining firm Elder Research, saw early drafts of the book and gave us detailed and helpful corrections and comments. Likewise, Anya McGuirk and Wei Xiao, statisticians at SAS, and Jay Hilfiger, fellow O'Reilly author, provided helpful feedback on initial drafts of the book. Toshiaki Kurokawa, who translated the first edition into Japanese, did a comprehensive job of reviewing and correcting in the process. Aaron Schumacher and Walter Paczkowski thoroughly reviewed the second edition of the book and provided numerous helpful and valuable suggestions for which we are extremely grateful. Needless to say, any errors that remain are ours alone.

At O'Reilly, Shannon Cutt has shepherded us through the publication process with good cheer and the right amount of prodding, while Kristen Brown smoothly took our book through the production phase. Rachel Monaghan and Eliahu Sussman corrected and improved our writing with care and patience, while Ellen Troutman-Zaig prepared the index. Nicole Tache took over the reins for the second edition and has both guided the process effectively and provided many good editorial suggestions to improve the readability of the book for a broad audience. We also thank Marie Beaugureau, who initiated our project at O'Reilly, as well as Ben Bengfort, O'Reilly author and Statistics.com instructor, who introduced us to O'Reilly.

We, and this book, have also benefited from the many conversations Peter has had over the years with Galit Shmueli, coauthor on other book projects.

Finally, we would like to especially thank Elizabeth Bruce and Deborah Donnell, whose patience and support made this endeavor possible.

CHAPTER 1

Exploratory Data Analysis

This chapter focuses on the first step in any data science project: exploring the data.

Classical statistics focused almost exclusively on *inference*, a sometimes complex set of procedures for drawing conclusions about large populations based on small samples. In 1962, John W. Tukey (*https://oreil.ly/LQw6q*) (Figure 1-1) called for a reformation of statistics in his seminal paper "The Future of Data Analysis" [Tukey-1962]. He proposed a new scientific discipline called *data analysis* that included statistical inference as just one component. Tukey forged links to the engineering and computer science communities (he coined the terms *bit*, short for binary digit, and *software*), and his original tenets are surprisingly durable and form part of the foundation for data science. The field of exploratory data analysis was established with Tukey's 1977 now-classic book *Exploratory Data Analysis* [Tukey-1977]. Tukey presented simple plots (e.g., boxplots, scatterplots) that, along with summary statistics (mean, median, quantiles, etc.), help paint a picture of a data set.

With the ready availability of computing power and expressive data analysis software, exploratory data analysis has evolved well beyond its original scope. Key drivers of this discipline have been the rapid development of new technology, access to more and bigger data, and the greater use of quantitative analysis in a variety of disciplines. David Donoho, professor of statistics at Stanford University and former undergraduate student of Tukey's, authored an excellent article based on his presentation at the Tukey Centennial workshop in Princeton, New Jersey [Donoho-2015]. Donoho traces the genesis of data science back to Tukey's pioneering work in data analysis.

Figure 1-1. John Tukey, the eminent statistician whose ideas developed over 50 years ago form the foundation of data science

Elements of Structured Data

Data comes from many sources: sensor measurements, events, text, images, and videos. The *Internet of Things* (IoT) is spewing out streams of information. Much of this data is unstructured: images are a collection of pixels, with each pixel containing RGB (red, green, blue) color information. Texts are sequences of words and nonword characters, often organized by sections, subsections, and so on. Clickstreams are sequences of actions by a user interacting with an app or a web page. In fact, a major challenge of data science is to harness this torrent of raw data into actionable information. To apply the statistical concepts covered in this book, unstructured raw data must be processed and manipulated into a structured form. One of the commonest forms of structured data is a table with rows and columns—as data might emerge from a relational database or be collected for a study.

There are two basic types of structured data: numeric and categorical. Numeric data comes in two forms: *continuous*, such as wind speed or time duration, and *discrete*, such as the count of the occurrence of an event. *Categorical* data takes only a fixed set of values, such as a type of TV screen (plasma, LCD, LED, etc.) or a state name (Alabama, Alaska, etc.). *Binary* data is an important special case of categorical data that takes on only one of two values, such as 0/1, yes/no, or true/false. Another useful type of categorical data is *ordinal* data in which the categories are ordered; an example of this is a numerical rating (1, 2, 3, 4, or 5).

Why do we bother with a taxonomy of data types? It turns out that for the purposes of data analysis and predictive modeling, the data type is important to help determine the type of visual display, data analysis, or statistical model. In fact, data science software, such as *R* and *Python*, uses these data types to improve computational performance. More important, the data type for a variable determines how software will handle computations for that variable.

Key Terms for Data Types

Numeric
: Data that are expressed on a numeric scale.

  Continuous
  : Data that can take on any value in an interval. (*Synonyms*: interval, float, numeric)

  Discrete
  : Data that can take on only integer values, such as counts. (*Synonyms*: integer, count)

Categorical
: Data that can take on only a specific set of values representing a set of possible categories. (*Synonyms*: enums, enumerated, factors, nominal)

  Binary
  : A special case of categorical data with just two categories of values, e.g., 0/1, true/false. (*Synonyms*: dichotomous, logical, indicator, boolean)

  Ordinal
  : Categorical data that has an explicit ordering. (*Synonym*: ordered factor)

Software engineers and database programmers may wonder why we even need the notion of *categorical* and *ordinal* data for analytics. After all, categories are merely a collection of text (or numeric) values, and the underlying database automatically handles the internal representation. However, explicit identification of data as categorical, as distinct from text, does offer some advantages:

- Knowing that data is categorical can act as a signal telling software how statistical procedures, such as producing a chart or fitting a model, should behave. In particular, ordinal data can be represented as an `ordered.factor` in *R*, preserving a user-specified ordering in charts, tables, and models. In *Python*, `scikit-learn` supports ordinal data with the `sklearn.preprocessing.OrdinalEncoder`.
- Storage and indexing can be optimized (as in a relational database).
- The possible values a given categorical variable can take are enforced in the software (like an enum).

The third "benefit" can lead to unintended or unexpected behavior: the default behavior of data import functions in *R* (e.g., `read.csv`) is to automatically convert a text column into a `factor`. Subsequent operations on that column will assume that the only allowable values for that column are the ones originally imported, and assigning a new text value will introduce a warning and produce an `NA` (missing value). The `pandas` package in *Python* will not make such a conversion automatically. However, you can specify a column as categorical explicitly in the `read_csv` function.

> **Key Ideas**
>
> - Data is typically classified in software by type.
> - Data types include numeric (continuous, discrete) and categorical (binary, ordinal).
> - Data typing in software acts as a signal to the software on how to process the data.

Further Reading

- The `pandas` documentation (*https://oreil.ly/UGX-4*) describes the different data types and how they can be manipulated in *Python*.
- Data types can be confusing, since types may overlap, and the taxonomy in one software may differ from that in another. The R Tutorial website (*https://oreil.ly/2YUoA*) covers the taxonomy for *R*. The `pandas` documentation (*https://oreil.ly/UGX-4*) describes the different data types and how they can be manipulated in *Python*.
- Databases are more detailed in their classification of data types, incorporating considerations of precision levels, fixed- or variable-length fields, and more; see the W3Schools guide to SQL (*https://oreil.ly/cThTM*).

Rectangular Data

The typical frame of reference for an analysis in data science is a *rectangular data* object, like a spreadsheet or database table.

Rectangular data is the general term for a two-dimensional matrix with rows indicating records (cases) and columns indicating features (variables); *data frame* is the specific format in *R* and *Python*. The data doesn't always start in this form: unstructured data (e.g., text) must be processed and manipulated so that it can be represented as a set of features in the rectangular data (see "Elements of Structured Data" on page 2). Data in relational databases must be extracted and put into a single table for most data analysis and modeling tasks.

Key Terms for Rectangular Data

Data frame
: Rectangular data (like a spreadsheet) is the basic data structure for statistical and machine learning models.

Feature
: A column within a table is commonly referred to as a *feature*.

  Synonyms
  : attribute, input, predictor, variable

Outcome
: Many data science projects involve predicting an *outcome*—often a yes/no outcome (in Table 1-1, it is "auction was competitive or not"). The *features* are sometimes used to predict the *outcome* in an experiment or a study.

  Synonyms
  : dependent variable, response, target, output

Records
: A row within a table is commonly referred to as a *record*.

  Synonyms
  : case, example, instance, observation, pattern, sample

Table 1-1. A typical data frame format

Category	currency	sellerRating	Duration	endDay	ClosePrice	OpenPrice	Competitive?
Music/Movie/Game	US	3249	5	Mon	0.01	0.01	0
Music/Movie/Game	US	3249	5	Mon	0.01	0.01	0
Automotive	US	3115	7	Tue	0.01	0.01	0
Automotive	US	3115	7	Tue	0.01	0.01	0
Automotive	US	3115	7	Tue	0.01	0.01	0
Automotive	US	3115	7	Tue	0.01	0.01	0
Automotive	US	3115	7	Tue	0.01	0.01	1
Automotive	US	3115	7	Tue	0.01	0.01	1

In Table 1-1, there is a mix of measured or counted data (e.g., duration and price) and categorical data (e.g., category and currency). As mentioned earlier, a special form of categorical variable is a binary (yes/no or 0/1) variable, seen in the rightmost column in Table 1-1—an indicator variable showing whether an auction was competitive (had multiple bidders) or not. This indicator variable also happens to be an *outcome* variable, when the scenario is to predict whether an auction is competitive or not.

Data Frames and Indexes

Traditional database tables have one or more columns designated as an index, essentially a row number. This can vastly improve the efficiency of certain database queries. In *Python*, with the `pandas` library, the basic rectangular data structure is a `DataFrame` object. By default, an automatic integer index is created for a `DataFrame` based on the order of the rows. In `pandas`, it is also possible to set multilevel/hierarchical indexes to improve the efficiency of certain operations.

In *R*, the basic rectangular data structure is a `data.frame` object. A `data.frame` also has an implicit integer index based on the row order. The native *R* `data.frame` does not support user-specified or multilevel indexes, though a custom key can be created through the `row.names` attribute. To overcome this deficiency, two new packages are gaining widespread use: `data.table` and `dplyr`. Both support multilevel indexes and offer significant speedups in working with a `data.frame`.

> **Terminology Differences**
>
> Terminology for rectangular data can be confusing. Statisticians and data scientists use different terms for the same thing. For a statistician, *predictor variables* are used in a model to predict a *response* or *dependent variable*. For a data scientist, *features* are used to predict a *target*. One synonym is particularly confusing: computer scientists will use the term *sample* for a single row; a *sample* to a statistician means a collection of rows.

Nonrectangular Data Structures

There are other data structures besides rectangular data.

Time series data records successive measurements of the same variable. It is the raw material for statistical forecasting methods, and it is also a key component of the data produced by devices—the Internet of Things.

Spatial data structures, which are used in mapping and location analytics, are more complex and varied than rectangular data structures. In the *object* representation, the focus of the data is an object (e.g., a house) and its spatial coordinates. The *field* view, by contrast, focuses on small units of space and the value of a relevant metric (pixel brightness, for example).

Graph (or network) data structures are used to represent physical, social, and abstract relationships. For example, a graph of a social network, such as Facebook or LinkedIn, may represent connections between people on the network. Distribution hubs connected by roads are an example of a physical network. Graph structures are useful for certain types of problems, such as network optimization and recommender systems.

Each of these data types has its specialized methodology in data science. The focus of this book is on rectangular data, the fundamental building block of predictive modeling.

Graphs in Statistics

In computer science and information technology, the term *graph* typically refers to a depiction of the connections among entities, and to the underlying data structure. In statistics, *graph* is used to refer to a variety of plots and *visualizations*, not just of connections among entities, and the term applies only to the visualization, not to the data structure.

Key Ideas

- The basic data structure in data science is a rectangular matrix in which rows are records and columns are variables (features).
- Terminology can be confusing; there are a variety of synonyms arising from the different disciplines that contribute to data science (statistics, computer science, and information technology).

Further Reading

- Documentation on data frames in *R* (*https://oreil.ly/NsONR*)
- Documentation on data frames in *Python* (*https://oreil.ly/oxDKQ*)

Estimates of Location

Variables with measured or count data might have thousands of distinct values. A basic step in exploring your data is getting a "typical value" for each feature (variable): an estimate of where most of the data is located (i.e., its central tendency).

Key Terms for Estimates of Location

Mean
: The sum of all values divided by the number of values.

  Synonym
  : average

Weighted mean
: The sum of all values times a weight divided by the sum of the weights.

  Synonym
  : weighted average

Median
: The value such that one-half of the data lies above and below.

  Synonym
  : 50th percentile

Percentile
: The value such that *P* percent of the data lies below.

  Synonym
  : quantile

Weighted median
: The value such that one-half of the sum of the weights lies above and below the sorted data.

Trimmed mean
: The average of all values after dropping a fixed number of extreme values.

  Synonym
  : truncated mean

Robust
: Not sensitive to extreme values.

  Synonym
  : resistant

Outlier
: A data value that is very different from most of the data.

  Synonym
  : extreme value

At first glance, summarizing data might seem fairly trivial: just take the *mean* of the data. In fact, while the mean is easy to compute and expedient to use, it may not always be the best measure for a central value. For this reason, statisticians have developed and promoted several alternative estimates to the mean.

> **Metrics and Estimates**
>
> Statisticians often use the term *estimate* for a value calculated from the data at hand, to draw a distinction between what we see from the data and the theoretical true or exact state of affairs. Data scientists and business analysts are more likely to refer to such a value as a *metric*. The difference reflects the approach of statistics versus that of data science: accounting for uncertainty lies at the heart of the discipline of statistics, whereas concrete business or organizational objectives are the focus of data science. Hence, statisticians estimate, and data scientists measure.

Mean

The most basic estimate of location is the mean, or *average* value. The mean is the sum of all values divided by the number of values. Consider the following set of numbers: {3 5 1 2}. The mean is (3 + 5 + 1 + 2) / 4 = 11 / 4 = 2.75. You will encounter the symbol $\bar{x}$ (pronounced "x-bar") being used to represent the mean of a sample from a population. The formula to compute the mean for a set of n values $x_1, x_2, ..., x_n$ is:

$$\text{Mean} = \bar{x} = \frac{\sum_{i=1}^{n} x_i}{n}$$

> *N* (or *n*) refers to the total number of records or observations. In statistics it is capitalized if it is referring to a population, and lowercase if it refers to a sample from a population. In data science, that distinction is not vital, so you may see it both ways.

A variation of the mean is a *trimmed mean*, which you calculate by dropping a fixed number of sorted values at each end and then taking an average of the remaining values. Representing the sorted values by $x_{(1)}, x_{(2)}, ..., x_{(n)}$ where $x_{(1)}$ is the smallest value and $x_{(n)}$ the largest, the formula to compute the trimmed mean with p smallest and largest values omitted is:

$$\text{Trimmed mean} = \bar{x} = \frac{\sum_{i=p+1}^{n-p} x_{(i)}}{n-2p}$$

A trimmed mean eliminates the influence of extreme values. For example, in international diving the top score and bottom score from five judges are dropped, and the final score is the average of the scores from the three remaining judges (*https://oreil.ly/uV4P0*). This makes it difficult for a single judge to manipulate the score, perhaps to favor their country's contestant. Trimmed means are widely used, and in many cases are preferable to using the ordinary mean—see "Median and Robust Estimates" on page 10 for further discussion.

Another type of mean is a *weighted mean*, which you calculate by multiplying each data value x_i by a user-specified weight w_i and dividing their sum by the sum of the weights. The formula for a weighted mean is:

$$\text{Weighted mean} = \bar{x}_w = \frac{\sum_{i=1}^{n} w_i x_i}{\sum_{i=1}^{n} w_i}$$

There are two main motivations for using a weighted mean:

- Some values are intrinsically more variable than others, and highly variable observations are given a lower weight. For example, if we are taking the average from multiple sensors and one of the sensors is less accurate, then we might downweight the data from that sensor.
- The data collected does not equally represent the different groups that we are interested in measuring. For example, because of the way an online experiment was conducted, we may not have a set of data that accurately reflects all groups in the user base. To correct that, we can give a higher weight to the values from the groups that were underrepresented.

Median and Robust Estimates

The *median* is the middle number on a sorted list of the data. If there is an even number of data values, the middle value is one that is not actually in the data set, but rather the average of the two values that divide the sorted data into upper and lower halves. Compared to the mean, which uses all observations, the median depends only on the values in the center of the sorted data. While this might seem to be a disadvantage, since the mean is much more sensitive to the data, there are many instances in which the median is a better metric for location. Let's say we want to look at typical household incomes in neighborhoods around Lake Washington in Seattle. In comparing the Medina neighborhood to the Windermere neighborhood, using the mean would produce very different results because Bill Gates lives in Medina. If we use the median, it won't matter how rich Bill Gates is—the position of the middle observation will remain the same.

For the same reasons that one uses a weighted mean, it is also possible to compute a *weighted median*. As with the median, we first sort the data, although each data value has an associated weight. Instead of the middle number, the weighted median is a value such that the sum of the weights is equal for the lower and upper halves of the sorted list. Like the median, the weighted median is robust to outliers.

Outliers

The median is referred to as a *robust* estimate of location since it is not influenced by *outliers* (extreme cases) that could skew the results. An outlier is any value that is very distant from the other values in a data set. The exact definition of an outlier is somewhat subjective, although certain conventions are used in various data summaries and plots (see "Percentiles and Boxplots" on page 20). Being an outlier in itself does not make a data value invalid or erroneous (as in the previous example with Bill Gates). Still, outliers are often the result of data errors such as mixing data of different units (kilometers versus meters) or bad readings from a sensor. When outliers are the result of bad data, the mean will result in a poor estimate of location, while the median will still be valid. In any case, outliers should be identified and are usually worthy of further investigation.

Anomaly Detection

In contrast to typical data analysis, where outliers are sometimes informative and sometimes a nuisance, in *anomaly detection* the points of interest are the outliers, and the greater mass of data serves primarily to define the "normal" against which anomalies are measured.

The median is not the only robust estimate of location. In fact, a trimmed mean is widely used to avoid the influence of outliers. For example, trimming the bottom and top 10% (a common choice) of the data will provide protection against outliers in all but the smallest data sets. The trimmed mean can be thought of as a compromise between the median and the mean: it is robust to extreme values in the data, but uses more data to calculate the estimate for location.

Other Robust Metrics for Location

Statisticians have developed a plethora of other estimators for location, primarily with the goal of developing an estimator more robust than the mean and also more efficient (i.e., better able to discern small location differences between data sets). While these methods are potentially useful for small data sets, they are not likely to provide added benefit for large or even moderately sized data sets.

Example: Location Estimates of Population and Murder Rates

Table 1-2 shows the first few rows in the data set containing population and murder rates (in units of murders per 100,000 people per year) for each US state (2010 Census).

Table 1-2. A few rows of the `data.frame` state of population and murder rate by state

	State	Population	Murder rate	Abbreviation
1	Alabama	4,779,736	5.7	AL
2	Alaska	710,231	5.6	AK
3	Arizona	6,392,017	4.7	AZ
4	Arkansas	2,915,918	5.6	AR
5	California	37,253,956	4.4	CA
6	Colorado	5,029,196	2.8	CO
7	Connecticut	3,574,097	2.4	CT
8	Delaware	897,934	5.8	DE

Compute the mean, trimmed mean, and median for the population using *R*:

```
> state <- read.csv('state.csv')
> mean(state[['Population']])
[1] 6162876
> mean(state[['Population']], trim=0.1)
[1] 4783697
> median(state[['Population']])
[1] 4436370
```

To compute mean and median in *Python* we can use the `pandas` methods of the data frame. The trimmed mean requires the `trim_mean` function in `scipy.stats`:

```
state = pd.read_csv('state.csv')
state['Population'].mean()
trim_mean(state['Population'], 0.1)
state['Population'].median()
```

The mean is bigger than the trimmed mean, which is bigger than the median.

This is because the trimmed mean excludes the largest and smallest five states (`trim=0.1` drops 10% from each end). If we want to compute the average murder rate for the country, we need to use a weighted mean or median to account for different populations in the states. Since base *R* doesn't have a function for weighted median, we need to install a package such as `matrixStats`:

```
> weighted.mean(state[['Murder.Rate']], w=state[['Population']])
[1] 4.445834
> library('matrixStats')
```

```
> weightedMedian(state[['Murder.Rate']], w=state[['Population']])
[1] 4.4
```

Weighted mean is available with `NumPy`. For weighted median, we can use the specialized package wquantiles (*https://oreil.ly/4SIPQ*):

```
np.average(state['Murder.Rate'], weights=state['Population'])
wquantiles.median(state['Murder.Rate'], weights=state['Population'])
```

In this case, the weighted mean and the weighted median are about the same.

> **Key Ideas**
>
> - The basic metric for location is the mean, but it can be sensitive to extreme values (outlier).
> - Other metrics (median, trimmed mean) are less sensitive to outliers and unusual distributions and hence are more robust.

Further Reading

- The Wikipedia article on central tendency (*https://oreil.ly/qUW2i*) contains an extensive discussion of various measures of location.
- John Tukey's 1977 classic *Exploratory Data Analysis* (Pearson) is still widely read.

Estimates of Variability

Location is just one dimension in summarizing a feature. A second dimension, *variability*, also referred to as *dispersion*, measures whether the data values are tightly clustered or spread out. At the heart of statistics lies variability: measuring it, reducing it, distinguishing random from real variability, identifying the various sources of real variability, and making decisions in the presence of it.

> **Key Terms for Variability Metrics**
>
> ***Deviations***
> The difference between the observed values and the estimate of location.
>
> *Synonyms*
> errors, residuals
>
> ***Variance***
> The sum of squared deviations from the mean divided by $n - 1$ where n is the number of data values.

Synonym
mean-squared-error

Standard deviation
The square root of the variance.

Mean absolute deviation
The mean of the absolute values of the deviations from the mean.

Synonyms
l1-norm, Manhattan norm

Median absolute deviation from the median
The median of the absolute values of the deviations from the median.

Range
The difference between the largest and the smallest value in a data set.

Order statistics
Metrics based on the data values sorted from smallest to biggest.

Synonym
ranks

Percentile
The value such that *P* percent of the values take on this value or less and (100–P) percent take on this value or more.

Synonym
quantile

Interquartile range
The difference between the 75th percentile and the 25th percentile.

Synonym
IQR

Just as there are different ways to measure location (mean, median, etc.), there are also different ways to measure variability.

Standard Deviation and Related Estimates

The most widely used estimates of variation are based on the differences, or *deviations*, between the estimate of location and the observed data. For a set of data {1, 4, 4}, the mean is 3 and the median is 4. The deviations from the mean are the differences: 1 – 3 = –2, 4 – 3 = 1, 4 – 3 = 1. These deviations tell us how dispersed the data is around the central value.

One way to measure variability is to estimate a typical value for these deviations. Averaging the deviations themselves would not tell us much—the negative deviations offset the positive ones. In fact, the sum of the deviations from the mean is precisely zero. Instead, a simple approach is to take the average of the absolute values of the deviations from the mean. In the preceding example, the absolute value of the deviations is {2 1 1}, and their average is (2 + 1 + 1) / 3 = 1.33. This is known as the *mean absolute deviation* and is computed with the formula:

$$\text{Mean absolute deviation} = \frac{\sum_{i=1}^{n} |x_i - \bar{x}|}{n}$$

where $\bar{x}$ is the sample mean.

The best-known estimates of variability are the *variance* and the *standard deviation*, which are based on squared deviations. The variance is an average of the squared deviations, and the standard deviation is the square root of the variance:

$$\text{Variance} = s^2 = \frac{\sum_{i=1}^{n} (x_i - \bar{x})^2}{n - 1}$$

$$\text{Standard deviation} = s = \sqrt{\text{Variance}}$$

The standard deviation is much easier to interpret than the variance since it is on the same scale as the original data. Still, with its more complicated and less intuitive formula, it might seem peculiar that the standard deviation is preferred in statistics over the mean absolute deviation. It owes its preeminence to statistical theory: mathematically, working with squared values is much more convenient than absolute values, especially for statistical models.

Degrees of Freedom, and *n* or *n* – 1?

In statistics books, there is always some discussion of why we have $n - 1$ in the denominator in the variance formula, instead of n, leading into the concept of *degrees of freedom*. This distinction is not important since n is generally large enough that it won't make much difference whether you divide by n or $n - 1$. But in case you are interested, here is the story. It is based on the premise that you want to make estimates about a population, based on a sample.

If you use the intuitive denominator of n in the variance formula, you will underestimate the true value of the variance and the standard deviation in the population. This is referred to as a *biased* estimate. However, if you divide by $n - 1$ instead of n, the variance becomes an *unbiased* estimate.

To fully explain why using n leads to a biased estimate involves the notion of degrees of freedom, which takes into account the number of constraints in computing an estimate. In this case, there are $n - 1$ degrees of freedom since there is one constraint: the standard deviation depends on calculating the sample mean. For most problems, data scientists do not need to worry about degrees of freedom.

Neither the variance, the standard deviation, nor the mean absolute deviation is robust to outliers and extreme values (see "Median and Robust Estimates" on page 10 for a discussion of robust estimates for location). The variance and standard deviation are especially sensitive to outliers since they are based on the squared deviations.

A robust estimate of variability is the *median absolute deviation from the median* or MAD:

$$\text{Median absolute deviation} = \text{Median}\left(\left|x_1 - m\right|, \left|x_2 - m\right|, ..., \left|x_N - m\right|\right)$$

where m is the median. Like the median, the MAD is not influenced by extreme values. It is also possible to compute a trimmed standard deviation analogous to the trimmed mean (see "Mean" on page 9).

The variance, the standard deviation, the mean absolute deviation, and the median absolute deviation from the median are not equivalent estimates, even in the case where the data comes from a normal distribution. In fact, the standard deviation is always greater than the mean absolute deviation, which itself is greater than the median absolute deviation. Sometimes, the median absolute deviation is multiplied by a constant scaling factor to put the MAD on the same scale as the standard deviation in the case of a normal distribution. The commonly used factor of 1.4826 means that 50% of the normal distribution fall within the range ±MAD (see, e.g., *https://oreil.ly/SfDk2*).

Estimates Based on Percentiles

A different approach to estimating dispersion is based on looking at the spread of the sorted data. Statistics based on sorted (ranked) data are referred to as *order statistics*. The most basic measure is the *range*: the difference between the largest and smallest numbers. The minimum and maximum values themselves are useful to know and are helpful in identifying outliers, but the range is extremely sensitive to outliers and not very useful as a general measure of dispersion in the data.

To avoid the sensitivity to outliers, we can look at the range of the data after dropping values from each end. Formally, these types of estimates are based on differences between *percentiles*. In a data set, the *P*th percentile is a value such that at least *P* percent of the values take on this value or less and at least (100 – *P*) percent of the values take on this value or more. For example, to find the 80th percentile, sort the data. Then, starting with the smallest value, proceed 80 percent of the way to the largest value. Note that the median is the same thing as the 50th percentile. The percentile is essentially the same as a *quantile*, with quantiles indexed by fractions (so the .8 quantile is the same as the 80th percentile).

A common measurement of variability is the difference between the 25th percentile and the 75th percentile, called the *interquartile range* (or IQR). Here is a simple example: {3,1,5,3,6,7,2,9}. We sort these to get {1,2,3,3,5,6,7,9}. The 25th percentile is at 2.5, and the 75th percentile is at 6.5, so the interquartile range is 6.5 – 2.5 = 4. Software can have slightly differing approaches that yield different answers (see the following tip); typically, these differences are smaller.

For very large data sets, calculating exact percentiles can be computationally very expensive since it requires sorting all the data values. Machine learning and statistical software use special algorithms, such as [Zhang-Wang-2007], to get an approximate percentile that can be calculated very quickly and is guaranteed to have a certain accuracy.

Percentile: Precise Definition

If we have an even number of data (*n* is even), then the percentile is ambiguous under the preceding definition. In fact, we could take on any value between the order statistics $x_{(j)}$ and $x_{(j+1)}$ where j satisfies:

$$100 * \frac{j}{n} \leq P < 100 * \frac{j+1}{n}$$

Formally, the percentile is the weighted average:

$$\text{Percentile}(P) = (1 - w)x_{(j)} + wx_{(j+1)}$$

for some weight *w* between 0 and 1. Statistical software has slightly differing approaches to choosing *w*. In fact, the *R* function `quantile` offers nine different alternatives to compute the quantile. Except for small data sets, you don't usually need to worry about the precise way a percentile is calculated. At the time of this writing, *Python*'s `numpy.quantile` supports only one approach, linear interpolation.

Example: Variability Estimates of State Population

Table 1-3 (repeated from Table 1-2 for convenience) shows the first few rows in the data set containing population and murder rates for each state.

Table 1-3. A few rows of the `data.frame` state of population and murder rate by state

	State	Population	Murder rate	Abbreviation
1	Alabama	4,779,736	5.7	AL
2	Alaska	710,231	5.6	AK
3	Arizona	6,392,017	4.7	AZ
4	Arkansas	2,915,918	5.6	AR
5	California	37,253,956	4.4	CA
6	Colorado	5,029,196	2.8	CO
7	Connecticut	3,574,097	2.4	CT
8	Delaware	897,934	5.8	DE

Using *R*'s built-in functions for the standard deviation, the interquartile range (IQR), and the median absolute deviation from the median (MAD), we can compute estimates of variability for the state population data:

```
> sd(state[['Population']])
[1] 6848235
> IQR(state[['Population']])
[1] 4847308
> mad(state[['Population']])
[1] 3849870
```

The `pandas` data frame provides methods for calculating standard deviation and quantiles. Using the quantiles, we can easily determine the IQR. For the robust MAD, we use the function `robust.scale.mad` from the `statsmodels` package:

```
state['Population'].std()
state['Population'].quantile(0.75) - state['Population'].quantile(0.25)
robust.scale.mad(state['Population'])
```

The standard deviation is almost twice as large as the MAD (in *R*, by default, the scale of the MAD is adjusted to be on the same scale as the mean). This is not surprising since the standard deviation is sensitive to outliers.

Key Ideas

- Variance and standard deviation are the most widespread and routinely reported statistics of variability.
- Both are sensitive to outliers.
- More robust metrics include mean absolute deviation, median absolute deviation from the median, and percentiles (quantiles).

Further Reading

- David Lane's online statistics resource has a section on percentiles (*https://oreil.ly/o2fBI*).
- Kevin Davenport has a useful post on *R*-Bloggers (*https://oreil.ly/E7zcG*) about deviations from the median and their robust properties.

Exploring the Data Distribution

Each of the estimates we've covered sums up the data in a single number to describe the location or variability of the data. It is also useful to explore how the data is distributed overall.

Key Terms for Exploring the Distribution

Boxplot
A plot introduced by Tukey as a quick way to visualize the distribution of data.

Synonym
box and whiskers plot

Frequency table
A tally of the count of numeric data values that fall into a set of intervals (bins).

Histogram
A plot of the frequency table with the bins on the x-axis and the count (or proportion) on the y-axis. While visually similar, bar charts should not be confused with histograms. See "Exploring Binary and Categorical Data" on page 27 for a discussion of the difference.

Density plot
A smoothed version of the histogram, often based on a *kernel density estimate*.

Percentiles and Boxplots

In "Estimates Based on Percentiles" on page 16, we explored how percentiles can be used to measure the spread of the data. Percentiles are also valuable for summarizing the entire distribution. It is common to report the quartiles (25th, 50th, and 75th percentiles) and the deciles (the 10th, 20th, ..., 90th percentiles). Percentiles are especially valuable for summarizing the *tails* (the outer range) of the distribution. Popular culture has coined the term *one-percenters* to refer to the people in the top 99th percentile of wealth.

Table 1-4 displays some percentiles of the murder rate by state. In *R*, this would be produced by the `quantile` function:

```
quantile(state[['Murder.Rate']], p=c(.05, .25, .5, .75, .95))
   5%   25%   50%   75%   95%
1.600 2.425 4.000 5.550 6.510
```

The `pandas` data frame method `quantile` provides it in *Python*:

```
state['Murder.Rate'].quantile([0.05, 0.25, 0.5, 0.75, 0.95])
```

Table 1-4. Percentiles of murder rate by state

5%	25%	50%	75%	95%
1.60	2.42	4.00	5.55	6.51

The median is 4 murders per 100,000 people, although there is quite a bit of variability: the 5th percentile is only 1.6 and the 95th percentile is 6.51.

Boxplots, introduced by Tukey [Tukey-1977], are based on percentiles and give a quick way to visualize the distribution of data. Figure 1-2 shows a boxplot of the population by state produced by *R*:

```
boxplot(state[['Population']]/1000000, ylab='Population (millions)')
```

`pandas` provides a number of basic exploratory plots for data frame; one of them is boxplots:

```
ax = (state['Population']/1_000_000).plot.box()
ax.set_ylabel('Population (millions)')
```

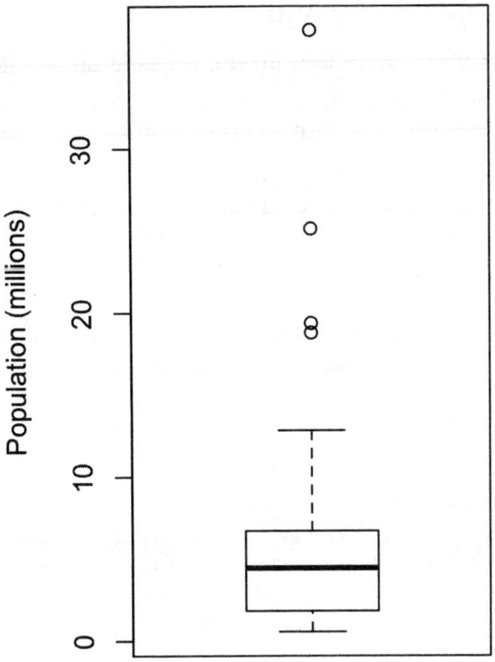

Figure 1-2. Boxplot of state populations

From this boxplot we can immediately see that the median state population is about 5 million, half the states fall between about 2 million and about 7 million, and there are some high population outliers. The top and bottom of the box are the 75th and 25th percentiles, respectively. The median is shown by the horizontal line in the box. The dashed lines, referred to as *whiskers*, extend from the top and bottom of the box to indicate the range for the bulk of the data. There are many variations of a boxplot; see, for example, the documentation for the *R* function `boxplot` [R-base-2015]. By default, the *R* function extends the whiskers to the furthest point beyond the box, except that it will not go beyond 1.5 times the IQR. *Matplotlib* uses the same implementation; other software may use a different rule.

Any data outside of the whiskers is plotted as single points or circles (often considered outliers).

Frequency Tables and Histograms

A frequency table of a variable divides up the variable range into equally spaced segments and tells us how many values fall within each segment. Table 1-5 shows a frequency table of the population by state computed in *R*:

```
breaks <- seq(from=min(state[['Population']]),
              to=max(state[['Population']]), length=11)
pop_freq <- cut(state[['Population']], breaks=breaks,
                right=TRUE, include.lowest=TRUE)
table(pop_freq)
```

The function `pandas.cut` creates a series that maps the values into the segments. Using the method `value_counts`, we get the frequency table:

```
binnedPopulation = pd.cut(state['Population'], 10)
binnedPopulation.value_counts()
```

Table 1-5. A frequency table of population by state

BinNumber	BinRange	Count	States
1	563,626–4,232,658	24	WY,VT,ND,AK,SD,DE,MT,RI,NH,ME,HI,ID,NE,WV,NM,NV,UT,KS,AR,MS,IA,CT,OK,OR
2	4,232,659–7,901,691	14	KY,LA,SC,AL,CO,MN,WI,MD,MO,TN,AZ,IN,MA,WA
3	7,901,692–11,570,724	6	VA,NJ,NC,GA,MI,OH
4	11,570,725–15,239,757	2	PA,IL
5	15,239,758–18,908,790	1	FL
6	18,908,791–22,577,823	1	NY
7	22,577,824–26,246,856	1	TX
8	26,246,857–29,915,889	0	
9	29,915,890–33,584,922	0	
10	33,584,923–37,253,956	1	CA

The least populous state is Wyoming, with 563,626 people, and the most populous is California, with 37,253,956 people. This gives us a range of 37,253,956 – 563,626 = 36,690,330, which we must divide up into equal size bins—let's say 10 bins. With 10 equal size bins, each bin will have a width of 3,669,033, so the first bin will span from 563,626 to 4,232,658. By contrast, the top bin, 33,584,923 to 37,253,956, has only one state: California. The two bins immediately below California are empty, until we reach Texas. It is important to include the empty bins; the fact that there are no values in those bins is useful information. It can also be useful to experiment with different bin sizes. If they are too large, important features of the distribution can be obscured. If they are too small, the result is too granular, and the ability to see the bigger picture is lost.

> Both frequency tables and percentiles summarize the data by creating bins. In general, quartiles and deciles will have the same count in each bin (equal-count bins), but the bin sizes will be different. The frequency table, by contrast, will have different counts in the bins (equal-size bins), and the bin sizes will be the same.

A histogram is a way to visualize a frequency table, with bins on the x-axis and the data count on the y-axis. In Figure 1-3, for example, the bin centered at 10 million (1e+07) runs from roughly 8 million to 12 million, and there are six states in that bin. To create a histogram corresponding to Table 1-5 in *R*, use the `hist` function with the `breaks` argument:

```
hist(state[['Population']], breaks=breaks)
```

`pandas` supports histograms for data frames with the `DataFrame.plot.hist` method. Use the keyword argument `bins` to define the number of bins. The various plot methods return an axis object that allows further fine-tuning of the visualization using `Matplotlib`:

```
ax = (state['Population'] / 1_000_000).plot.hist(figsize=(4, 4))
ax.set_xlabel('Population (millions)')
```

The histogram is shown in Figure 1-3. In general, histograms are plotted such that:

- Empty bins are included in the graph.
- Bins are of equal width.
- The number of bins (or, equivalently, bin size) is up to the user.
- Bars are contiguous—no empty space shows between bars, unless there is an empty bin.

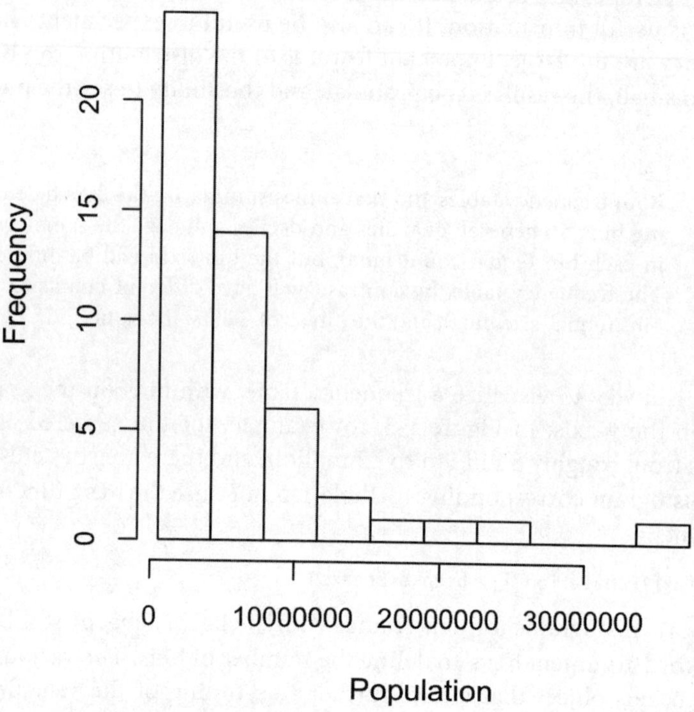

Figure 1-3. Histogram of state populations

> **Statistical Moments**
>
> In statistical theory, location and variability are referred to as the first and second *moments* of a distribution. The third and fourth moments are called *skewness* and *kurtosis*. Skewness refers to whether the data is skewed to larger or smaller values, and kurtosis indicates the propensity of the data to have extreme values. Generally, metrics are not used to measure skewness and kurtosis; instead, these are discovered through visual displays such as Figures 1-2 and 1-3.

Density Plots and Estimates

Related to the histogram is a density plot, which shows the distribution of data values as a continuous line. A density plot can be thought of as a smoothed histogram, although it is typically computed directly from the data through a *kernel density estimate* (see [Duong-2001] for a short tutorial). Figure 1-4 displays a density estimate superposed on a histogram. In *R*, you can compute a density estimate using the `density` function:

```
hist(state[['Murder.Rate']], freq=FALSE)
lines(density(state[['Murder.Rate']]), lwd=3, col='blue')
```

`pandas` provides the `density` method to create a density plot. Use the argument `bw_method` to control the smoothness of the density curve:

```
ax = state['Murder.Rate'].plot.hist(density=True, xlim=[0,12], bins=range(1,12))
state['Murder.Rate'].plot.density(ax=ax) ❶
ax.set_xlabel('Murder Rate (per 100,000)')
```

❶ Plot functions often take an optional axis (`ax`) argument, which will cause the plot to be added to the same graph.

A key distinction from the histogram plotted in Figure 1-3 is the scale of the y-axis: a density plot corresponds to plotting the histogram as a proportion rather than counts (you specify this in *R* using the argument `freq=FALSE`). Note that the total area under the density curve = 1, and instead of counts in bins you calculate areas under the curve between any two points on the x-axis, which correspond to the proportion of the distribution lying between those two points.

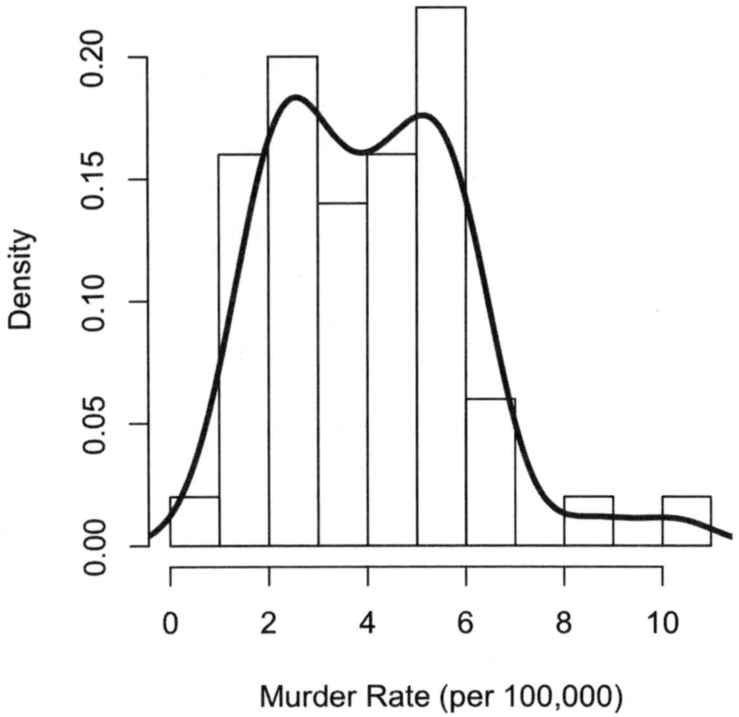

Figure 1-4. Density of state murder rates

Density Estimation

Density estimation is a rich topic with a long history in statistical literature. In fact, over 20 *R* packages have been published that offer functions for density estimation. [Deng-Wickham-2011] give a comprehensive review of *R* packages, with a particular recommendation for `ASH` or `KernSmooth`. The density estimation methods in `pandas` and `scikit-learn` also offer good implementations. For many data science problems, there is no need to worry about the various types of density estimates; it suffices to use the base functions.

Key Ideas

- A frequency histogram plots frequency counts on the y-axis and variable values on the x-axis; it gives a sense of the distribution of the data at a glance.
- A frequency table is a tabular version of the frequency counts found in a histogram.
- A boxplot—with the top and bottom of the box at the 75th and 25th percentiles, respectively—also gives a quick sense of the distribution of the data; it is often used in side-by-side displays to compare distributions.
- A density plot is a smoothed version of a histogram; it requires a function to estimate a plot based on the data (multiple estimates are possible, of course).

Further Reading

- A SUNY Oswego professor provides a step-by-step guide to creating a boxplot (*https://oreil.ly/wTpnE*).
- Density estimation in *R* is covered in Henry Deng and Hadley Wickham's paper of the same name (*https://oreil.ly/TbWYS*).
- *R*-Bloggers has a useful post on histograms in *R* (*https://oreil.ly/Ynp-n*), including customization elements, such as binning (breaks).
- *R*-Bloggers also has a similar post on boxplots in *R* (*https://oreil.ly/0DSb2*).
- Matthew Conlen published an interactive presentation (*https://oreil.ly/bC9nu*) that demonstrates the effect of choosing different kernels and bandwidth on kernel density estimates.

Exploring Binary and Categorical Data

For categorical data, simple proportions or percentages tell the story of the data.

Key Terms for Exploring Categorical Data

Mode
: The most commonly occurring category or value in a data set.

Expected value
: When the categories can be associated with a numeric value, this gives an average value based on a category's probability of occurrence.

Bar charts
: The frequency or proportion for each category plotted as bars.

Pie charts
: The frequency or proportion for each category plotted as wedges in a pie.

Getting a summary of a binary variable or a categorical variable with a few categories is a fairly easy matter: we just figure out the proportion of 1s, or the proportions of the important categories. For example, Table 1-6 shows the percentage of delayed flights by the cause of delay at Dallas/Fort Worth Airport since 2010. Delays are categorized as being due to factors under carrier control, air traffic control (ATC) system delays, weather, security, or a late inbound aircraft.

Table 1-6. Percentage of delays by cause at Dallas/Fort Worth Airport

Carrier	ATC	Weather	Security	Inbound
23.02	30.40	4.03	0.12	42.43

Bar charts, seen often in the popular press, are a common visual tool for displaying a single categorical variable. Categories are listed on the x-axis, and frequencies or proportions on the y-axis. Figure 1-5 shows the airport delays per year by cause for Dallas/Fort Worth (DFW), and it is produced with the *R* function `barplot`:

```
barplot(as.matrix(dfw) / 6, cex.axis=0.8, cex.names=0.7,
        xlab='Cause of delay', ylab='Count')
```

`pandas` also supports bar charts for data frames:

```
ax = dfw.transpose().plot.bar(figsize=(4, 4), legend=False)
ax.set_xlabel('Cause of delay')
ax.set_ylabel('Count')
```

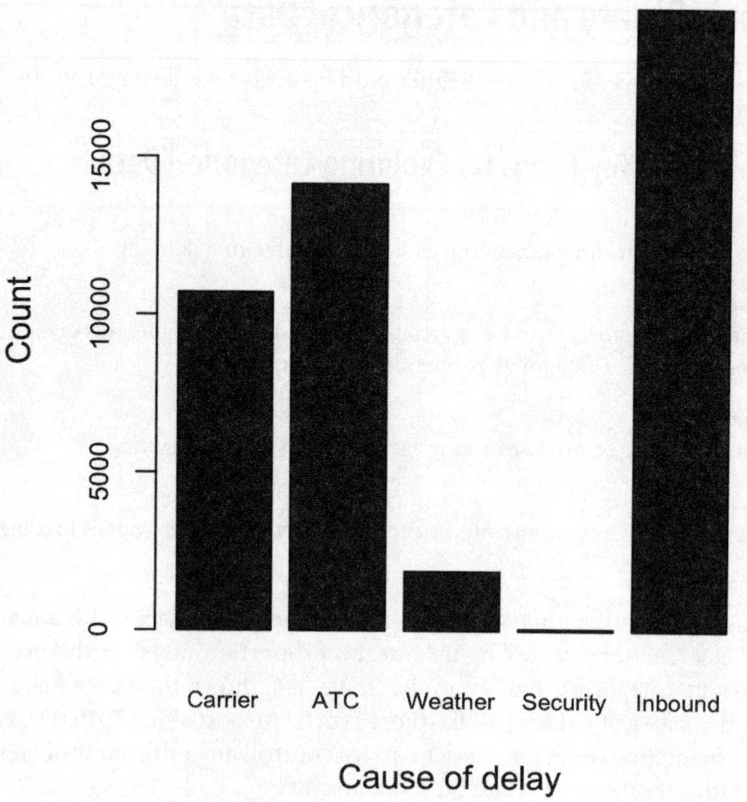

Figure 1-5. Bar chart of airline delays at DFW by cause

Note that a bar chart resembles a histogram; in a bar chart the x-axis represents different categories of a factor variable, while in a histogram the x-axis represents values of a single variable on a numeric scale. In a histogram, the bars are typically shown touching each other, with gaps indicating values that did not occur in the data. In a bar chart, the bars are shown separate from one another.

Pie charts are an alternative to bar charts, although statisticians and data visualization experts generally eschew pie charts as less visually informative (see [Few-2007]).

Numerical Data as Categorical Data

In "Frequency Tables and Histograms" on page 22, we looked at frequency tables based on binning the data. This implicitly converts the numeric data to an ordered factor. In this sense, histograms and bar charts are similar, except that the categories on the x-axis in the bar chart are not ordered. Converting numeric data to categorical data is an important and widely used step in data analysis since it reduces the complexity (and size) of the data. This aids in the discovery of relationships between features, particularly at the initial stages of an analysis.

Mode

The mode is the value—or values in case of a tie—that appears most often in the data. For example, the mode of the cause of delay at Dallas/Fort Worth airport is "Inbound." As another example, in most parts of the United States, the mode for religious preference would be Christian. The mode is a simple summary statistic for categorical data, and it is generally not used for numeric data.

Expected Value

A special type of categorical data is data in which the categories represent or can be mapped to discrete values on the same scale. A marketer for a new cloud technology, for example, offers two levels of service, one priced at $300/month and another at $50/month. The marketer offers free webinars to generate leads, and the firm figures that 5% of the attendees will sign up for the $300 service, 15% will sign up for the $50 service, and 80% will not sign up for anything. This data can be summed up, for financial purposes, in a single "expected value," which is a form of weighted mean, in which the weights are probabilities.

The expected value is calculated as follows:

1. Multiply each outcome by its probability of occurrence.
2. Sum these values.

In the cloud service example, the expected value of a webinar attendee is thus $22.50 per month, calculated as follows:

$$EV = (0.05)(300) + (0.15)(50) + (0.80)(0) = 22.5$$

The expected value is really a form of weighted mean: it adds the ideas of future expectations and probability weights, often based on subjective judgment. Expected value is a fundamental concept in business valuation and capital budgeting—for example, the expected value of five years of profits from a new acquisition, or the expected cost savings from new patient management software at a clinic.

Probability

We referred above to the *probability* of a value occurring. Most people have an intuitive understanding of probability, encountering the concept frequently in weather forecasts (the chance of rain) or sports analysis (the probability of winning). Sports and games are more often expressed as odds, which are readily convertible to probabilities (if the odds that a team will win are 2 to 1, its probability of winning is 2/(2+1) = 2/3). Surprisingly, though, the concept of probability can be the source of deep philosophical discussion when it comes to defining it. Fortunately, we do not need a formal mathematical or philosophical definition here. For our purposes, the probability that an event will happen is the proportion of times it will occur if the situation could be repeated over and over, countless times. Most often this is an imaginary construction, but it is an adequate operational understanding of probability.

Key Ideas

- Categorical data is typically summed up in proportions and can be visualized in a bar chart.
- Categories might represent distinct things (apples and oranges, male and female), levels of a factor variable (low, medium, and high), or numeric data that has been binned.
- Expected value is the sum of values times their probability of occurrence, often used to sum up factor variable levels.

Further Reading

No statistics course is complete without a lesson on misleading graphs (*https://oreil.ly/rDMuT*), which often involves bar charts and pie charts.

Correlation

Exploratory data analysis in many modeling projects (whether in data science or in research) involves examining correlation among predictors, and between predictors and a target variable. Variables X and Y (each with measured data) are said to be positively correlated if high values of X go with high values of Y, and low values of X go with low values of Y. If high values of X go with low values of Y, and vice versa, the variables are negatively correlated.

> ### Key Terms for Correlation
>
> *Correlation coefficient*
> : A metric that measures the extent to which numeric variables are associated with one another (ranges from –1 to +1).
>
> *Correlation matrix*
> : A table where the variables are shown on both rows and columns, and the cell values are the correlations between the variables.
>
> *Scatterplot*
> : A plot in which the x-axis is the value of one variable, and the y-axis the value of another.

Consider these two variables, perfectly correlated in the sense that each goes from low to high:

v1: {1, 2, 3}
v2: {4, 5, 6}

The vector sum of products is $1 \cdot 4 + 2 \cdot 5 + 3 \cdot 6 = 32$. Now try shuffling one of them and recalculating—the vector sum of products will never be higher than 32. So this sum of products could be used as a metric; that is, the observed sum of 32 could be compared to lots of random shufflings (in fact, this idea relates to a resampling-based estimate; see "Permutation Test" on page 97). Values produced by this metric, though, are not that meaningful, except by reference to the resampling distribution.

More useful is a standardized variant: the *correlation coefficient*, which gives an estimate of the correlation between two variables that always lies on the same scale. To compute *Pearson's correlation coefficient*, we multiply deviations from the mean for variable 1 times those for variable 2, and divide by the product of the standard deviations:

$$r = \frac{\sum_{i=1}^{n} (x_i - \bar{x})(y_i - \bar{y})}{(n-1)s_x s_y}$$

Note that we divide by $n - 1$ instead of n; see "Degrees of Freedom, and n or $n - 1$?" on page 15 for more details. The correlation coefficient always lies between +1 (perfect positive correlation) and –1 (perfect negative correlation); 0 indicates no correlation.

Variables can have an association that is not linear, in which case the correlation coefficient may not be a useful metric. The relationship between tax rates and revenue raised is an example: as tax rates increase from zero, the revenue raised also increases. However, once tax rates reach a high level and approach 100%, tax avoidance increases and tax revenue actually declines.

Table 1-7, called a *correlation matrix*, shows the correlation between the daily returns for telecommunication stocks from July 2012 through June 2015. From the table, you can see that Verizon (VZ) and ATT (T) have the highest correlation. Level 3 (LVLT), which is an infrastructure company, has the lowest correlation with the others. Note the diagonal of 1s (the correlation of a stock with itself is 1) and the redundancy of the information above and below the diagonal.

Table 1-7. Correlation between telecommunication stock returns

	T	CTL	FTR	VZ	LVLT
T	1.000	0.475	0.328	0.678	0.279
CTL	0.475	1.000	0.420	0.417	0.287
FTR	0.328	0.420	1.000	0.287	0.260
VZ	0.678	0.417	0.287	1.000	0.242
LVLT	0.279	0.287	0.260	0.242	1.000

A table of correlations like Table 1-7 is commonly plotted to visually display the relationship between multiple variables. Figure 1-6 shows the correlation between the daily returns for major exchange-traded funds (ETFs). In *R*, we can easily create this using the package `corrplot`:

```
etfs <- sp500_px[row.names(sp500_px) > '2012-07-01',
                 sp500_sym[sp500_sym$sector == 'etf', 'symbol']]
library(corrplot)
corrplot(cor(etfs), method='ellipse')
```

It is possible to create the same graph in *Python*, but there is no implementation in the common packages. However, most support the visualization of correlation matrices using heatmaps. The following code demonstrates this using the `seaborn.heatmap` package. In the accompanying source code repository, we include *Python* code to generate the more comprehensive visualization:

```
etfs = sp500_px.loc[sp500_px.index > '2012-07-01',
                    sp500_sym[sp500_sym['sector'] == 'etf']['symbol']]
sns.heatmap(etfs.corr(), vmin=-1, vmax=1,
            cmap=sns.diverging_palette(20, 220, as_cmap=True))
```

The ETFs for the S&P 500 (SPY) and the Dow Jones Index (DIA) have a high correlation. Similarly, the QQQ and the XLK, composed mostly of technology companies, are positively correlated. Defensive ETFs, such as those tracking gold prices (GLD), oil prices (USO), or market volatility (VXX), tend to be weakly or negatively correlated with the other ETFs. The orientation of the ellipse indicates whether two variables are positively correlated (ellipse is pointed to the top right) or negatively correlated (ellipse is pointed to the top left). The shading and width of the ellipse indicate the strength of the association: thinner and darker ellipses correspond to stronger relationships.

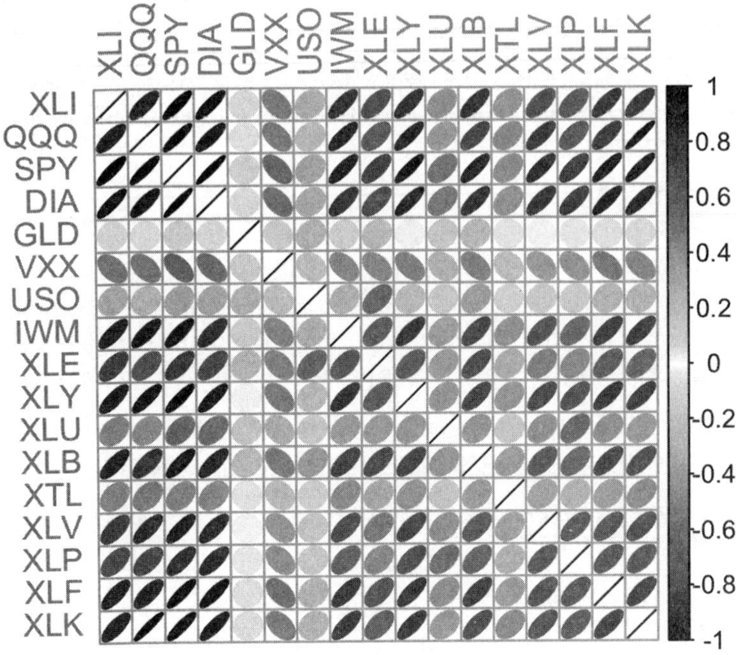

Figure 1-6. Correlation between ETF returns

Like the mean and standard deviation, the correlation coefficient is sensitive to outliers in the data. Software packages offer robust alternatives to the classical correlation coefficient. For example, the *R* package `robust` (*https://oreil.ly/isORz*) uses the function `covRob` to compute a robust estimate of correlation. The methods in the `scikit-learn` module *sklearn.covariance* (*https://oreil.ly/su7wi*) implement a variety of approaches.

Other Correlation Estimates

Statisticians long ago proposed other types of correlation coefficients, such as *Spearman's rho* or *Kendall's tau*. These are correlation coefficients based on the rank of the data. Since they work with ranks rather than values, these estimates are robust to outliers and can handle certain types of nonlinearities. However, data scientists can generally stick to Pearson's correlation coefficient, and its robust alternatives, for exploratory analysis. The appeal of rank-based estimates is mostly for smaller data sets and specific hypothesis tests.

Scatterplots

The standard way to visualize the relationship between two measured data variables is with a scatterplot. The x-axis represents one variable and the y-axis another, and each point on the graph is a record. See Figure 1-7 for a plot of the correlation between the daily returns for ATT and Verizon. This is produced in *R* with the command:

```
plot(telecom$T, telecom$VZ, xlab='ATT (T)', ylab='Verizon (VZ)')
```

The same graph can be generated in *Python* using the `pandas` scatter method:

```
ax = telecom.plot.scatter(x='T', y='VZ', figsize=(4, 4), marker='$\u25EF$')
ax.set_xlabel('ATT (T)')
ax.set_ylabel('Verizon (VZ)')
ax.axhline(0, color='grey', lw=1)
ax.axvline(0, color='grey', lw=1)
```

The returns have a positive relationship: while they cluster around zero, on most days, the stocks go up or go down in tandem (upper-right and lower-left quadrants). There are fewer days where one stock goes down significantly while the other stock goes up, or vice versa (lower-right and upper-left quadrants).

While the plot Figure 1-7 displays only 754 data points, it's already obvious how difficult it is to identify details in the middle of the plot. We will see later how adding transparency to the points, or using hexagonal binning and density plots, can help to find additional structure in the data.

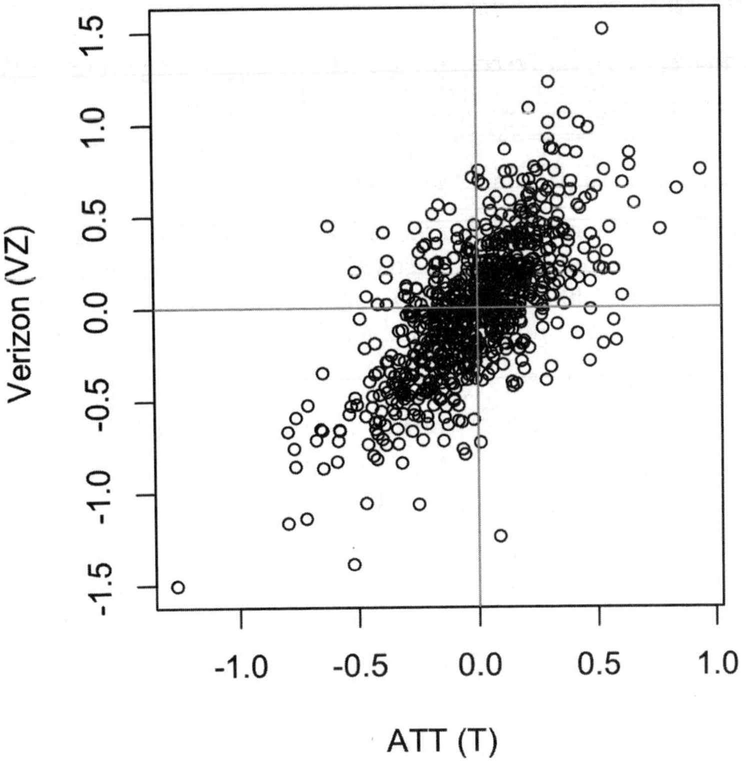

Figure 1-7. Scatterplot of correlation between returns for ATT and Verizon

> **Key Ideas**
>
> - The correlation coefficient measures the extent to which two paired variables (e.g., height and weight for individuals) are associated with one another.
> - When high values of v1 go with high values of v2, v1 and v2 are positively associated.
> - When high values of v1 go with low values of v2, v1 and v2 are negatively associated.
> - The correlation coefficient is a standardized metric, so that it always ranges from –1 (perfect negative correlation) to +1 (perfect positive correlation).
> - A correlation coefficient of zero indicates no correlation, but be aware that random arrangements of data will produce both positive and negative values for the correlation coefficient just by chance.

Further Reading

Statistics, 4th ed., by David Freedman, Robert Pisani, and Roger Purves (W. W. Norton, 2007) has an excellent discussion of correlation.

Exploring Two or More Variables

Familiar estimators like mean and variance look at variables one at a time (*univariate analysis*). Correlation analysis (see "Correlation" on page 30) is an important method that compares two variables (*bivariate analysis*). In this section we look at additional estimates and plots, and at more than two variables (*multivariate analysis*).

> **Key Terms for Exploring Two or More Variables**
>
> ***Contingency table***
> A tally of counts between two or more categorical variables.
>
> ***Hexagonal binning***
> A plot of two numeric variables with the records binned into hexagons.
>
> ***Contour plot***
> A plot showing the density of two numeric variables like a topographical map.
>
> ***Violin plot***
> Similar to a boxplot but showing the density estimate.

Like univariate analysis, bivariate analysis involves both computing summary statistics and producing visual displays. The appropriate type of bivariate or multivariate analysis depends on the nature of the data: numeric versus categorical.

Hexagonal Binning and Contours (Plotting Numeric Versus Numeric Data)

Scatterplots are fine when there is a relatively small number of data values. The plot of stock returns in Figure 1-7 involves only about 750 points. For data sets with hundreds of thousands or millions of records, a scatterplot will be too dense, so we need a different way to visualize the relationship. To illustrate, consider the data set `kc_tax`, which contains the tax-assessed values for residential properties in King County, Washington. In order to focus on the main part of the data, we strip out very expensive and very small or large residences using the `subset` function:

```
kc_tax0 <- subset(kc_tax, TaxAssessedValue < 750000 &
                  SqFtTotLiving > 100 &
                  SqFtTotLiving < 3500)
nrow(kc_tax0)
432693
```

In `pandas`, we filter the data set as follows:

```
kc_tax0 = kc_tax.loc[(kc_tax.TaxAssessedValue < 750000) &
                     (kc_tax.SqFtTotLiving > 100) &
                     (kc_tax.SqFtTotLiving < 3500), :]
kc_tax0.shape
(432693, 3)
```

Figure 1-8 is a *hexagonal binning* plot of the relationship between the finished square feet and the tax-assessed value for homes in King County. Rather than plotting points, which would appear as a monolithic dark cloud, we grouped the records into hexagonal bins and plotted the hexagons with a color indicating the number of records in that bin. In this chart, the positive relationship between square feet and tax-assessed value is clear. An interesting feature is the hint of additional bands above the main (darkest) band at the bottom, indicating homes that have the same square footage as those in the main band but a higher tax-assessed value.

Figure 1-8 was generated by the powerful *R* package `ggplot2`, developed by Hadley Wickham [ggplot2]. `ggplot2` is one of several new software libraries for advanced exploratory visual analysis of data; see "Visualizing Multiple Variables" on page 43:

```
ggplot(kc_tax0, (aes(x=SqFtTotLiving, y=TaxAssessedValue))) +
  stat_binhex(color='white') +
  theme_bw() +
  scale_fill_gradient(low='white', high='black') +
  labs(x='Finished Square Feet', y='Tax-Assessed Value')
```

In *Python*, hexagonal binning plots are readily available using the `pandas` data frame method `hexbin`:

```
ax = kc_tax0.plot.hexbin(x='SqFtTotLiving', y='TaxAssessedValue',
                         gridsize=30, sharex=False, figsize=(5, 4))
ax.set_xlabel('Finished Square Feet')
ax.set_ylabel('Tax-Assessed Value')
```

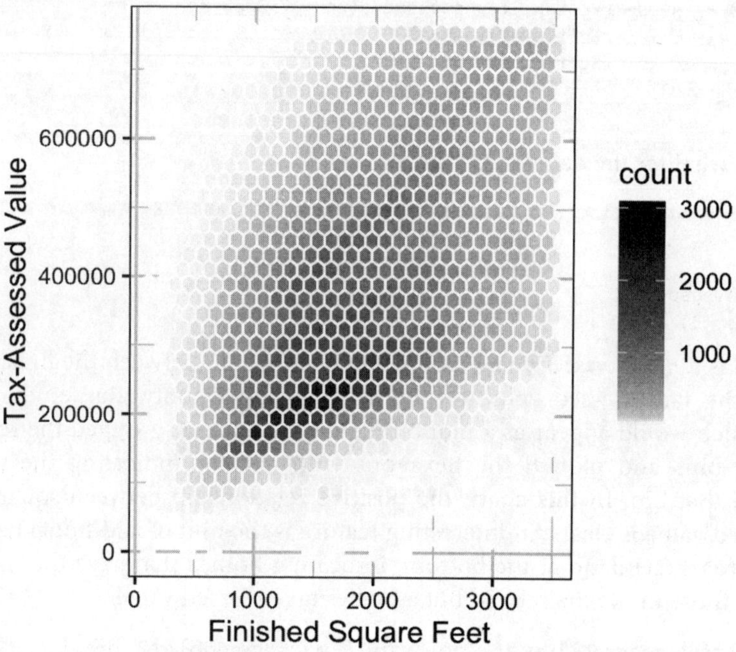

Figure 1-8. Hexagonal binning for tax-assessed value versus finished square feet

Figure 1-9 uses contours overlaid onto a scatterplot to visualize the relationship between two numeric variables. The contours are essentially a topographical map to two variables; each contour band represents a specific density of points, increasing as one nears a "peak." This plot shows a similar story as Figure 1-8: there is a secondary peak "north" of the main peak. This chart was also created using `ggplot2` with the built-in `geom_density2d` function:

```
ggplot(kc_tax0, aes(SqFtTotLiving, TaxAssessedValue)) +
  theme_bw() +
  geom_point(alpha=0.1) +
  geom_density2d(color='white') +
  labs(x='Finished Square Feet', y='Tax-Assessed Value')
```

The `seaborn` `kdeplot` function in *Python* creates a contour plot:

```
ax = sns.kdeplot(kc_tax0.SqFtTotLiving, kc_tax0.TaxAssessedValue, ax=ax)
ax.set_xlabel('Finished Square Feet')
ax.set_ylabel('Tax-Assessed Value')
```

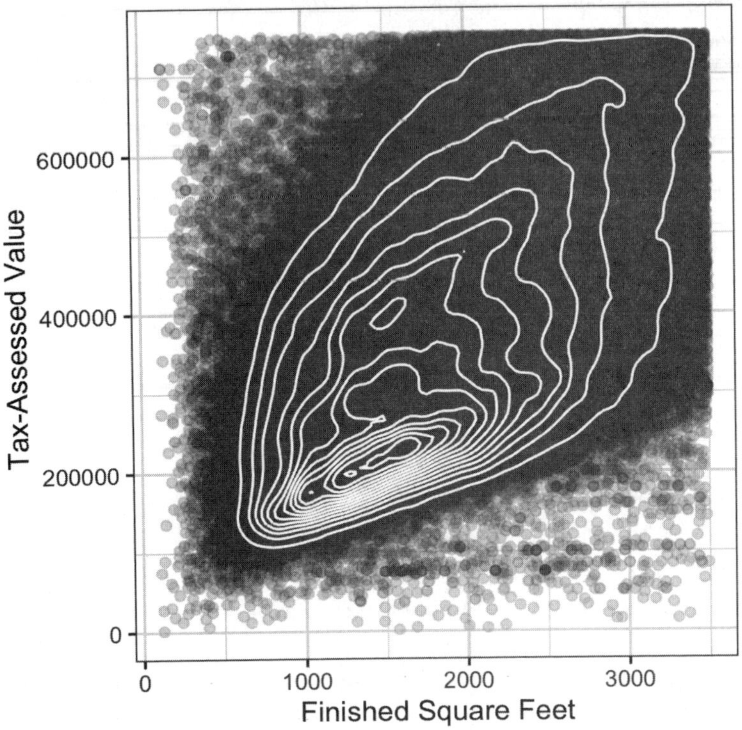

Figure 1-9. Contour plot for tax-assessed value versus finished square feet

Other types of charts are used to show the relationship between two numeric variables, including *heat maps*. Heat maps, hexagonal binning, and contour plots all give a visual representation of a two-dimensional density. In this way, they are natural analogs to histograms and density plots.

Two Categorical Variables

A useful way to summarize two categorical variables is a contingency table—a table of counts by category. Table 1-8 shows the contingency table between the grade of a personal loan and the outcome of that loan. This is taken from data provided by Lending Club, a leader in the peer-to-peer lending business. The grade goes from A (high) to G (low). The outcome is either fully paid, current, late, or charged off (the balance of the loan is not expected to be collected). This table shows the count and row percentages. High-grade loans have a very low late/charge-off percentage as compared with lower-grade loans.

Table 1-8. Contingency table of loan grade and status

Grade	Charged off	Current	Fully paid	Late	Total
A	1562	50051	20408	469	72490
	0.022	0.690	0.282	0.006	0.161
B	5302	93852	31160	2056	132370
	0.040	0.709	0.235	0.016	0.294
C	6023	88928	23147	2777	120875
	0.050	0.736	0.191	0.023	0.268
D	5007	53281	13681	2308	74277
	0.067	0.717	0.184	0.031	0.165
E	2842	24639	5949	1374	34804
	0.082	0.708	0.171	0.039	0.077
F	1526	8444	2328	606	12904
	0.118	0.654	0.180	0.047	0.029
G	409	1990	643	199	3241
	0.126	0.614	0.198	0.061	0.007
Total	22671	321185	97316	9789	450961

Contingency tables can look only at counts, or they can also include column and total percentages. Pivot tables in Excel are perhaps the most common tool used to create contingency tables. In *R*, the `CrossTable` function in the `descr` package produces contingency tables, and the following code was used to create Table 1-8:

```
library(descr)
x_tab <- CrossTable(lc_loans$grade, lc_loans$status,
                    prop.c=FALSE, prop.chisq=FALSE, prop.t=FALSE)
```

The `pivot_table` method creates the pivot table in *Python*. The `aggfunc` argument allows us to get the counts. Calculating the percentages is a bit more involved:

```
crosstab = lc_loans.pivot_table(index='grade', columns='status',
                                aggfunc=lambda x: len(x), margins=True) ❶

df = crosstab.loc['A':'G',:].copy() ❷
df.loc[:,'Charged Off':'Late'] = df.loc[:,'Charged Off':'Late'].div(df['All'],
                                                                    axis=0) ❸
df['All'] = df['All'] / sum(df['All']) ❹
perc_crosstab = df
```

❶ The `margins` keyword argument will add the column and row sums.

❷ We create a copy of the pivot table, ignoring the column sums.

❸ We divide the rows with the row sum.

❹ We divide the 'All' column by its sum.

Categorical and Numeric Data

Boxplots (see "Percentiles and Boxplots" on page 20) are a simple way to visually compare the distributions of a numeric variable grouped according to a categorical variable. For example, we might want to compare how the percentage of flight delays varies across airlines. Figure 1-10 shows the percentage of flights in a month that were delayed where the delay was within the carrier's control:

```
boxplot(pct_carrier_delay ~ airline, data=airline_stats, ylim=c(0, 50))
```

The pandas boxplot method takes the by argument that splits the data set into groups and creates the individual boxplots:

```
ax = airline_stats.boxplot(by='airline', column='pct_carrier_delay')
ax.set_xlabel('')
ax.set_ylabel('Daily % of Delayed Flights')
plt.suptitle('')
```

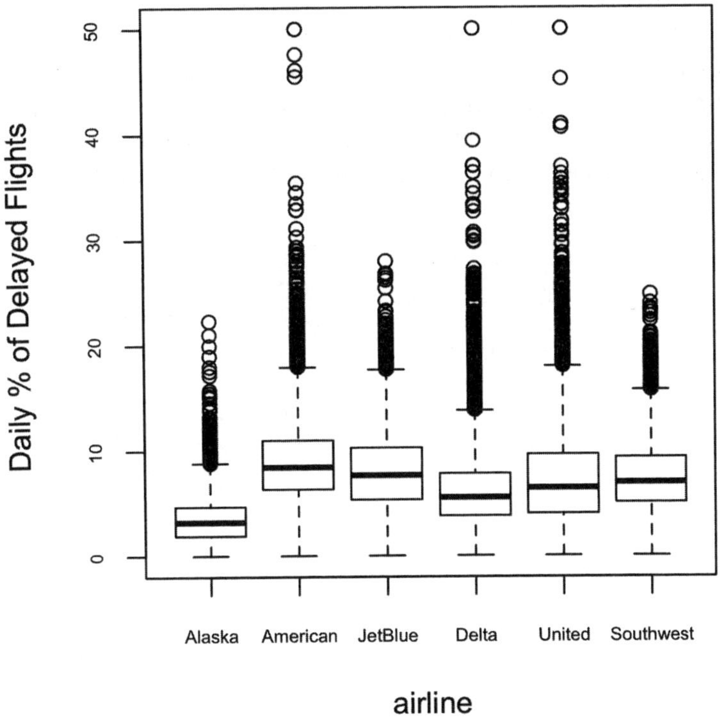

Figure 1-10. Boxplot of percent of airline delays by carrier

Alaska stands out as having the fewest delays, while American has the most delays: the lower quartile for American is higher than the upper quartile for Alaska.

A *violin plot*, introduced by [Hintze-Nelson-1998], is an enhancement to the boxplot and plots the density estimate with the density on the y-axis. The density is mirrored and flipped over, and the resulting shape is filled in, creating an image resembling a violin. The advantage of a violin plot is that it can show nuances in the distribution that aren't perceptible in a boxplot. On the other hand, the boxplot more clearly shows the outliers in the data. In `ggplot2`, the function `geom_violin` can be used to create a violin plot as follows:

```
ggplot(data=airline_stats, aes(airline, pct_carrier_delay)) +
  ylim(0, 50) +
  geom_violin() +
  labs(x='', y='Daily % of Delayed Flights')
```

Violin plots are available with the `violinplot` method of the `seaborn` package:

```
ax = sns.violinplot(airline_stats.airline, airline_stats.pct_carrier_delay,
                    inner='quartile', color='white')
ax.set_xlabel('')
ax.set_ylabel('Daily % of Delayed Flights')
```

The corresponding plot is shown in Figure 1-11. The violin plot shows a concentration in the distribution near zero for Alaska and, to a lesser extent, Delta. This phenomenon is not as obvious in the boxplot. You can combine a violin plot with a boxplot by adding `geom_boxplot` to the plot (although this works best when colors are used).

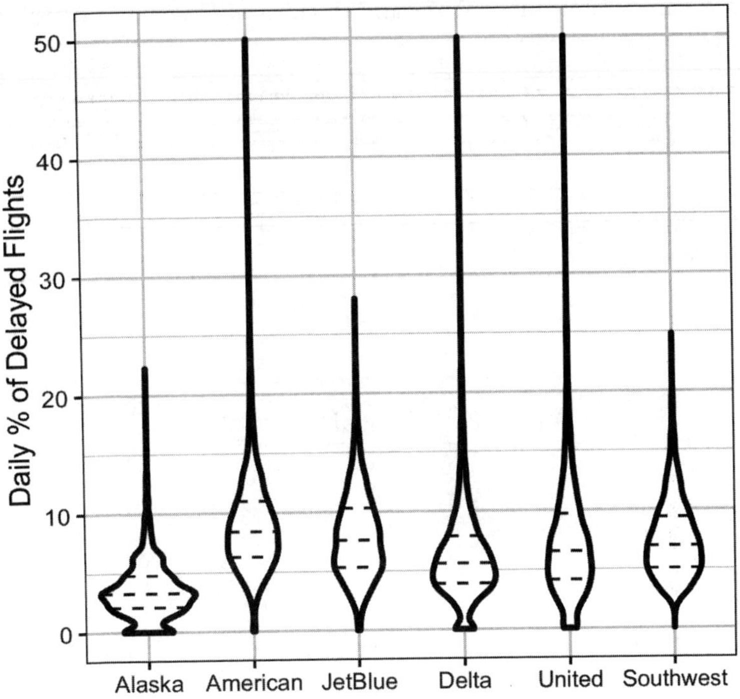

Figure 1-11. Violin plot of percent of airline delays by carrier

Visualizing Multiple Variables

The types of charts used to compare two variables—scatterplots, hexagonal binning, and boxplots—are readily extended to more variables through the notion of *conditioning*. As an example, look back at Figure 1-8, which showed the relationship between homes' finished square feet and their tax-assessed values. We observed that there appears to be a cluster of homes that have higher tax-assessed value per square foot. Diving deeper, Figure 1-12 accounts for the effect of location by plotting the data for a set of zip codes. Now the picture is much clearer: tax-assessed value is much higher in some zip codes (98105, 98126) than in others (98108, 98188). This disparity gives rise to the clusters observed in Figure 1-8.

We created Figure 1-12 using `ggplot2` and the idea of *facets*, or a conditioning variable (in this case, zip code):

```
ggplot(subset(kc_tax0, ZipCode %in% c(98188, 98105, 98108, 98126)),
         aes(x=SqFtTotLiving, y=TaxAssessedValue)) +
  stat_binhex(color='white') +
  theme_bw() +
  scale_fill_gradient(low='white', high='blue') +
  labs(x='Finished Square Feet', y='Tax-Assessed Value') +
  facet_wrap('ZipCode') ❶
```

❶ Use the `ggplot` functions `facet_wrap` and `facet_grid` to specify the conditioning variable.

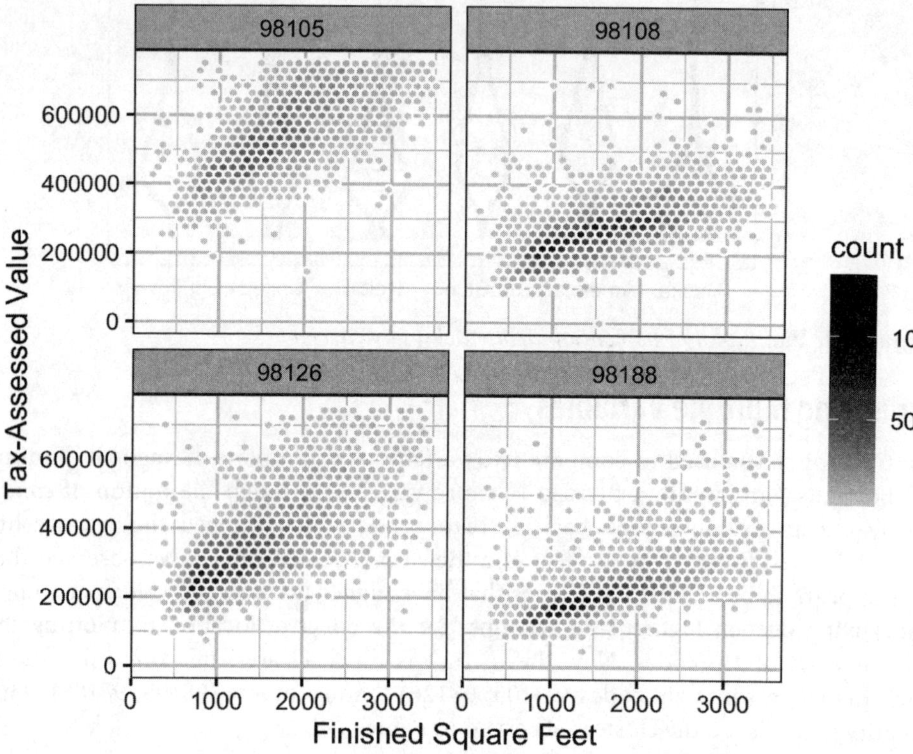

Figure 1-12. Tax-assessed value versus finished square feet by zip code

Most *Python* packages base their visualizations on `Matplotlib`. While it is in principle possible to create faceted graphs using `Matplotlib`, the code can get complicated. Fortunately, `seaborn` has a relatively straightforward way of creating these graphs:

```
zip_codes = [98188, 98105, 98108, 98126]
kc_tax_zip = kc_tax0.loc[kc_tax0.ZipCode.isin(zip_codes),:]
kc_tax_zip

def hexbin(x, y, color, **kwargs):
    cmap = sns.light_palette(color, as_cmap=True)
    plt.hexbin(x, y, gridsize=25, cmap=cmap, **kwargs)

g = sns.FacetGrid(kc_tax_zip, col='ZipCode', col_wrap=2) ❶
g.map(hexbin, 'SqFtTotLiving', 'TaxAssessedValue',
      extent=[0, 3500, 0, 700000]) ❷
g.set_axis_labels('Finished Square Feet', 'Tax-Assessed Value')
g.set_titles('Zip code {col_name:.0f}')
```

❶ Use the arguments `col` and `row` to specify the conditioning variables. For a single conditioning variable, use `col` together with `col_wrap` to wrap the faceted graphs into multiple rows.

❷ The `map` method calls the `hexbin` function with subsets of the original data set for the different zip codes. `extent` defines the limits of the x- and y-axes.

The concept of conditioning variables in a graphics system was pioneered with *Trellis graphics*, developed by Rick Becker, Bill Cleveland, and others at Bell Labs [Trellis-Graphics]. This idea has propagated to various modern graphics systems, such as the `lattice` [lattice] and `ggplot2` packages in *R* and the `seaborn` [seaborn] and `Bokeh` [bokeh] modules in *Python*. Conditioning variables are also integral to business intelligence platforms such as Tableau and Spotfire. With the advent of vast computing power, modern visualization platforms have moved well beyond the humble beginnings of exploratory data analysis. However, key concepts and tools developed a half century ago (e.g., simple boxplots) still form a foundation for these systems.

Key Ideas

- Hexagonal binning and contour plots are useful tools that permit graphical examination of two numeric variables at a time, without being overwhelmed by huge amounts of data.
- Contingency tables are the standard tool for looking at the counts of two categorical variables.
- Boxplots and violin plots allow you to plot a numeric variable against a categorical variable.

Further Reading

- *Modern Data Science with R* by Benjamin Baumer, Daniel Kaplan, and Nicholas Horton (Chapman & Hall/CRC Press, 2017) has an excellent presentation of "a grammar for graphics" (the "gg" in `ggplot`).
- *ggplot2: Elegant Graphics for Data Analysis* by Hadley Wickham (Springer, 2009) is an excellent resource from the creator of `ggplot2`.
- Josef Fruehwald has a web-based tutorial on `ggplot2` (*https://oreil.ly/zB2Dz*).

Summary

Exploratory data analysis (EDA), pioneered by John Tukey, set a foundation for the field of data science. The key idea of EDA is that the first and most important step in any project based on data is to *look at the data*. By summarizing and visualizing the data, you can gain valuable intuition and understanding of the project.

This chapter has reviewed concepts ranging from simple metrics, such as estimates of location and variability, to rich visual displays that explore the relationships between multiple variables, as in Figure 1-12. The diverse set of tools and techniques being developed by the open source community, combined with the expressiveness of the *R* and *Python* languages, has created a plethora of ways to explore and analyze data. Exploratory analysis should be a cornerstone of any data science project.

CHAPTER 2
Data and Sampling Distributions

A popular misconception holds that the era of big data means the end of a need for sampling. In fact, the proliferation of data of varying quality and relevance reinforces the need for sampling as a tool to work efficiently with a variety of data and to minimize bias. Even in a big data project, predictive models are typically developed and piloted with samples. Samples are also used in tests of various sorts (e.g., comparing the effect of web page designs on clicks).

Figure 2-1 shows a schematic that underpins the concepts we will discuss in this chapter—data and sampling distributions. The lefthand side represents a population that, in statistics, is assumed to follow an underlying but *unknown* distribution. All that is available is the *sample* data and its empirical distribution, shown on the righthand side. To get from the lefthand side to the righthand side, a *sampling* procedure is used (represented by an arrow). Traditional statistics focused very much on the lefthand side, using theory based on strong assumptions about the population. Modern statistics has moved to the righthand side, where such assumptions are not needed.

In general, data scientists need not worry about the theoretical nature of the lefthand side and instead should focus on the sampling procedures and the data at hand. There are some notable exceptions. Sometimes data is generated from a physical process that can be modeled. The simplest example is flipping a coin: this follows a binomial distribution. Any real-life binomial situation (buy or don't buy, fraud or no fraud, click or don't click) can be modeled effectively by a coin (with modified probability of landing heads, of course). In these cases, we can gain additional insight by using our understanding of the population.

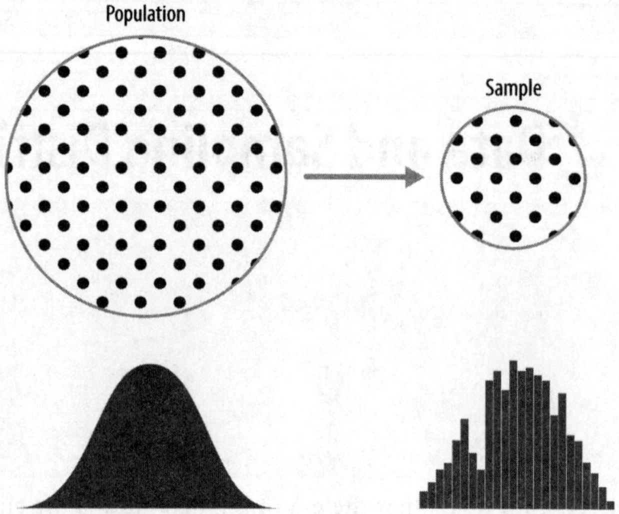

Figure 2-1. Population versus sample

Random Sampling and Sample Bias

A *sample* is a subset of data from a larger data set; statisticians call this larger data set the *population*. A population in statistics is not the same thing as in biology—it is a large, defined (but sometimes theoretical or imaginary) set of data.

Random sampling is a process in which each available member of the population being sampled has an equal chance of being chosen for the sample at each draw. The sample that results is called a *simple random sample*. Sampling can be done *with replacement*, in which observations are put back in the population after each draw for possible future reselection. Or it can be done *without replacement*, in which case observations, once selected, are unavailable for future draws.

Data quality often matters more than data quantity when making an estimate or a model based on a sample. Data quality in data science involves completeness, consistency of format, cleanliness, and accuracy of individual data points. Statistics adds the notion of *representativeness*.

Key Terms for Random Sampling

Sample
: A subset from a larger data set.

Population
: The larger data set or idea of a data set.

N (n)
: The size of the population (sample).

Random sampling
: Drawing elements into a sample at random.

Stratified sampling
: Dividing the population into strata and randomly sampling from each strata.

Stratum (pl., strata)
: A homogeneous subgroup of a population with common characteristics.

Simple random sample
: The sample that results from random sampling without stratifying the population.

Bias
: Systematic error.

Sample bias
: A sample that misrepresents the population.

The classic example is the *Literary Digest* poll of 1936 that predicted a victory of Alf Landon over Franklin Roosevelt. The *Literary Digest*, a leading periodical of the day, polled its entire subscriber base plus additional lists of individuals, a total of over 10 million people, and predicted a landslide victory for Landon. George Gallup, founder of the Gallup Poll, conducted biweekly polls of just 2,000 people and accurately predicted a Roosevelt victory. The difference lay in the selection of those polled.

The *Literary Digest* opted for quantity, paying little attention to the method of selection. They ended up polling those with relatively high socioeconomic status (their own subscribers, plus those who, by virtue of owning luxuries like telephones and automobiles, appeared in marketers' lists). The result was *sample bias*; that is, the sample was different in some meaningful and nonrandom way from the larger population it was meant to represent. The term *nonrandom* is important—hardly any sample, including random samples, will be exactly representative of the population. Sample bias occurs when the difference is meaningful, and it can be expected to continue for other samples drawn in the same way as the first.

Self-Selection Sampling Bias

The reviews of restaurants, hotels, cafés, and so on that you read on social media sites like Yelp are prone to bias because the people submitting them are not randomly selected; rather, they themselves have taken the initiative to write. This leads to self-selection bias—the people motivated to write reviews may have had poor experiences, may have an association with the establishment, or may simply be a different type of person from those who do not write reviews. Note that while self-selection samples can be unreliable indicators of the true state of affairs, they may be more reliable in simply comparing one establishment to a similar one; the same self-selection bias might apply to each.

Bias

Statistical bias refers to measurement or sampling errors that are systematic and produced by the measurement or sampling process. An important distinction should be made between errors due to random chance and errors due to bias. Consider the physical process of a gun shooting at a target. It will not hit the absolute center of the target every time, or even much at all. An unbiased process will produce error, but it is random and does not tend strongly in any direction (see Figure 2-2). The results shown in Figure 2-3 show a biased process—there is still random error in both the x and y direction, but there is also a bias. Shots tend to fall in the upper-right quadrant.

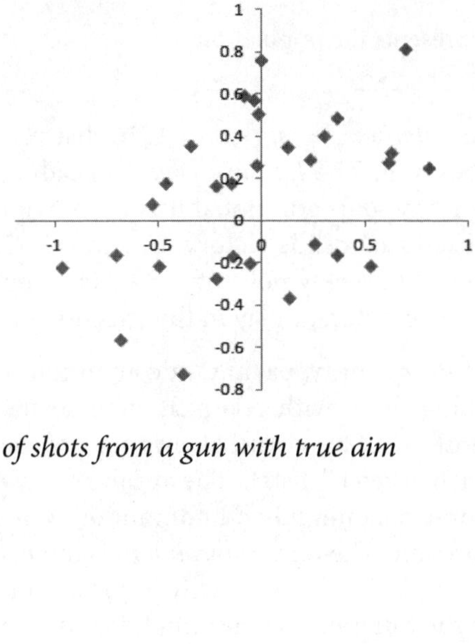

Figure 2-2. Scatterplot of shots from a gun with true aim

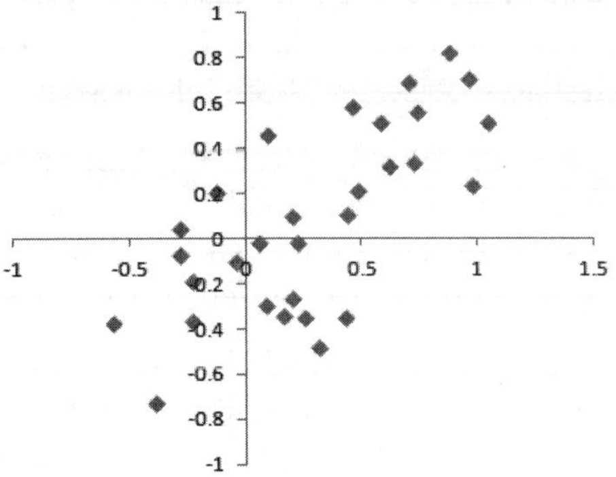

Figure 2-3. Scatterplot of shots from a gun with biased aim

Bias comes in different forms, and may be observable or invisible. When a result does suggest bias (e.g., by reference to a benchmark or actual values), it is often an indicator that a statistical or machine learning model has been misspecified, or an important variable left out.

Random Selection

To avoid the problem of sample bias that led the *Literary Digest* to predict Landon over Roosevelt, George Gallup (shown in Figure 2-4) opted for more scientifically chosen methods to achieve a sample that was representative of the US voting electorate. There are now a variety of methods to achieve representativeness, but at the heart of all of them lies *random sampling*.

Figure 2-4. George Gallup, catapulted to fame by the Literary Digest's "big data" failure

Random sampling is not always easy. Proper definition of an accessible population is key. Suppose we want to generate a representative profile of customers and we need to conduct a pilot customer survey. The survey needs to be representative but is labor intensive.

First, we need to define who a customer is. We might select all customer records where purchase amount > 0. Do we include all past customers? Do we include refunds? Internal test purchases? Resellers? Both billing agent and customer?

Next, we need to specify a sampling procedure. It might be "select 100 customers at random." Where a sampling from a flow is involved (e.g., real-time customer transactions or web visitors), timing considerations may be important (e.g., a web visitor at 10 a.m. on a weekday may be different from a web visitor at 10 p.m. on a weekend).

In *stratified sampling*, the population is divided up into *strata*, and random samples are taken from each stratum. Political pollsters might seek to learn the electoral preferences of whites, blacks, and Hispanics. A simple random sample taken from the population would yield too few blacks and Hispanics, so those strata could be overweighted in stratified sampling to yield equivalent sample sizes.

Size Versus Quality: When Does Size Matter?

In the era of big data, it is sometimes surprising that smaller is better. Time and effort spent on random sampling not only reduces bias but also allows greater attention to data exploration and data quality. For example, missing data and outliers may contain useful information. It might be prohibitively expensive to track down missing values or evaluate outliers in millions of records, but doing so in a sample of several thousand records may be feasible. Data plotting and manual inspection bog down if there is too much data.

So when *are* massive amounts of data needed?

The classic scenario for the value of big data is when the data is not only big but sparse as well. Consider the search queries received by Google, where columns are terms, rows are individual search queries, and cell values are either 0 or 1, depending on whether a query contains a term. The goal is to determine the best predicted search destination for a given query. There are over 150,000 words in the English language, and Google processes over one trillion queries per year. This yields a huge matrix, the vast majority of whose entries are "0."

This is a true big data problem—only when such enormous quantities of data are accumulated can effective search results be returned for most queries. And the more data accumulates, the better the results. For popular search terms this is not such a problem—effective data can be found fairly quickly for the handful of extremely popular topics trending at a particular time. The real value of modern search technology lies in the ability to return detailed and useful results for a huge variety of search queries, including those that occur with a frequency, say, of only one in a million.

Consider the search phrase "Ricky Ricardo and Little Red Riding Hood." In the early days of the internet, this query would probably have returned results on the bandleader Ricky Ricardo, the television show *I Love Lucy* in which that character appeared, and the children's story *Little Red Riding Hood*. Both of those individual items would have had many searches to refer to, but the combination would have had very few. Later, now that trillions of search queries have been accumulated, this search query returns the exact *I Love Lucy* episode in which Ricky narrates, in dramatic fashion, the *Little Red Riding Hood* story to his infant son in a comic mix of English and Spanish.

Keep in mind that the number of actual *pertinent* records—ones in which this exact search query, or something very similar, appears (together with information on what link people ultimately clicked on)—might need only be in the thousands to be effective. However, many trillions of data points are needed to obtain these pertinent records (and random sampling, of course, will not help). See also "Long-Tailed Distributions" on page 73.

Sample Mean Versus Population Mean

The symbol $\bar{x}$ (pronounced "x-bar") is used to represent the mean of a sample from a population, whereas μ is used to represent the mean of a population. Why make the distinction? Information about samples is observed, and information about large populations is often inferred from smaller samples. Statisticians like to keep the two things separate in the symbology.

Key Ideas

- Even in the era of big data, random sampling remains an important arrow in the data scientist's quiver.
- Bias occurs when measurements or observations are systematically in error because they are not representative of the full population.
- Data quality is often more important than data quantity, and random sampling can reduce bias and facilitate quality improvement that would otherwise be prohibitively expensive.

Further Reading

- A useful review of sampling procedures can be found in Ronald Fricker's chapter "Sampling Methods for Online Surveys" in *The SAGE Handbook of Online Research Methods*, 2nd ed., edited by Nigel G. Fielding, Raymond M. Lee, and Grant Blank (SAGE Publications, 2016). This chapter includes a review of the modifications to random sampling that are often used for practical reasons of cost or feasibility.

- The story of the *Literary Digest* poll failure can be found on the Capital Century website (*https://oreil.ly/iSoQT*).

Selection Bias

To paraphrase Yogi Berra: if you don't know what you're looking for, look hard enough and you'll find it.

Selection bias refers to the practice of selectively choosing data—consciously or unconsciously—in a way that leads to a conclusion that is misleading or ephemeral.

Key Terms for Selection Bias

Selection bias
Bias resulting from the way in which observations are selected.

Data snooping
Extensive hunting through data in search of something interesting.

Vast search effect
Bias or nonreproducibility resulting from repeated data modeling, or modeling data with large numbers of predictor variables.

If you specify a hypothesis and conduct a well-designed experiment to test it, you can have high confidence in the conclusion. This is frequently not what occurs, however. Often, one looks at available data and tries to discern patterns. But are the patterns real? Or are they just the product of *data snooping*—that is, extensive hunting through the data until something interesting emerges? There is a saying among statisticians: "If you torture the data long enough, sooner or later it will confess."

The difference between a phenomenon that you verify when you test a hypothesis using an experiment and a phenomenon that you discover by perusing available data can be illuminated with the following thought experiment.

Imagine that someone tells you they can flip a coin and have it land heads on the next 10 tosses. You challenge them (the equivalent of an experiment), and they proceed to toss the coin 10 times, with all flips landing heads. Clearly you ascribe some special talent to this person—the probability that 10 coin tosses will land heads just by chance is 1 in 1,000.

Now imagine that the announcer at a sports stadium asks the 20,000 people in attendance each to toss a coin 10 times, and to report to an usher if they get 10 heads in a row. The chance that *somebody* in the stadium will get 10 heads is extremely high (more than 99%—it's 1 minus the probability that nobody gets 10 heads). Clearly, selecting after the fact the person (or persons) who gets 10 heads at the stadium does not indicate they have any special talent—it's most likely luck.

Since repeated review of large data sets is a key value proposition in data science, selection bias is something to worry about. A form of selection bias of particular concern to data scientists is what John Elder (founder of Elder Research, a respected data mining consultancy) calls the *vast search effect*. If you repeatedly run different models and ask different questions with a large data set, you are bound to find something interesting. But is the result you found truly something interesting, or is it the chance outlier?

We can guard against this by using a holdout set, and sometimes more than one holdout set, against which to validate performance. Elder also advocates the use of what he calls *target shuffling* (a permutation test, in essence) to test the validity of predictive associations that a data mining model suggests.

Typical forms of selection bias in statistics, in addition to the vast search effect, include nonrandom sampling (see "Random Sampling and Sample Bias" on page 48), cherry-picking data, selection of time intervals that accentuate a particular statistical effect, and stopping an experiment when the results look "interesting."

Regression to the Mean

Regression to the mean refers to a phenomenon involving successive measurements on a given variable: extreme observations tend to be followed by more central ones. Attaching special focus and meaning to the extreme value can lead to a form of selection bias.

Sports fans are familiar with the "rookie of the year, sophomore slump" phenomenon. Among the athletes who begin their career in a given season (the rookie class), there is always one who performs better than all the rest. Generally, this "rookie of the year" does not do as well in his second year. Why not?

In nearly all major sports, at least those played with a ball or puck, there are two elements that play a role in overall performance:

- Skill
- Luck

Regression to the mean is a consequence of a particular form of selection bias. When we select the rookie with the best performance, skill and good luck are probably contributing. In his next season, the skill will still be there, but very often the luck will not be, so his performance will decline—it will regress. The phenomenon was first identified by Francis Galton in 1886 [Galton-1886], who wrote of it in connection with genetic tendencies; for example, the children of extremely tall men tend not to be as tall as their father (see Figure 2-5).

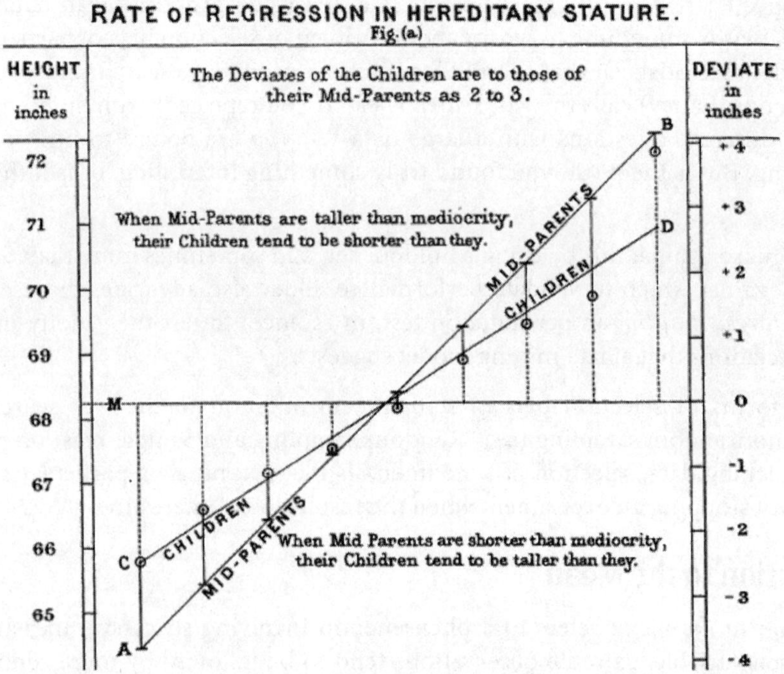

Figure 2-5. Galton's study that identified the phenomenon of regression to the mean

Regression to the mean, meaning to "go back," is distinct from the statistical modeling method of linear regression, in which a linear relationship is estimated between predictor variables and an outcome variable.

Key Ideas

- Specifying a hypothesis and then collecting data following randomization and random sampling principles ensures against bias.
- All other forms of data analysis run the risk of bias resulting from the data collection/analysis process (repeated running of models in data mining, data snooping in research, and after-the-fact selection of interesting events).

Further Reading

- Christopher J. Pannucci and Edwin G. Wilkins' article "Identifying and Avoiding Bias in Research" in (surprisingly not a statistics journal) *Plastic and Reconstructive Surgery* (August 2010) has an excellent review of various types of bias that can enter into research, including selection bias.
- Michael Harris's article "Fooled by Randomness Through Selection Bias" (*https://oreil.ly/v_Q0u*) provides an interesting review of selection bias considerations in stock market trading schemes, from the perspective of traders.

Sampling Distribution of a Statistic

The term *sampling distribution* of a statistic refers to the distribution of some sample statistic over many samples drawn from the same population. Much of classical statistics is concerned with making inferences from (small) samples to (very large) populations.

Key Terms for Sampling Distribution

Sample statistic
: A metric calculated for a sample of data drawn from a larger population.

Data distribution
: The frequency distribution of individual *values* in a data set.

Sampling distribution
: The frequency distribution of a *sample statistic* over many samples or resamples.

Central limit theorem
: The tendency of the sampling distribution to take on a normal shape as sample size rises.

Standard error
: The variability (standard deviation) of a sample *statistic* over many samples (not to be confused with *standard deviation*, which by itself, refers to variability of individual data *values*).

Typically, a sample is drawn with the goal of measuring something (with a *sample statistic*) or modeling something (with a statistical or machine learning model). Since our estimate or model is based on a sample, it might be in error; it might be different if we were to draw a different sample. We are therefore interested in how different it might be—a key concern is *sampling variability*. If we had lots of data, we could draw additional samples and observe the distribution of a sample statistic directly.

Typically, we will calculate our estimate or model using as much data as is easily available, so the option of drawing additional samples from the population is not readily available.

It is important to distinguish between the distribution of the individual data points, known as *the data distribution*, and the distribution of a sample statistic, known as the *sampling distribution*.

The distribution of a sample statistic such as the mean is likely to be more regular and bell-shaped than the distribution of the data itself. The larger the sample the statistic is based on, the more this is true. Also, the larger the sample, the narrower the distribution of the sample statistic.

This is illustrated in an example using annual income for loan applicants to LendingClub (see "A Small Example: Predicting Loan Default" on page 239 for a description of the data). Take three samples from this data: a sample of 1,000 values, a sample of 1,000 means of 5 values, and a sample of 1,000 means of 20 values. Then plot a histogram of each sample to produce Figure 2-6.

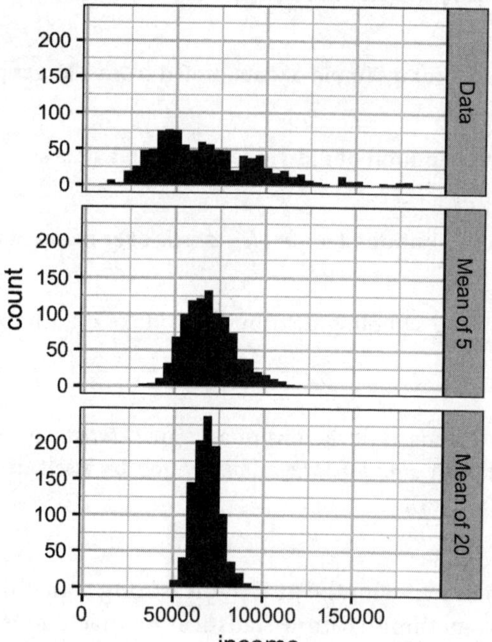

Figure 2-6. Histogram of annual incomes of 1,000 loan applicants (top), then 1,000 means of n=5 applicants (middle), and finally 1,000 means of n=20 applicants (bottom)

The histogram of the individual data values is broadly spread out and skewed toward higher values, as is to be expected with income data. The histograms of the means of 5 and 20 are increasingly compact and more bell-shaped. Here is the *R* code to generate these histograms, using the visualization package `ggplot2`:

```
library(ggplot2)
# take a simple random sample
samp_data <- data.frame(income=sample(loans_income, 1000),
                        type='data_dist')
# take a sample of means of 5 values
samp_mean_05 <- data.frame(
  income = tapply(sample(loans_income, 1000*5),
                  rep(1:1000, rep(5, 1000)), FUN=mean),
  type = 'mean_of_5')
# take a sample of means of 20 values
samp_mean_20 <- data.frame(
  income = tapply(sample(loans_income, 1000*20),
                  rep(1:1000, rep(20, 1000)), FUN=mean),
  type = 'mean_of_20')
# bind the data.frames and convert type to a factor
income <- rbind(samp_data, samp_mean_05, samp_mean_20)
income$type = factor(income$type,
                     levels=c('data_dist', 'mean_of_5', 'mean_of_20'),
                     labels=c('Data', 'Mean of 5', 'Mean of 20'))
# plot the histograms
ggplot(income, aes(x=income)) +
  geom_histogram(bins=40) +
  facet_grid(type ~ .)
```

The *Python* code uses seaborn's `FacetGrid` to show the three histograms:

```
import pandas as pd
import seaborn as sns

sample_data = pd.DataFrame({
    'income': loans_income.sample(1000),
    'type': 'Data',
})
sample_mean_05 = pd.DataFrame({
    'income': [loans_income.sample(5).mean() for _ in range(1000)],
    'type': 'Mean of 5',
})
sample_mean_20 = pd.DataFrame({
    'income': [loans_income.sample(20).mean() for _ in range(1000)],
    'type': 'Mean of 20',
})
results = pd.concat([sample_data, sample_mean_05, sample_mean_20])

g = sns.FacetGrid(results, col='type', col_wrap=1, height=2, aspect=2)
g.map(plt.hist, 'income', range=[0, 200000], bins=40)
```

```
g.set_axis_labels('Income', 'Count')
g.set_titles('{col_name}')
```

Central Limit Theorem

The phenomenon we've just described is termed the *central limit theorem*. It says that the means drawn from multiple samples will resemble the familiar bell-shaped normal curve (see "Normal Distribution" on page 69), even if the source population is not normally distributed, provided that the sample size is large enough and the departure of the data from normality is not too great. The central limit theorem allows normal-approximation formulas like the t-distribution to be used in calculating sampling distributions for inference—that is, confidence intervals and hypothesis tests.

The central limit theorem receives a lot of attention in traditional statistics texts because it underlies the machinery of hypothesis tests and confidence intervals, which themselves consume half the space in such texts. Data scientists should be aware of this role; however, since formal hypothesis tests and confidence intervals play a small role in data science, and the *bootstrap* (see "The Bootstrap" on page 61) is available in any case, the central limit theorem is not so central in the practice of data science.

Standard Error

The *standard error* is a single metric that sums up the variability in the sampling distribution for a statistic. The standard error can be estimated using a statistic based on the standard deviation s of the sample values, and the sample size n:

$$\text{Standard error} = SE = \frac{s}{\sqrt{n}}$$

As the sample size increases, the standard error decreases, corresponding to what was observed in Figure 2-6. The relationship between standard error and sample size is sometimes referred to as the *square root of n* rule: to reduce the standard error by a factor of 2, the sample size must be increased by a factor of 4.

The validity of the standard error formula arises from the central limit theorem. In fact, you don't need to rely on the central limit theorem to understand standard error. Consider the following approach to measuring standard error:

1. Collect a number of brand-new samples from the population.
2. For each new sample, calculate the statistic (e.g., mean).

3. Calculate the standard deviation of the statistics computed in step 2; use this as your estimate of standard error.

In practice, this approach of collecting new samples to estimate the standard error is typically not feasible (and statistically very wasteful). Fortunately, it turns out that it is not necessary to draw brand new samples; instead, you can use *bootstrap* resamples. In modern statistics, the bootstrap has become the standard way to estimate standard error. It can be used for virtually any statistic and does not rely on the central limit theorem or other distributional assumptions.

Standard Deviation Versus Standard Error

Do not confuse standard deviation (which measures the variability of individual data points) with standard error (which measures the variability of a sample metric).

Key Ideas

- The frequency distribution of a sample statistic tells us how that metric would turn out differently from sample to sample.
- This sampling distribution can be estimated via the bootstrap, or via formulas that rely on the central limit theorem.
- A key metric that sums up the variability of a sample statistic is its standard error.

Further Reading

David Lane's online multimedia resource in statistics (*https://oreil.ly/pe7ra*) has a useful simulation that allows you to select a sample statistic, a sample size, and the number of iterations and visualize a histogram of the resulting frequency distribution.

The Bootstrap

One easy and effective way to estimate the sampling distribution of a statistic, or of model parameters, is to draw additional samples, with replacement, from the sample itself and recalculate the statistic or model for each resample. This procedure is called the *bootstrap*, and it does not necessarily involve any assumptions about the data or the sample statistic being normally distributed.

Key Terms for the Bootstrap

Bootstrap sample
A sample taken with replacement from an observed data set.

Resampling
The process of taking repeated samples from observed data; includes both bootstrap and permutation (shuffling) procedures.

Conceptually, you can imagine the bootstrap as replicating the original sample thousands or millions of times so that you have a hypothetical population that embodies all the knowledge from your original sample (it's just larger). You can then draw samples from this hypothetical population for the purpose of estimating a sampling distribution; see Figure 2-7.

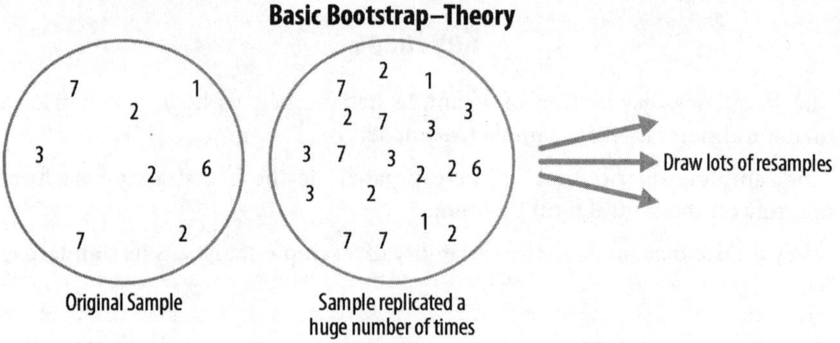

Figure 2-7. The idea of the bootstrap

In practice, it is not necessary to actually replicate the sample a huge number of times. We simply replace each observation after each draw; that is, we *sample with replacement*. In this way we effectively create an infinite population in which the probability of an element being drawn remains unchanged from draw to draw. The algorithm for a bootstrap resampling of the mean, for a sample of size *n*, is as follows:

1. Draw a sample value, record it, and then replace it.
2. Repeat *n* times.
3. Record the mean of the *n* resampled values.
4. Repeat steps 1–3 *R* times.
5. Use the *R* results to:

a. Calculate their standard deviation (this estimates sample mean standard error).

b. Produce a histogram or boxplot.

c. Find a confidence interval.

R, the number of iterations of the bootstrap, is set somewhat arbitrarily. The more iterations you do, the more accurate the estimate of the standard error, or the confidence interval. The result from this procedure is a bootstrap set of sample statistics or estimated model parameters, which you can then examine to see how variable they are.

The *R* package `boot` combines these steps in one function. For example, the following applies the bootstrap to the incomes of people taking out loans:

```
library(boot)
stat_fun <- function(x, idx) median(x[idx])
boot_obj <- boot(loans_income, R=1000, statistic=stat_fun)
```

The function `stat_fun` computes the median for a given sample specified by the index `idx`. The result is as follows:

```
Bootstrap Statistics :
    original   bias    std. error
t1*    62000 -70.5595    209.1515
```

The original estimate of the median is $62,000. The bootstrap distribution indicates that the estimate has a *bias* of about –$70 and a standard error of $209. The results will vary slightly between consecutive runs of the algorithm.

The major *Python* packages don't provide implementations of the bootstrap approach. It can be implemented using the `scikit-learn` method `resample`:

```
results = []
for nrepeat in range(1000):
    sample = resample(loans_income)
    results.append(sample.median())
results = pd.Series(results)
print('Bootstrap Statistics:')
print(f'original: {loans_income.median()}')
print(f'bias: {results.mean() - loans_income.median()}')
print(f'std. error: {results.std()}')
```

The bootstrap can be used with multivariate data, where the rows are sampled as units (see Figure 2-8). A model might then be run on the bootstrapped data, for example, to estimate the stability (variability) of model parameters, or to improve predictive power. With classification and regression trees (also called *decision trees*), running multiple trees on bootstrap samples and then averaging their predictions (or, with classification, taking a majority vote) generally performs better than using a single tree. This process is called *bagging* (short for "bootstrap aggregating"; see "Bagging and the Random Forest" on page 259).

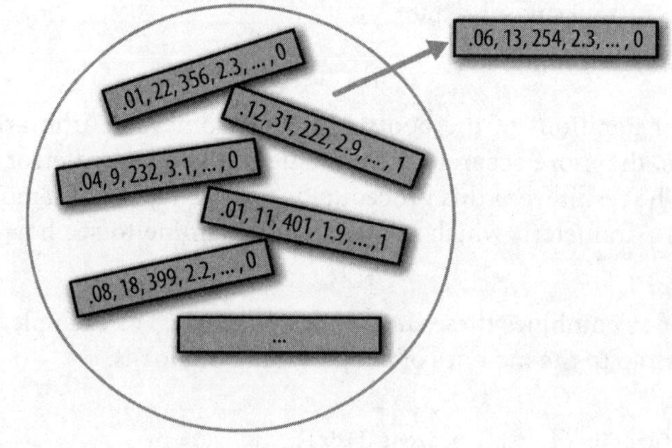

Figure 2-8. Multivariate bootstrap sampling

The repeated resampling of the bootstrap is conceptually simple, and Julian Simon, an economist and demographer, published a compendium of resampling examples, including the bootstrap, in his 1969 text *Basic Research Methods in Social Science* (Random House). However, it is also computationally intensive and was not a feasible option before the widespread availability of computing power. The technique gained its name and took off with the publication of several journal articles and a book by Stanford statistician Bradley Efron in the late 1970s and early 1980s. It was particularly popular among researchers who use statistics but are not statisticians, and for use with metrics or models where mathematical approximations are not readily available. The sampling distribution of the mean has been well established since 1908; the sampling distribution of many other metrics has not. The bootstrap can be used for sample size determination; experiment with different values for n to see how the sampling distribution is affected.

The bootstrap was met with considerable skepticism when it was first introduced; it had the aura to many of spinning gold from straw. This skepticism stemmed from a misunderstanding of the bootstrap's purpose.

> The bootstrap does not compensate for a small sample size; it does not create new data, nor does it fill in holes in an existing data set. It merely informs us about how lots of additional samples would behave when drawn from a population like our original sample.

Resampling Versus Bootstrapping

Sometimes the term *resampling* is used synonymously with the term *bootstrapping*, as just outlined. More often, the term *resampling* also includes permutation procedures (see "Permutation Test" on page 97), where multiple samples are combined and the sampling may be done without replacement. In any case, the term *bootstrap* always implies sampling with replacement from an observed data set.

Key Ideas

- The bootstrap (sampling with replacement from a data set) is a powerful tool for assessing the variability of a sample statistic.
- The bootstrap can be applied in similar fashion in a wide variety of circumstances, without extensive study of mathematical approximations to sampling distributions.
- It also allows us to estimate sampling distributions for statistics where no mathematical approximation has been developed.
- When applied to predictive models, aggregating multiple bootstrap sample predictions (bagging) outperforms the use of a single model.

Further Reading

- *An Introduction to the Bootstrap* by Bradley Efron and Robert Tibshirani (Chapman & Hall, 1993) was the first book-length treatment of the bootstrap. It is still widely read.
- The retrospective on the bootstrap in the May 2003 issue of *Statistical Science* (vol. 18, no. 2), discusses (among other antecedents, in Peter Hall's "A Short Prehistory of the Bootstrap") Julian Simon's initial publication of the bootstrap in 1969.
- See *An Introduction to Statistical Learning* by Gareth James, Daniela Witten, Trevor Hastie, and Robert Tibshirani (Springer, 2013) for sections on the bootstrap and, in particular, bagging.

Confidence Intervals

Frequency tables, histograms, boxplots, and standard errors are all ways to understand the potential error in a sample estimate. Confidence intervals are another.

Key Terms for Confidence Intervals

Confidence level
: The percentage of confidence intervals, constructed in the same way from the same population, that are expected to contain the statistic of interest.

Interval endpoints
: The top and bottom of the confidence interval.

There is a natural human aversion to uncertainty; people (especially experts) say "I don't know" far too rarely. Analysts and managers, while acknowledging uncertainty, nonetheless place undue faith in an estimate when it is presented as a single number (a *point estimate*). Presenting an estimate not as a single number but as a range is one way to counteract this tendency. Confidence intervals do this in a manner grounded in statistical sampling principles.

Confidence intervals always come with a coverage level, expressed as a (high) percentage, say 90% or 95%. One way to think of a 90% confidence interval is as follows: it is the interval that encloses the central 90% of the bootstrap sampling distribution of a sample statistic (see "The Bootstrap" on page 61). More generally, an x% confidence interval around a sample estimate should, on average, contain similar sample estimates x% of the time (when a similar sampling procedure is followed).

Given a sample of size n, and a sample statistic of interest, the algorithm for a bootstrap confidence interval is as follows:

1. Draw a random sample of size n with replacement from the data (a resample).
2. Record the statistic of interest for the resample.
3. Repeat steps 1–2 many (R) times.
4. For an x% confidence interval, trim [(100-x) / 2]% of the R resample results from either end of the distribution.
5. The trim points are the endpoints of an x% bootstrap confidence interval.

Figure 2-9 shows a 90% confidence interval for the mean annual income of loan applicants, based on a sample of 20 for which the mean was $62,231.

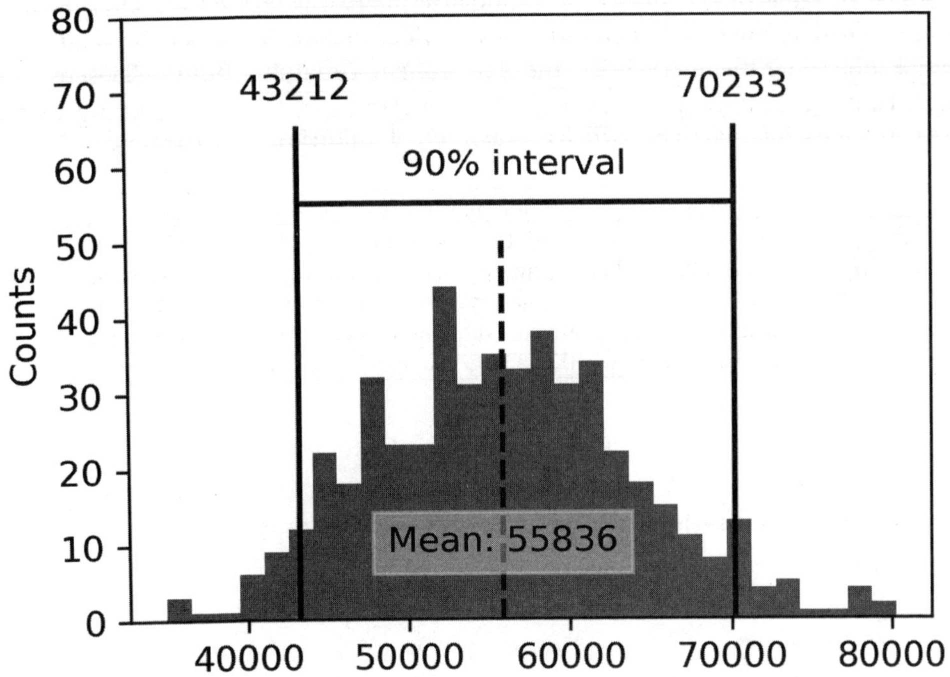

Figure 2-9. Bootstrap confidence interval for the annual income of loan applicants, based on a sample of 20

The bootstrap is a general tool that can be used to generate confidence intervals for most statistics, or model parameters. Statistical textbooks and software, with roots in over a half century of computerless statistical analysis, will also reference confidence intervals generated by formulas, especially the t-distribution (see "Student's t-Distribution" on page 75).

Of course, what we are really interested in when we have a sample result is, "What is the probability that the true value lies within a certain interval?" This is not really the question that a confidence interval answers, but it ends up being how most people interpret the answer.

The probability question associated with a confidence interval starts out with the phrase "Given a sampling procedure and a population, what is the probability that…" To go in the opposite direction, "Given a sample result, what is the probability that (something is true about the population)?" involves more complex calculations and deeper imponderables.

The percentage associated with the confidence interval is termed the *level of confidence*. The higher the level of confidence, the wider the interval. Also, the smaller the sample, the wider the interval (i.e., the greater the uncertainty). Both make sense: the more confident you want to be, and the less data you have, the wider you must make the confidence interval to be sufficiently assured of capturing the true value.

> For a data scientist, a confidence interval is a tool that can be used to get an idea of how variable a sample result might be. Data scientists would use this information not to publish a scholarly paper or submit a result to a regulatory agency (as a researcher might) but most likely to communicate the potential error in an estimate, and perhaps to learn whether a larger sample is needed.

Key Ideas

- Confidence intervals are the typical way to present estimates as an interval range.
- The more data you have, the less variable a sample estimate will be.
- The lower the level of confidence you can tolerate, the narrower the confidence interval will be.
- The bootstrap is an effective way to construct confidence intervals.

Further Reading

- For a bootstrap approach to confidence intervals, see *Introductory Statistics and Analytics: A Resampling Perspective* by Peter Bruce (Wiley, 2014) or *Statistics: Unlocking the Power of Data*, 2nd ed., by Robin Lock and four other Lock family members (Wiley, 2016).
- Engineers, who have a need to understand the precision of their measurements, use confidence intervals perhaps more than most disciplines, and *Modern Engineering Statistics* by Thomas Ryan (Wiley, 2007) discusses confidence intervals. It also reviews a tool that is just as useful and gets less attention: *prediction intervals* (intervals around a single value, as opposed to a mean or other summary statistic).

Normal Distribution

The bell-shaped normal distribution is iconic in traditional statistics.[1] The fact that distributions of sample statistics are often normally shaped has made it a powerful tool in the development of mathematical formulas that approximate those distributions.

> ### Key Terms for Normal Distribution
>
> ***Error***
> The difference between a data point and a predicted or average value.
>
> ***Standardize***
> Subtract the mean and divide by the standard deviation.
>
> ***z-score***
> The result of standardizing an individual data point.
>
> ***Standard normal***
> A normal distribution with mean = 0 and standard deviation = 1.
>
> ***QQ-Plot***
> A plot to visualize how close a sample distribution is to a specified distribution, e.g., the normal distribution.

In a normal distribution (Figure 2-10), 68% of the data lies within one standard deviation of the mean, and 95% lies within two standard deviations.

> It is a common misconception that the normal distribution is called that because most data follows a normal distribution—that is, it is the normal thing. Most of the variables used in a typical data science project—in fact, most raw data as a whole—are *not* normally distributed: see "Long-Tailed Distributions" on page 73. The utility of the normal distribution derives from the fact that many statistics *are* normally distributed in their sampling distribution. Even so, assumptions of normality are generally a last resort, used when empirical probability distributions, or bootstrap distributions, are not available.

1 The bell curve is iconic but perhaps overrated. George W. Cobb, the Mount Holyoke statistician noted for his contribution to the philosophy of teaching introductory statistics, argued in a November 2015 editorial in the *American Statistician* that the "standard introductory course, which puts the normal distribution at its center, had outlived the usefulness of its centrality."

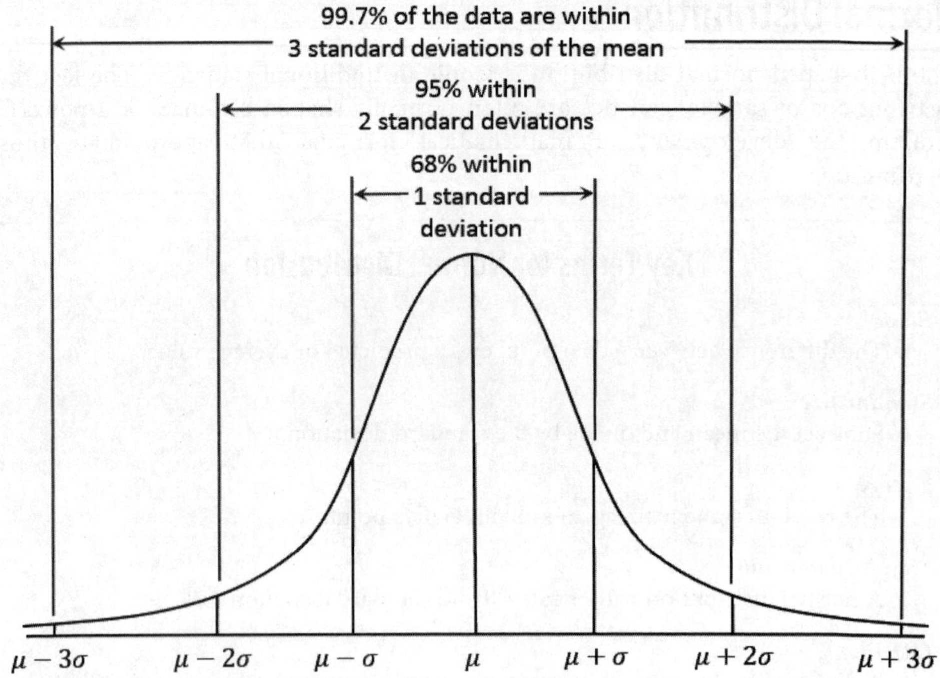

Figure 2-10. Normal curve

The normal distribution is also referred to as a *Gaussian* distribution after Carl Friedrich Gauss, a prodigious German mathematician from the late 18th and early 19th centuries. Another name previously used for the normal distribution was the "error" distribution. Statistically speaking, an *error* is the difference between an actual value and a statistical estimate like the sample mean. For example, the standard deviation (see "Estimates of Variability" on page 13) is based on the errors from the mean of the data. Gauss's development of the normal distribution came from his study of the errors of astronomical measurements that were found to be normally distributed.

Standard Normal and QQ-Plots

A *standard normal* distribution is one in which the units on the x-axis are expressed in terms of standard deviations away from the mean. To compare data to a standard normal distribution, you subtract the mean and then divide by the standard deviation; this is also called *normalization* or *standardization* (see "Standardization (Normalization, z-Scores)" on page 243). Note that "standardization" in this sense is unrelated to database record standardization (conversion to a common format). The transformed value is termed a *z-score*, and the normal distribution is sometimes called the *z-distribution*.

A *QQ-Plot* is used to visually determine how close a sample is to a specified distribution—in this case, the normal distribution. The QQ-Plot orders the *z*-scores from low to high and plots each value's *z*-score on the y-axis; the x-axis is the corresponding quantile of a normal distribution for that value's rank. Since the data is normalized, the units correspond to the number of standard deviations away from the mean. If the points roughly fall on the diagonal line, then the sample distribution can be considered close to normal. Figure 2-11 shows a QQ-Plot for a sample of 100 values randomly generated from a normal distribution; as expected, the points closely follow the line. This figure can be produced in *R* with the `qqnorm` function:

```
norm_samp <- rnorm(100)
qqnorm(norm_samp)
abline(a=0, b=1, col='grey')
```

In *Python*, use the method `scipy.stats.probplot` to create the QQ-Plot:

```
fig, ax = plt.subplots(figsize=(4, 4))
norm_sample = stats.norm.rvs(size=100)
stats.probplot(norm_sample, plot=ax)
```

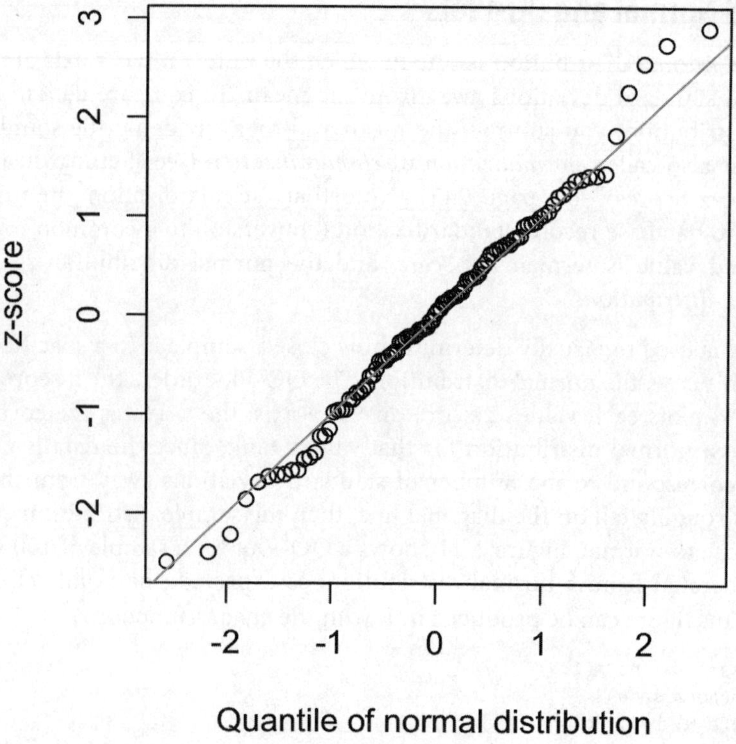

Figure 2-11. QQ-Plot of a sample of 100 values drawn from a standard normal distribution

Converting data to *z*-scores (i.e., standardizing or normalizing the data) does *not* make the data normally distributed. It just puts the data on the same scale as the standard normal distribution, often for comparison purposes.

Key Ideas

- The normal distribution was essential to the historical development of statistics, as it permitted mathematical approximation of uncertainty and variability.
- While raw data is typically not normally distributed, errors often are, as are averages and totals in large samples.
- To convert data to *z*-scores, you subtract the mean of the data and divide by the standard deviation; you can then compare the data to a normal distribution.

Long-Tailed Distributions

Despite the importance of the normal distribution historically in statistics, and in contrast to what the name would suggest, data is generally not normally distributed.

Key Terms for Long-Tailed Distributions

Tail
: The long narrow portion of a frequency distribution, where relatively extreme values occur at low frequency.

Skew
: Where one tail of a distribution is longer than the other.

While the normal distribution is often appropriate and useful with respect to the distribution of errors and sample statistics, it typically does not characterize the distribution of raw data. Sometimes, the distribution is highly *skewed* (asymmetric), such as with income data; or the distribution can be discrete, as with binomial data. Both symmetric and asymmetric distributions may have *long tails*. The tails of a distribution correspond to the extreme values (small and large). Long tails, and guarding against them, are widely recognized in practical work. Nassim Taleb has proposed the *black swan* theory, which predicts that anomalous events, such as a stock market crash, are much more likely to occur than would be predicted by the normal distribution.

A good example to illustrate the long-tailed nature of data is stock returns. Figure 2-12 shows the QQ-Plot for the daily stock returns for Netflix (NFLX). This is generated in *R* by:

```
nflx <- sp500_px[,'NFLX']
nflx <- diff(log(nflx[nflx>0]))
qqnorm(nflx)
abline(a=0, b=1, col='grey')
```

The corresponding *Python* code is:

```
nflx = sp500_px.NFLX
nflx = np.diff(np.log(nflx[nflx>0]))
fig, ax = plt.subplots(figsize=(4, 4))
stats.probplot(nflx, plot=ax)
```

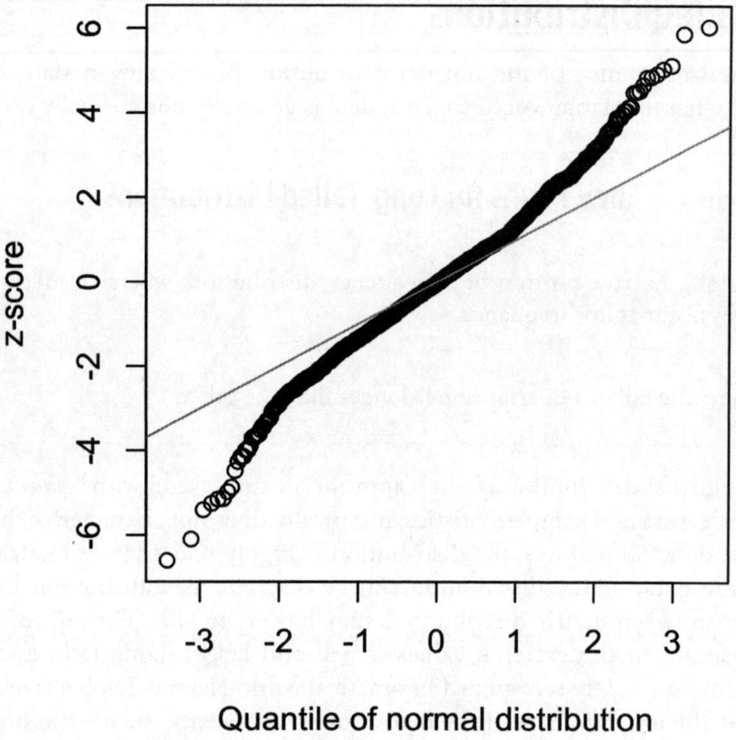

Figure 2-12. QQ-Plot of the returns for Netflix (NFLX)

In contrast to Figure 2-11, the points are far below the line for low values and far above the line for high values, indicating the data are not normally distributed. This means that we are much more likely to observe extreme values than would be expected if the data had a normal distribution. Figure 2-12 shows another common phenomenon: the points are close to the line for the data within one standard deviation of the mean. Tukey refers to this phenomenon as data being "normal in the middle" but having much longer tails (see [Tukey-1987]).

> There is much statistical literature about the task of fitting statistical distributions to observed data. Beware an excessively data-centric approach to this job, which is as much art as science. Data is variable, and often consistent, on its face, with more than one shape and type of distribution. It is typically the case that domain and statistical knowledge must be brought to bear to determine what type of distribution is appropriate to model a given situation. For example, we might have data on the level of internet traffic on a server over many consecutive five-second periods. It is useful to know that the best distribution to model "events per time period" is the Poisson (see "Poisson Distributions" on page 83).

Key Ideas

- Most data is not normally distributed.
- Assuming a normal distribution can lead to underestimation of extreme events ("black swans").

Further Reading

- *The Black Swan*, 2nd ed., by Nassim Nicholas Taleb (Random House, 2010)
- *Handbook of Statistical Distributions with Applications*, 2nd ed., by K. Krishnamoorthy (Chapman & Hall/CRC Press, 2016)

Student's t-Distribution

The *t-distribution* is a normally shaped distribution, except that it is a bit thicker and longer on the tails. It is used extensively in depicting distributions of sample statistics. Distributions of sample means are typically shaped like a t-distribution, and there is a family of t-distributions that differ depending on how large the sample is. The larger the sample, the more normally shaped the t-distribution becomes.

Key Terms for Student's t-Distribution

n
: Sample size.

Degrees of freedom
: A parameter that allows the t-distribution to adjust to different sample sizes, statistics, and numbers of groups.

The t-distribution is often called *Student's t* because it was published in 1908 in *Biometrika* by W. S. Gosset under the name "Student." Gosset's employer, the Guinness brewery, did not want competitors to know that it was using statistical methods, so it insisted that Gosset not use his name on the article.

Gosset wanted to answer the question "What is the sampling distribution of the mean of a sample, drawn from a larger population?" He started out with a resampling experiment—drawing random samples of 4 from a data set of 3,000 measurements of criminals' height and left-middle-finger length. (This being the era of eugenics, there was much interest in data on criminals, and in discovering correlations between criminal tendencies and physical or psychological attributes.) Gosset plotted the standardized results (the *z*-scores) on the x-axis and the frequency on the y-axis. Separately, he had derived a function, now known as *Student's t*, and he fit this function over the sample results, plotting the comparison (see Figure 2-13).

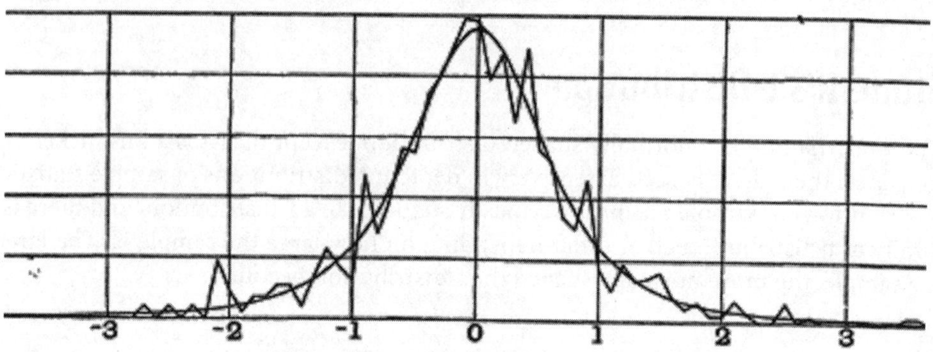

Figure 2-13. Gosset's resampling experiment results and fitted t-curve (from his 1908 Biometrika paper)

A number of different statistics can be compared, after standardization, to the t-distribution, to estimate confidence intervals in light of sampling variation. Consider a sample of size n for which the sample mean $\bar{x}$ has been calculated. If s is the sample standard deviation, a 90% confidence interval around the sample mean is given by:

$$\bar{x} \pm t_{n-1}(0.05) \cdot \frac{s}{\sqrt{n}}$$

where $t_{n-1}(.05)$ is the value of the t-statistic, with $(n - 1)$ degrees of freedom (see "Degrees of Freedom" on page 116), that "chops off" 5% of the t-distribution at either end. The t-distribution has been used as a reference for the distribution of a sample mean, the difference between two sample means, regression parameters, and other statistics.

Had computing power been widely available in 1908, statistics would no doubt have relied much more heavily on computationally intensive resampling methods from the start. Lacking computers, statisticians turned to mathematics and functions such as the t-distribution to approximate sampling distributions. Computer power enabled practical resampling experiments in the 1980s, but by then, use of the t-distribution and similar distributions had become deeply embedded in textbooks and software.

The t-distribution's accuracy in depicting the behavior of a sample statistic requires that the distribution of that statistic for that sample be shaped like a normal distribution. It turns out that sample statistics *are* often normally distributed, even when the underlying population data is not (a fact which led to widespread application of the t-distribution). This brings us back to the phenomenon known as the *central limit theorem* (see "Central Limit Theorem" on page 60).

What do data scientists need to know about the t-distribution and the central limit theorem? Not a whole lot. The t-distribution is used in classical statistical inference but is not as central to the purposes of data science. Understanding and quantifying uncertainty and variation are important to data scientists, but empirical bootstrap sampling can answer most questions about sampling error. However, data scientists will routinely encounter t-statistics in output from statistical software and statistical procedures in *R*—for example, in A/B tests and regressions—so familiarity with its purpose is helpful.

Key Ideas

- The t-distribution is actually a family of distributions resembling the normal distribution but with thicker tails.
- The t-distribution is widely used as a reference basis for the distribution of sample means, differences between two sample means, regression parameters, and more.

Further Reading

- The original W.S. Gosset paper as published in *Biometrika* in 1908 is available as a PDF (*https://oreil.ly/J6gDg*).
- A standard treatment of the t-distribution can be found in David Lane's online resource (*https://oreil.ly/QxUkA*).

Binomial Distribution

Yes/no (binomial) outcomes lie at the heart of analytics since they are often the culmination of a decision or other process; buy/don't buy, click/don't click, survive/die, and so on. Central to understanding the binomial distribution is the idea of a set of *trials*, each trial having two possible outcomes with definite probabilities.

For example, flipping a coin 10 times is a binomial experiment with 10 trials, each trial having two possible outcomes (heads or tails); see Figure 2-14. Such yes/no or 0/1 outcomes are termed *binary* outcomes, and they need not have 50/50 probabilities. Any probabilities that sum to 1.0 are possible. It is conventional in statistics to term the "1" outcome the *success* outcome; it is also common practice to assign "1" to the more rare outcome. Use of the term *success* does not imply that the outcome is desirable or beneficial, but it does tend to indicate the outcome of interest. For example, loan defaults or fraudulent transactions are relatively uncommon events that we may be interested in predicting, so they are termed "1s" or "successes."

Figure 2-14. The tails side of a buffalo nickel

Key Terms for Binomial Distribution

Trial
: An event with a discrete outcome (e.g., a coin flip).

Success
: The outcome of interest for a trial.

  Synonym
  : "1" (as opposed to "0")

Binomial
: Having two outcomes.

  Synonyms
  : yes/no, 0/1, binary

Binomial trial
: A trial with two outcomes.

  Synonym
  : Bernoulli trial

Binomial distribution
: Distribution of number of successes in x trials.

  Synonym
  : Bernoulli distribution

The binomial distribution is the frequency distribution of the number of successes (x) in a given number of trials (n) with specified probability (p) of success in each trial. There is a family of binomial distributions, depending on the values of n and p. The binomial distribution would answer a question like:

> If the probability of a click converting to a sale is 0.02, what is the probability of observing 0 sales in 200 clicks?

The *R* function `dbinom` calculates binomial probabilities. For example:

```
dbinom(x=2, size=5, p=0.1)
```

would return 0.0729, the probability of observing exactly $x = 2$ successes in $size = 5$ trials, where the probability of success for each trial is $p = 0.1$. For our example above, we use $x = 0$, $size = 200$, and $p = 0.02$. With these arguments, `dbinom` returns a probability of 0.0176.

Often we are interested in determining the probability of x or fewer successes in n trials. In this case, we use the function `pbinom`:

```
pbinom(2, 5, 0.1)
```

This would return 0.9914, the probability of observing two or fewer successes in five trials, where the probability of success for each trial is 0.1.

The `scipy.stats` module implements a large variety of statistical distributions. For the binomial distribution, use the functions `stats.binom.pmf` and `stats.binom.cdf`:

```
stats.binom.pmf(2, n=5, p=0.1)
stats.binom.cdf(2, n=5, p=0.1)
```

The mean of a binomial distribution is $n \times p$; you can also think of this as the expected number of successes in n trials, for success probability = p.

The variance is $n \times p(1 - p)$. With a large enough number of trials (particularly when p is close to 0.50), the binomial distribution is virtually indistinguishable from the normal distribution. In fact, calculating binomial probabilities with large sample sizes is computationally demanding, and most statistical procedures use the normal distribution, with mean and variance, as an approximation.

Key Ideas

- Binomial outcomes are important to model, since they represent, among other things, fundamental decisions (buy or don't buy, click or don't click, survive or die, etc.).
- A binomial trial is an experiment with two possible outcomes: one with probability p and the other with probability $1 - p$.
- With large n, and provided p is not too close to 0 or 1, the binomial distribution can be approximated by the normal distribution.

Further Reading

- Read about the "quincunx" (*https://oreil.ly/nmkcs*), a pinball-like simulation device for illustrating the binomial distribution.
- The binomial distribution is a staple of introductory statistics, and all introductory statistics texts will have a chapter or two on it.

Chi-Square Distribution

An important idea in statistics is *departure from expectation*, especially with respect to category counts. Expectation is defined loosely as "nothing unusual or of note in the data" (e.g., no correlation between variables or predictable patterns). This is also termed the "null hypothesis" or "null model" (see "The Null Hypothesis" on page 94). For example, you might want to test whether one variable (say, a row variable representing gender) is independent of another (say, a column variable representing "was promoted in job"), and you have counts of the number in each of the cells of the data table. The statistic that measures the extent to which results depart from the null expectation of independence is the chi-square statistic. It is the difference between the observed and expected values, divided by the square root of the expected value, squared, then summed across all categories. This process standardizes the statistic so it can be compared to a reference distribution. A more general way of putting this is to note that the chi-square statistic is a measure of the extent to which a set of observed values "fits" a specified distribution (a "goodness-of-fit" test). It is useful for determining whether multiple treatments (an "A/B/C... test") differ from one another in their effects.

The chi-square distribution is the distribution of this statistic under repeated resampled draws from the null model—see "Chi-Square Test" on page 124 for a detailed algorithm, and the chi-square formula for a data table. A low chi-square value for a set of counts indicates that they closely follow the expected distribution. A high chi-square indicates that they differ markedly from what is expected. There are a variety of chi-square distributions associated with different degrees of freedom (e.g., number of observations—see "Degrees of Freedom" on page 116).

Key Ideas

- The chi-square distribution is typically concerned with counts of subjects or items falling into categories.
- The chi-square statistic measures the extent of departure from what you would expect in a null model.

Further Reading

- The chi-square distribution owes its place in modern statistics to the great statistician Karl Pearson and the birth of hypothesis testing—read about this and more in David Salsburg's *The Lady Tasting Tea: How Statistics Revolutionized Science in the Twentieth Century* (W. H. Freeman, 2001).
- For a more detailed exposition, see the section in this book on the chi-square test ("Chi-Square Test" on page 124).

F-Distribution

A common procedure in scientific experimentation is to test multiple treatments across groups—say, different fertilizers on different blocks of a field. This is similar to the A/B/C test referred to in the chi-square distribution (see "Chi-Square Distribution" on page 80), except we are dealing with measured continuous values rather than counts. In this case we are interested in the extent to which differences among group means are greater than we might expect under normal random variation. The F-statistic measures this and is the ratio of the variability among the group means to the variability within each group (also called residual variability). This comparison is termed an *analysis of variance* (see "ANOVA" on page 118). The distribution of the F-statistic is the frequency distribution of all the values that would be produced by randomly permuting data in which all the group means are equal (i.e., a null model). There are a variety of F-distributions associated with different degrees of freedom (e.g., numbers of groups—see "Degrees of Freedom" on page 116). The calculation of F is illustrated in the section on ANOVA. The F-statistic is also used in linear regression to compare the variation accounted for by the regression model to the overall variation in the data. F-statistics are produced automatically by *R* and *Python* as part of regression and ANOVA routines.

Key Ideas

- The F-distribution is used with experiments and linear models involving measured data.
- The F-statistic compares variation due to factors of interest to overall variation.

Further Reading

George Cobb's *Introduction to Design and Analysis of Experiments* (Wiley, 2008) contains an excellent exposition of the decomposition of variance components, which helps in understanding ANOVA and the F-statistic.

Poisson and Related Distributions

Many processes produce events randomly at a given overall rate—visitors arriving at a website, or cars arriving at a toll plaza (events spread over time); imperfections in a square meter of fabric, or typos per 100 lines of code (events spread over space).

Key Terms for Poisson and Related Distributions

Lambda
: The rate (per unit of time or space) at which events occur.

Poisson distribution
: The frequency distribution of the number of events in sampled units of time or space.

Exponential distribution
: The frequency distribution of the time or distance from one event to the next event.

Weibull distribution
: A generalized version of the exponential distribution in which the event rate is allowed to shift over time.

Poisson Distributions

From prior aggregate data (for example, number of flu infections per year), we can estimate the average number of events per unit of time or space (e.g., infections per day, or per census unit). We might also want to know how different this might be from one unit of time/space to another. The Poisson distribution tells us the distribution of events per unit of time or space when we sample many such units. It is useful when addressing queuing questions such as "How much capacity do we need to be 95% sure of fully processing the internet traffic that arrives on a server in any five-second period?"

The key parameter in a Poisson distribution is λ, or lambda. This is the mean number of events that occurs in a specified interval of time or space. The variance for a Poisson distribution is also λ.

A common technique is to generate random numbers from a Poisson distribution as part of a queuing simulation. The `rpois` function in *R* does this, taking only two arguments—the quantity of random numbers sought, and lambda:

```
rpois(100, lambda=2)
```

The corresponding `scipy` function is `stats.poisson.rvs`:

```
stats.poisson.rvs(2, size=100)
```

This code will generate 100 random numbers from a Poisson distribution with $\lambda = 2$. For example, if incoming customer service calls average two per minute, this code will simulate 100 minutes, returning the number of calls in each of those 100 minutes.

Exponential Distribution

Using the same parameter λ that we used in the Poisson distribution, we can also model the distribution of the time between events: time between visits to a website or between cars arriving at a toll plaza. It is also used in engineering to model time to failure, and in process management to model, for example, the time required per service call. The *R* code to generate random numbers from an exponential distribution takes two arguments: `n` (the quantity of numbers to be generated) and `rate` (the number of events per time period). For example:

```
rexp(n=100, rate=0.2)
```

In the function `stats.expon.rvs`, the order of the arguments is reversed:

```
stats.expon.rvs(0.2, size=100)
```

This code would generate 100 random numbers from an exponential distribution where the mean number of events per time period is 0.2. So you could use it to simulate 100 intervals, in minutes, between service calls, where the average rate of incoming calls is 0.2 per minute.

A key assumption in any simulation study for either the Poisson or exponential distribution is that the rate, λ, remains constant over the period being considered. This is rarely reasonable in a global sense; for example, traffic on roads or data networks varies by time of day and day of week. However, the time periods, or areas of space, can usually be divided into segments that are sufficiently homogeneous so that analysis or simulation within those periods is valid.

Estimating the Failure Rate

In many applications, the event rate, λ, is known or can be estimated from prior data. However, for rare events, this is not necessarily so. Aircraft engine failure, for example, is sufficiently rare (thankfully) that, for a given engine type, there may be little data on which to base an estimate of time between failures. With no data at all, there is little basis on which to estimate an event rate. However, you can make some guesses: if no events have been seen after 20 hours, you can be pretty sure that the rate is not 1 per hour. Via simulation, or direct calculation of probabilities, you can assess different hypothetical event rates and estimate threshold values below which the rate is very unlikely to fall. If there is some data but not enough to provide a precise, reliable estimate of the rate, a goodness-of-fit test (see "Chi-Square Test" on page 124) can be applied to various rates to determine how well they fit the observed data.

Weibull Distribution

In many cases, the event rate does not remain constant over time. If the period over which it changes is much longer than the typical interval between events, there is no problem; you just subdivide the analysis into the segments where rates are relatively constant, as mentioned before. If, however, the event rate changes over the time of the interval, the exponential (or Poisson) distributions are no longer useful. This is likely to be the case in mechanical failure—the risk of failure increases as time goes by. The *Weibull* distribution is an extension of the exponential distribution in which the event rate is allowed to change, as specified by a *shape parameter*, β. If $\beta > 1$, the probability of an event increases over time; if $\beta < 1$, the probability decreases. Because the Weibull distribution is used with time-to-failure analysis instead of event rate, the second parameter is expressed in terms of characteristic life, rather than in terms of the rate of events per interval. The symbol used is η, the Greek letter eta. It is also called the *scale* parameter.

With the Weibull, the estimation task now includes estimation of both parameters, β and η. Software is used to model the data and yield an estimate of the best-fitting Weibull distribution.

The *R* code to generate random numbers from a Weibull distribution takes three arguments: `n` (the quantity of numbers to be generated), `shape`, and `scale`. For example, the following code would generate 100 random numbers (lifetimes) from a Weibull distribution with shape of 1.5 and characteristic life of 5,000:

```
rweibull(100, 1.5, 5000)
```

To achieve the same in *Python*, use the function `stats.weibull_min.rvs`:

```
stats.weibull_min.rvs(1.5, scale=5000, size=100)
```

Key Ideas

- For events that occur at a constant rate, the number of events per unit of time or space can be modeled as a Poisson distribution.
- You can also model the time or distance between one event and the next as an exponential distribution.
- A changing event rate over time (e.g., an increasing probability of device failure) can be modeled with the Weibull distribution.

Further Reading

- *Modern Engineering Statistics* by Thomas Ryan (Wiley, 2007) has a chapter devoted to the probability distributions used in engineering applications.
- Read an engineering-based perspective on the use of the Weibull distribution here (*https://oreil.ly/1x-ga*) and here (*https://oreil.ly/9bn-U*).

Summary

In the era of big data, the principles of random sampling remain important when accurate estimates are needed. Random selection of data can reduce bias and yield a higher quality data set than would result from just using the conveniently available data. Knowledge of various sampling and data-generating distributions allows us to quantify potential errors in an estimate that might be due to random variation. At the same time, the bootstrap (sampling with replacement from an observed data set) is an attractive "one size fits all" method to determine possible error in sample estimates.

CHAPTER 3

Statistical Experiments and Significance Testing

Design of experiments is a cornerstone of the practice of statistics, with applications in virtually all areas of research. The goal is to design an experiment in order to confirm or reject a hypothesis. Data scientists often need to conduct continual experiments, particularly regarding user interface and product marketing. This chapter reviews traditional experimental design and discusses some common challenges in data science. It also covers some oft-cited concepts in statistical inference and explains their meaning and relevance (or lack of relevance) to data science.

Whenever you see references to statistical significance, t-tests, or p-values, it is typically in the context of the classical statistical inference "pipeline" (see Figure 3-1). This process starts with a hypothesis ("drug A is better than the existing standard drug," or "price A is more profitable than the existing price B"). An experiment (it might be an A/B test) is designed to test the hypothesis—designed in such a way that it hopefully will deliver conclusive results. The data is collected and analyzed, and then a conclusion is drawn. The term *inference* reflects the intention to apply the experiment results, which involve a limited set of data, to a larger process or population.

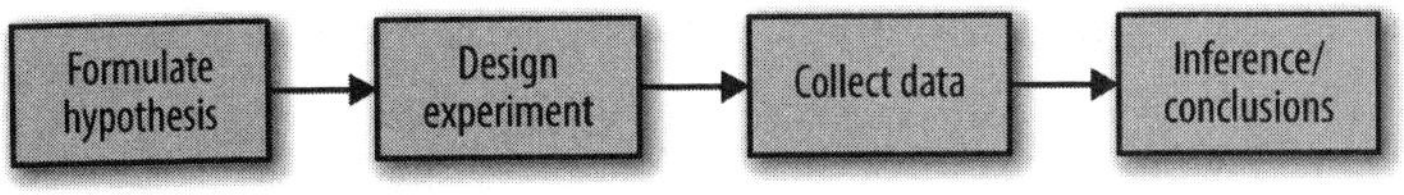

Figure 3-1. The classical statistical inference pipeline

A/B Testing

An A/B test is an experiment with two groups to establish which of two treatments, products, procedures, or the like is superior. Often one of the two treatments is the standard existing treatment, or no treatment. If a standard (or no) treatment is used, it is called the *control*. A typical hypothesis is that a new treatment is better than the control.

Key Terms for A/B Testing

Treatment
: Something (drug, price, web headline) to which a subject is exposed.

Treatment group
: A group of subjects exposed to a specific treatment.

Control group
: A group of subjects exposed to no (or standard) treatment.

Randomization
: The process of randomly assigning subjects to treatments.

Subjects
: The items (web visitors, patients, etc.) that are exposed to treatments.

Test statistic
: The metric used to measure the effect of the treatment.

A/B tests are common in web design and marketing, since results are so readily measured. Some examples of A/B testing include:

- Testing two soil treatments to determine which produces better seed germination
- Testing two therapies to determine which suppresses cancer more effectively
- Testing two prices to determine which yields more net profit
- Testing two web headlines to determine which produces more clicks (Figure 3-2)
- Testing two web ads to determine which generates more conversions

Figure 3-2. Marketers continually test one web presentation against another

A proper A/B test has *subjects* that can be assigned to one treatment or another. The subject might be a person, a plant seed, a web visitor; the key is that the subject is exposed to the treatment. Ideally, subjects are *randomized* (assigned randomly) to treatments. In this way, you know that any difference between the treatment groups is due to one of two things:

- The effect of the different treatments
- Luck of the draw in which subjects are assigned to which treatments (i.e., the random assignment may have resulted in the naturally better-performing subjects being concentrated in A or B)

You also need to pay attention to the *test statistic* or metric you use to compare group A to group B. Perhaps the most common metric in data science is a binary variable: click or no-click, buy or don't buy, fraud or no fraud, and so on. Those results would be summed up in a 2×2 table. Table 3-1 is a 2×2 table for an actual price test (see "Statistical Significance and p-Values" on page 103 for further discussion of these results).

Table 3-1. 2×2 table for ecommerce experiment results

Outcome	Price A	Price B
Conversion	200	182
No conversion	23,539	22,406

If the metric is a continuous variable (purchase amount, profit, etc.) or a count (e.g., days in hospital, pages visited), the result might be displayed differently. If one were interested not in conversion but in revenue per page view, the results of the price test in Table 3-1 might look like this in typical default software output:

Revenue/page view with price A: mean = 3.87, SD = 51.10

Revenue/page view with price B: mean = 4.11, SD = 62.98

"SD" refers to the standard deviation of the values within each group.

Just because statistical software—including *R* and *Python*—generates output by default does not mean that all the output is useful or relevant. You can see that the preceding standard deviations are not that useful; on their face they suggest that numerous values might be negative, when negative revenue is not feasible. This data consists of a small set of relatively high values (page views with conversions) and a huge number of 0-values (page views with no conversion). It is difficult to sum up the variability of such data with a single number, though the mean absolute deviation from the mean (7.68 for A and 8.15 for B) is more reasonable than the standard deviation.

Why Have a Control Group?

Why not skip the control group and just run an experiment applying the treatment of interest to only one group, and compare the outcome to prior experience?

Without a control group, there is no assurance that "all other things are equal" and that any difference is really due to the treatment (or to chance). When you have a control group, it is subject to the same conditions (except for the treatment of interest) as the treatment group. If you simply make a comparison to "baseline" or prior experience, other factors, besides the treatment, might differ.

> **Blinding in studies**
>
> A *blind study* is one in which the subjects are unaware of whether they are getting treatment A or treatment B. Awareness of receiving a particular treatment can affect response. A *double-blind* study is one in which the investigators and facilitators (e.g., doctors and nurses in a medical study) also are unaware which subjects are getting which treatment. Blinding is not possible when the nature of the treatment is transparent—for example, cognitive therapy from a computer versus a psychologist.

A/B testing in data science is typically used in a web context. Treatments might be the design of a web page, the price of a product, the wording of a headline, or some other item. Some thought is required to preserve the principles of randomization. Typically the subject in the experiment is the web visitor, and the outcomes we are interested in measuring are clicks, purchases, visit duration, number of pages visited, whether a particular page is visited, and the like. In a standard A/B experiment, you need to decide on one metric ahead of time. Multiple behavior metrics might be collected and be of interest, but if the experiment is expected to lead to a decision between treatment A and treatment B, a single metric, or *test statistic*, needs to be established beforehand. Selecting a test statistic *after* the experiment is conducted opens the door to researcher bias.

Why Just A/B? Why Not C, D,…?

A/B tests are popular in the marketing and ecommerce worlds, but are far from the only type of statistical experiment. Additional treatments can be included. Subjects might have repeated measurements taken. Pharmaceutical trials where subjects are scarce, expensive, and acquired over time are sometimes designed with multiple opportunities to stop the experiment and reach a conclusion.

Traditional statistical experimental designs focus on answering a static question about the efficacy of specified treatments. Data scientists are less interested in the question:

> Is the difference between price A and price B statistically significant?

than in the question:

> Which, out of multiple possible prices, is best?

For this, a relatively new type of experimental design is used: the *multi-arm bandit* (see "Multi-Arm Bandit Algorithm" on page 131).

Getting Permission

In scientific and medical research involving human subjects, it is typically necessary to get their permission, as well as obtain the approval of an institutional review board. Experiments in business that are done as a part of ongoing operations almost never do this. In most cases (e.g., pricing experiments, or experiments about which headline to show or which offer should be made), this practice is widely accepted. Facebook, however, ran afoul of this general acceptance in 2014 when it experimented with the emotional tone in users' newsfeeds. Facebook used sentiment analysis to classify newsfeed posts as positive or negative, and then altered the positive/negative balance in what it showed users. Some randomly selected users experienced more positive posts, while others experienced more negative posts. Facebook found that the users who experienced a more positive newsfeed were more likely to post positively themselves, and vice versa. The magnitude of the effect was small, however, and Facebook faced much criticism for conducting the experiment without users' knowledge. Some users speculated that Facebook might have pushed some extremely depressed users over the edge if they got the negative version of their feed.

Key Ideas

- Subjects are assigned to two (or more) groups that are treated exactly alike, except that the treatment under study differs from one group to another.
- Ideally, subjects are assigned randomly to the groups.

Further Reading

- Two-group comparisons (A/B tests) are a staple of traditional statistics, and just about any introductory statistics text will have extensive coverage of design principles and inference procedures. For a discussion that places A/B tests in more of a data science context and uses resampling, see *Introductory Statistics and Analytics: A Resampling Perspective* by Peter Bruce (Wiley, 2014).
- For web testing, the logistical aspects of testing can be just as challenging as the statistical ones. A good place to start is the Google Analytics help section on experiments (*https://oreil.ly/mAbqF*).
- Beware advice found in the ubiquitous guides to A/B testing that you see on the web, such as these words in one such guide: "Wait for about 1,000 total visitors and make sure you run the test for a week." Such general rules of thumb are not

statistically meaningful; see "Power and Sample Size" on page 135 for more detail.

Hypothesis Tests

Hypothesis tests, also called *significance tests*, are ubiquitous in the traditional statistical analysis of published research. Their purpose is to help you learn whether random chance might be responsible for an observed effect.

> ### Key Terms for Hypothesis Tests
>
> ***Null hypothesis***
> The hypothesis that chance is to blame.
>
> ***Alternative hypothesis***
> Counterpoint to the null (what you hope to prove).
>
> ***One-way test***
> Hypothesis test that counts chance results only in one direction.
>
> ***Two-way test***
> Hypothesis test that counts chance results in two directions.

An A/B test (see "A/B Testing" on page 88) is typically constructed with a hypothesis in mind. For example, the hypothesis might be that price B produces higher profit. Why do we need a hypothesis? Why not just look at the outcome of the experiment and go with whichever treatment does better?

The answer lies in the tendency of the human mind to underestimate the scope of natural random behavior. One manifestation of this is the failure to anticipate extreme events, or so-called "black swans" (see "Long-Tailed Distributions" on page 73). Another manifestation is the tendency to misinterpret random events as having patterns of some significance. Statistical hypothesis testing was invented as a way to protect researchers from being fooled by random chance.

> ### Misinterpreting Randomness
>
> You can observe the human tendency to underestimate randomness in this experiment. Ask several friends to invent a series of 50 coin flips: have them write down a series of random Hs and Ts. Then ask them to actually flip a coin 50 times and write down the results. Have them put the real coin flip results in one pile, and the made-up results in another. It is easy to tell which results are real: the real ones will have longer runs of Hs or Ts. In a set of 50 *real* coin flips, it is not at all unusual to see five

or six Hs or Ts in a row. However, when most of us are inventing random coin flips and we have gotten three or four Hs in a row, we tell ourselves that, for the series to look random, we had better switch to T.

The other side of this coin, so to speak, is that when we *do* see the real-world equivalent of six Hs in a row (e.g., when one headline outperforms another by 10%), we are inclined to attribute it to something real, not just to chance.

In a properly designed A/B test, you collect data on treatments A and B in such a way that any observed difference between A and B must be due to either:

- Random chance in assignment of subjects
- A true difference between A and B

A statistical hypothesis test is further analysis of an A/B test, or any randomized experiment, to assess whether random chance is a reasonable explanation for the observed difference between groups A and B.

The Null Hypothesis

Hypothesis tests use the following logic: "Given the human tendency to react to unusual but random behavior and interpret it as something meaningful and real, in our experiments we will require proof that the difference between groups is more extreme than what chance might reasonably produce." This involves a baseline assumption that the treatments are equivalent, and any difference between the groups is due to chance. This baseline assumption is termed the *null hypothesis*. Our hope, then, is that we can in fact prove the null hypothesis *wrong* and show that the outcomes for groups A and B are more different than what chance might produce.

One way to do this is via a resampling permutation procedure, in which we shuffle together the results from groups A and B and then repeatedly deal out the data in groups of similar sizes, and then observe how often we get a difference as extreme as the observed difference. The combined shuffled results from groups A and B, and the procedure of resampling from them, embodies the null hypothesis of groups A and B being equivalent and interchangeable and is termed the null model. See "Resampling" on page 96 for more detail.

Alternative Hypothesis

Hypothesis tests by their nature involve not just a null hypothesis but also an offsetting alternative hypothesis. Here are some examples:

- Null = "no difference between the means of group A and group B"; alternative = "A is different from B" (could be bigger or smaller)
- Null = "A ≤ B"; alternative = "A > B"
- Null = "B is not X% greater than A"; alternative = "B is X% greater than A"

Taken together, the null and alternative hypotheses must account for all possibilities. The nature of the null hypothesis determines the structure of the hypothesis test.

One-Way Versus Two-Way Hypothesis Tests

Often in an A/B test, you are testing a new option (say, B) against an established default option (A), and the presumption is that you will stick with the default option unless the new option proves itself definitively better. In such a case, you want a hypothesis test to protect you from being fooled by chance in the direction favoring B. You don't care about being fooled by chance in the other direction, because you would be sticking with A unless B proves definitively better. So you want a *directional* alternative hypothesis (B is better than A). In such a case, you use a *one-way* (or one-tail) hypothesis test. This means that extreme chance results in only one direction count toward the p-value.

If you want a hypothesis test to protect you from being fooled by chance in either direction, the alternative hypothesis is *bidirectional* (A is different from B; could be bigger or smaller). In such a case, you use a *two-way* (or two-tail) hypothesis. This means that extreme chance results in either direction count toward the p-value.

A one-tail hypothesis test often fits the nature of A/B decision making, in which a decision is required and one option is typically assigned "default" status unless the other proves better. Software, however, including *R* and `scipy` in *Python*, typically provides a two-tail test in its default output, and many statisticians opt for the more conservative two-tail test just to avoid argument. One-tail versus two-tail is a confusing subject, and not that relevant for data science, where the precision of p-value calculations is not terribly important.

Key Ideas

- A null hypothesis is a logical construct embodying the notion that nothing special has happened, and any effect you observe is due to random chance.
- The hypothesis test assumes that the null hypothesis is true, creates a "null model" (a probability model), and tests whether the effect you observe is a reasonable outcome of that model.

Further Reading

- *The Drunkard's Walk* by Leonard Mlodinow (Pantheon, 2008) is a readable survey of the ways in which "randomness rules our lives."
- David Freedman, Robert Pisani, and Roger Purves's classic statistics text *Statistics*, 4th ed. (W. W. Norton, 2007), has excellent nonmathematical treatments of most statistics topics, including hypothesis testing.
- *Introductory Statistics and Analytics: A Resampling Perspective* by Peter Bruce (Wiley, 2014) develops hypothesis testing concepts using resampling.

Resampling

Resampling in statistics means to repeatedly sample values from observed data, with a general goal of assessing random variability in a statistic. It can also be used to assess and improve the accuracy of some machine-learning models (e.g., the predictions from decision tree models built on multiple bootstrapped data sets can be averaged in a process known as *bagging*—see "Bagging and the Random Forest" on page 259).

There are two main types of resampling procedures: the *bootstrap* and *permutation* tests. The bootstrap is used to assess the reliability of an estimate; it was discussed in the previous chapter (see "The Bootstrap" on page 61). Permutation tests are used to test hypotheses, typically involving two or more groups, and we discuss those in this section.

Key Terms for Resampling

Permutation test

The procedure of combining two or more samples together and randomly (or exhaustively) reallocating the observations to resamples.

Synonyms

Randomization test, random permutation test, exact test

Resampling

Drawing additional samples ("resamples") from an observed data set.

With or without replacement

In sampling, whether or not an item is returned to the sample before the next draw.

Permutation Test

In a *permutation* procedure, two or more samples are involved, typically the groups in an A/B or other hypothesis test. *Permute* means to change the order of a set of values. The first step in a *permutation test* of a hypothesis is to combine the results from groups A and B (and, if used, C, D,…). This is the logical embodiment of the null hypothesis that the treatments to which the groups were exposed do not differ. We then test that hypothesis by randomly drawing groups from this combined set and seeing how much they differ from one another. The permutation procedure is as follows:

1. Combine the results from the different groups into a single data set.
2. Shuffle the combined data and then randomly draw (without replacement) a resample of the same size as group A (clearly it will contain some data from the other groups).
3. From the remaining data, randomly draw (without replacement) a resample of the same size as group B.
4. Do the same for groups C, D, and so on. You have now collected one set of resamples that mirror the sizes of the original samples.
5. Whatever statistic or estimate was calculated for the original samples (e.g., difference in group proportions), calculate it now for the resamples, and record; this constitutes one permutation iteration.
6. Repeat the previous steps *R* times to yield a permutation distribution of the test statistic.

Now go back to the observed difference between groups and compare it to the set of permuted differences. If the observed difference lies well within the set of permuted differences, then we have not proven anything—the observed difference is within the range of what chance might produce. However, if the observed difference lies outside most of the permutation distribution, then we conclude that chance is *not* responsible. In technical terms, the difference is *statistically significant*. (See “Statistical Significance and p-Values” on page 103.)

Example: Web Stickiness

A company selling a relatively high-value service wants to test which of two web presentations does a better selling job. Due to the high value of the service being sold, sales are infrequent and the sales cycle is lengthy; it would take too long to accumulate enough sales to know which presentation is superior. So the company decides to measure the results with a proxy variable, using the detailed interior page that describes the service.

> A *proxy* variable is one that stands in for the true variable of interest, which may be unavailable, too costly, or too time-consuming to measure. In climate research, for example, the oxygen content of ancient ice cores is used as a proxy for temperature. It is useful to have at least *some* data on the true variable of interest, so the strength of its association with the proxy can be assessed.

One potential proxy variable for our company is the number of clicks on the detailed landing page. A better one is how long people spend on the page. It is reasonable to think that a web presentation (page) that holds people's attention longer will lead to more sales. Hence, our metric is average session time, comparing page A to page B.

Due to the fact that this is an interior, special-purpose page, it does not receive a huge number of visitors. Also note that Google Analytics, which is how we measure session time, cannot measure session time for the last session a person visits. Instead of deleting that session from the data, though, Google Analytics records it as a zero, so the data requires additional processing to remove those sessions. The result is a total of 36 sessions for the two different presentations, 21 for page A and 15 for page B. Using `ggplot`, we can visually compare the session times using side-by-side boxplots:

```
ggplot(session_times, aes(x=Page, y=Time)) +
  geom_boxplot()
```

The pandas boxplot command uses the keyword argument by to create the figure:

```
ax = session_times.boxplot(by='Page', column='Time')
ax.set_xlabel('')
ax.set_ylabel('Time (in seconds)')
plt.suptitle('')
```

The boxplot, shown in Figure 3-3, indicates that page B leads to longer sessions than page A. The means for each group can be computed in *R* as follows:

```
mean_a <- mean(session_times[session_times['Page'] == 'Page A', 'Time'])
mean_b <- mean(session_times[session_times['Page'] == 'Page B', 'Time'])
mean_b - mean_a
[1] 35.66667
```

In *Python*, we filter the pandas data frame first by page and then determine the mean of the Time column:

```
mean_a = session_times[session_times.Page == 'Page A'].Time.mean()
mean_b = session_times[session_times.Page == 'Page B'].Time.mean()
mean_b - mean_a
```

Page B has session times that are greater than those of page A by 35.67 seconds, on average. The question is whether this difference is within the range of what random chance might produce, i.e., is statistically significant. One way to answer this is to apply a permutation test—combine all the session times together and then repeatedly shuffle and divide them into groups of 21 (recall that $n_A = 21$ for page A) and 15 ($n_B = 15$ for page B).

To apply a permutation test, we need a function to randomly assign the 36 session times to a group of 21 (page A) and a group of 15 (page B). The *R* version of this function is:

```
perm_fun <- function(x, nA, nB)
{
  n <- nA + nB
  idx_b <- sample(1:n, nB)
  idx_a <- setdiff(1:n, idx_b)
  mean_diff <- mean(x[idx_b]) - mean(x[idx_a])
  return(mean_diff)
}
```

The *Python* version of this permutation test is the following:

```
def perm_fun(x, nA, nB):
    n = nA + nB
    idx_B = set(random.sample(range(n), nB))
    idx_A = set(range(n)) - idx_B
    return x.loc[idx_B].mean() - x.loc[idx_A].mean()
```

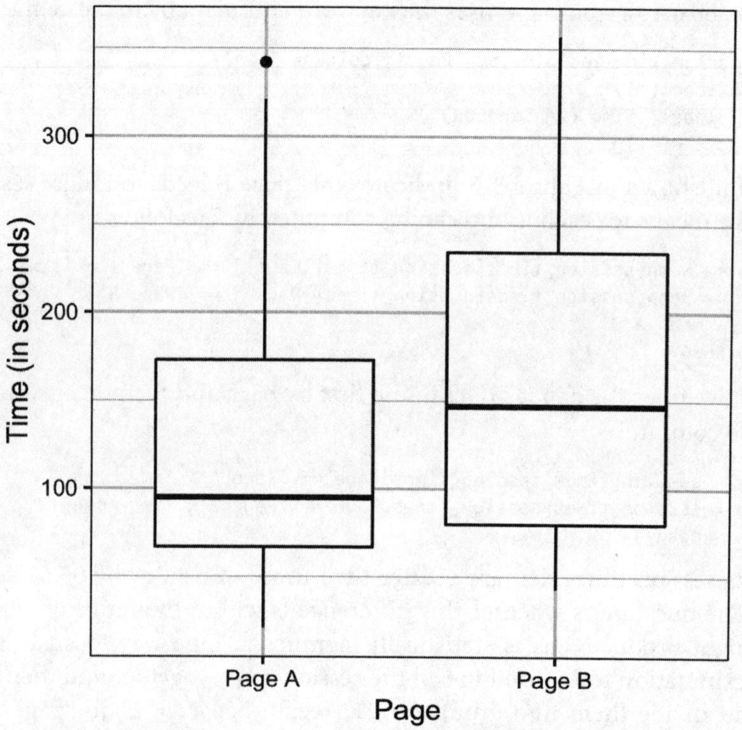

Figure 3-3. Session times for web pages A and B

This function works by sampling (without replacement) n_B indices and assigning them to the B group; the remaining n_A indices are assigned to group A. The difference between the two means is returned. Calling this function R = 1,000 times and specifying $n_A = 21$ and $n_B = 15$ leads to a distribution of differences in the session times that can be plotted as a histogram. In *R* this is done as follows using the `hist` function:

```
perm_diffs <- rep(0, 1000)
for (i in 1:1000) {
  perm_diffs[i] = perm_fun(session_times[, 'Time'], 21, 15)
}
hist(perm_diffs, xlab='Session time differences (in seconds)')
abline(v=mean_b - mean_a)
```

In *Python*, we can create a similar graph using `matplotlib`:

```
perm_diffs = [perm_fun(session_times.Time, nA, nB) for _ in range(1000)]

fig, ax = plt.subplots(figsize=(5, 5))
ax.hist(perm_diffs, bins=11, rwidth=0.9)
ax.axvline(x = mean_b - mean_a, color='black', lw=2)
```

```
ax.text(50, 190, 'Observed\ndifference', bbox={'facecolor':'white'})
ax.set_xlabel('Session time differences (in seconds)')
ax.set_ylabel('Frequency')
```

The histogram, in Figure 3-4 shows that mean difference of random permutations often exceeds the observed difference in session times (the vertical line). For our results, this happens in 12.6% of the cases:

```
mean(perm_diffs > (mean_b - mean_a))
---
0.126
```

As the simulation uses random numbers, the percentage will vary. For example, in the *Python* version, we got 12.1%:

```
np.mean(perm_diffs > mean_b - mean_a)
---
0.121
```

This suggests that the observed difference in session time between page A and page B is well within the range of chance variation and thus is not statistically significant.

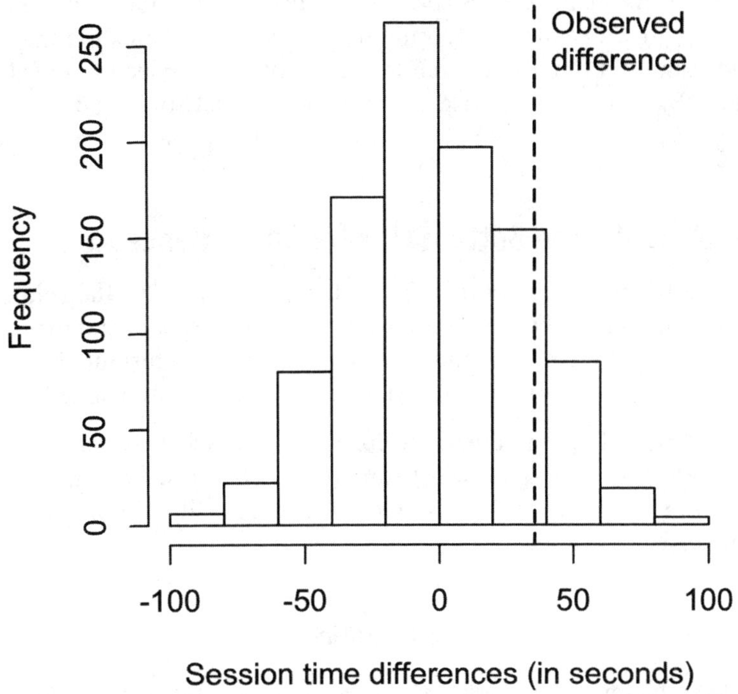

Figure 3-4. Frequency distribution for session time differences between pages A and B; the vertical line shows the observed difference

Exhaustive and Bootstrap Permutation Tests

In addition to the preceding random shuffling procedure, also called a *random permutation test* or a *randomization test*, there are two variants of the permutation test:

- An *exhaustive permutation test*
- A *bootstrap permutation test*

In an exhaustive permutation test, instead of just randomly shuffling and dividing the data, we actually figure out all the possible ways it could be divided. This is practical only for relatively small sample sizes. With a large number of repeated shufflings, the random permutation test results approximate those of the exhaustive permutation test, and approach them in the limit. Exhaustive permutation tests are also sometimes called *exact tests*, due to their statistical property of guaranteeing that the null model will not test as "significant" more than the alpha level of the test (see "Statistical Significance and p-Values" on page 103).

In a bootstrap permutation test, the draws outlined in steps 2 and 3 of the random permutation test are made *with replacement* instead of without replacement. In this way the resampling procedure models not just the random element in the assignment of treatment to subject but also the random element in the selection of subjects from a population. Both procedures are encountered in statistics, and the distinction between them is somewhat convoluted and not of consequence in the practice of data science.

Permutation Tests: The Bottom Line for Data Science

Permutation tests are useful heuristic procedures for exploring the role of random variation. They are relatively easy to code, interpret, and explain, and they offer a useful detour around the formalism and "false determinism" of formula-based statistics, in which the precision of formula "answers" tends to imply unwarranted certainty.

One virtue of resampling, in contrast to formula approaches, is that it comes much closer to a one-size-fits-all approach to inference. Data can be numeric or binary. Sample sizes can be the same or different. Assumptions about normally distributed data are not needed.

Key Ideas

- In a permutation test, multiple samples are combined and then shuffled.
- The shuffled values are then divided into resamples, and the statistic of interest is calculated.

- This process is then repeated, and the resampled statistic is tabulated.
- Comparing the observed value of the statistic to the resampled distribution allows you to judge whether an observed difference between samples might occur by chance.

Further Reading

- *Randomization Tests*, 4th ed., by Eugene Edgington and Patrick Onghena (Chapman & Hall/CRC Press, 2007)—but don't get too drawn into the thicket of nonrandom sampling
- *Introductory Statistics and Analytics: A Resampling Perspective* by Peter Bruce (Wiley, 2014)

Statistical Significance and p-Values

Statistical significance is how statisticians measure whether an experiment (or even a study of existing data) yields a result more extreme than what chance might produce. If the result is beyond the realm of chance variation, it is said to be statistically significant.

Key Terms for Statistical Significance and p-Values

p-value
: Given a chance model that embodies the null hypothesis, the p-value is the probability of obtaining results as unusual or extreme as the observed results.

Alpha
: The probability threshold of "unusualness" that chance results must surpass for actual outcomes to be deemed statistically significant.

Type 1 error
: Mistakenly concluding an effect is real (when it is due to chance).

Type 2 error
: Mistakenly concluding an effect is due to chance (when it is real).

Consider in Table 3-2 the results of the web test shown earlier.

Table 3-2. 2×2 table for ecommerce experiment results

Outcome	Price A	Price B
Conversion	200	182
No conversion	23,539	22,406

Price A converts almost 5% better than price B (0.8425% = 200/(23539+200)*100, versus 0.8057% = 182/(22406+182)*100—a difference of 0.0368 percentage points), big enough to be meaningful in a high-volume business. We have over 45,000 data points here, and it is tempting to consider this as "big data," not requiring tests of statistical significance (needed mainly to account for sampling variability in small samples). However, the conversion rates are so low (less than 1%) that the actual meaningful values—the conversions—are only in the 100s, and the sample size needed is really determined by these conversions. We can test whether the difference in conversions between prices A and B is within the range of *chance variation*, using a resampling procedure. By chance variation, we mean the random variation produced by a probability model that embodies the null hypothesis that there is no difference between the rates (see "The Null Hypothesis" on page 94). The following permutation procedure asks, "If the two prices share the same conversion rate, could chance variation produce a difference as big as 5%?"

1. Put cards labeled 1 and 0 in a box: this represents the supposed shared conversion rate of 382 ones and 45,945 zeros = 0.008246 = 0.8246%.
2. Shuffle and draw out a resample of size 23,739 (same *n* as price A), and record how many 1s.
3. Record the number of 1s in the remaining 22,588 (same *n* as price B).
4. Record the difference in proportion of 1s.
5. Repeat steps 2–4.
6. How often was the difference >= 0.0368?

Reusing the function perm_fun defined in "Example: Web Stickiness" on page 98, we can create a histogram of randomly permuted differences in conversion rate in *R*:

```
obs_pct_diff <- 100 * (200 / 23739 - 182 / 22588)
conversion <- c(rep(0, 45945), rep(1, 382))
perm_diffs <- rep(0, 1000)
for (i in 1:1000) {
  perm_diffs[i] = 100 * perm_fun(conversion, 23739, 22588)
}
hist(perm_diffs, xlab='Conversion rate (percent)', main='')
abline(v=obs_pct_diff)
```

The corresponding *Python* code is:

```
obs_pct_diff = 100 * (200 / 23739 - 182 / 22588)
print(f'Observed difference: {obs_pct_diff:.4f}%')
conversion = [0] * 45945
conversion.extend([1] * 382)
conversion = pd.Series(conversion)

perm_diffs = [100 * perm_fun(conversion, 23739, 22588)
              for _ in range(1000)]

fig, ax = plt.subplots(figsize=(5, 5))
ax.hist(perm_diffs, bins=11, rwidth=0.9)
ax.axvline(x=obs_pct_diff, color='black', lw=2)
ax.text(0.06, 200, 'Observed\ndifference', bbox={'facecolor':'white'})
ax.set_xlabel('Conversion rate (percent)')
ax.set_ylabel('Frequency')
```

See the histogram of 1,000 resampled results in Figure 3-5: as it happens, in this case the observed difference of 0.0368% is well within the range of chance variation.

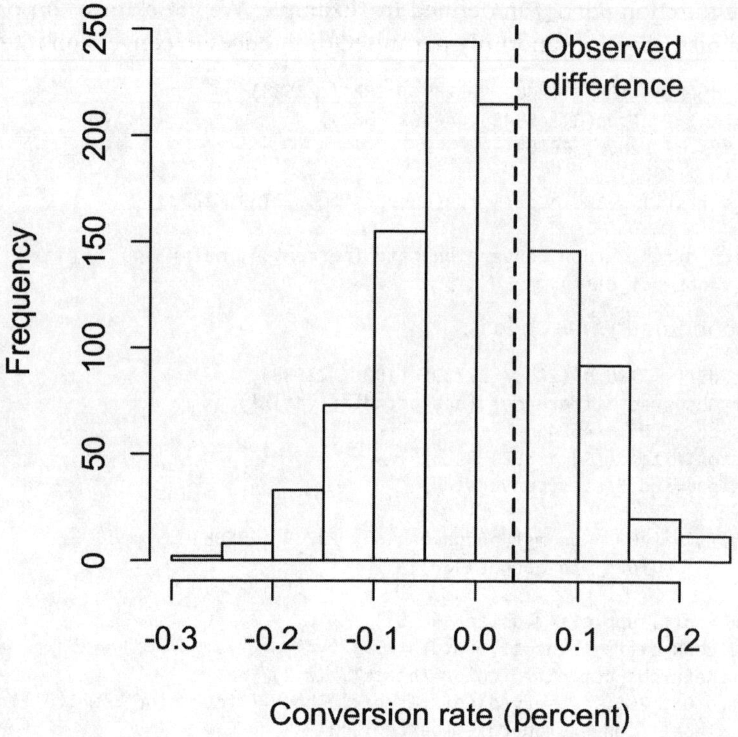

Figure 3-5. Frequency distribution for the difference in conversion rates between prices A and B

p-Value

Simply looking at the graph is not a very precise way to measure statistical significance, so of more interest is the *p-value*. This is the frequency with which the chance model produces a result more extreme than the observed result. We can estimate a p-value from our permutation test by taking the proportion of times that the permutation test produces a difference equal to or greater than the observed difference:

```
mean(perm_diffs > obs_pct_diff)
[1] 0.308
```

```
np.mean([diff > obs_pct_diff for diff in perm_diffs])
```

Here, both *R* and *Python* use the fact that true is interpreted as 1 and false as 0.

The p-value is 0.308, which means that we would expect to achieve a result as extreme as this, or a more extreme result, by random chance over 30% of the time.

In this case, we didn't need to use a permutation test to get a p-value. Since we have a binomial distribution, we can approximate the p-value. In *R* code, we do this using the function `prop.test`:

```
> prop.test(x=c(200, 182), n=c(23739, 22588), alternative='greater')

        2-sample test for equality of proportions with continuity correction

data:  c(200, 182) out of c(23739, 22588)
X-squared = 0.14893, df = 1, p-value = 0.3498
alternative hypothesis: greater
95 percent confidence interval:
 -0.001057439  1.000000000
sample estimates:
     prop 1      prop 2
0.008424955 0.008057376
```

The argument `x` is the number of successes for each group, and the argument `n` is the number of trials.

The method `scipy.stats.chi2_contingency` takes the values as shown in Table 3-2:

```
survivors = np.array([[200, 23739 - 200], [182, 22588 - 182]])
chi2, p_value, df, _ = stats.chi2_contingency(survivors)

print(f'p-value for single sided test: {p_value / 2:.4f}')
```

The normal approximation yields a p-value of 0.3498, which is close to the p-value obtained from the permutation test.

Alpha

Statisticians frown on the practice of leaving it to the researcher's discretion to determine whether a result is "too unusual" to happen by chance. Rather, a threshold is specified in advance, as in "more extreme than 5% of the chance (null hypothesis) results"; this threshold is known as *alpha*. Typical alpha levels are 5% and 1%. Any chosen level is an arbitrary decision—there is nothing about the process that will guarantee correct decisions x% of the time. This is because the probability question being answered is *not* "What is the probability that this happened by chance?" but rather "Given a chance model, what is the probability of a result this extreme?" We then deduce backward about the appropriateness of the chance model, but that judgment does not carry a probability. This point has been the subject of much confusion.

p-value controversy

Considerable controversy has surrounded the use of the p-value in recent years. One psychology journal has gone so far as to "ban" the use of p-values in submitted papers on the grounds that publication decisions based solely on the p-value were resulting in the publication of poor research. Too many researchers, only dimly aware of what a p-value really means, root around in the data, and among different possible hypotheses to test, until they find a combination that yields a significant p-value and, hence, a paper suitable for publication.

The real problem is that people want more meaning from the p-value than it contains. Here's what we would *like* the p-value to convey:

> The probability that the result is due to chance.

We hope for a low value, so we can conclude that we've proved something. This is how many journal editors were interpreting the p-value. But here's what the p-value *actually* represents:

> The probability that, *given a chance model*, results as extreme as the observed results could occur.

The difference is subtle but real. A significant p-value does not carry you quite as far along the road to "proof" as it seems to promise. The logical foundation for the conclusion "statistically significant" is somewhat weaker when the real meaning of the p-value is understood.

In March 2016, the American Statistical Association, after much internal deliberation, revealed the extent of misunderstanding about p-values when it issued a cautionary statement regarding their use. The ASA statement (*https://oreil.ly/WVfYU*) stressed six principles for researchers and journal editors:

1. P-values can indicate how incompatible the data are with a specified statistical model.
2. P-values do not measure the probability that the studied hypothesis is true, or the probability that the data were produced by random chance alone.
3. Scientific conclusions and business or policy decisions should not be based only on whether a p-value passes a specific threshold.
4. Proper inference requires full reporting and transparency.
5. A p-value, or statistical significance, does not measure the size of an effect or the importance of a result.
6. By itself, a p-value does not provide a good measure of evidence regarding a model or hypothesis.

Practical significance

Even if a result is statistically significant, that does not mean it has practical significance. A small difference that has no practical meaning can be statistically significant if it arose from large enough samples. Large samples ensure that small, non-meaningful effects can nonetheless be big enough to rule out chance as an explanation. Ruling out chance does not magically render important a result that is, in its essence, unimportant.

Type 1 and Type 2 Errors

In assessing statistical significance, two types of error are possible:

- A Type 1 error, in which you mistakenly conclude an effect is real, when it is really just due to chance
- A Type 2 error, in which you mistakenly conclude that an effect is not real (i.e., due to chance), when it actually is real

Actually, a Type 2 error is not so much an error as a judgment that the sample size is too small to detect the effect. When a p-value falls short of statistical significance (e.g., it exceeds 5%), what we are really saying is "effect not proven." It could be that a larger sample would yield a smaller p-value.

The basic function of significance tests (also called *hypothesis tests*) is to protect against being fooled by random chance; thus they are typically structured to minimize Type 1 errors.

Data Science and p-Values

The work that data scientists do is typically not destined for publication in scientific journals, so the debate over the value of a p-value is somewhat academic. For a data scientist, a p-value is a useful metric in situations where you want to know whether a model result that appears interesting and useful is within the range of normal chance variability. As a decision tool in an experiment, a p-value should not be considered controlling, but merely another point of information bearing on a decision. For example, p-values are sometimes used as intermediate inputs in some statistical or machine learning models—a feature might be included in or excluded from a model depending on its p-value.

Key Ideas

- Significance tests are used to determine whether an observed effect is within the range of chance variation for a null hypothesis model.
- The p-value is the probability that results as extreme as the observed results might occur, given a null hypothesis model.
- The alpha value is the threshold of "unusualness" in a null hypothesis chance model.
- Significance testing has been much more relevant for formal reporting of research than for data science (but has been fading recently, even for the former).

Further Reading

- Stephen Stigler, "Fisher and the 5% Level," *Chance* 21, no. 4 (2008): 12. This article is a short commentary on Ronald Fisher's 1925 book *Statistical Methods for Research Workers* (Oliver & Boyd), and on Fisher's emphasis on the 5% level of significance.
- See also "Hypothesis Tests" on page 93 and the further reading mentioned there.

t-Tests

There are numerous types of significance tests, depending on whether the data comprises count data or measured data, how many samples there are, and what's being measured. A very common one is the *t-test*, named after Student's t-distribution, originally developed by W. S. Gosset to approximate the distribution of a single sample mean (see "Student's t-Distribution" on page 75).

Key Terms for t-Tests

Test statistic
A metric for the difference or effect of interest.

t-statistic
A standardized version of common test statistics such as means.

t-distribution
A reference distribution (in this case derived from the null hypothesis), to which the observed t-statistic can be compared.

All significance tests require that you specify a *test statistic* to measure the effect you are interested in and help you determine whether that observed effect lies within the range of normal chance variation. In a resampling test (see the discussion of permutation in "Permutation Test" on page 97), the scale of the data does not matter. You create the reference (null hypothesis) distribution from the data itself and use the test statistic as is.

In the 1920s and 1930s, when statistical hypothesis testing was being developed, it was not feasible to randomly shuffle data thousands of times to do a resampling test. Statisticians found that a good approximation to the permutation (shuffled) distribution was the t-test, based on Gosset's t-distribution. It is used for the very common two-sample comparison—A/B test—in which the data is numeric. But in order for the t-distribution to be used without regard to scale, a standardized form of the test statistic must be used.

A classic statistics text would at this stage show various formulas that incorporate Gosset's distribution and demonstrate how to standardize your data to compare it to the standard t-distribution. These formulas are not shown here because all statistical software, as well as *R* and *Python*, includes commands that embody the formula. In *R*, the function is `t.test`:

```
> t.test(Time ~ Page, data=session_times, alternative='less')

        Welch Two Sample t-test

data:  Time by Page
t = -1.0983, df = 27.693, p-value = 0.1408
alternative hypothesis: true difference in means is less than 0
95 percent confidence interval:
     -Inf 19.59674
sample estimates:
mean in group Page A mean in group Page B
            126.3333             162.0000
```

The function `scipy.stats.ttest_ind` can be used in *Python*:

```
res = stats.ttest_ind(session_times[session_times.Page == 'Page A'].Time,
                      session_times[session_times.Page == 'Page B'].Time,
                      equal_var=False)
print(f'p-value for single sided test: {res.pvalue / 2:.4f}')
```

The alternative hypothesis is that the session time mean for page A is less than that for page B. The p-value of 0.1408 is fairly close to the permutation test p-values of 0.121 and 0.126 (see "Example: Web Stickiness" on page 98).

In a resampling mode, we structure the solution to reflect the observed data and the hypothesis to be tested, not worrying about whether the data is numeric or binary, whether or not sample sizes are balanced, sample variances, or a variety of other factors. In the formula world, many variations present themselves, and they can be bewildering. Statisticians need to navigate that world and learn its map, but data scientists do not—they are typically not in the business of sweating the details of hypothesis tests and confidence intervals the way a researcher preparing a paper for presentation might.

Key Ideas

- Before the advent of computers, resampling tests were not practical, and statisticians used standard reference distributions.
- A test statistic could then be standardized and compared to the reference distribution.
- One such widely used standardized statistic is the t-statistic.

Further Reading

- Any introductory statistics text will have illustrations of the t-statistic and its uses; two good ones are *Statistics*, 4th ed., by David Freedman, Robert Pisani, and Roger Purves (W. W. Norton, 2007), and *The Basic Practice of Statistics*, 8th ed., by David S. Moore, William I. Notz, and Michael A. Fligner (W. H. Freeman, 2017).
- For a treatment of both the t-test and resampling procedures in parallel, see *Introductory Statistics and Analytics: A Resampling Perspective* by Peter Bruce (Wiley, 2014) or *Statistics: Unlocking the Power of Data*, 2nd ed., by Robin Lock and four other Lock family members (Wiley, 2016).

Multiple Testing

As we've mentioned previously, there is a saying in statistics: "Torture the data long enough, and it will confess." This means that if you look at the data through enough different perspectives and ask enough questions, you almost invariably will find a statistically significant effect.

For example, if you have 20 predictor variables and one outcome variable, all *randomly* generated, the odds are pretty good that at least one predictor will (falsely) turn out to be statistically significant if you do a series of 20 significance tests at the alpha = 0.05 level. As previously discussed, this is called a *Type 1 error*. You can calculate this probability by first finding the probability that all will *correctly* test nonsignificant at the 0.05 level. The probability that *one* will correctly test nonsignificant is 0.95, so the probability that all 20 will correctly test nonsignificant is 0.95 × 0.95 × 0.95…, or

$0.95^{20} = 0.36$.[1] The probability that at least one predictor will (falsely) test significant is the flip side of this probability, or 1 – (*probability that all will be nonsignificant*) = 0.64. This is known as *alpha inflation*.

This issue is related to the problem of overfitting in data mining, or "fitting the model to the noise." The more variables you add, or the more models you run, the greater the probability that something will emerge as "significant" just by chance.

Key Terms for Multiple Testing

Type 1 error
Mistakenly concluding that an effect is statistically significant.

False discovery rate
Across multiple tests, the rate of making a Type 1 error.

Alpha inflation
The multiple testing phenomenon, in which *alpha*, the probability of making a Type 1 error, increases as you conduct more tests.

Adjustment of p-values
Accounting for doing multiple tests on the same data.

Overfitting
Fitting the noise.

In supervised learning tasks, a holdout set where models are assessed on data that the model has not seen before mitigates this risk. In statistical and machine learning tasks not involving a labeled holdout set, the risk of reaching conclusions based on statistical noise persists.

In statistics, there are some procedures intended to deal with this problem in very specific circumstances. For example, if you are comparing results across multiple treatment groups, you might ask multiple questions. So, for treatments A–C, you might ask:

- Is A different from B?
- Is B different from C?
- Is A different from C?

1 The multiplication rule states that the probability of *n* independent events all happening is the product of the individual probabilities. For example, if you and I each flip a coin once, the probability that your coin and my coin will both land heads is $0.5 \times 0.5 = 0.25$.

Or, in a clinical trial, you might want to look at results from a therapy at multiple stages. In each case, you are asking multiple questions, and with each question, you are increasing the chance of being fooled by chance. Adjustment procedures in statistics can compensate for this by setting the bar for statistical significance more stringently than it would be set for a single hypothesis test. These adjustment procedures typically involve "dividing up the alpha" according to the number of tests. This results in a smaller alpha (i.e., a more stringent bar for statistical significance) for each test. One such procedure, the Bonferroni adjustment, simply divides the alpha by the number of comparisons. Another, used in comparing multiple group means, is Tukey's "honest significant difference," or *Tukey's HSD*. This test applies to the maximum difference among group means, comparing it to a benchmark based on the *t-distribution* (roughly equivalent to shuffling all the values together, dealing out resampled groups of the same sizes as the original groups, and finding the maximum difference among the resampled group means).

However, the problem of multiple comparisons goes beyond these highly structured cases and is related to the phenomenon of repeated data "dredging" that gives rise to the saying about torturing the data. Put another way, given sufficiently complex data, if you haven't found something interesting, you simply haven't looked long and hard enough. More data is available now than ever before, and the number of journal articles published nearly doubled between 2002 and 2010. This gives rise to lots of opportunities to find something interesting in the data, including multiplicity issues such as:

- Checking for multiple pairwise differences across groups
- Looking at multiple subgroup results ("we found no significant treatment effect overall, but we did find an effect for unmarried women younger than 30")
- Trying lots of statistical models
- Including lots of variables in models
- Asking a number of different questions (i.e., different possible outcomes)

False Discovery Rate

The term *false discovery rate* was originally used to describe the rate at which a given set of hypothesis tests would falsely identify a significant effect. It became particularly useful with the advent of genomic research, in which massive numbers of statistical tests might be conducted as part of a gene sequencing project. In these cases, the term applies to the testing protocol, and a single false "discovery" refers to the outcome of a hypothesis test (e.g., between two samples). Researchers sought to set the parameters of the testing process to control the false discovery rate at a specified level. The term has also been used for classification in data mining; it is the misclassification rate within the class 1 predictions. Or, put another way, it is the probability that a "discovery" (labeling a record as a "1") is false. Here we typically are dealing with the case where 0s are abundant and 1s are interesting and rare (see Chapter 5 and "The Rare Class Problem" on page 223).

For a variety of reasons, including especially this general issue of "multiplicity," more research does not necessarily mean better research. For example, the pharmaceutical company Bayer found in 2011 that when it tried to replicate 67 scientific studies, it could fully replicate only 14 of them. Nearly two-thirds could not be replicated at all.

In any case, the adjustment procedures for highly defined and structured statistical tests are too specific and inflexible to be of general use to data scientists. The bottom line for data scientists on multiplicity is:

- For predictive modeling, the risk of getting an illusory model whose apparent efficacy is largely a product of random chance is mitigated by cross-validation (see "Cross-Validation" on page 155) and use of a holdout sample.
- For other procedures without a labeled holdout set to check the model, you must rely on:
  - Awareness that the more you query and manipulate the data, the greater the role that chance might play.
  - Resampling and simulation heuristics to provide random chance benchmarks against which observed results can be compared.

Key Ideas

- Multiplicity in a research study or data mining project (multiple comparisons, many variables, many models, etc.) increases the risk of concluding that something is significant just by chance.
- For situations involving multiple statistical comparisons (i.e., multiple tests of significance), there are statistical adjustment procedures.
- In a data mining situation, use of a holdout sample with labeled outcome variables can help avoid misleading results.

Further Reading

- For a short exposition of one procedure (Dunnett's test) to adjust for multiple comparisons, see David Lane's online statistics text (*https://oreil.ly/hd_62*).
- Megan Goldman offers a slightly longer treatment of the Bonferroni adjustment procedure (*https://oreil.ly/Dt4Vi*).
- For an in-depth treatment of more flexible statistical procedures for adjusting p-values, see *Resampling-Based Multiple Testing* by Peter Westfall and Stanley Young (Wiley, 1993).
- For a discussion of data partitioning and the use of holdout samples in predictive modeling, see Chapter 2 of *Data Mining for Business Analytics*, by Galit Shmueli, Peter Bruce, Nitin Patel, Peter Gedeck, Inbal Yahav, and Kenneth Lichtendahl (Wiley, 2007–2020, with editions for *R*, *Python*, Excel, and JMP).

Degrees of Freedom

In the documentation and settings for many statistical tests and probability distributions, you will see a reference to "degrees of freedom." The concept is applied to statistics calculated from sample data, and refers to the number of values free to vary. For example, if you know the mean for a sample of 10 values, there are 9 degrees of freedom (once you know 9 of the sample values, the 10th can be calculated and is not free to vary). The degrees of freedom parameter, as applied to many probability distributions, affects the shape of the distribution.

The number of degrees of freedom is an input to many statistical tests. For example, degrees of freedom is the name given to the $n - 1$ denominator seen in the calculations for variance and standard deviation. Why does it matter? When you use a sample to estimate the variance for a population, you will end up with an estimate that is slightly biased downward if you use n in the denominator. If you use $n - 1$ in the denominator, the estimate will be free of that bias.

Key Terms for Degrees of Freedom

***n* or sample size**
: The number of observations (also called *rows* or *records*) in the data.

d.f.
: Degrees of freedom.

A large share of a traditional statistics course or text is consumed by various standard tests of hypotheses (t-test, F-test, etc.). When sample statistics are standardized for use in traditional statistical formulas, degrees of freedom is part of the standardization calculation to ensure that your standardized data matches the appropriate reference distribution (t-distribution, F-distribution, etc.).

Is it important for data science? Not really, at least in the context of significance testing. For one thing, formal statistical tests are used only sparingly in data science. For another, the data size is usually large enough that it rarely makes a real difference for a data scientist whether, for example, the denominator has n or $n - 1$. (As n gets large, the bias that would come from using n in the denominator disappears.)

There is one context, though, in which it is relevant: the use of factored variables in regression (including logistic regression). Some regression algorithms choke if exactly redundant predictor variables are present. This most commonly occurs when factoring categorical variables into binary indicators (dummies). Consider the variable "day of week." Although there are seven days of the week, there are only six degrees of freedom in specifying day of week. For example, once you know that day of week is not Monday through Saturday, you know it must be Sunday. Inclusion of the Mon–Sat indicators thus means that *also* including Sunday would cause the regression to fail, due to a *multicollinearity* error.

Key Ideas

- The number of degrees of freedom (d.f.) forms part of the calculation to standardize test statistics so they can be compared to reference distributions (t-distribution, F-distribution, etc.).
- The concept of degrees of freedom lies behind the factoring of categorical variables into $n - 1$ indicator or dummy variables when doing a regression (to avoid multicollinearity).

Further Reading

There are several web tutorials on degrees of freedom (*https://oreil.ly/VJyts*).

ANOVA

Suppose that, instead of an A/B test, we had a comparison of multiple groups, say A/B/C/D, each with numeric data. The statistical procedure that tests for a statistically significant difference among the groups is called *analysis of variance*, or *ANOVA*.

Key Terms for ANOVA

Pairwise comparison
A hypothesis test (e.g., of means) between two groups among multiple groups.

Omnibus test
A single hypothesis test of the overall variance among multiple group means.

Decomposition of variance
Separation of components contributing to an individual value (e.g., from the overall average, from a treatment mean, and from a residual error).

F-statistic
A standardized statistic that measures the extent to which differences among group means exceed what might be expected in a chance model.

SS
"Sum of squares," referring to deviations from some average value.

Table 3-3 shows the stickiness of four web pages, defined as the number of seconds a visitor spent on the page. The four pages are switched out so that each web visitor receives one at random. There are a total of five visitors for each page, and in Table 3-3, each column is an independent set of data. The first viewer for page 1 has no connection to the first viewer for page 2. Note that in a web test like this, we cannot fully implement the classic randomized sampling design in which each visitor is selected at random from some huge population. We must take the visitors as they come. Visitors may systematically differ depending on time of day, time of week, season of the year, conditions of their internet, what device they are using, and so on. These factors should be considered as potential bias when the experiment results are reviewed.

Table 3-3. Stickiness (in seconds) of four web pages

	Page 1	Page 2	Page 3	Page 4
	164	178	175	155
	172	191	193	166
	177	182	171	164
	156	185	163	170
	195	177	176	168
Average	172	185	176	162
Grand average				173.75

Now we have a conundrum (see Figure 3-6). When we were comparing just two groups, it was a simple matter; we merely looked at the difference between the means of each group. With four means, there are six possible comparisons between groups:

- Page 1 compared to page 2
- Page 1 compared to page 3
- Page 1 compared to page 4
- Page 2 compared to page 3
- Page 2 compared to page 4
- Page 3 compared to page 4

The more such *pairwise* comparisons we make, the greater the potential for being fooled by random chance (see "Multiple Testing" on page 112). Instead of worrying about all the different comparisons between individual pages we could possibly make, we can do a single overall test that addresses the question, "Could all the pages have the same underlying stickiness, and the differences among them be due to the random way in which a common set of session times got allocated among the four pages?"

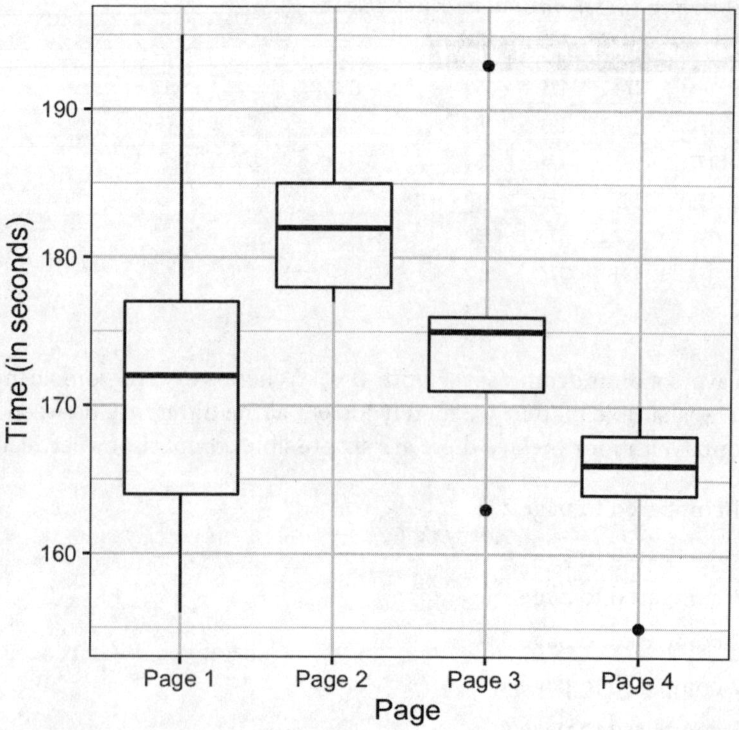

Figure 3-6. Boxplots of the four groups show considerable differences among them

The procedure used to test this is ANOVA. The basis for it can be seen in the following resampling procedure (specified here for the A/B/C/D test of web page stickiness):

1. Combine all the data together in a single box.
2. Shuffle and draw out four resamples of five values each.
3. Record the mean of each of the four groups.
4. Record the variance among the four group means.
5. Repeat steps 2–4 many (say, 1,000) times.

What proportion of the time did the resampled variance exceed the observed variance? This is the p-value.

This type of permutation test is a bit more involved than the type used in "Permutation Test" on page 97. Fortunately, the `aovp` function in the `lmPerm` package computes a permutation test for this case:

```
> library(lmPerm)
> summary(aovp(Time ~ Page, data=four_sessions))
[1] "Settings:  unique SS "
Component 1 :
            Df R Sum Sq R Mean Sq Iter Pr(Prob)
Page         3    831.4    277.13 3104  0.09278 .
Residuals   16   1618.4    101.15
---
Signif. codes:  0 '***' 0.001 '**' 0.01 '*' 0.05 '.' 0.1 ' ' 1
```

The p-value, given by `Pr(Prob)`, is 0.09278. In other words, given the same underlying stickiness, 9.3% of the time the response rate among four pages might differ as much as was actually observed, just by chance. This degree of improbability falls short of the traditional statistical threshold of 5%, so we conclude that the difference among the four pages could have arisen by chance.

The column `Iter` lists the number of iterations taken in the permutation test. The other columns correspond to a traditional ANOVA table and are described next.

In *Python*, we can compute the permutation test using the following code:

```
observed_variance = four_sessions.groupby('Page').mean().var()[0]
print('Observed means:', four_sessions.groupby('Page').mean().values.ravel())
print('Variance:', observed_variance)

def perm_test(df):
    df = df.copy()
    df['Time'] = np.random.permutation(df['Time'].values)
    return df.groupby('Page').mean().var()[0]

perm_variance = [perm_test(four_sessions) for _ in range(3000)]
print('Pr(Prob)', np.mean([var > observed_variance for var in perm_variance]))
```

F-Statistic

Just like the t-test can be used instead of a permutation test for comparing the mean of two groups, there is a statistical test for ANOVA based on the *F-statistic*. The F-statistic is based on the ratio of the variance across group means (i.e., the treatment effect) to the variance due to residual error. The higher this ratio, the more statistically significant the result. If the data follows a normal distribution, then statistical theory dictates that the statistic should have a certain distribution. Based on this, it is possible to compute a p-value.

In *R*, we can compute an *ANOVA table* using the aov function:

```
> summary(aov(Time ~ Page, data=four_sessions))
            Df Sum Sq Mean Sq F value Pr(>F)
Page         3  831.4   277.1    2.74 0.0776 .
Residuals   16 1618.4   101.2
---
Signif. codes:  0 '***' 0.001 '**' 0.01 '*' 0.05 '.' 0.1 ' ' 1
```

The statsmodels package provides an ANOVA implementation in *Python*:

```
model = smf.ols('Time ~ Page', data=four_sessions).fit()

aov_table = sm.stats.anova_lm(model)
aov_table
```

The output from the *Python* code is almost identical to that from *R*.

Df is "degrees of freedom," Sum Sq is "sum of squares," Mean Sq is "mean squares" (short for mean-squared deviations), and F value is the F-statistic. For the grand average, sum of squares is the departure of the grand average from 0, squared, times 20 (the number of observations). The degrees of freedom for the grand average is 1, by definition.

For the treatment means, the degrees of freedom is 3 (once three values are set, and then the grand average is set, the other treatment mean cannot vary). Sum of squares for the treatment means is the sum of squared departures between the treatment means and the grand average.

For the residuals, degrees of freedom is 20 (all observations can vary), and SS is the sum of squared difference between the individual observations and the treatment means. Mean squares (MS) is the sum of squares divided by the degrees of freedom.

The F-statistic is MS(treatment)/MS(error). The F value thus depends only on this ratio and can be compared to a standard F-distribution to determine whether the differences among treatment means are greater than would be expected in random chance variation.

Decomposition of Variance

Observed values in a data set can be considered sums of different components. For any observed data value within a data set, we can break it down into the grand average, the treatment effect, and the residual error. We call this a "decomposition of variance":

1. Start with grand average (173.75 for web page stickiness data).
2. Add treatment effect, which might be negative (independent variable = web page).
3. Add residual error, which might be negative.

Thus the decomposition of the variance for the top-left value in the A/B/C/D test table is as follows:

1. Start with grand average: 173.75.
2. Add treatment (group) effect: –1.75 (172 – 173.75).
3. Add residual: –8 (164 – 172).
4. Equals: 164.

Two-Way ANOVA

The A/B/C/D test just described is a "one-way" ANOVA, in which we have one factor (group) that is varying. We could have a second factor involved—say, "weekend versus weekday"—with data collected on each combination (group A weekend, group A weekday, group B weekend, etc.). This would be a "two-way ANOVA," and we would handle it in similar fashion to the one-way ANOVA by identifying the "interaction effect." After identifying the grand average effect and the treatment effect, we then separate the weekend and weekday observations for each group and find the difference between the averages for those subsets and the treatment average.

You can see that ANOVA and then two-way ANOVA are the first steps on the road toward a full statistical model, such as regression and logistic regression, in which multiple factors and their effects can be modeled (see Chapter 4).

Key Ideas

- ANOVA is a statistical procedure for analyzing the results of an experiment with multiple groups.
- It is the extension of similar procedures for the A/B test, used to assess whether the overall variation among groups is within the range of chance variation.

- A useful outcome of ANOVA is the identification of variance components associated with group treatments, interaction effects, and errors.

Further Reading

- *Introductory Statistics and Analytics: A Resampling Perspective* by Peter Bruce (Wiley, 2014) has a chapter on ANOVA.
- *Introduction to Design and Analysis of Experiments* by George Cobb (Wiley, 2008) is a comprehensive and readable treatment of its subject.

Chi-Square Test

Web testing often goes beyond A/B testing and tests multiple treatments at once. The chi-square test is used with count data to test how well it fits some expected distribution. The most common use of the *chi-square* statistic in statistical practice is with $r \times c$ contingency tables, to assess whether the null hypothesis of independence among variables is reasonable (see also "Chi-Square Distribution" on page 80).

The chi-square test was originally developed by Karl Pearson in 1900 (*https://oreil.ly/cEubO*). The term *chi* comes from the Greek letter Χ used by Pearson in the article.

Key Terms for Chi-Square Test

Chi-square statistic
: A measure of the extent to which some observed data departs from expectation.

Expectation or expected
: How we would expect the data to turn out under some assumption, typically the null hypothesis.

> $r \times c$ means "rows by columns"—a 2 × 3 table has two rows and three columns.

Chi-Square Test: A Resampling Approach

Suppose you are testing three different headlines—A, B, and C—and you run them each on 1,000 visitors, with the results shown in Table 3-4.

Table 3-4. Web testing results for three different headlines

	Headline A	Headline B	Headline C
Click	14	8	12
No-click	986	992	988

The headlines certainly appear to differ. Headline A returns nearly twice the click rate of B. The actual numbers are small, though. A resampling procedure can test whether the click rates differ to an extent greater than chance might cause. For this test, we need to have the "expected" distribution of clicks, and in this case, that would be under the null hypothesis assumption that all three headlines share the same click rate, for an overall click rate of 34/3,000. Under this assumption, our contingency table would look like Table 3-5.

Table 3-5. Expected if all three headlines have the same click rate (null hypothesis)

	Headline A	Headline B	Headline C
Click	11.33	11.33	11.33
No-click	988.67	988.67	988.67

The *Pearson residual* is defined as:

$$R = \frac{\text{Observed} - \text{Expected}}{\sqrt{\text{Expected}}}$$

R measures the extent to which the actual counts differ from these expected counts (see Table 3-6).

Table 3-6. Pearson residuals

	Headline A	Headline B	Headline C
Click	0.792	–0.990	0.198
No-click	–0.085	0.106	–0.021

The chi-square statistic is defined as the sum of the squared Pearson residuals:

$$X = \sum_{i}^{r} \sum_{j}^{c} R^2$$

where r and c are the number of rows and columns, respectively. The chi-square statistic for this example is 1.666. Is that more than could reasonably occur in a chance model?

We can test with this resampling algorithm:

1. Constitute a box with 34 ones (clicks) and 2,966 zeros (no clicks).
2. Shuffle, take three separate samples of 1,000, and count the clicks in each.
3. Find the squared differences between the shuffled counts and the expected counts and sum them.
4. Repeat steps 2 and 3, say, 1,000 times.
5. How often does the resampled sum of squared deviations exceed the observed? That's the p-value.

The function `chisq.test` can be used to compute a resampled chi-square statistic in *R*. For the click data, the chi-square test is:

```
> chisq.test(clicks, simulate.p.value=TRUE)

        Pearson's Chi-squared test with simulated p-value (based on 2000 replicates)

data:  clicks
X-squared = 1.6659, df = NA, p-value = 0.4853
```

The test shows that this result could easily have been obtained by randomness.

To run a permutation test in *Python*, use the following implementation:

```
box = [1] * 34
box.extend([0] * 2966)
random.shuffle(box)

def chi2(observed, expected):
    pearson_residuals = []
    for row, expect in zip(observed, expected):
        pearson_residuals.append([(observe - expect) ** 2 / expect
                                  for observe in row])
    # return sum of squares
    return np.sum(pearson_residuals)

expected_clicks = 34 / 3
expected_noclicks = 1000 - expected_clicks
expected = [34 / 3, 1000 - 34 / 3]
chi2observed = chi2(clicks.values, expected)

def perm_fun(box):
    sample_clicks = [sum(random.sample(box, 1000)),
                     sum(random.sample(box, 1000)),
                     sum(random.sample(box, 1000))]
    sample_noclicks = [1000 - n for n in sample_clicks]
    return chi2([sample_clicks, sample_noclicks], expected)

perm_chi2 = [perm_fun(box) for _ in range(2000)]
```

```
resampled_p_value = sum(perm_chi2 > chi2observed) / len(perm_chi2)
print(f'Observed chi2: {chi2observed:.4f}')
print(f'Resampled p-value: {resampled_p_value:.4f}')
```

Chi-Square Test: Statistical Theory

Asymptotic statistical theory shows that the distribution of the chi-square statistic can be approximated by a *chi-square distribution* (see "Chi-Square Distribution" on page 80). The appropriate standard chi-square distribution is determined by the *degrees of freedom* (see "Degrees of Freedom" on page 116). For a contingency table, the degrees of freedom are related to the number of rows (r) and columns (c) as follows:

$$\text{degrees of freedom} = (r - 1) \times (c - 1)$$

The chi-square distribution is typically skewed, with a long tail to the right; see Figure 3-7 for the distribution with 1, 2, 5, and 20 degrees of freedom. The further out on the chi-square distribution the observed statistic is, the lower the p-value.

The function `chisq.test` can be used to compute the p-value using the chi-square distribution as a reference:

```
> chisq.test(clicks, simulate.p.value=FALSE)

        Pearson's Chi-squared test

data:  clicks
X-squared = 1.6659, df = 2, p-value = 0.4348
```

In *Python*, use the function `scipy.stats.chi2_contingency`:

```
chisq, pvalue, df, expected = stats.chi2_contingency(clicks)
print(f'Observed chi2: {chi2observed:.4f}')
print(f'p-value: {pvalue:.4f}')
```

The p-value is a little less than the resampling p-value; this is because the chi-square distribution is only an approximation of the actual distribution of the statistic.

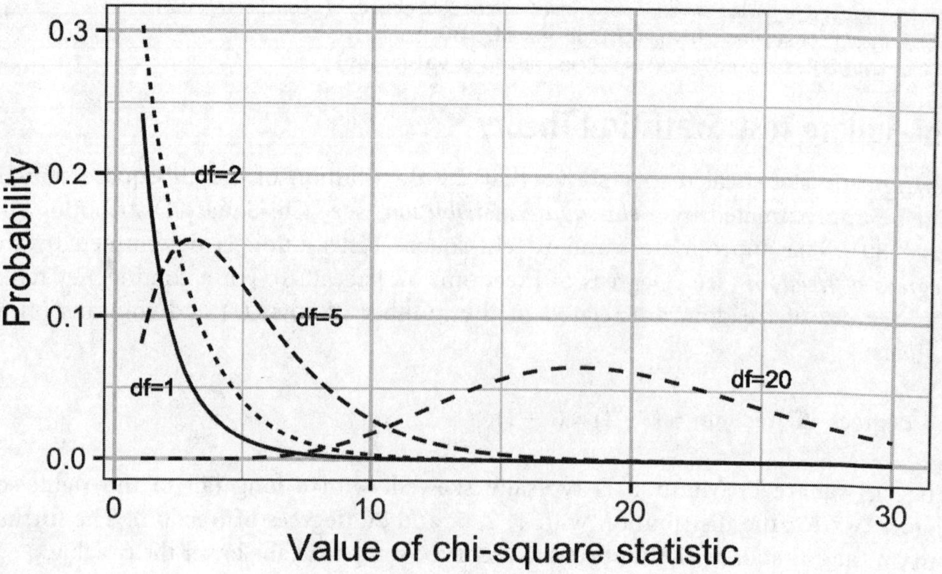

Figure 3-7. Chi-square distribution with various degrees of freedom

Fisher's Exact Test

The chi-square distribution is a good approximation of the shuffled resampling test just described, except when counts are extremely low (single digits, especially five or fewer). In such cases, the resampling procedure will yield more accurate p-values. In fact, most statistical software has a procedure to actually enumerate *all* the possible rearrangements (permutations) that can occur, tabulate their frequencies, and determine exactly how extreme the observed result is. This is called *Fisher's exact test* after the great statistician R. A. Fisher. *R* code for Fisher's exact test is simple in its basic form:

```
> fisher.test(clicks)

        Fisher's Exact Test for Count Data

data:  clicks
p-value = 0.4824
alternative hypothesis: two.sided
```

The p-value is very close to the p-value of 0.4853 obtained using the resampling method.

Where some counts are very low but others are quite high (e.g., the denominator in a conversion rate), it may be necessary to do a shuffled permutation test instead of a full exact test, due to the difficulty of calculating all possible permutations. The preceding *R* function has several arguments that control whether to use this approximation (`simulate.p.value=TRUE or FALSE`), how many iterations should be used (`B=...`), and a computational constraint (`workspace=...`) that limits how far calculations for the *exact* result should go.

There is no implementation of Fisher's exact test easily available in *Python*.

Detecting Scientific Fraud

An interesting example is provided by the case of Tufts University researcher Thereza Imanishi-Kari, who was accused in 1991 of fabricating data in her research. Congressman John Dingell became involved, and the case eventually led to the resignation of her colleague, David Baltimore, from the presidency of Rockefeller University.

One element in the case rested on statistical evidence regarding the expected distribution of digits in her laboratory data, where each observation had many digits. Investigators focused on the *interior* digits (ignoring the first digit and last digit of a number), which would be expected to follow a *uniform random* distribution. That is, they would occur randomly, with each digit having equal probability of occurring (the lead digit might be predominantly one value, and the final digits might be affected by rounding). Table 3-7 lists the frequencies of interior digits from the actual data in the case.

Table 3-7. Frequency of interior digits in laboratory data

Digit	Frequency
0	14
1	71
2	7
3	65
4	23
5	19
6	12
7	45
8	53
9	6

The distribution of the 315 digits, shown in Figure 3-8, certainly looks nonrandom.

Investigators calculated the departure from expectation (31.5—that's how often each digit would occur in a strictly uniform distribution) and used a chi-square test (a resampling procedure could equally have been used) to show that the actual distribution was well beyond the range of normal chance variation, indicating the data might have been fabricated. (Note: Imanishi-Kari was ultimately exonerated after a lengthy proceeding.)

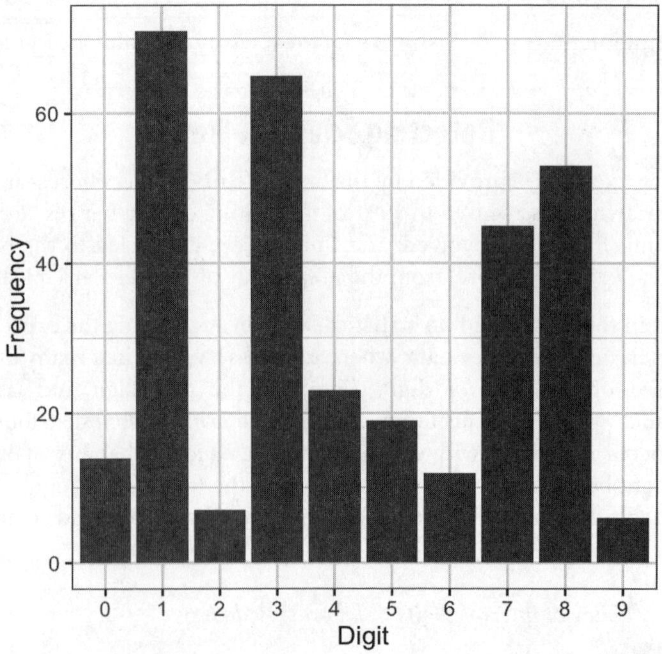

Figure 3-8. Frequency histogram for Imanishi-Kari lab data

Relevance for Data Science

The chi-square test, or Fisher's exact test, is used when you want to know whether an effect is for real or might be the product of chance. In most classical statistical applications of the chi-square test, its role is to establish statistical significance, which is typically needed before a study or an experiment can be published. This is not so important for data scientists. In most data science experiments, whether A/B or A/B/C…, the goal is not simply to establish statistical significance but rather to arrive at the best treatment. For this purpose, multi-armed bandits (see "Multi-Arm Bandit Algorithm" on page 131) offer a more complete solution.

One data science application of the chi-square test, especially Fisher's exact version, is in determining appropriate sample sizes for web experiments. These experiments often have very low click rates, and despite thousands of exposures, count rates might be too small to yield definitive conclusions in an experiment. In such cases, Fisher's exact test, the chi-square test, and other tests can be useful as a component of power and sample size calculations (see "Power and Sample Size" on page 135).

Chi-square tests are used widely in research by investigators in search of the elusive statistically significant p-value that will allow publication. Chi-square tests, or similar resampling simulations, are used in data science applications more as a filter to determine whether an effect or a feature is worthy of further consideration than as a formal test of significance. For example, they are used in spatial statistics and mapping to determine whether spatial data conforms to a specified null distribution (e.g., are crimes concentrated in a certain area to a greater degree than random chance would allow?). They can also be used in automated feature selection in machine learning, to assess class prevalence across features and identify features where the prevalence of a certain class is unusually high or low, in a way that is not compatible with random variation.

Key Ideas

- A common procedure in statistics is to test whether observed data counts are consistent with an assumption of independence (e.g., propensity to buy a particular item is independent of gender).
- The chi-square distribution is the reference distribution (which embodies the assumption of independence) to which the observed calculated chi-square statistic must be compared.

Further Reading

- R. A. Fisher's famous "Lady Tasting Tea" example from the beginning of the 20th century remains a simple and effective illustration of his exact test. Google "Lady Tasting Tea," and you will find a number of good writeups.
- Stat Trek offers a good tutorial on the chi-square test (*https://oreil.ly/77DUf*).

Multi-Arm Bandit Algorithm

Multi-arm bandits offer an approach to testing, especially web testing, that allows explicit optimization and more rapid decision making than the traditional statistical approach to designing experiments.

Key Terms for Multi-Arm Bandits

Multi-arm bandit
: An imaginary slot machine with multiple arms for the customer to choose from, each with different payoffs, here taken to be an analogy for a multitreatment experiment.

Arm
: A treatment in an experiment (e.g., "headline A in a web test").

Win
: The experimental analog of a win at the slot machine (e.g., "customer clicks on the link").

A traditional A/B test involves data collected in an experiment, according to a specified design, to answer a specific question such as, "Which is better, treatment A or treatment B?" The presumption is that once we get an answer to that question, the experimenting is over and we proceed to act on the results.

You can probably perceive several difficulties with that approach. First, our answer may be inconclusive: "effect not proven." In other words, the results from the experiment may suggest an effect, but if there is an effect, we don't have a big enough sample to prove it (to the satisfaction of the traditional statistical standards). What decision do we take? Second, we might want to begin taking advantage of results that come in prior to the conclusion of the experiment. Third, we might want the right to change our minds or to try something different based on additional data that comes in after the experiment is over. The traditional approach to experiments and hypothesis tests dates from the 1920s and is rather inflexible. The advent of computer power and software has enabled more powerful flexible approaches. Moreover, data science (and business in general) is not so worried about statistical significance, but concerned more with optimizing overall effort and results.

Bandit algorithms, which are very popular in web testing, allow you to test multiple treatments at once and reach conclusions faster than traditional statistical designs. They take their name from slot machines used in gambling, also termed one-armed bandits (since they are configured in such a way that they extract money from the gambler in a steady flow). If you imagine a slot machine with more than one arm, each arm paying out at a different rate, you would have a multi-armed bandit, which is the full name for this algorithm.

Your goal is to win as much money as possible and, more specifically, to identify and settle on the winning arm sooner rather than later. The challenge is that you don't know at what overall rate the arms pay out—you only know the results of individual pulls on the arms. Suppose each "win" is for the same amount, no matter which arm.

What differs is the probability of a win. Suppose further that you initially try each arm 50 times and get the following results:

Arm A: 10 wins out of 50
Arm B: 2 win out of 50
Arm C: 4 wins out of 50

One extreme approach is to say, "Looks like arm A is a winner—let's quit trying the other arms and stick with A." This takes full advantage of the information from the initial trial. If A is truly superior, we get the benefit of that early on. On the other hand, if B or C is truly better, we lose any opportunity to discover that. Another extreme approach is to say, "This all looks to be within the realm of chance—let's keep pulling them all equally." This gives maximum opportunity for alternates to A to show themselves. However, in the process, we are deploying what seem to be inferior treatments. How long do we permit that? Bandit algorithms take a hybrid approach: we start pulling A more often, to take advantage of its apparent superiority, but we don't abandon B and C. We just pull them less often. If A continues to outperform, we continue to shift resources (pulls) away from B and C and pull A more often. If, on the other hand, C starts to do better, and A starts to do worse, we can shift pulls from A back to C. If one of them turns out to be superior to A and this was hidden in the initial trial due to chance, it now has an opportunity to emerge with further testing.

Now think of applying this to web testing. Instead of multiple slot machine arms, you might have multiple offers, headlines, colors, and so on being tested on a website. Customers either click (a "win" for the merchant) or don't click. Initially, the offers are shown randomly and equally. If, however, one offer starts to outperform the others, it can be shown ("pulled") more often. But what should the parameters of the algorithm that modifies the pull rates be? What "pull rates" should we change to, and when should we change?

Here is one simple algorithm, the epsilon-greedy algorithm for an A/B test:

1. Generate a uniformly distributed random number between 0 and 1.
2. If the number lies between 0 and epsilon (where epsilon is a number between 0 and 1, typically fairly small), flip a fair coin (50/50 probability), and:
    a. If the coin is heads, show offer A.
    b. If the coin is tails, show offer B.
3. If the number is ≥ epsilon, show whichever offer has had the highest response rate to date.

Epsilon is the single parameter that governs this algorithm. If epsilon is 1, we end up with a standard simple A/B experiment (random allocation between A and B for each subject). If epsilon is 0, we end up with a purely *greedy* algorithm—one that chooses the best available immediate option (a local optimum). It seeks no further experimentation, simply assigning subjects (web visitors) to the best-performing treatment.

A more sophisticated algorithm uses "Thompson's sampling." This procedure "samples" (pulls a bandit arm) at each stage to maximize the probability of choosing the best arm. Of course you don't know which is the best arm—that's the whole problem!—but as you observe the payoff with each successive draw, you gain more information. Thompson's sampling uses a Bayesian approach: some prior distribution of rewards is assumed initially, using what is called a *beta distribution* (this is a common mechanism for specifying prior information in a Bayesian problem). As information accumulates from each draw, this information can be updated, allowing the selection of the next draw to be better optimized as far as choosing the right arm.

Bandit algorithms can efficiently handle 3+ treatments and move toward optimal selection of the "best." For traditional statistical testing procedures, the complexity of decision making for 3+ treatments far outstrips that of the traditional A/B test, and the advantage of bandit algorithms is much greater.

Key Ideas

- Traditional A/B tests envision a random sampling process, which can lead to excessive exposure to the inferior treatment.
- Multi-arm bandits, in contrast, alter the sampling process to incorporate information learned during the experiment and reduce the frequency of the inferior treatment.
- They also facilitate efficient treatment of more than two treatments.
- There are different algorithms for shifting sampling probability away from the inferior treatment(s) and to the (presumed) superior one.

Further Reading

- An excellent short treatment of multi-arm bandit algorithms is found in *Bandit Algorithms for Website Optimization*, by John Myles White (O'Reilly, 2012). White includes *Python* code, as well as the results of simulations to assess the performance of bandits.
- For more (somewhat technical) information about Thompson sampling, see "Analysis of Thompson Sampling for the Multi-armed Bandit Problem" (*https://oreil.ly/OgWrG*) by Shipra Agrawal and Navin Goyal.

Power and Sample Size

If you run a web test, how do you decide how long it should run (i.e., how many impressions per treatment are needed)? Despite what you may read in many guides to web testing, there is no good general guidance—it depends, mainly, on the frequency with which the desired goal is attained.

> ### Key Terms for Power and Sample Size
>
> ***Effect size***
> The minimum size of the effect that you hope to be able to detect in a statistical test, such as "a 20% improvement in click rates."
>
> ***Power***
> The probability of detecting a given effect size with a given sample size.
>
> ***Significance level***
> The statistical significance level at which the test will be conducted.

One step in statistical calculations for sample size is to ask "Will a hypothesis test actually reveal a difference between treatments A and B?" The outcome of a hypothesis test—the p-value—depends on what the real difference is between treatment A and treatment B. It also depends on the luck of the draw—who gets selected for the groups in the experiment. But it makes sense that the bigger the actual difference between treatments A and B, the greater the probability that our experiment will reveal it; and the smaller the difference, the more data will be needed to detect it. To distinguish between a .350 hitter and a .200 hitter in baseball, not that many at-bats are needed. To distinguish between a .300 hitter and a .280 hitter, a good many more at-bats will be needed.

Power is the probability of detecting a specified *effect size* with specified sample characteristics (size and variability). For example, we might say (hypothetically) that the probability of distinguishing between a .330 hitter and a .200 hitter in 25 at-bats is 0.75. The effect size here is a difference of .130. And "detecting" means that a hypothesis test will reject the null hypothesis of "no difference" and conclude there is a real effect. So the experiment of 25 at-bats (n = 25) for two hitters, with an effect size of 0.130, has (hypothetical) power of 0.75, or 75%.

You can see that there are several moving parts here, and it is easy to get tangled up in the numerous statistical assumptions and formulas that will be needed (to specify sample variability, effect size, sample size, alpha-level for the hypothesis test, etc., and to calculate power). Indeed, there is special-purpose statistical software to calculate power. Most data scientists will not need to go through all the formal steps needed to report power, for example, in a published paper. However, they may face occasions where they want to collect some data for an A/B test, and collecting or processing the data involves some cost. In that case, knowing approximately how much data to collect can help avoid the situation where you collect data at some effort, and the result ends up being inconclusive. Here's a fairly intuitive alternative approach:

1. Start with some hypothetical data that represents your best guess about the data that will result (perhaps based on prior data)—for example, a box with 20 ones and 80 zeros to represent a .200 hitter, or a box with some observations of "time spent on website."
2. Create a second sample simply by adding the desired effect size to the first sample—for example, a second box with 33 ones and 67 zeros, or a second box with 25 seconds added to each initial "time spent on website."
3. Draw a bootstrap sample of size *n* from each box.
4. Conduct a permutation (or formula-based) hypothesis test on the two bootstrap samples and record whether the difference between them is statistically significant.
5. Repeat the preceding two steps many times and determine how often the difference was significant—that's the estimated power.

Sample Size

The most common use of power calculations is to estimate how big a sample you will need.

For example, suppose you are looking at click-through rates (clicks as a percentage of exposures), and testing a new ad against an existing ad. How many clicks do you need to accumulate in the study? If you are interested only in results that show a huge difference (say, a 50% difference), a relatively small sample might do the trick. If, on the other hand, even a minor difference would be of interest, then a much larger sample is needed. A standard approach is to establish a policy that a new ad must do better than an existing ad by some percentage, say, 10%; otherwise, the existing ad will remain in place. This goal, the "effect size," then drives the sample size.

For example, suppose current click-through rates are about 1.1%, and you are seeking a 10% boost to 1.21%. So we have two boxes: box A with 1.1% ones (say, 110 ones and 9,890 zeros), and box B with 1.21% ones (say, 121 ones and 9,879 zeros). For starters, let's try 300 draws from each box (this would be like 300 "impressions" for each ad). Suppose our first draw yields the following:

Box A: 3 ones
Box B: 5 ones

Right away we can see that any hypothesis test would reveal this difference (5 versus 3) to be well within the range of chance variation. This combination of sample size ($n = 300$ in each group) and effect size (10% difference) is too small for any hypothesis test to reliably show a difference.

So we can try increasing the sample size (let's try 2,000 impressions), and require a larger improvement (50% instead of 10%).

For example, suppose current click-through rates are still 1.1%, but we are now seeking a 50% boost to 1.65%. So we have two boxes: box A still with 1.1% ones (say, 110 ones and 9,890 zeros), and box B with 1.65% ones (say, 165 ones and 9,868 zeros). Now we'll try 2,000 draws from each box. Suppose our first draw yields the following:

Box A: 19 ones
Box B: 34 ones

A significance test on this difference (34–19) shows it still registers as "not significant" (though much closer to significance than the earlier difference of 5–3). To calculate power, we would need to repeat the previous procedure many times, or use statistical software that can calculate power, but our initial draw suggests to us that even detecting a 50% improvement will require several thousand ad impressions.

In summary, for calculating power or required sample size, there are four moving parts:

- Sample size
- Effect size you want to detect
- Significance level (alpha) at which the test will be conducted
- Power

Specify any three of them, and the fourth can be calculated. Most commonly, you would want to calculate sample size, so you must specify the other three. With *R* and *Python*, you also have to specify the alternative hypothesis as "greater" or "larger" to get a one-sided test; see "One-Way Versus Two-Way Hypothesis Tests" on page 95 for more discussion of one-way versus two-way tests. Here is *R* code for a test involving two proportions, where both samples are the same size (this uses the `pwr` package):

```
effect_size = ES.h(p1=0.0121, p2=0.011)
pwr.2p.test(h=effect_size, sig.level=0.05, power=0.8, alternative='greater’)
--
     Difference of proportion power calculation for binomial distribution
                                                       (arcsine transformation)

              h = 0.01029785
              n = 116601.7
      sig.level = 0.05
```

```
              power = 0.8
        alternative = greater

NOTE: same sample sizes
```

The function `ES.h` calculates the effect size. We see that if we want a power of 80%, we require a sample size of almost 120,000 impressions. If we are seeking a 50% boost (`p1=0.0165`), the sample size is reduced to 5,500 impressions.

The `statsmodels` package contains several methods for power calculation. Here, we use `proportion_effectsize` to calculate the effect size and `TTestIndPower` to solve for the sample size:

```
effect_size = sm.stats.proportion_effectsize(0.0121, 0.011)
analysis = sm.stats.TTestIndPower()
result = analysis.solve_power(effect_size=effect_size,
                              alpha=0.05, power=0.8, alternative='larger')
print('Sample Size: %.3f' % result)
--
Sample Size: 116602.393
```

Key Ideas

- Finding out how big a sample size you need requires thinking ahead to the statistical test you plan to conduct.
- You must specify the minimum size of the effect that you want to detect.
- You must also specify the required probability of detecting that effect size (power).
- Finally, you must specify the significance level (alpha) at which the test will be conducted.

Further Reading

- *Sample Size Determination and Power* by Thomas Ryan (Wiley, 2013) is a comprehensive and readable review of this subject.
- Steve Simon, a statistical consultant, has written a very engaging narrative-style post on the subject (*https://oreil.ly/18mtp*).

Summary

The principles of experimental design—randomization of subjects into two or more groups receiving different treatments—allow us to draw valid conclusions about how well the treatments work. It is best to include a control treatment of "making no change." The subject of formal statistical inference—hypothesis testing, p-values, t-tests, and much more along these lines—occupies much time and space in a traditional statistics course or text, and the formality is mostly unneeded from a data science perspective. However, it remains important to recognize the role that random variation can play in fooling the human brain. Intuitive resampling procedures (permutation and bootstrap) allow data scientists to gauge the extent to which chance variation can play a role in their data analysis.

CHAPTER 4

Regression and Prediction

Perhaps the most common goal in statistics is to answer the question "Is the variable X (or more likely, $X_1, ..., X_p$) associated with a variable Y, and if so, what is the relationship and can we use it to predict Y?"

Nowhere is the nexus between statistics and data science stronger than in the realm of prediction—specifically, the prediction of an outcome (target) variable based on the values of other "predictor" variables. This process of training a model on data where the outcome is known, for subsequent application to data where the outcome is not known, is termed *supervised learning*. Another important connection between data science and statistics is in the area of *anomaly detection*, where regression diagnostics originally intended for data analysis and improving the regression model can be used to detect unusual records.

Simple Linear Regression

Simple linear regression provides a model of the relationship between the magnitude of one variable and that of a second—for example, as X increases, Y also increases. Or as X increases, Y decreases.[1] Correlation is another way to measure how two variables are related—see the section "Correlation" on page 30. The difference is that while correlation measures the *strength* of an association between two variables, regression quantifies the *nature* of the relationship.

1 This and subsequent sections in this chapter © 2020 Datastats, LLC, Peter Bruce, Andrew Bruce, and Peter Gedeck; used by permission.

Key Terms for Simple Linear Regression

Response
: The variable we are trying to predict.

  Synonyms
  : dependent variable, *Y* variable, target, outcome

Independent variable
: The variable used to predict the response.

  Synonyms
  : *X* variable, feature, attribute, predictor

Record
: The vector of predictor and outcome values for a specific individual or case.

  Synonyms
  : row, case, instance, example

Intercept
: The intercept of the regression line—that is, the predicted value when $X = 0$.

  Synonyms
  : b_0, β_0

Regression coefficient
: The slope of the regression line.

  Synonyms
  : slope, b_1, β_1, parameter estimates, weights

Fitted values
: The estimates $\hat{Y}_i$ obtained from the regression line.

  Synonym
  : predicted values

Residuals
: The difference between the observed values and the fitted values.

  Synonym
  : errors

Least squares

The method of fitting a regression by minimizing the sum of squared residuals.

Synonyms

ordinary least squares, OLS

The Regression Equation

Simple linear regression estimates how much Y will change when X changes by a certain amount. With the correlation coefficient, the variables X and Y are interchangeable. With regression, we are trying to predict the Y variable from X using a linear relationship (i.e., a line):

$$Y = b_0 + b_1 X$$

We read this as "Y equals b_1 times X, plus a constant b_0." The symbol b_0 is known as the *intercept* (or constant), and the symbol b_1 as the *slope* for X. Both appear in *R* output as *coefficients*, though in general use the term *coefficient* is often reserved for b_1. The Y variable is known as the *response* or *dependent* variable since it depends on X. The X variable is known as the *predictor* or *independent* variable. The machine learning community tends to use other terms, calling Y the *target* and X a *feature* vector. Throughout this book, we will use the terms *predictor* and *feature* interchangeably.

Consider the scatterplot in Figure 4-1 displaying the number of years a worker was exposed to cotton dust (`Exposure`) versus a measure of lung capacity (`PEFR` or "peak expiratory flow rate"). How is `PEFR` related to `Exposure`? It's hard to tell based just on the picture.

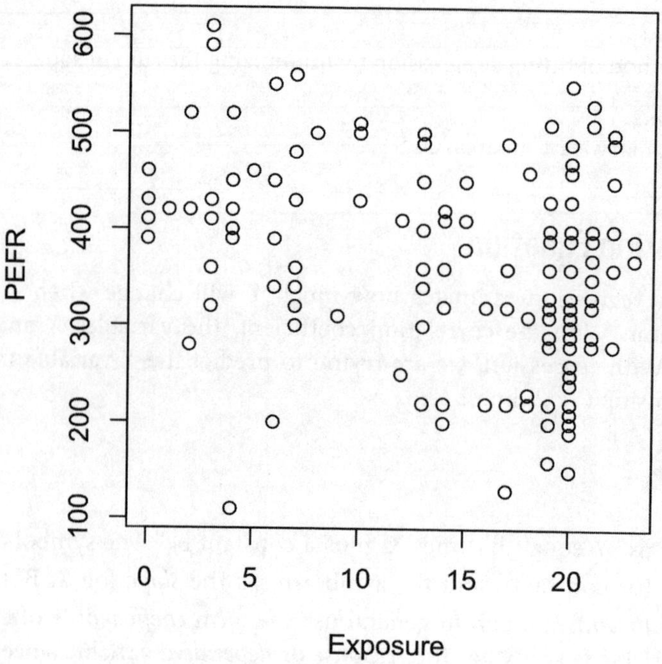

Figure 4-1. Cotton exposure versus lung capacity

Simple linear regression tries to find the "best" line to predict the response `PEFR` as a function of the predictor variable `Exposure`:

$$\text{PEFR} = b_0 + b_1 \text{Exposure}$$

The `lm` function in *R* can be used to fit a linear regression:

```
model <- lm(PEFR ~ Exposure, data=lung)
```

`lm` stands for *linear model*, and the ~ symbol denotes that `PEFR` is predicted by `Exposure`. With this model definition, the intercept is automatically included and fitted. If you want to exclude the intercept from the model, you need to write the model definition as follows:

```
PEFR ~ Exposure - 1
```

Printing the `model` object produces the following output:

```
Call:
lm(formula = PEFR ~ Exposure, data = lung)

Coefficients:
(Intercept)     Exposure
    424.583       -4.185
```

The intercept, or b_0, is 424.583 and can be interpreted as the predicted `PEFR` for a worker with zero years exposure. The regression coefficient, or b_1, can be interpreted as follows: for each additional year that a worker is exposed to cotton dust, the worker's `PEFR` measurement is reduced by –4.185.

In *Python*, we can use `LinearRegression` from the `scikit-learn` package. (the `statsmodels` package has a linear regression implementation that is more similar to *R* (`sm.OLS`); we will use it later in this chapter):

```
predictors = ['Exposure']
outcome = 'PEFR'

model = LinearRegression()
model.fit(lung[predictors], lung[outcome])

print(f'Intercept: {model.intercept_:.3f}')
print(f'Coefficient Exposure: {model.coef_[0]:.3f}')
```

The regression line from this model is displayed in Figure 4-2.

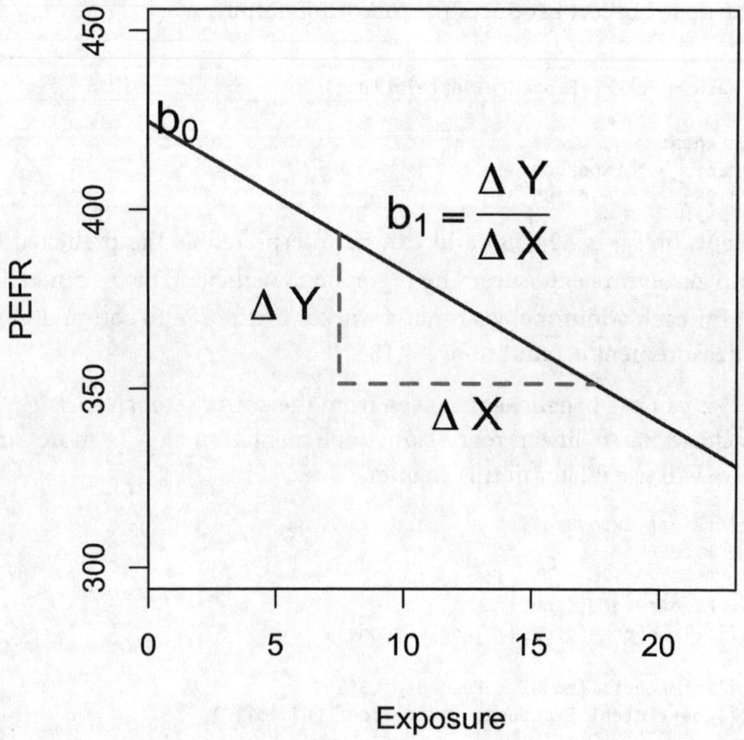

Figure 4-2. Slope and intercept for the regression fit to the lung data

Fitted Values and Residuals

Important concepts in regression analysis are the *fitted values* (the predictions) and *residuals* (prediction errors). In general, the data doesn't fall exactly on a line, so the regression equation should include an explicit error term e_i:

$$Y_i = b_0 + b_1 X_i + e_i$$

The fitted values, also referred to as the *predicted values*, are typically denoted by $\hat{Y}_i$ (Y-hat). These are given by:

$$\hat{Y}_i = \hat{b}_0 + \hat{b}_1 X_i$$

The notation $\hat{b}_0$ and $\hat{b}_1$ indicates that the coefficients are estimated versus known.

Hat Notation: Estimates Versus Known Values

The "hat" notation is used to differentiate between estimates and known values. So the symbol $\hat{b}$ ("b-hat") is an estimate of the unknown parameter b. Why do statisticians differentiate between the estimate and the true value? The estimate has uncertainty, whereas the true value is fixed.[2]

We compute the residuals $\hat{e}_i$ by subtracting the *predicted* values from the original data:

$$\hat{e}_i = Y_i - \hat{Y}_i$$

In *R*, we can obtain the fitted values and residuals using the functions `predict` and `residuals`:

```
fitted <- predict(model)
resid <- residuals(model)
```

With `scikit-learn`'s `LinearRegression` model, we use the `predict` method on the training data to get the `fitted` values and subsequently the `residuals`. As we will see, this is a general pattern that all models in `scikit-learn` follow:

```
fitted = model.predict(lung[predictors])
residuals = lung[outcome] - fitted
```

Figure 4-3 illustrates the residuals from the regression line fit to the lung data. The residuals are the length of the vertical dashed lines from the data to the line.

2 In Bayesian statistics, the true value is assumed to be a random variable with a specified distribution. In the Bayesian context, instead of estimates of unknown parameters, there are posterior and prior distributions.

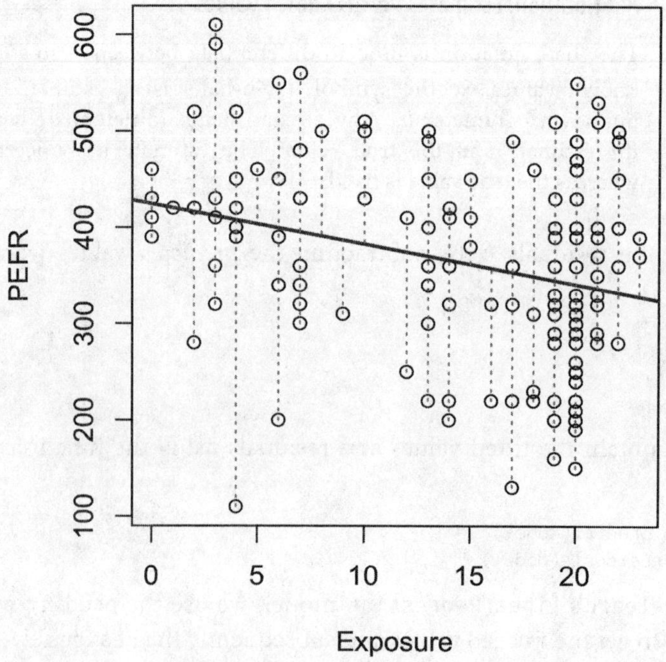

Figure 4-3. Residuals from a regression line (to accommodate all the data, the y-axis scale differs from Figure 4-2, hence the apparently different slope)

Least Squares

How is the model fit to the data? When there is a clear relationship, you could imagine fitting the line by hand. In practice, the regression line is the estimate that minimizes the sum of squared residual values, also called the *residual sum of squares* or *RSS*:

$$
\begin{aligned}
RSS &= \sum_{i=1}^{n} \left(Y_i - \hat{Y}_i\right)^2 \\
&= \sum_{i=1}^{n} \left(Y_i - \hat{b}_0 - \hat{b}_1 X_i\right)^2
\end{aligned}
$$

The estimates $\hat{b}_0$ and $\hat{b}_1$ are the values that minimize RSS.

The method of minimizing the sum of the squared residuals is termed *least squares* regression, or *ordinary least squares* (OLS) regression. It is often attributed to Carl Friedrich Gauss, the German mathematician, but was first published by the French mathematician Adrien-Marie Legendre in 1805. Least squares regression can be computed quickly and easily with any standard statistical software.

Historically, computational convenience is one reason for the widespread use of least squares in regression. With the advent of big data, computational speed is still an important factor. Least squares, like the mean (see "Median and Robust Estimates" on page 10), are sensitive to outliers, although this tends to be a significant problem only in small or moderate-sized data sets. See "Outliers" on page 177 for a discussion of outliers in regression.

Regression Terminology

When analysts and researchers use the term *regression* by itself, they are typically referring to linear regression; the focus is usually on developing a linear model to explain the relationship between predictor variables and a numeric outcome variable. In its formal statistical sense, regression also includes nonlinear models that yield a functional relationship between predictors and outcome variables. In the machine learning community, the term is also occasionally used loosely to refer to the use of any predictive model that produces a predicted numeric outcome (as opposed to classification methods that predict a binary or categorical outcome).

Prediction Versus Explanation (Profiling)

Historically, a primary use of regression was to illuminate a supposed linear relationship between predictor variables and an outcome variable. The goal has been to understand a relationship and explain it using the data that the regression was fit to. In this case, the primary focus is on the estimated slope of the regression equation, $\hat{b}$. Economists want to know the relationship between consumer spending and GDP growth. Public health officials might want to understand whether a public information campaign is effective in promoting safe sex practices. In such cases, the focus is not on predicting individual cases but rather on understanding the overall relationship among variables.

With the advent of big data, regression is widely used to form a model to predict individual outcomes for new data (i.e., a predictive model) rather than explain data in hand. In this instance, the main items of interest are the fitted values $\hat{Y}$. In marketing, regression can be used to predict the change in revenue in response to the size of an ad campaign. Universities use regression to predict students' GPA based on their SAT scores.

A regression model that fits the data well is set up such that changes in X lead to changes in Y. However, by itself, the regression equation does not prove the direction of causation. Conclusions about causation must come from a broader understanding about the relationship. For example, a regression equation might show a definite relationship between number of clicks on a web ad and number of conversions. It is our knowledge of the marketing process, not the regression equation, that leads us to the conclusion that clicks on the ad lead to sales, and not vice versa.

> ### Key Ideas
>
> - The regression equation models the relationship between a response variable Y and a predictor variable X as a line.
> - A regression model yields fitted values and residuals—predictions of the response and the errors of the predictions.
> - Regression models are typically fit by the method of least squares.
> - Regression is used both for prediction and explanation.

Further Reading

For an in-depth treatment of prediction versus explanation, see Galit Shmueli's article "To Explain or to Predict?" (*https://oreil.ly/4fVUY*).

Multiple Linear Regression

When there are multiple predictors, the equation is simply extended to accommodate them:

$$Y = b_0 + b_1 X_1 + b_2 X_2 + \ldots + b_p X_p + e$$

Instead of a line, we now have a linear model—the relationship between each coefficient and its variable (feature) is linear.

> ### Key Terms for Multiple Linear Regression
>
> ***Root mean squared error***
> The square root of the average squared error of the regression (this is the most widely used metric to compare regression models).
>
> *Synonym*
> RMSE
>
> ***Residual standard error***
> The same as the root mean squared error, but adjusted for degrees of freedom.

Synonym

RSE

R-squared

The proportion of variance explained by the model, from 0 to 1.

Synonyms

coefficient of determination, R^2

t-statistic

The coefficient for a predictor, divided by the standard error of the coefficient, giving a metric to compare the importance of variables in the model. See "t-Tests" on page 110.

Weighted regression

Regression with the records having different weights.

All of the other concepts in simple linear regression, such as fitting by least squares and the definition of fitted values and residuals, extend to the multiple linear regression setting. For example, the fitted values are given by:

$$\hat{Y}_i = \hat{b}_0 + \hat{b}_1 X_{1,i} + \hat{b}_2 X_{2,i} + \dots + \hat{b}_p X_{p,i}$$

Example: King County Housing Data

An example of using multiple linear regression is in estimating the value of houses. County assessors must estimate the value of a house for the purposes of assessing taxes. Real estate professionals and home buyers consult popular websites such as Zillow (*https://zillow.com*) to ascertain a fair price. Here are a few rows of housing data from King County (Seattle), Washington, from the `house data.frame`:

```
head(house[, c('AdjSalePrice', 'SqFtTotLiving', 'SqFtLot', 'Bathrooms',
               'Bedrooms', 'BldgGrade')])
Source: local data frame [6 x 6]

  AdjSalePrice SqFtTotLiving SqFtLot Bathrooms Bedrooms BldgGrade
         (dbl)         (int)   (int)     (dbl)    (int)     (int)
1       300805          2400    9373      3.00        6         7
2      1076162          3764   20156      3.75        4        10
3       761805          2060   26036      1.75        4         8
4       442065          3200    8618      3.75        5         7
5       297065          1720    8620      1.75        4         7
6       411781           930    1012      1.50        2         8
```

The `head` method of `pandas` data frame lists the top rows:

```
subset = ['AdjSalePrice', 'SqFtTotLiving', 'SqFtLot', 'Bathrooms',
          'Bedrooms', 'BldgGrade']
house[subset].head()
```

The goal is to predict the sales price from the other variables. The `lm` function handles the multiple regression case simply by including more terms on the righthand side of the equation; the argument `na.action=na.omit` causes the model to drop records that have missing values:

```
house_lm <- lm(AdjSalePrice ~ SqFtTotLiving + SqFtLot + Bathrooms +
               Bedrooms + BldgGrade,
               data=house, na.action=na.omit)
```

`scikit-learn`'s `LinearRegression` can be used for multiple linear regression as well:

```
predictors = ['SqFtTotLiving', 'SqFtLot', 'Bathrooms', 'Bedrooms', 'BldgGrade']
outcome = 'AdjSalePrice'

house_lm = LinearRegression()
house_lm.fit(house[predictors], house[outcome])
```

Printing `house_lm` object produces the following output:

```
house_lm

Call:
lm(formula = AdjSalePrice ~ SqFtTotLiving + SqFtLot + Bathrooms +
    Bedrooms + BldgGrade, data = house, na.action = na.omit)

Coefficients:
  (Intercept)  SqFtTotLiving        SqFtLot      Bathrooms
   -5.219e+05      2.288e+02     -6.047e-02     -1.944e+04
     Bedrooms      BldgGrade
   -4.777e+04      1.061e+05
```

For a `LinearRegression` model, intercept and coefficients are the fields `intercept_` and `coef_` of the fitted model:

```
print(f'Intercept: {house_lm.intercept_:.3f}')
print('Coefficients:')
for name, coef in zip(predictors, house_lm.coef_):
    print(f' {name}: {coef}')
```

The interpretation of the coefficients is as with simple linear regression: the predicted value $\hat{Y}$ changes by the coefficient b_j for each unit change in X_j assuming all the other variables, X_k for $k \neq j$, remain the same. For example, adding an extra finished square foot to a house increases the estimated value by roughly \$229; adding 1,000 finished square feet implies the value will increase by \$228,800.

Assessing the Model

The most important performance metric from a data science perspective is *root mean squared error*, or *RMSE*. RMSE is the square root of the average squared error in the predicted $\hat{y}_i$ values:

$$RMSE = \sqrt{\frac{\sum_{i=1}^{n}\left(y_i - \hat{y}_i\right)^2}{n}}$$

This measures the overall accuracy of the model and is a basis for comparing it to other models (including models fit using machine learning techniques). Similar to RMSE is the *residual standard error*, or *RSE*. In this case we have *p* predictors, and the RSE is given by:

$$RSE = \sqrt{\frac{\sum_{i=1}^{n}\left(y_i - \hat{y}_i\right)^2}{(n - p - 1)}}$$

The only difference is that the denominator is the degrees of freedom, as opposed to number of records (see "Degrees of Freedom" on page 116). In practice, for linear regression, the difference between RMSE and RSE is very small, particularly for big data applications.

The `summary` function in *R* computes RSE as well as other metrics for a regression model:

```
summary(house_lm)

Call:
lm(formula = AdjSalePrice ~ SqFtTotLiving + SqFtLot + Bathrooms +
    Bedrooms + BldgGrade, data = house, na.action = na.omit)

Residuals:
     Min       1Q   Median       3Q      Max
-1199479  -118908   -20977    87435  9473035

Coefficients:
                Estimate Std. Error t value Pr(>|t|)
(Intercept)   -5.219e+05  1.565e+04 -33.342  < 2e-16 ***
SqFtTotLiving  2.288e+02  3.899e+00  58.694  < 2e-16 ***
SqFtLot       -6.047e-02  6.118e-02  -0.988    0.323
Bathrooms     -1.944e+04  3.625e+03  -5.363 8.27e-08 ***
Bedrooms      -4.777e+04  2.490e+03 -19.187  < 2e-16 ***
BldgGrade      1.061e+05  2.396e+03  44.277  < 2e-16 ***
---
Signif. codes:  0 '***' 0.001 '**' 0.01 '*' 0.05 '.' 0.1 ' ' 1
```

```
Residual standard error: 261300 on 22681 degrees of freedom
Multiple R-squared:  0.5406,    Adjusted R-squared:  0.5405
F-statistic:  5338 on 5 and 22681 DF,  p-value: < 2.2e-16
```

`scikit-learn` provides a number of metrics for regression and classification. Here, we use `mean_squared_error` to get RMSE and `r2_score` for the coefficient of determination:

```
fitted = house_lm.predict(house[predictors])
RMSE = np.sqrt(mean_squared_error(house[outcome], fitted))
r2 = r2_score(house[outcome], fitted)
print(f'RMSE: {RMSE:.0f}')
print(f'r2: {r2:.4f}')
```

Use `statsmodels` to get a more detailed analysis of the regression model in *Python*:

```
model = sm.OLS(house[outcome], house[predictors].assign(const=1))
results = model.fit()
results.summary()
```

The `pandas` method `assign`, as used here, adds a constant column with value 1 to the predictors. This is required to model the intercept.

Another useful metric that you will see in software output is the *coefficient of determination*, also called the *R-squared* statistic or R^2. R-squared ranges from 0 to 1 and measures the proportion of variation in the data that is accounted for in the model. It is useful mainly in explanatory uses of regression where you want to assess how well the model fits the data. The formula for R^2 is:

$$R^2 = 1 - \frac{\sum_{i=1}^{n}(y_i - \hat{y}_i)^2}{\sum_{i=1}^{n}(y_i - \bar{y})^2}$$

The denominator is proportional to the variance of Y. The output from *R* also reports an *adjusted R-squared*, which adjusts for the degrees of freedom, effectively penalizing the addition of more predictors to a model. Seldom is this significantly different from *R-squared* in multiple regression with large data sets.

Along with the estimated coefficients, *R* and `statsmodels` report the standard error of the coefficients (SE) and a *t-statistic*:

$$t_b = \frac{\hat{b}}{\text{SE}(\hat{b})}$$

The t-statistic—and its mirror image, the p-value—measures the extent to which a coefficient is "statistically significant"—that is, outside the range of what a random chance arrangement of predictor and target variable might produce. The higher the t-statistic (and the lower the p-value), the more significant the predictor. Since parsimony is a valuable model feature, it is useful to have a tool like this to guide choice of variables to include as predictors (see “Model Selection and Stepwise Regression” on page 156).

> In addition to the t-statistic, *R* and other packages will often report a *p-value* (`Pr(>|t|)` in the *R* output) and *F-statistic*. Data scientists do not generally get too involved with the interpretation of these statistics, nor with the issue of statistical significance. Data scientists primarily focus on the t-statistic as a useful guide for whether to include a predictor in a model or not. High t-statistics (which go with p-values near 0) indicate a predictor should be retained in a model, while very low t-statistics indicate a predictor could be dropped. See “p-Value” on page 106 for more discussion.

Cross-Validation

Classic statistical regression metrics (R^2, F-statistics, and p-values) are all “in-sample” metrics—they are applied to the same data that was used to fit the model. Intuitively, you can see that it would make a lot of sense to set aside some of the original data, not use it to fit the model, and then apply the model to the set-aside (holdout) data to see how well it does. Normally, you would use a majority of the data to fit the model and use a smaller portion to test the model.

This idea of “out-of-sample” validation is not new, but it did not really take hold until larger data sets became more prevalent; with a small data set, analysts typically want to use all the data and fit the best possible model.

Using a holdout sample, though, leaves you subject to some uncertainty that arises simply from variability in the small holdout sample. How different would the assessment be if you selected a different holdout sample?

Cross-validation extends the idea of a holdout sample to multiple sequential holdout samples. The algorithm for basic *k-fold cross-validation* is as follows:

1. Set aside *1/k* of the data as a holdout sample.
2. Train the model on the remaining data.
3. Apply (score) the model to the *1/k* holdout, and record needed model assessment metrics.
4. Restore the first *1/k* of the data, and set aside the next *1/k* (excluding any records that got picked the first time).
5. Repeat steps 2 and 3.

6. Repeat until each record has been used in the holdout portion.
7. Average or otherwise combine the model assessment metrics.

The division of the data into the training sample and the holdout sample is also called a *fold*.

Model Selection and Stepwise Regression

In some problems, many variables could be used as predictors in a regression. For example, to predict house value, additional variables such as the basement size or year built could be used. In *R*, these are easy to add to the regression equation:

```
house_full <- lm(AdjSalePrice ~ SqFtTotLiving + SqFtLot + Bathrooms +
                 Bedrooms + BldgGrade + PropertyType + NbrLivingUnits +
                 SqFtFinBasement + YrBuilt + YrRenovated +
                 NewConstruction,
               data=house, na.action=na.omit)
```

In *Python*, we need to convert the categorical and boolean variables into numbers:

```
predictors = ['SqFtTotLiving', 'SqFtLot', 'Bathrooms', 'Bedrooms', 'BldgGrade',
              'PropertyType', 'NbrLivingUnits', 'SqFtFinBasement', 'YrBuilt',
              'YrRenovated', 'NewConstruction']

X = pd.get_dummies(house[predictors], drop_first=True)
X['NewConstruction'] = [1 if nc else 0 for nc in X['NewConstruction']]

house_full = sm.OLS(house[outcome], X.assign(const=1))
results = house_full.fit()
results.summary()
```

Adding more variables, however, does not necessarily mean we have a better model. Statisticians use the principle of *Occam's razor* to guide the choice of a model: all things being equal, a simpler model should be used in preference to a more complicated model.

Including additional variables always reduces RMSE and increases R^2 for the training data. Hence, these are not appropriate to help guide the model choice. One approach to including model complexity is to use the adjusted R^2:

$$R_{adj}^2 = 1 - (1 - R^2)\frac{n - 1}{n - P - 1}$$

Here, n is the number of records and P is the number of variables in the model.

In the 1970s, Hirotugu Akaike, the eminent Japanese statistician, developed a metric called *AIC* (Akaike's Information Criteria) that penalizes adding terms to a model. In the case of regression, AIC has the form:

$$\mathrm{AIC} = 2P + n \log(\mathtt{RSS}/n)$$

where P is the number of variables and n is the number of records. The goal is to find the model that minimizes AIC; models with k more extra variables are penalized by $2k$.

AIC, BIC, and Mallows Cp

The formula for AIC may seem a bit mysterious, but in fact it is based on asymptotic results in information theory. There are several variants to AIC:

AICc
: A version of AIC corrected for small sample sizes.

BIC or Bayesian information criteria
: Similar to AIC, with a stronger penalty for including additional variables to the model.

Mallows Cp
: A variant of AIC developed by Colin Mallows.

These are typically reported as in-sample metrics (i.e., on the training data), and data scientists using holdout data for model assessment do not need to worry about the differences among them or the underlying theory behind them.

How do we find the model that minimizes AIC or maximizes adjusted R^2? One way is to search through all possible models, an approach called *all subset regression*. This is computationally expensive and is not feasible for problems with large data and many variables. An attractive alternative is to use *stepwise regression*. It could start with a full model and successively drop variables that don't contribute meaningfully. This is called *backward elimination*. Alternatively one could start with a constant model and successively add variables (*forward selection*). As a third option we can also successively add and drop predictors to find a model that lowers AIC or adjusted R^2. The `MASS` in *R* package by Venebles and Ripley offers a stepwise regression function called `stepAIC`:

```
library(MASS)
step <- stepAIC(house_full, direction="both")
step

Call:
```

```
lm(formula = AdjSalePrice ~ SqFtTotLiving + Bathrooms + Bedrooms +
    BldgGrade + PropertyType + SqFtFinBasement + YrBuilt, data = house,
    na.action = na.omit)

Coefficients:
              (Intercept)                SqFtTotLiving
                6.179e+06                    1.993e+02
                Bathrooms                     Bedrooms
                4.240e+04                   -5.195e+04
                BldgGrade  PropertyTypeSingle Family
                1.372e+05                    2.291e+04
    PropertyTypeTownhouse              SqFtFinBasement
                8.448e+04                    7.047e+00
                  YrBuilt
               -3.565e+03
```

`scikit-learn` has no implementation for stepwise regression. We implemented functions `stepwise_selection`, `forward_selection`, and `backward_elimination` in our `dmba` package:

```
y = house[outcome]

def train_model(variables): ❶
    if len(variables) == 0:
        return None
    model = LinearRegression()
    model.fit(X[variables], y)
    return model

def score_model(model, variables): ❷
    if len(variables) == 0:
        return AIC_score(y, [y.mean()] * len(y), model, df=1)
    return AIC_score(y, model.predict(X[variables]), model)

best_model, best_variables = stepwise_selection(X.columns, train_model,
                                                score_model, verbose=True)

print(f'Intercept: {best_model.intercept_:.3f}')
print('Coefficients:')
for name, coef in zip(best_variables, best_model.coef_):
    print(f' {name}: {coef}')
```

❶ Define a function that returns a fitted model for a given set of variables.

❷ Define a function that returns a score for a given model and set of variables. In this case, we use the `AIC_score` implemented in the `dmba` package.

The function chose a model in which several variables were dropped from `house_full`: `SqFtLot`, `NbrLivingUnits`, `YrRenovated`, and `NewConstruction`.

Simpler yet are *forward selection* and *backward selection*. In forward selection, you start with no predictors and add them one by one, at each step adding the predictor that has the largest contribution to R^2, and stopping when the contribution is no longer statistically significant. In backward selection, or *backward elimination*, you start with the full model and take away predictors that are not statistically significant until you are left with a model in which all predictors are statistically significant.

Penalized regression is similar in spirit to AIC. Instead of explicitly searching through a discrete set of models, the model-fitting equation incorporates a constraint that penalizes the model for too many variables (parameters). Rather than eliminating predictor variables entirely—as with stepwise, forward, and backward selection—penalized regression applies the penalty by reducing coefficients, in some cases to near zero. Common penalized regression methods are *ridge regression* and *lasso regression*.

Stepwise regression and all subset regression are *in-sample* methods to assess and tune models. This means the model selection is possibly subject to overfitting (fitting the noise in the data) and may not perform as well when applied to new data. One common approach to avoid this is to use cross-validation to validate the models. In linear regression, overfitting is typically not a major issue, due to the simple (linear) global structure imposed on the data. For more sophisticated types of models, particularly iterative procedures that respond to local data structure, cross-validation is a very important tool; see "Cross-Validation" on page 155 for details.

Weighted Regression

Weighted regression is used by statisticians for a variety of purposes; in particular, it is important for analysis of complex surveys. Data scientists may find weighted regression useful in two cases:

- Inverse-variance weighting when different observations have been measured with different precision; the higher variance ones receiving lower weights.
- Analysis of data where rows represent multiple cases; the weight variable encodes how many original observations each row represents.

For example, with the housing data, older sales are less reliable than more recent sales. Using the `DocumentDate` to determine the year of the sale, we can compute a `Weight` as the number of years since 2005 (the beginning of the data):

R

```
library(lubridate)
house$Year = year(house$DocumentDate)
house$Weight = house$Year - 2005
```

Python

```
house['Year'] = [int(date.split('-')[0]) for date in house.DocumentDate]
house['Weight'] = house.Year - 2005
```

We can compute a weighted regression with the `lm` function using the `weight` argument:

```
house_wt <- lm(AdjSalePrice ~ SqFtTotLiving + SqFtLot + Bathrooms +
                 Bedrooms + BldgGrade,
               data=house, weight=Weight)
round(cbind(house_lm=house_lm$coefficients,
            house_wt=house_wt$coefficients), digits=3)

                 house_lm    house_wt
(Intercept)   -521871.368 -584189.329
SqFtTotLiving     228.831     245.024
SqFtLot            -0.060      -0.292
Bathrooms      -19442.840  -26085.970
Bedrooms       -47769.955  -53608.876
BldgGrade      106106.963  115242.435
```

The coefficients in the weighted regression are slightly different from the original regression.

Most models in `scikit-learn` accept weights as the keyword argument `sample_weight` in the call of the `fit` method:

```
predictors = ['SqFtTotLiving', 'SqFtLot', 'Bathrooms', 'Bedrooms', 'BldgGrade']
outcome = 'AdjSalePrice'

house_wt = LinearRegression()
house_wt.fit(house[predictors], house[outcome], sample_weight=house.Weight)
```

Key Ideas

- Multiple linear regression models the relationship between a response variable Y and multiple predictor variables $X_1, ..., X_p$.
- The most important metrics to evaluate a model are root mean squared error (RMSE) and R-squared (R^2).
- The standard error of the coefficients can be used to measure the reliability of a variable's contribution to a model.
- Stepwise regression is a way to automatically determine which variables should be included in the model.
- Weighted regression is used to give certain records more or less weight in fitting the equation.

Further Reading

An excellent treatment of cross-validation and resampling can be found in *An Introduction to Statistical Learning* by Gareth James, Daniela Witten, Trevor Hastie, and Robert Tibshirani (Springer, 2013).

Prediction Using Regression

The primary purpose of regression in data science is prediction. This is useful to keep in mind, since regression, being an old and established statistical method, comes with baggage that is more relevant to its traditional role as a tool for explanatory modeling than to prediction.

> ### Key Terms for Prediction Using Regression
>
> ***Prediction interval***
> An uncertainty interval around an individual predicted value.
>
> ***Extrapolation***
> Extension of a model beyond the range of the data used to fit it.

The Dangers of Extrapolation

Regression models should not be used to extrapolate beyond the range of the data (leaving aside the use of regression for time series forecasting.). The model is valid only for predictor values for which the data has sufficient values (even in the case that sufficient data is available, there could be other problems—see "Regression Diagnostics" on page 176). As an extreme case, suppose `model_lm` is used to predict the value of a 5,000-square-foot empty lot. In such a case, all the predictors related to the building would have a value of 0, and the regression equation would yield an absurd prediction of $-521{,}900 + 5{,}000 \times -.0605 = -\$522{,}202$. Why did this happen? The data contains only parcels with buildings—there are no records corresponding to vacant land. Consequently, the model has no information to tell it how to predict the sales price for vacant land.

Confidence and Prediction Intervals

Much of statistics involves understanding and measuring variability (uncertainty). The t-statistics and p-values reported in regression output deal with this in a formal way, which is sometimes useful for variable selection (see "Assessing the Model" on page 153). More useful metrics are confidence intervals, which are uncertainty intervals placed around regression coefficients and predictions. An easy way to understand this is via the bootstrap (see "The Bootstrap" on page 61 for more details about the general bootstrap procedure). The most common regression confidence intervals encountered in software output are those for regression parameters (coefficients). Here is a bootstrap algorithm for generating confidence intervals for regression parameters (coefficients) for a data set with P predictors and n records (rows):

1. Consider each row (including outcome variable) as a single "ticket" and place all the n tickets in a box.
2. Draw a ticket at random, record the values, and replace it in the box.
3. Repeat step 2 n times; you now have one bootstrap resample.
4. Fit a regression to the bootstrap sample, and record the estimated coefficients.
5. Repeat steps 2 through 4, say, 1,000 times.
6. You now have 1,000 bootstrap values for each coefficient; find the appropriate percentiles for each one (e.g., 5th and 95th for a 90% confidence interval).

You can use the `Boot` function in *R* to generate actual bootstrap confidence intervals for the coefficients, or you can simply use the formula-based intervals that are a routine *R* output. The conceptual meaning and interpretation are the same, and not of central importance to data scientists, because they concern the regression coefficients. Of greater interest to data scientists are intervals around predicted y values ($\hat{Y}_i$). The uncertainty around $\hat{Y}_i$ comes from two sources:

- Uncertainty about what the relevant predictor variables and their coefficients are (see the preceding bootstrap algorithm)
- Additional error inherent in individual data points

The individual data point error can be thought of as follows: even if we knew for certain what the regression equation was (e.g., if we had a huge number of records to fit it), the *actual* outcome values for a given set of predictor values will vary. For example, several houses—each with 8 rooms, a 6,500-square-foot lot, 3 bathrooms, and a basement—might have different values. We can model this individual error with the residuals from the fitted values. The bootstrap algorithm for modeling both the regression model error and the individual data point error would look as follows:

1. Take a bootstrap sample from the data (spelled out in greater detail earlier).
2. Fit the regression, and predict the new value.
3. Take a single residual at random from the original regression fit, add it to the predicted value, and record the result.
4. Repeat steps 1 through 3, say, 1,000 times.
5. Find the 2.5th and the 97.5th percentiles of the results.

Key Ideas

- Extrapolation beyond the range of the data can lead to error.
- Confidence intervals quantify uncertainty around regression coefficients.
- Prediction intervals quantify uncertainty in individual predictions.
- Most software, *R* included, will produce prediction and confidence intervals in default or specified output, using formulas.
- The bootstrap can also be used to produce prediction and confidence intervals; the interpretation and idea are the same.

Prediction Interval or Confidence Interval?

A prediction interval pertains to uncertainty around a single value, while a confidence interval pertains to a mean or other statistic calculated from multiple values. Thus, a prediction interval will typically be much wider than a confidence interval for the same value. We model this individual value error in the bootstrap model by selecting an individual residual to tack on to the predicted value. Which should you use? That depends on the context and the purpose of the analysis, but, in general, data scientists are interested in specific individual predictions, so a prediction interval would be more appropriate. Using a confidence interval when you should be using a prediction interval will greatly underestimate the uncertainty in a given predicted value.

Factor Variables in Regression

Factor variables, also termed *categorical* variables, take on a limited number of discrete values. For example, a loan purpose can be "debt consolidation," "wedding," "car," and so on. The binary (yes/no) variable, also called an *indicator* variable, is a special case of a factor variable. Regression requires numerical inputs, so factor variables need to be recoded to use in the model. The most common approach is to convert a variable into a set of binary *dummy* variables.

Key Terms for Factor Variables

Dummy variables
: Binary 0–1 variables derived by recoding factor data for use in regression and other models.

Reference coding
: The most common type of coding used by statisticians, in which one level of a factor is used as a reference and other factors are compared to that level.

  Synonym
  : treatment coding

One hot encoder
: A common type of coding used in the machine learning community in which all factor levels are retained. While useful for certain machine learning algorithms, this approach is not appropriate for multiple linear regression.

Deviation coding
: A type of coding that compares each level against the overall mean as opposed to the reference level.

  Synonym
  : sum contrasts

Dummy Variables Representation

In the King County housing data, there is a factor variable for the property type; a small subset of six records is shown below:

R:

```
head(house[, 'PropertyType'])
Source: local data frame [6 x 1]

   PropertyType
         (fctr)
1     Multiplex
2 Single Family
3 Single Family
4 Single Family
5 Single Family
6     Townhouse
```

Python:

```
house.PropertyType.head()
```

There are three possible values: `Multiplex`, `Single Family`, and `Townhouse`. To use this factor variable, we need to convert it to a set of binary variables. We do this by creating a binary variable for each possible value of the factor variable. To do this in *R*, we use the `model.matrix` function:[3]

```
prop_type_dummies <- model.matrix(~PropertyType -1, data=house)
head(prop_type_dummies)
  PropertyTypeMultiplex PropertyTypeSingle Family PropertyTypeTownhouse
1                     1                         0                     0
2                     0                         1                     0
3                     0                         1                     0
4                     0                         1                     0
5                     0                         1                     0
6                     0                         0                     1
```

The function `model.matrix` converts a data frame into a matrix suitable to a linear model. The factor variable `PropertyType`, which has three distinct levels, is represented as a matrix with three columns. In the machine learning community, this representation is referred to as *one hot encoding* (see "One Hot Encoder" on page 242).

In *Python*, we can convert categorical variables to dummies using the `pandas` method `get_dummies`:

```
pd.get_dummies(house['PropertyType']).head() ❶
pd.get_dummies(house['PropertyType'], drop_first=True).head() ❷
```

❶ By default, returns one hot encoding of the categorical variable.

❷ The keyword argument `drop_first` will return $P - 1$ columns. Use this to avoid the problem of multicollinearity.

In certain machine learning algorithms, such as nearest neighbors and tree models, one hot encoding is the standard way to represent factor variables (for example, see "Tree Models" on page 249).

In the regression setting, a factor variable with P distinct levels is usually represented by a matrix with only $P - 1$ columns. This is because a regression model typically includes an intercept term. With an intercept, once you have defined the values for $P - 1$ binaries, the value for the Pth is known and could be considered redundant. Adding the Pth column will cause a multicollinearity error (see "Multicollinearity" on page 172).

3 The `-1` argument in the `model.matrix` produces one hot encoding representation (by removing the intercept, hence the "-"). Otherwise, the default in *R* is to produce a matrix with $P - 1$ columns with the first factor level as a reference.

The default representation in *R* is to use the first factor level as a *reference* and interpret the remaining levels relative to that factor:

```
lm(AdjSalePrice ~ SqFtTotLiving + SqFtLot + Bathrooms +
       Bedrooms + BldgGrade + PropertyType, data=house)

Call:
lm(formula = AdjSalePrice ~ SqFtTotLiving + SqFtLot + Bathrooms +
    Bedrooms + BldgGrade + PropertyType, data = house)

Coefficients:
               (Intercept)               SqFtTotLiving
                -4.468e+05                   2.234e+02
                   SqFtLot                   Bathrooms
                -7.037e-02                  -1.598e+04
                  Bedrooms                   BldgGrade
                -5.089e+04                   1.094e+05
PropertyTypeSingle Family      PropertyTypeTownhouse
                -8.468e+04                  -1.151e+05
```

The method `get_dummies` takes the optional keyword argument `drop_first` to exclude the first factor as *reference*:

```
predictors = ['SqFtTotLiving', 'SqFtLot', 'Bathrooms', 'Bedrooms',
              'BldgGrade', 'PropertyType']

X = pd.get_dummies(house[predictors], drop_first=True)

house_lm_factor = LinearRegression()
house_lm_factor.fit(X, house[outcome])

print(f'Intercept: {house_lm_factor.intercept_:.3f}')
print('Coefficients:')
for name, coef in zip(X.columns, house_lm_factor.coef_):
    print(f' {name}: {coef}')
```

The output from the *R* regression shows two coefficients corresponding to `PropertyType`: `PropertyTypeSingle Family` and `PropertyTypeTownhouse`. There is no coefficient of `Multiplex` since it is implicitly defined when `PropertyTypeSingle Family == 0` and `PropertyTypeTownhouse == 0`. The coefficients are interpreted as relative to `Multiplex`, so a home that is `Single Family` is worth almost $85,000 less, and a home that is `Townhouse` is worth over $150,000 less.[4]

4 This is unintuitive, but can be explained by the impact of location as a confounding variable; see "Confounding Variables" on page 172.

> **Different Factor Codings**
>
> There are several different ways to encode factor variables, known as *contrast coding* systems. For example, *deviation coding*, also known as *sum contrasts*, compares each level against the overall mean. Another contrast is *polynomial coding*, which is appropriate for ordered factors; see the section "Ordered Factor Variables" on page 169. With the exception of ordered factors, data scientists will generally not encounter any type of coding besides reference coding or one hot encoder.

Factor Variables with Many Levels

Some factor variables can produce a huge number of binary dummies—zip codes are a factor variable, and there are 43,000 zip codes in the US. In such cases, it is useful to explore the data, and the relationships between predictor variables and the outcome, to determine whether useful information is contained in the categories. If so, you must further decide whether it is useful to retain all factors, or whether the levels should be consolidated.

In King County, there are 80 zip codes with a house sale:

```
table(house$ZipCode)

98001 98002 98003 98004 98005 98006 98007 98008 98010 98011 98014 98019
  358   180   241   293   133   460   112   291    56   163    85   242
98022 98023 98024 98027 98028 98029 98030 98031 98032 98033 98034 98038
  188   455    31   366   252   475   263   308   121   517   575   788
98039 98040 98042 98043 98045 98047 98050 98051 98052 98053 98055 98056
   47   244   641     1   222    48     7    32   614   499   332   402
98057 98058 98059 98065 98068 98070 98072 98074 98075 98077 98092 98102
    4   420   513   430     1    89   245   502   388   204   289   106
98103 98105 98106 98107 98108 98109 98112 98113 98115 98116 98117 98118
  671   313   361   296   155   149   357     1   620   364   619   492
98119 98122 98125 98126 98133 98136 98144 98146 98148 98155 98166 98168
  260   380   409   473   465   310   332   287    40   358   193   332
98177 98178 98188 98198 98199 98224 98288 98354
  216   266   101   225   393     3     4     9
```

The `value_counts` method of `pandas` data frames returns the same information:

```
pd.DataFrame(house['ZipCode'].value_counts()).transpose()
```

`ZipCode` is an important variable, since it is a proxy for the effect of location on the value of a house. Including all levels requires 79 coefficients corresponding to 79 degrees of freedom. The original model `house_lm` has only 5 degrees of freedom; see "Assessing the Model" on page 153. Moreover, several zip codes have only one sale. In some problems, you can consolidate a zip code using the first two or three digits, corresponding to a submetropolitan geographic region. For King County, almost all of the sales occur in 980xx or 981xx, so this doesn't help.

An alternative approach is to group the zip codes according to another variable, such as sale price. Even better is to form zip code groups using the residuals from an initial model. The following `dplyr` code in *R* consolidates the 80 zip codes into five groups based on the median of the residual from the `house_lm` regression:

```
zip_groups <- house %>%
  mutate(resid = residuals(house_lm)) %>%
  group_by(ZipCode) %>%
  summarize(med_resid = median(resid),
            cnt = n()) %>%
  arrange(med_resid) %>%
  mutate(cum_cnt = cumsum(cnt),
         ZipGroup = ntile(cum_cnt, 5))
house <- house %>%
  left_join(select(zip_groups, ZipCode, ZipGroup), by='ZipCode')
```

The median residual is computed for each zip, and the `ntile` function is used to split the zip codes, sorted by the median, into five groups. See "Confounding Variables" on page 172 for an example of how this is used as a term in a regression improving upon the original fit.

In *Python* we can calculate this information as follows:

```
zip_groups = pd.DataFrame([
    *pd.DataFrame({
        'ZipCode': house['ZipCode'],
        'residual' : house[outcome] - house_lm.predict(house[predictors]),
    })
    .groupby(['ZipCode'])
    .apply(lambda x: {
        'ZipCode': x.iloc[0,0],
        'count': len(x),
        'median_residual': x.residual.median()
    })
]).sort_values('median_residual')
zip_groups['cum_count'] = np.cumsum(zip_groups['count'])
zip_groups['ZipGroup'] = pd.qcut(zip_groups['cum_count'], 5, labels=False,
                                 retbins=False)

to_join = zip_groups[['ZipCode', 'ZipGroup']].set_index('ZipCode')
house = house.join(to_join, on='ZipCode')
house['ZipGroup'] = house['ZipGroup'].astype('category')
```

The concept of using the residuals to help guide the regression fitting is a fundamental step in the modeling process; see "Regression Diagnostics" on page 176.

Ordered Factor Variables

Some factor variables reflect levels of a factor; these are termed *ordered factor variables* or *ordered categorical variables*. For example, the loan grade could be A, B, C, and so on—each grade carries more risk than the prior grade. Often, ordered factor variables can be converted to numerical values and used as is. For example, the variable `BldgGrade` is an ordered factor variable. Several of the types of grades are shown in Table 4-1. While the grades have specific meaning, the numeric value is ordered from low to high, corresponding to higher-grade homes. With the regression model `house_lm`, fit in "Multiple Linear Regression" on page 150, `BldgGrade` was treated as a numeric variable.

Table 4-1. Building grades and numeric equivalents

Value	Description
1	Cabin
2	Substandard
5	Fair
10	Very good
12	Luxury
13	Mansion

Treating ordered factors as a numeric variable preserves the information contained in the ordering that would be lost if it were converted to a factor.

Key Ideas

- Factor variables need to be converted into numeric variables for use in a regression.
- The most common method to encode a factor variable with P distinct values is to represent them using P – 1 dummy variables.
- A factor variable with many levels, even in very big data sets, may need to be consolidated into a variable with fewer levels.
- Some factors have levels that are ordered and can be represented as a single numeric variable.

Interpreting the Regression Equation

In data science, the most important use of regression is to predict some dependent (outcome) variable. In some cases, however, gaining insight from the equation itself to understand the nature of the relationship between the predictors and the outcome can be of value. This section provides guidance on examining the regression equation and interpreting it.

Key Terms for Interpreting the Regression Equation

Correlated variables
: When the predictor variables are highly correlated, it is difficult to interpret the individual coefficients.

Multicollinearity
: When the predictor variables have perfect, or near-perfect, correlation, the regression can be unstable or impossible to compute.

  Synonym
  : collinearity

Confounding variables
: An important predictor that, when omitted, leads to spurious relationships in a regression equation.

Main effects
: The relationship between a predictor and the outcome variable, independent of other variables.

Interactions
: An interdependent relationship between two or more predictors and the response.

Correlated Predictors

In multiple regression, the predictor variables are often correlated with each other. As an example, examine the regression coefficients for the model `step_lm`, fit in "Model Selection and Stepwise Regression" on page 156.

R:

```
step_lm$coefficients
              (Intercept)             SqFtTotLiving                 Bathrooms
             6.178645e+06              1.992776e+02              4.239616e+04
                 Bedrooms                 BldgGrade PropertyTypeSingle Family
            -5.194738e+04              1.371596e+05              2.291206e+04
    PropertyTypeTownhouse            SqFtFinBasement                   YrBuilt
             8.447916e+04              7.046975e+00             -3.565425e+03
```

Python:

```
print(f'Intercept: {best_model.intercept_:.3f}')
print('Coefficients:')
for name, coef in zip(best_variables, best_model.coef_):
    print(f' {name}: {coef}')
```

The coefficient for `Bedrooms` is negative! This implies that adding a bedroom to a house will reduce its value. How can this be? This is because the predictor variables are correlated: larger houses tend to have more bedrooms, and it is the size that drives house value, not the number of bedrooms. Consider two homes of the exact same size: it is reasonable to expect that a home with more but smaller bedrooms would be considered less desirable.

Having correlated predictors can make it difficult to interpret the sign and value of regression coefficients (and can inflate the standard error of the estimates). The variables for bedrooms, house size, and number of bathrooms are all correlated. This is illustrated by the following example in *R*, which fits another regression removing the variables `SqFtTotLiving`, `SqFtFinBasement`, and `Bathrooms` from the equation:

```
update(step_lm, . ~ . - SqFtTotLiving - SqFtFinBasement - Bathrooms)

Call:
lm(formula = AdjSalePrice ~ Bedrooms + BldgGrade + PropertyType +
    YrBuilt, data = house, na.action = na.omit)

Coefficients:
              (Intercept)                   Bedrooms
                  4913973                      27151
                BldgGrade  PropertyTypeSingle Family
                   248998                     -19898
    PropertyTypeTownhouse                    YrBuilt
                   -47355                      -3212
```

The `update` function can be used to add or remove variables from a model. Now the coefficient for bedrooms is positive—in line with what we would expect (though it is really acting as a proxy for house size, now that those variables have been removed).

In *Python*, there is no equivalent to *R*'s `update` function. We need to refit the model with the modified predictor list:

```
predictors = ['Bedrooms', 'BldgGrade', 'PropertyType', 'YrBuilt']
outcome = 'AdjSalePrice'

X = pd.get_dummies(house[predictors], drop_first=True)

reduced_lm = LinearRegression()
reduced_lm.fit(X, house[outcome])
```

Correlated variables are only one issue with interpreting regression coefficients. In `house_lm`, there is no variable to account for the location of the home, and the model is mixing together very different types of regions. Location may be a *confounding* variable; see "Confounding Variables" on page 172 for further discussion.

Multicollinearity

An extreme case of correlated variables produces multicollinearity—a condition in which there is redundance among the predictor variables. Perfect multicollinearity occurs when one predictor variable can be expressed as a linear combination of others. Multicollinearity occurs when:

- A variable is included multiple times by error.
- *P* dummies, instead of *P* – 1 dummies, are created from a factor variable (see "Factor Variables in Regression" on page 163).
- Two variables are nearly perfectly correlated with one another.

Multicollinearity in regression must be addressed—variables should be removed until the multicollinearity is gone. A regression does not have a well-defined solution in the presence of perfect multicollinearity. Many software packages, including *R* and *Python*, automatically handle certain types of multicollinearity. For example, if `SqFtTotLiving` is included twice in the regression of the `house` data, the results are the same as for the `house_lm` model. In the case of nonperfect multicollinearity, the software may obtain a solution, but the results may be unstable.

> Multicollinearity is not such a problem for nonlinear regression methods like trees, clustering, and nearest-neighbors, and in such methods it may be advisable to retain *P* dummies (instead of *P* – 1). That said, even in those methods, nonredundancy in predictor variables is still a virtue.

Confounding Variables

With correlated variables, the problem is one of commission: including different variables that have a similar predictive relationship with the response. With *confounding variables*, the problem is one of omission: an important variable is not included in the regression equation. Naive interpretation of the equation coefficients can lead to invalid conclusions.

Take, for example, the King County regression equation `house_lm` from "Example: King County Housing Data" on page 151. The regression coefficients of `SqFtLot`, `Bathrooms`, and `Bedrooms` are all negative. The original regression model does not contain a variable to represent location—a very important predictor of house price.

To model location, include a variable ZipGroup that categorizes the zip code into one of five groups, from least expensive (1) to most expensive (5):[5]

```
lm(formula = AdjSalePrice ~ SqFtTotLiving + SqFtLot + Bathrooms +
    Bedrooms + BldgGrade + PropertyType + ZipGroup, data = house,
    na.action = na.omit)

Coefficients:
                 (Intercept)             SqFtTotLiving
                  -6.666e+05                 2.106e+02
                     SqFtLot                 Bathrooms
                   4.550e-01                 5.928e+03
                    Bedrooms                 BldgGrade
                  -4.168e+04                 9.854e+04
PropertyTypeSingle Family     PropertyTypeTownhouse
                   1.932e+04                -7.820e+04
                   ZipGroup2                 ZipGroup3
                   5.332e+04                 1.163e+05
                   ZipGroup4                 ZipGroup5
                   1.784e+05                 3.384e+05
```

The same model in *Python*:

```
predictors = ['SqFtTotLiving', 'SqFtLot', 'Bathrooms', 'Bedrooms',
              'BldgGrade', 'PropertyType', 'ZipGroup']
outcome = 'AdjSalePrice'

X = pd.get_dummies(house[predictors], drop_first=True)

confounding_lm = LinearRegression()
confounding_lm.fit(X, house[outcome])

print(f'Intercept: {confounding_lm.intercept_:.3f}')
print('Coefficients:')
for name, coef in zip(X.columns, confounding_lm.coef_):
    print(f' {name}: {coef}')
```

ZipGroup is clearly an important variable: a home in the most expensive zip code group is estimated to have a higher sales price by almost $340,000. The coefficients of SqFtLot and Bathrooms are now positive, and adding a bathroom increases the sale price by $5,928.

The coefficient for Bedrooms is still negative. While this is unintuitive, this is a well-known phenomenon in real estate. For homes of the same livable area and number of bathrooms, having more and therefore smaller bedrooms is associated with less valuable homes.

5 There are 80 zip codes in King County, several with just a handful of sales. An alternative to directly using zip code as a factor variable, ZipGroup clusters similar zip codes into a single group. See "Factor Variables with Many Levels" on page 167 for details.

Interactions and Main Effects

Statisticians like to distinguish between *main effects*, or independent variables, and the *interactions* between the main effects. Main effects are what are often referred to as the *predictor variables* in the regression equation. An implicit assumption when only main effects are used in a model is that the relationship between a predictor variable and the response is independent of the other predictor variables. This is often not the case.

For example, the model fit to the King County Housing Data in "Confounding Variables" on page 172 includes several variables as main effects, including `ZipCode`. Location in real estate is everything, and it is natural to presume that the relationship between, say, house size and the sale price depends on location. A big house built in a low-rent district is not going to retain the same value as a big house built in an expensive area. You include interactions between variables in *R* using the `*` operator. For the King County data, the following fits an interaction between `SqFtTotLiving` and `ZipGroup`:

```
lm(formula = AdjSalePrice ~ SqFtTotLiving * ZipGroup + SqFtLot +
    Bathrooms + Bedrooms + BldgGrade + PropertyType, data = house,
    na.action = na.omit)

Coefficients:
              (Intercept)              SqFtTotLiving
               -4.853e+05                  1.148e+02
                ZipGroup2                  ZipGroup3
               -1.113e+04                  2.032e+04
                ZipGroup4                  ZipGroup5
                2.050e+04                 -1.499e+05
                  SqFtLot                  Bathrooms
                6.869e-01                 -3.619e+03
                 Bedrooms                  BldgGrade
               -4.180e+04                  1.047e+05
PropertyTypeSingle Family       PropertyTypeTownhouse
                1.357e+04                 -5.884e+04
  SqFtTotLiving:ZipGroup2     SqFtTotLiving:ZipGroup3
                3.260e+01                  4.178e+01
  SqFtTotLiving:ZipGroup4     SqFtTotLiving:ZipGroup5
                6.934e+01                  2.267e+02
```

The resulting model has four new terms: `SqFtTotLiving:ZipGroup2`, `SqFtTotLiving:ZipGroup3`, and so on.

In *Python*, we need to use the `statsmodels` package to train linear regression models with interactions. This package was designed similar to *R* and allows defining models using a formula interface:

```
model = smf.ols(formula='AdjSalePrice ~ SqFtTotLiving*ZipGroup + SqFtLot + ' +
     'Bathrooms + Bedrooms + BldgGrade + PropertyType', data=house)
```

```
results = model.fit()
results.summary()
```

The `statsmodels` package takes care of categorical variables (e.g., `ZipGroup[T.1]`, `PropertyType[T.Single Family]`) and interaction terms (e.g., `SqFtTotLiving:ZipGroup[T.1]`).

Location and house size appear to have a strong interaction. For a home in the lowest `ZipGroup`, the slope is the same as the slope for the main effect `SqFtTotLiving`, which is \$118 per square foot (this is because *R* uses *reference* coding for factor variables; see "Factor Variables in Regression" on page 163). For a home in the highest `ZipGroup`, the slope is the sum of the main effect plus `SqFtTotLiving:ZipGroup5`, or \$115 + \$227 = \$342 per square foot. In other words, adding a square foot in the most expensive zip code group boosts the predicted sale price by a factor of almost three, compared to the average boost from adding a square foot.

Model Selection with Interaction Terms

In problems involving many variables, it can be challenging to decide which interaction terms should be included in the model. Several different approaches are commonly taken:

- In some problems, prior knowledge and intuition can guide the choice of which interaction terms to include in the model.
- Stepwise selection (see "Model Selection and Stepwise Regression" on page 156) can be used to sift through the various models.
- Penalized regression can automatically fit to a large set of possible interaction terms.
- Perhaps the most common approach is to use *tree models*, as well as their descendants, *random forest* and *gradient boosted trees*. This class of models automatically searches for optimal interaction terms; see "Tree Models" on page 249.

Key Ideas

- Because of correlation between predictors, care must be taken in the interpretation of the coefficients in multiple linear regression.
- Multicollinearity can cause numerical instability in fitting the regression equation.
- A confounding variable is an important predictor that is omitted from a model and can lead to a regression equation with spurious relationships.

- An interaction term between two variables is needed if the relationship between the variables and the response is interdependent.

Regression Diagnostics

In explanatory modeling (i.e., in a research context), various steps, in addition to the metrics mentioned previously (see "Assessing the Model" on page 153), are taken to assess how well the model fits the data; most are based on analysis of the residuals. These steps do not directly address predictive accuracy, but they can provide useful insight in a predictive setting.

Key Terms for Regression Diagnostics

Standardized residuals
Residuals divided by the standard error of the residuals.

Outliers
Records (or outcome values) that are distant from the rest of the data (or the predicted outcome).

Influential value
A value or record whose presence or absence makes a big difference in the regression equation.

Leverage
The degree of influence that a single record has on a regression equation.

Synonym
hat-value

Non-normal residuals
Non-normally distributed residuals can invalidate some technical requirements of regression but are usually not a concern in data science.

Heteroskedasticity
When some ranges of the outcome experience residuals with higher variance (may indicate a predictor missing from the equation).

Partial residual plots
A diagnostic plot to illuminate the relationship between the outcome variable and a single predictor.

Synonym
added variables plot

Outliers

Generally speaking, an extreme value, also called an *outlier*, is one that is distant from most of the other observations. Just as outliers need to be handled for estimates of location and variability (see "Estimates of Location" on page 7 and "Estimates of Variability" on page 13), outliers can cause problems with regression models. In regression, an outlier is a record whose actual *y* value is distant from the predicted value. You can detect outliers by examining the *standardized residual*, which is the residual divided by the standard error of the residuals.

There is no statistical theory that separates outliers from nonoutliers. Rather, there are (arbitrary) rules of thumb for how distant from the bulk of the data an observation needs to be in order to be called an outlier. For example, with the boxplot, outliers are those data points that are too far above or below the box boundaries (see "Percentiles and Boxplots" on page 20), where "too far" = "more than 1.5 times the interquartile range." In regression, the standardized residual is the metric that is typically used to determine whether a record is classified as an outlier. Standardized residuals can be interpreted as "the number of standard errors away from the regression line."

Let's fit a regression to the King County house sales data for all sales in zip code 98105 in *R*:

```
house_98105 <- house[house$ZipCode == 98105,]
lm_98105 <- lm(AdjSalePrice ~ SqFtTotLiving + SqFtLot + Bathrooms +
                 Bedrooms + BldgGrade, data=house_98105)
```

In *Python*:

```
house_98105 = house.loc[house['ZipCode'] == 98105, ]

predictors = ['SqFtTotLiving', 'SqFtLot', 'Bathrooms', 'Bedrooms', 'BldgGrade']
outcome = 'AdjSalePrice'

house_outlier = sm.OLS(house_98105[outcome],
                       house_98105[predictors].assign(const=1))
result_98105 = house_outlier.fit()
```

We extract the standardized residuals in *R* using the `rstandard` function and obtain the index of the smallest residual using the `order` function:

```
sresid <- rstandard(lm_98105)
idx <- order(sresid)
sresid[idx[1]]
    20429
-4.326732
```

In `statsmodels`, use `OLSInfluence` to analyze the residuals:

```
influence = OLSInfluence(result_98105)
sresiduals = influence.resid_studentized_internal
sresiduals.idxmin(), sresiduals.min()
```

The biggest overestimate from the model is more than four standard errors above the regression line, corresponding to an overestimate of $757,754. The original data record corresponding to this outlier is as follows in *R*:

```
house_98105[idx[1], c('AdjSalePrice', 'SqFtTotLiving', 'SqFtLot',
              'Bathrooms', 'Bedrooms', 'BldgGrade')]

AdjSalePrice SqFtTotLiving SqFtLot Bathrooms Bedrooms BldgGrade
        (dbl)         (int)   (int)     (dbl)    (int)     (int)
20429  119748          2900    7276         3        6         7
```

In *Python*:

```
outlier = house_98105.loc[sresiduals.idxmin(), :]
print('AdjSalePrice', outlier[outcome])
print(outlier[predictors])
```

In this case, it appears that there is something wrong with the record: a house of that size typically sells for much more than $119,748 in that zip code. Figure 4-4 shows an excerpt from the statutory deed from this sale: it is clear that the sale involved only partial interest in the property. In this case, the outlier corresponds to a sale that is anomalous and should not be included in the regression. Outliers could also be the result of other problems, such as a "fat-finger" data entry or a mismatch of units (e.g., reporting a sale in thousands of dollars rather than simply in dollars).

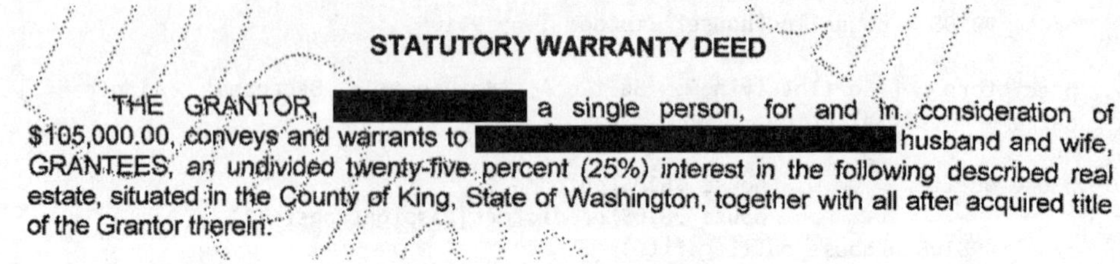
STATUTORY WARRANTY DEED

THE GRANTOR, [redacted] a single person, for and in consideration of $105,000.00, conveys and warrants to [redacted] husband and wife, GRANTEES, an undivided twenty-five percent (25%) interest in the following described real estate, situated in the County of King, State of Washington, together with all after acquired title of the Grantor therein:

Figure 4-4. Statutory warrany deed for the largest negative residual

For big data problems, outliers are generally not a problem in fitting the regression to be used in predicting new data. However, outliers are central to anomaly detection, where finding outliers is the whole point. The outlier could also correspond to a case of fraud or an accidental action. In any case, detecting outliers can be a critical business need.

Influential Values

A value whose absence would significantly change the regression equation is termed an *influential observation*. In regression, such a value need not be associated with a large residual. As an example, consider the regression lines in Figure 4-5. The solid line corresponds to the regression with all the data, while the dashed line corresponds to the regression with the point in the upper-right corner removed. Clearly, that data value has a huge influence on the regression even though it is not associated with a large outlier (from the full regression). This data value is considered to have high *leverage* on the regression.

In addition to standardized residuals (see "Outliers" on page 177), statisticians have developed several metrics to determine the influence of a single record on a regression. A common measure of leverage is the *hat-value*; values above $2(P+1)/n$ indicate a high-leverage data value.[6]

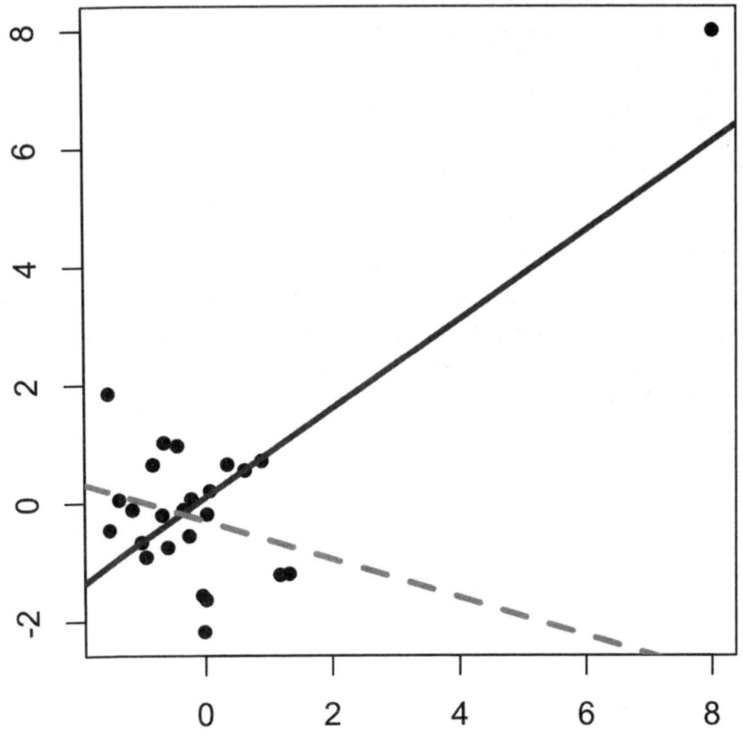

Figure 4-5. An example of an influential data point in regression

6 The term *hat-value* comes from the notion of the hat matrix in regression. Multiple linear regression can be expressed by the formula $\hat{Y} = HY$ where H is the hat matrix. The hat-values correspond to the diagonal of H.

Another metric is *Cook's distance*, which defines influence as a combination of leverage and residual size. A rule of thumb is that an observation has high influence if Cook's distance exceeds $4/(n - P - 1)$.

An *influence plot* or *bubble plot* combines standardized residuals, the hat-value, and Cook's distance in a single plot. Figure 4-6 shows the influence plot for the King County house data and can be created by the following *R* code:

```
std_resid <- rstandard(lm_98105)
cooks_D <- cooks.distance(lm_98105)
hat_values <- hatvalues(lm_98105)
plot(subset(hat_values, cooks_D > 0.08), subset(std_resid, cooks_D > 0.08),
     xlab='hat_values', ylab='std_resid',
     cex=10*sqrt(subset(cooks_D, cooks_D > 0.08)), pch=16, col='lightgrey')
points(hat_values, std_resid, cex=10*sqrt(cooks_D))
abline(h=c(-2.5, 2.5), lty=2)
```

Here is the *Python* code to create a similar figure:

```
influence = OLSInfluence(result_98105)
fig, ax = plt.subplots(figsize=(5, 5))
ax.axhline(-2.5, linestyle='--', color='C1')
ax.axhline(2.5, linestyle='--', color='C1')
ax.scatter(influence.hat_matrix_diag, influence.resid_studentized_internal,
           s=1000 * np.sqrt(influence.cooks_distance[0]),
           alpha=0.5)
ax.set_xlabel('hat values')
ax.set_ylabel('studentized residuals')
```

There are apparently several data points that exhibit large influence in the regression. Cook's distance can be computed using the function `cooks.distance`, and you can use `hatvalues` to compute the diagnostics. The hat values are plotted on the x-axis, the residuals are plotted on the y-axis, and the size of the points is related to the value of Cook's distance.

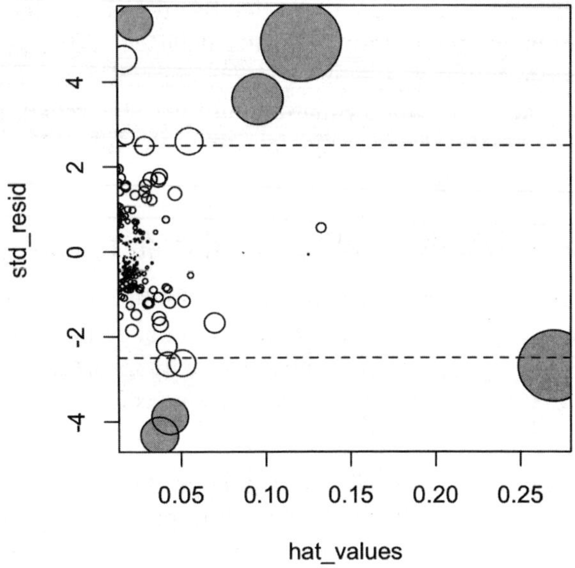

Figure 4-6. A plot to determine which observations have high influence; points with Cook's distance greater than 0.08 are highlighted in grey

Table 4-2 compares the regression with the full data set and with highly influential data points removed (Cook's distance > 0.08).

The regression coefficient for `Bathrooms` changes quite dramatically.[7]

Table 4-2. Comparison of regression coefficients with the full data and with influential data removed

	Original	Influential removed
(Intercept)	−772,550	−647,137
SqFtTotLiving	210	230
SqFtLot	39	33
Bathrooms	2282	−16,132
Bedrooms	−26,320	−22,888
BldgGrade	130,000	114,871

7 The coefficient for `Bathrooms` becomes negative, which is unintuitive. Location has not been taken into account, and the zip code 98105 contains areas of disparate types of homes. See "Confounding Variables" on page 172 for a discussion of confounding variables.

For purposes of fitting a regression that reliably predicts future data, identifying influential observations is useful only in smaller data sets. For regressions involving many records, it is unlikely that any one observation will carry sufficient weight to cause extreme influence on the fitted equation (although the regression may still have big outliers). For purposes of anomaly detection, though, identifying influential observations can be very useful.

Heteroskedasticity, Non-Normality, and Correlated Errors

Statisticians pay considerable attention to the distribution of the residuals. It turns out that ordinary least squares (see "Least Squares" on page 148) are unbiased, and in some cases are the "optimal" estimator, under a wide range of distributional assumptions. This means that in most problems, data scientists do not need to be too concerned with the distribution of the residuals.

The distribution of the residuals is relevant mainly for the validity of formal statistical inference (hypothesis tests and p-values), which is of minimal importance to data scientists concerned mainly with predictive accuracy. Normally distributed errors are a sign that the model is complete; errors that are not normally distributed indicate the model may be missing something. For formal inference to be fully valid, the residuals are assumed to be normally distributed, have the same variance, and be independent. One area where this may be of concern to data scientists is the standard calculation of confidence intervals for predicted values, which are based upon the assumptions about the residuals (see "Confidence and Prediction Intervals" on page 161).

Heteroskedasticity is the lack of constant residual variance across the range of the predicted values. In other words, errors are greater for some portions of the range than for others. Visualizing the data is a convenient way to analyze residuals.

The following code in *R* plots the absolute residuals versus the predicted values for the `lm_98105` regression fit in "Outliers" on page 177:

```
df <- data.frame(resid = residuals(lm_98105), pred = predict(lm_98105))
ggplot(df, aes(pred, abs(resid))) + geom_point() + geom_smooth()
```

Figure 4-7 shows the resulting plot. Using `geom_smooth`, it is easy to superpose a smooth of the absolute residuals. The function calls the `loess` method (locally estimated scatterplot smoothing) to produce a smoothed estimate of the relationship between the variables on the x-axis and y-axis in a scatterplot (see "Scatterplot Smoothers" on page 185).

In *Python*, the `seaborn` package has the `regplot` function to create a similar figure:

```
fig, ax = plt.subplots(figsize=(5, 5))
sns.regplot(result_98105.fittedvalues, np.abs(result_98105.resid),
            scatter_kws={'alpha': 0.25}, line_kws={'color': 'C1'},
            lowess=True, ax=ax)
```

```
ax.set_xlabel('predicted')
ax.set_ylabel('abs(residual)')
```

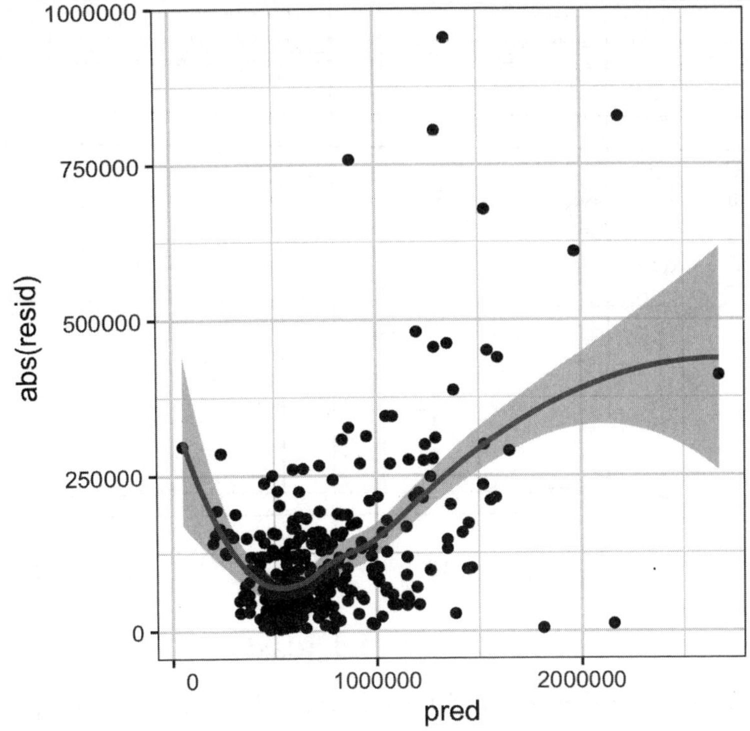

Figure 4-7. A plot of the absolute value of the residuals versus the predicted values

Evidently, the variance of the residuals tends to increase for higher-valued homes but is also large for lower-valued homes. This plot indicates that `lm_98105` has *heteroskedastic* errors.

> **Why Would a Data Scientist Care About Heteroskedasticity?**
>
> Heteroskedasticity indicates that prediction errors differ for different ranges of the predicted value, and may suggest an incomplete model. For example, the heteroskedasticity in `lm_98105` may indicate that the regression has left something unaccounted for in high- and low-range homes.

Figure 4-8 is a histogram of the standardized residuals for the `lm_98105` regression. The distribution has decidedly longer tails than the normal distribution and exhibits mild skewness toward larger residuals.

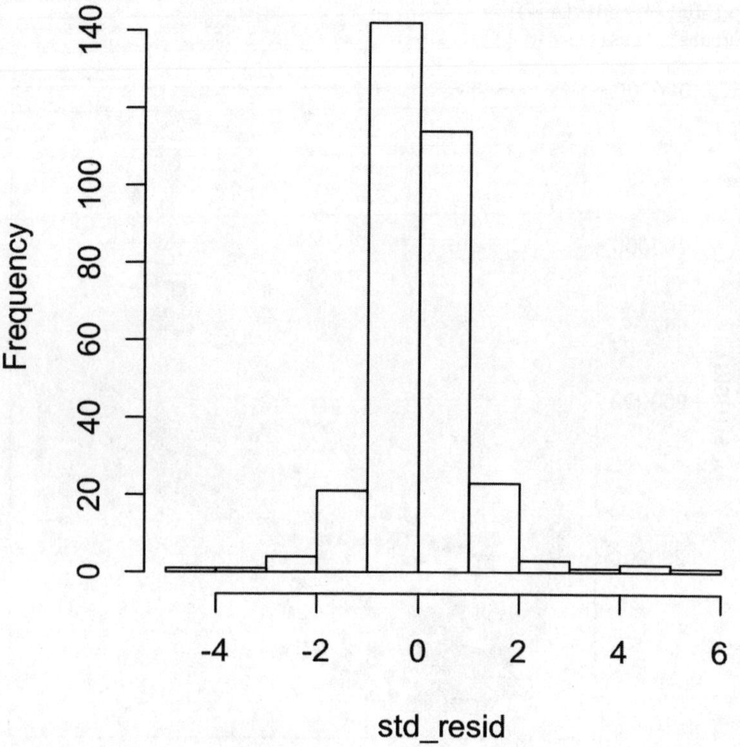

Figure 4-8. A histogram of the residuals from the regression of the housing data

Statisticians may also check the assumption that the errors are independent. This is particularly true for data that is collected over time or space. The *Durbin-Watson* statistic can be used to detect if there is significant autocorrelation in a regression involving time series data. If the errors from a regression model are correlated, then this information can be useful in making short-term forecasts and should be built into the model. See *Practical Time Series Forecasting with R*, 2nd ed., by Galit Shmueli and Kenneth Lichtendahl (Axelrod Schnall, 2018) to learn more about how to build autocorrelation information into regression models for time series data. If longer-term forecasts or explanatory models are the goal, excess autocorrelated data at the microlevel may distract. In that case, smoothing, or less granular collection of data in the first place, may be in order.

Even though a regression may violate one of the distributional assumptions, should we care? Most often in data science, the interest is primarily in predictive accuracy, so some review of heteroskedasticity may be in order. You may discover that there is some signal in the data that your model has not captured. However, satisfying distributional assumptions simply for the sake of validating formal statistical inference (p-values, F-statistics, etc.) is not that important for the data scientist.

Scatterplot Smoothers

Regression is about modeling the relationship between the response and predictor variables. In evaluating a regression model, it is useful to use a *scatterplot smoother* to visually highlight relationships between two variables.

For example, in Figure 4-7, a smooth of the relationship between the absolute residuals and the predicted value shows that the variance of the residuals depends on the value of the residual. In this case, the `loess` function was used; `loess` works by repeatedly fitting a series of local regressions to contiguous subsets to come up with a smooth. While `loess` is probably the most commonly used smoother, other scatterplot smoothers are available in *R*, such as super smooth (`supsmu`) and kernel smoothing (`ksmooth`). In *Python*, we can find additional smoothers in `scipy` (`wiener` or `sav`) and `statsmodels` (`kernel_regression`). For the purposes of evaluating a regression model, there is typically no need to worry about the details of these scatterplot smooths.

Partial Residual Plots and Nonlinearity

Partial residual plots are a way to visualize how well the estimated fit explains the relationship between a predictor and the outcome. The basic idea of a partial residual plot is to isolate the relationship between a predictor variable and the response, *taking into account all of the other predictor variables*. A partial residual might be thought of as a "synthetic outcome" value, combining the prediction based on a single predictor with the actual residual from the full regression equation. A partial residual for predictor X_i is the ordinary residual plus the regression term associated with X_i:

$$\text{Partial residual} = \text{Residual} + \hat{b}_i X_i$$

where $\hat{b}_i$ is the estimated regression coefficient. The `predict` function in *R* has an option to return the individual regression terms $\hat{b}_i X_i$:

```
terms <- predict(lm_98105, type='terms')
partial_resid <- resid(lm_98105) + terms
```

The partial residual plot displays the X_i predictor on the x-axis and the partial residuals on the y-axis. Using `ggplot2` makes it easy to superpose a smooth of the partial residuals:

```
df <- data.frame(SqFtTotLiving = house_98105[, 'SqFtTotLiving'],
                 Terms = terms[, 'SqFtTotLiving'],
                 PartialResid = partial_resid[, 'SqFtTotLiving'])
ggplot(df, aes(SqFtTotLiving, PartialResid)) +
```

```
geom_point(shape=1) + scale_shape(solid = FALSE) +
geom_smooth(linetype=2) +
geom_line(aes(SqFtTotLiving, Terms))
```

The `statsmodels` package has the method `sm.graphics.plot_ccpr` that creates a similar partial residual plot:

```
sm.graphics.plot_ccpr(result_98105, 'SqFtTotLiving')
```

The *R* and *Python* graphs differ by a constant shift. In *R*, a constant is added so that the mean of the terms is zero.

The resulting plot is shown in Figure 4-9. The partial residual is an estimate of the contribution that `SqFtTotLiving` adds to the sales price. The relationship between `SqFtTotLiving` and the sales price is evidently nonlinear (dashed line). The regression line (solid line) underestimates the sales price for homes less than 1,000 square feet and overestimates the price for homes between 2,000 and 3,000 square feet. There are too few data points above 4,000 square feet to draw conclusions for those homes.

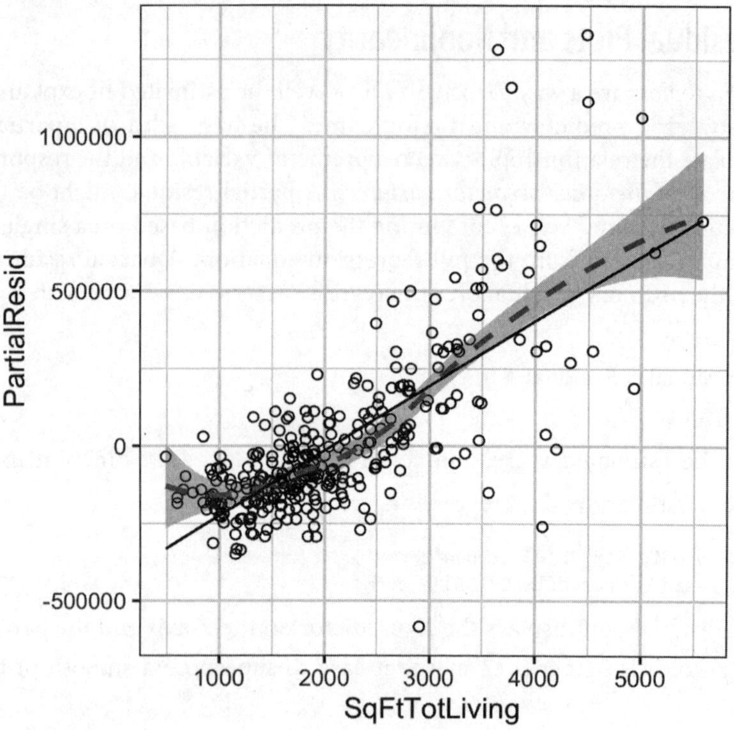

Figure 4-9. A partial residual plot for the variable `SqFtTotLiving`

This nonlinearity makes sense in this case: adding 500 feet in a small home makes a much bigger difference than adding 500 feet in a large home. This suggests that, instead of a simple linear term for `SqFtTotLiving`, a nonlinear term should be considered (see "Polynomial and Spline Regression" on page 187).

Key Ideas

- While outliers can cause problems for small data sets, the primary interest with outliers is to identify problems with the data, or locate anomalies.
- Single records (including regression outliers) can have a big influence on a regression equation with small data, but this effect washes out in big data.
- If the regression model is used for formal inference (p-values and the like), then certain assumptions about the distribution of the residuals should be checked. In general, however, the distribution of residuals is not critical in data science.
- The partial residuals plot can be used to qualitatively assess the fit for each regression term, possibly leading to alternative model specification.

Polynomial and Spline Regression

The relationship between the response and a predictor variable isn't necessarily linear. The response to the dose of a drug is often nonlinear: doubling the dosage generally doesn't lead to a doubled response. The demand for a product isn't a linear function of marketing dollars spent; at some point, demand is likely to be saturated. There are many ways that regression can be extended to capture these nonlinear effects.

Key Terms for Nonlinear Regression

Polynomial regression
: Adds polynomial terms (squares, cubes, etc.) to a regression.

Spline regression
: Fitting a smooth curve with a series of polynomial segments.

Knots
: Values that separate spline segments.

Generalized additive models
: Spline models with automated selection of knots.

Synonym
: GAM

Nonlinear Regression

When statisticians talk about *nonlinear regression*, they are referring to models that can't be fit using least squares. What kind of models are nonlinear? Essentially all models where the response cannot be expressed as a linear combination of the predictors or some transform of the predictors. Nonlinear regression models are harder and computationally more intensive to fit, since they require numerical optimization. For this reason, it is generally preferred to use a linear model if possible.

Polynomial

Polynomial regression involves including polynomial terms in a regression equation. The use of polynomial regression dates back almost to the development of regression itself with a paper by Gergonne in 1815. For example, a quadratic regression between the response Y and the predictor X would take the form:

$$Y = b_0 + b_1 X + b_2 X^2 + e$$

Polynomial regression can be fit in *R* through the `poly` function. For example, the following fits a quadratic polynomial for `SqFtTotLiving` with the King County housing data:

```
lm(AdjSalePrice ~  poly(SqFtTotLiving, 2) + SqFtLot +
                BldgGrade + Bathrooms + Bedrooms,
                    data=house_98105)

Call:
lm(formula = AdjSalePrice ~ poly(SqFtTotLiving, 2) + SqFtLot +
   BldgGrade + Bathrooms + Bedrooms, data = house_98105)

Coefficients:
           (Intercept)  poly(SqFtTotLiving, 2)1  poly(SqFtTotLiving, 2)2
            -402530.47               3271519.49                776934.02
               SqFtLot                BldgGrade                Bathrooms
                 32.56                135717.06                 -1435.12
              Bedrooms
              -9191.94
```

In `statsmodels`, we add the squared term to the model definition using `I(SqFtTotLiving**2)`:

```
model_poly = smf.ols(formula='AdjSalePrice ~  SqFtTotLiving + ' +
                '+ I(SqFtTotLiving**2) + ' +
                'SqFtLot + Bathrooms + Bedrooms + BldgGrade', data=house_98105)
result_poly = model_poly.fit()
result_poly.summary()  ❶
```

❶ The intercept and the polynomial coefficients are different compared to *R*. This is due to different implementations. The remaining coefficients and the predictions are equivalent.

There are now two coefficients associated with `SqFtTotLiving`: one for the linear term and one for the quadratic term.

The partial residual plot (see "Partial Residual Plots and Nonlinearity" on page 185) indicates some curvature in the regression equation associated with `SqFtTotLiving`. The fitted line more closely matches the smooth (see "Splines" on page 189) of the partial residuals as compared to a linear fit (see Figure 4-10).

The `statsmodels` implementation works only for linear terms. The accompanying source code gives an implementation that will work for polynomial regression as well.

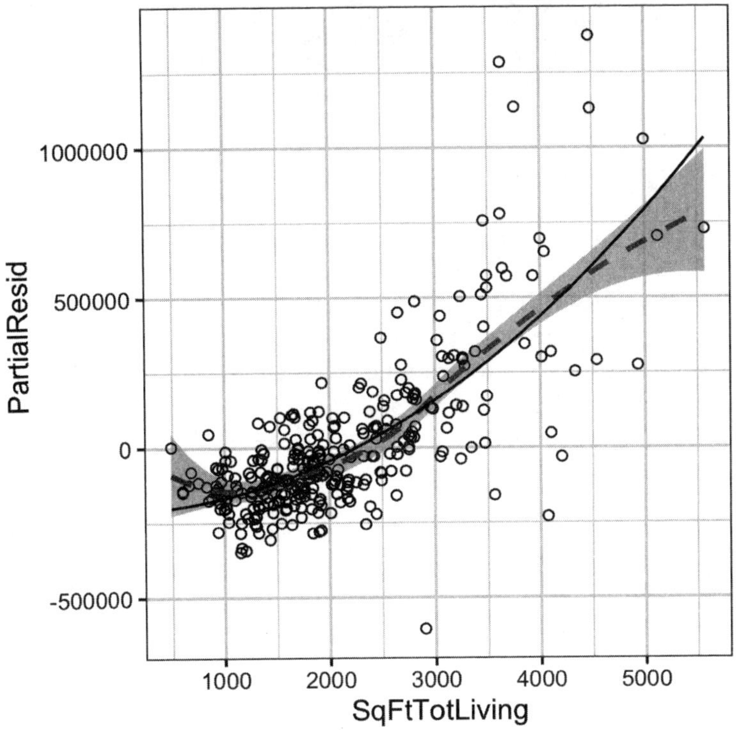

Figure 4-10. A polynomial regression fit for the variable `SqFtTotLiving` (solid line) versus a smooth (dashed line; see the following section about splines)

Splines

Polynomial regression captures only a certain amount of curvature in a nonlinear relationship. Adding in higher-order terms, such as a cubic quartic polynomial, often leads to undesirable "wiggliness" in the regression equation. An alternative, and often superior, approach to modeling nonlinear relationships is to use *splines*. *Splines* provide a way to smoothly interpolate between fixed points. Splines were originally used by draftsmen to draw a smooth curve, particularly in ship and aircraft building.

The splines were created by bending a thin piece of wood using weights, referred to as "ducks"; see Figure 4-11.

Figure 4-11. Splines were originally created using bendable wood and "ducks" and were used as a draftsman's tool to fit curves (photo courtesy of Bob Perry)

The technical definition of a spline is a series of piecewise continuous polynomials. They were first developed during World War II at the US Aberdeen Proving Grounds by I. J. Schoenberg, a Romanian mathematician. The polynomial pieces are smoothly connected at a series of fixed points in a predictor variable, referred to as *knots*. Formulation of splines is much more complicated than polynomial regression; statistical software usually handles the details of fitting a spline. The *R* package `splines` includes the function `bs` to create a *b-spline* (basis spline) term in a regression model. For example, the following adds a b-spline term to the house regression model:

```
library(splines)
knots <- quantile(house_98105$SqFtTotLiving, p=c(.25, .5, .75))
lm_spline <- lm(AdjSalePrice ~ bs(SqFtTotLiving, knots=knots, degree=3) +
  SqFtLot + Bathrooms + Bedrooms + BldgGrade,  data=house_98105)
```

Two parameters need to be specified: the degree of the polynomial and the location of the knots. In this case, the predictor `SqFtTotLiving` is included in the model using a cubic spline (`degree=3`). By default, `bs` places knots at the boundaries; in addition, knots were also placed at the lower quartile, the median quartile, and the upper quartile.

The `statsmodels` formula interface supports the use of splines in a similar way to *R*. Here, we specify the *b-spline* using `df`, the degrees of freedom. This will create `df` – `degree` = 6 – 3 = 3 internal knots with positions calculated in the same way as in the *R* code above:

```
formula = 'AdjSalePrice ~ bs(SqFtTotLiving, df=6, degree=3) + ' +
          'SqFtLot + Bathrooms + Bedrooms + BldgGrade'
model_spline = smf.ols(formula=formula, data=house_98105)
result_spline = model_spline.fit()
```

In contrast to a linear term, for which the coefficient has a direct meaning, the coefficients for a spline term are not interpretable. Instead, it is more useful to use the visual display to reveal the nature of the spline fit. Figure 4-12 displays the partial residual plot from the regression. In contrast to the polynomial model, the spline model more closely matches the smooth, demonstrating the greater flexibility of splines. In this case, the line more closely fits the data. Does this mean the spline regression is a better model? Not necessarily: it doesn't make economic sense that very small homes (less than 1,000 square feet) would have higher value than slightly larger homes. This is possibly an artifact of a confounding variable; see "Confounding Variables" on page 172.

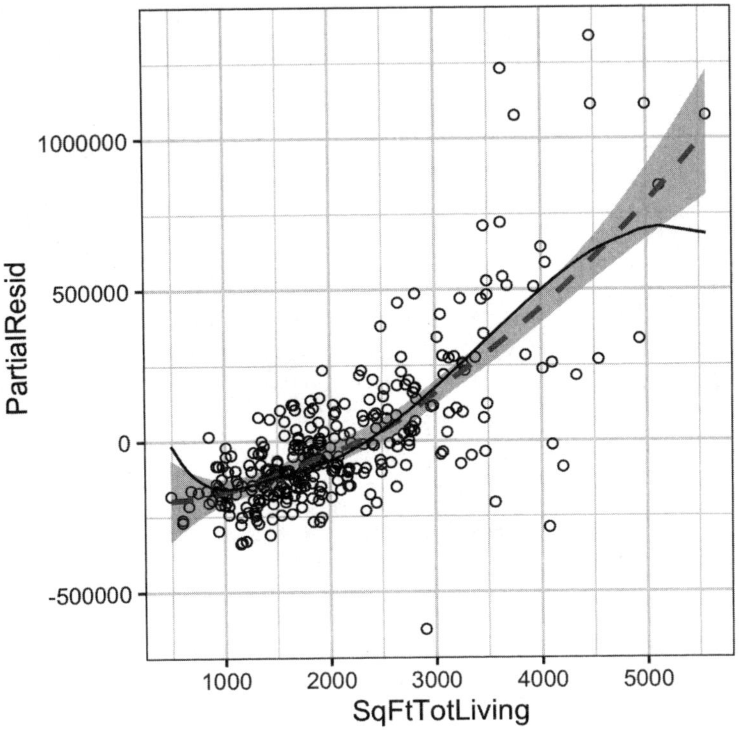

Figure 4-12. A spline regression fit for the variable `SqFtTotLiving` (solid line) compared to a smooth (dashed line)

Generalized Additive Models

Suppose you suspect a nonlinear relationship between the response and a predictor variable, either by a priori knowledge or by examining the regression diagnostics. Polynomial terms may not be flexible enough to capture the relationship, and spline terms require specifying the knots. *Generalized additive models*, or *GAM*, are a flexible modeling technique that can be used to automatically fit a spline regression. The `mgcv` package in *R* can be used to fit a GAM model to the housing data:

```
library(mgcv)
lm_gam <- gam(AdjSalePrice ~ s(SqFtTotLiving) + SqFtLot +
                    Bathrooms +  Bedrooms + BldgGrade,
                    data=house_98105)
```

The term `s(SqFtTotLiving)` tells the `gam` function to find the "best" knots for a spline term (see Figure 4-13).

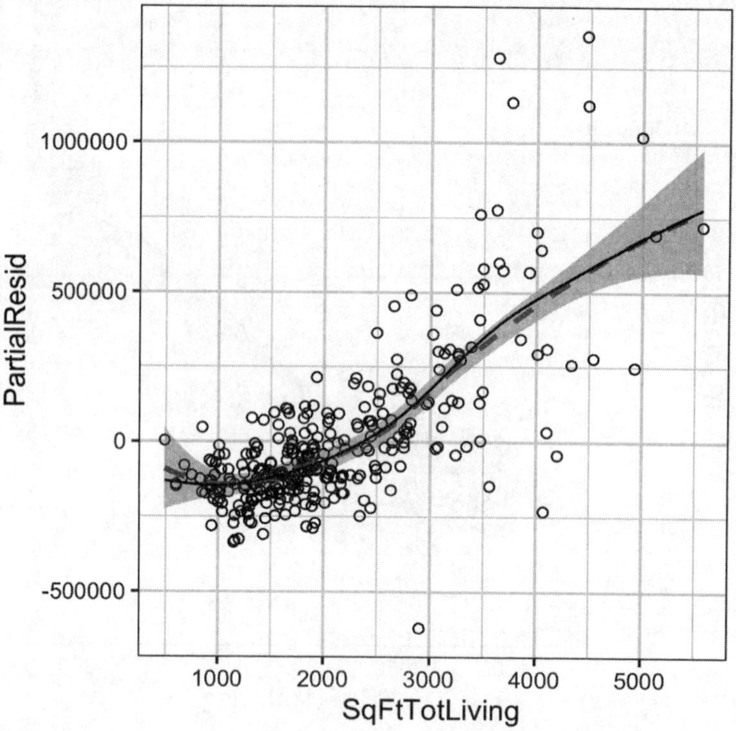

Figure 4-13. A GAM regression fit for the variable `SqFtTotLiving` (solid line) compared to a smooth (dashed line)

In *Python*, we can use the `pyGAM` package. It provides methods for regression and classification. Here, we use `LinearGAM` to create a regression model:

```
predictors = ['SqFtTotLiving', 'SqFtLot', 'Bathrooms',  'Bedrooms', 'BldgGrade']
outcome = 'AdjSalePrice'
X = house_98105[predictors].values
y = house_98105[outcome]

gam = LinearGAM(s(0, n_splines=12) + l(1) + l(2) + l(3) + l(4))  ❶
gam.gridsearch(X, y)
```

❶ The default value for `n_splines` is 20. This leads to overfitting for larger `SqFtTotLiving` values. A value of 12 leads to a more reasonable fit.

> **Key Ideas**
>
> - Outliers in a regression are records with a large residual.
> - Multicollinearity can cause numerical instability in fitting the regression equation.
> - A confounding variable is an important predictor that is omitted from a model and can lead to a regression equation with spurious relationships.
> - An interaction term between two variables is needed if the effect of one variable depends on the level or magnitude of the other.
> - Polynomial regression can fit nonlinear relationships between predictors and the outcome variable.
> - Splines are series of polynomial segments strung together, joining at knots.
> - We can automate the process of specifying the knots in splines using generalized additive models (GAM).

Further Reading

- For more on spline models and GAMs, see *The Elements of Statistical Learning*, 2nd ed., by Trevor Hastie, Robert Tibshirani, and Jerome Friedman (2009), and its shorter cousin based on *R*, *An Introduction to Statistical Learning* by Gareth James, Daniela Witten, Trevor Hastie, and Robert Tibshirani (2013); both are Springer books.
- To learn more about using regression models for time series forecasting, see *Practical Time Series Forecasting with R* by Galit Shmueli and Kenneth Lichtendahl (Axelrod Schnall, 2018).

Summary

Perhaps no other statistical method has seen greater use over the years than regression—the process of establishing a relationship between multiple predictor variables and an outcome variable. The fundamental form is linear: each predictor variable has a coefficient that describes a linear relationship between the predictor and the outcome. More advanced forms of regression, such as polynomial and spline regression, permit the relationship to be nonlinear. In classical statistics, the emphasis is on finding a good fit to the observed data to explain or describe some phenomenon, and the strength of this fit is how traditional *in-sample* metrics are used to assess the model. In data science, by contrast, the goal is typically to predict values for new data, so metrics based on predictive accuracy for out-of-sample data are used. Variable selection methods are used to reduce dimensionality and create more compact models.

CHAPTER 5

Classification

Data scientists are often tasked with automating decisions for business problems. Is an email an attempt at phishing? Is a customer likely to churn? Is the web user likely to click on an advertisement? These are all *classification* problems, a form of *supervised learning* in which we first train a model on data where the outcome is known and then apply the model to data where the outcome is not known. Classification is perhaps the most important form of prediction: the goal is to predict whether a record is a 1 or a 0 (phishing/not-phishing, click/don't click, churn/don't churn), or in some cases, one of several categories (for example, Gmail's filtering of your inbox into "primary," "social," "promotional," or "forums").

Often, we need more than a simple binary classification: we want to know the predicted probability that a case belongs to a class. Rather than having a model simply assign a binary classification, most algorithms can return a probability score (propensity) of belonging to the class of interest. In fact, with logistic regression, the default output from *R* is on the log-odds scale, and this must be transformed to a propensity. In *Python*'s `scikit-learn`, logistic regression, like most classification methods, provides two prediction methods: `predict` (which returns the class) and `predict_proba` (which returns probabilities for each class). A sliding cutoff can then be used to convert the propensity score to a decision. The general approach is as follows:

1. Establish a cutoff probability for the class of interest, above which we consider a record as belonging to that class.
2. Estimate (with any model) the probability that a record belongs to the class of interest.
3. If that probability is above the cutoff probability, assign the new record to the class of interest.

The higher the cutoff, the fewer the records predicted as 1—that is, as belonging to the class of interest. The lower the cutoff, the more the records predicted as 1.

This chapter covers several key techniques for classification and estimating propensities; additional methods that can be used both for classification and for numerical prediction are described in the next chapter.

More Than Two Categories?

The vast majority of problems involve a binary response. Some classification problems, however, involve a response with more than two possible outcomes. For example, at the anniversary of a customer's subscription contract, there might be three outcomes: the customer leaves or "churns" ($Y = 2$), goes on a month-to-month contract ($Y = 1$), or signs a new long-term contract ($Y = 0$). The goal is to predict $Y = j$ for $j = 0$, 1, or 2. Most of the classification methods in this chapter can be applied, either directly or with modest adaptations, to responses that have more than two outcomes. Even in the case of more than two outcomes, the problem can often be recast into a series of binary problems using conditional probabilities. For example, to predict the outcome of the contract, you can solve two binary prediction problems:

- Predict whether $Y = 0$ or $Y > 0$.
- Given that $Y > 0$, predict whether $Y = 1$ or $Y = 2$.

In this case, it makes sense to break up the problem into two cases: (1) whether the customer churns; and (2) if they don't churn, what type of contract they will choose. From a model-fitting viewpoint, it is often advantageous to convert the multiclass problem to a series of binary problems. This is particularly true when one category is much more common than the other categories.

Naive Bayes

The naive Bayes algorithm uses the probability of observing predictor values, given an outcome, to estimate what is really of interest: the probability of observing outcome $Y = i$, given a set of predictor values.[1]

1 This and subsequent sections in this chapter © 2020 Datastats, LLC, Peter Bruce, Andrew Bruce, and Peter Gedeck; used with permission.

Key Terms for Naive Bayes

Conditional probability
: The probability of observing some event (say, $X = i$) given some other event (say, $Y = i$), written as $P(X_i | Y_i)$.

Posterior probability
: The probability of an outcome after the predictor information has been incorporated (in contrast to the *prior probability* of outcomes, not taking predictor information into account).

To understand naive Bayesian classification, we can start out by imagining complete or exact Bayesian classification. For each record to be classified:

1. Find all the other records with the same predictor profile (i.e., where the predictor values are the same).
2. Determine what classes those records belong to and which class is most prevalent (i.e., probable).
3. Assign that class to the new record.

The preceding approach amounts to finding all the records in the sample that are exactly like the new record to be classified in the sense that all the predictor values are identical.

> Predictor variables must be categorical (factor) variables in the standard naive Bayes algorithm. See "Numeric Predictor Variables" on page 200 for two workarounds for using continuous variables.

Why Exact Bayesian Classification Is Impractical

When the number of predictor variables exceeds a handful, many of the records to be classified will be without exact matches. Consider a model to predict voting on the basis of demographic variables. Even a sizable sample may not contain even a single match for a new record who is a male Hispanic with high income from the US Midwest who voted in the last election, did not vote in the prior election, has three daughters and one son, and is divorced. And this is with just eight variables, a small number for most classification problems. The addition of just a single new variable with five equally frequent categories reduces the probability of a match by a factor of 5.

The Naive Solution

In the naive Bayes solution, we no longer restrict the probability calculation to those records that match the record to be classified. Instead, we use the entire data set. The naive Bayes modification is as follows:

1. For a binary response $Y = i$ ($i = 0$ or 1), estimate the individual conditional probabilities for each predictor $P(X_j \mid Y = i)$; these are the probabilities that the predictor value is in the record when we observe $Y = i$. This probability is estimated by the proportion of X_j values among the $Y = i$ records in the training set.
2. Multiply these probabilities by each other, and then by the proportion of records belonging to $Y = i$.
3. Repeat steps 1 and 2 for all the classes.
4. Estimate a probability for outcome i by taking the value calculated in step 2 for class i and dividing it by the sum of such values for all classes.
5. Assign the record to the class with the highest probability for this set of predictor values.

This naive Bayes algorithm can also be stated as an equation for the probability of observing outcome $Y = i$, given a set of predictor values $X_1, \cdots, X_p$:

$$P(Y = i \mid X_1, X_2, \ldots, X_p)$$

Here is the full formula for calculating class probabilities using exact Bayes classification:

$$P(Y = i \mid X_1, X_2, \ldots, X_p) = \frac{P(Y = i)P(X_1, \ldots, X_p \mid Y = i)}{P(Y = 0)P(X_1, \ldots, X_p \mid Y = 0) + P(Y = 1)P(X_1, \ldots, X_p \mid Y = 1)}$$

Under the naive Bayes assumption of conditional independence, this equation changes into:

$$P(Y = i \mid X_1, X_2, \ldots, X_p)$$
$$= \frac{P(Y = i)P(X_1 \mid Y = i)\ldots P(X_p \mid Y = i)}{P(Y = 0)P(X_1 \mid Y = 0)\ldots P(X_p \mid Y = 0) + P(Y = 1)P(X_1 \mid Y = 1)\ldots P(X_p \mid Y = 1)}$$

Why is this formula called "naive"? We have made a simplifying assumption that the *exact conditional probability* of a vector of predictor values, given observing an outcome, is sufficiently well estimated by the product of the individual conditional probabilities $P(X_j \mid Y = i)$. In other words, in estimating $P(X_j \mid Y = i)$ instead of $P(X_1, X_2, \cdots X_p \mid Y = i)$, we are assuming X_j is *independent* of all the other predictor variables X_k for $k \neq j$.

Several packages in *R* can be used to estimate a naive Bayes model. The following fits a model to the loan payment data using the `klaR` package:

```
library(klaR)
naive_model <- NaiveBayes(outcome ~ purpose_ + home_ + emp_len_,
                          data = na.omit(loan_data))

naive_model$table
$purpose_
          var
grouping   credit_card debt_consolidation home_improvement major_purchase
  paid off  0.18759649         0.55215915       0.07150104     0.05359270
  default   0.15151515         0.57571347       0.05981209     0.03727229
          var
grouping      medical      other small_business
  paid off 0.01424728 0.09990737     0.02099599
  default  0.01433549 0.11561025     0.04574126

$home_
          var
grouping    MORTGAGE       OWN      RENT
  paid off 0.4894800 0.0808963 0.4296237
  default  0.4313440 0.0832782 0.4853778

$emp_len_
          var
grouping     < 1 Year   > 1 Year
  paid off 0.03105289 0.96894711
  default  0.04728508 0.95271492
```

The output from the model is the conditional probabilities $P(X_j \mid Y = i)$.

In *Python* we can use `sklearn.naive_bayes.MultinomialNB` from `scikit-learn`. We need to convert the categorical features to dummy variables before we fit the model:

```
predictors = ['purpose_', 'home_', 'emp_len_']
outcome = 'outcome'
X = pd.get_dummies(loan_data[predictors], prefix='', prefix_sep='')
y = loan_data[outcome]

naive_model = MultinomialNB(alpha=0.01, fit_prior=True)
naive_model.fit(X, y)
```

It is possible to derive the conditional probabilities from the fitted model using the property `feature_log_prob_`.

The model can be used to predict the outcome of a new loan. We use the last value of the data set for testing:

```
new_loan <- loan_data[147, c('purpose_', 'home_', 'emp_len_')]
row.names(new_loan) <- NULL
new_loan
          purpose_    home_  emp_len_
         1 small_business MORTGAGE  > 1 Year
```

In *Python*, we get this value as follows:

```
new_loan = X.loc[146:146, :]
```

In this case, the model predicts a default (*R*):

```
predict(naive_model, new_loan)
$class
[1] default
Levels: paid off default

$posterior
      paid off   default
[1,] 0.3463013 0.6536987
```

As we discussed, `scikit-learn`'s classification models have two methods—`predict`, which returns the predicted class, and `predict_proba`, which returns the class probabilities:

```
print('predicted class: ', naive_model.predict(new_loan)[0])

probabilities = pd.DataFrame(naive_model.predict_proba(new_loan),
                             columns=loan_data[outcome].cat.categories)
print('predicted probabilities', probabilities)
--
predicted class:  default
predicted probabilities
    default  paid off
0  0.653696  0.346304
```

The prediction also returns a `posterior` estimate of the probability of default. The naive Bayesian classifier is known to produce *biased* estimates. However, where the goal is to *rank* records according to the probability that $Y = 1$, unbiased estimates of probability are not needed, and naive Bayes produces good results.

Numeric Predictor Variables

The Bayesian classifier works only with categorical predictors (e.g., with spam classification, where the presence or absence of words, phrases, characters, and so on lies at the heart of the predictive task). To apply naive Bayes to numerical predictors, one of two approaches must be taken:

- Bin and convert the numerical predictors to categorical predictors and apply the algorithm of the previous section.
- Use a probability model—for example, the normal distribution (see "Normal Distribution" on page 69)—to estimate the conditional probability $P(X_j \mid Y = i)$.

> When a predictor category is absent in the training data, the algorithm assigns *zero probability* to the outcome variable in new data, rather than simply ignoring this variable and using the information from other variables, as other methods might. Most implementations of Naive Bayes use a smoothing parameter (Laplace Smoothing) to prevent this.

Key Ideas

- Naive Bayes works with categorical (factor) predictors and outcomes.
- It asks, "Within each outcome category, which predictor categories are most probable?"
- That information is then inverted to estimate probabilities of outcome categories, given predictor values.

Further Reading

- *The Elements of Statistical Learning*, 2nd ed., by Trevor Hastie, Robert Tibshirani, and Jerome Friedman (Springer, 2009).
- There is a full chapter on naive Bayes in *Data Mining for Business Analytics* by Galit Shmueli, Peter Bruce, Nitin Patel, Peter Gedeck, Inbal Yahav, and Kenneth Lichtendahl (Wiley, 2007–2020, with editions for *R*, *Python*, Excel, and JMP).

Discriminant Analysis

Discriminant analysis is the earliest statistical classifier; it was introduced by R. A. Fisher in 1936 in an article published in the *Annals of Eugenics* journal.[2]

2 It is certainly surprising that the first article on statistical classification was published in a journal devoted to eugenics. Indeed, there is a disconcerting connection between the early development of statistics and eugenics (*https://oreil.ly/eUJvR*).

Key Terms for Discriminant Analysis

Covariance
: A measure of the extent to which one variable varies in concert with another (i.e., similar magnitude and direction).

Discriminant function
: The function that, when applied to the predictor variables, maximizes the separation of the classes.

Discriminant weights
: The scores that result from the application of the discriminant function and are used to estimate probabilities of belonging to one class or another.

While discriminant analysis encompasses several techniques, the most commonly used is *linear discriminant analysis*, or *LDA*. The original method proposed by Fisher was actually slightly different from LDA, but the mechanics are essentially the same. LDA is now less widely used with the advent of more sophisticated techniques, such as tree models and logistic regression.

However, you may still encounter LDA in some applications, and it has links to other more widely used methods (such as principal components analysis; see "Principal Components Analysis" on page 284).

Linear discriminant analysis should not be confused with Latent Dirichlet Allocation, also referred to as LDA. Latent Dirichlet Allocation is used in text and natural language processing and is unrelated to linear discriminant analysis.

Covariance Matrix

To understand discriminant analysis, it is first necessary to introduce the concept of *covariance* between two or more variables. The covariance measures the relationship between two variables x and z. Denote the mean for each variable by $\bar{x}$ and $\bar{z}$ (see "Mean" on page 9). The covariance $s_{x,z}$ between x and z is given by:

$$s_{x,z} = \frac{\sum_{i=1}^{n} (x_i - \bar{x})(z_i - \bar{z})}{n - 1}$$

where n is the number of records (note that we divide by $n - 1$ instead of n; see "Degrees of Freedom, and n or $n - 1$?" on page 15).

As with the correlation coefficient (see "Correlation" on page 30), positive values indicate a positive relationship and negative values indicate a negative relationship. Correlation, however, is constrained to be between –1 and 1, whereas covariance scale depends on the scale of the variables x and z. The *covariance matrix* Σ for x and z consists of the individual variable variances, s_x^2 and s_z^2, on the diagonal (where row and column are the same variable) and the covariances between variable pairs on the off-diagonals:

$$\hat{\Sigma} = \begin{bmatrix} s_x^2 & s_{x,z} \\ s_{z,x} & s_z^2 \end{bmatrix}$$

> Recall that the standard deviation is used to normalize a variable to a z-score; the covariance matrix is used in a multivariate extension of this standardization process. This is known as Mahalanobis distance (see "Other Distance Metrics" on page 242) and is related to the LDA function.

Fisher's Linear Discriminant

For simplicity, let's focus on a classification problem in which we want to predict a binary outcome y using just two continuous numeric variables (x, z). Technically, discriminant analysis assumes the predictor variables are normally distributed continuous variables, but, in practice, the method works well even for nonextreme departures from normality, and for binary predictors. Fisher's linear discriminant distinguishes variation *between* groups, on the one hand, from variation *within* groups on the other. Specifically, seeking to divide the records into two groups, linear discriminant analysis (LDA) focuses on maximizing the "between" sum of squares SS_{between} (measuring the variation between the two groups) relative to the "within" sum of squares SS_{within} (measuring the within-group variation). In this case, the two groups correspond to the records (x_0, z_0) for which $y = 0$ and the records (x_1, z_1) for which $y = 1$. The method finds the linear combination $w_x x + w_z z$ that maximizes that sum of squares ratio:

$$\frac{SS_{\text{between}}}{SS_{\text{within}}}$$

The between sum of squares is the squared distance between the two group means, and the within sum of squares is the spread around the means within each group, weighted by the covariance matrix. Intuitively, by maximizing the between sum of squares and minimizing the within sum of squares, this method yields the greatest separation between the two groups.

A Simple Example

The `MASS` package, associated with the book *Modern Applied Statistics with S* by W. N. Venables and B. D. Ripley (Springer, 1994), provides a function for LDA with *R*. The following applies this function to a sample of loan data using two predictor variables, `borrower_score` and `payment_inc_ratio`, and prints out the estimated linear discriminator weights:

```
library(MASS)
loan_lda <- lda(outcome ~ borrower_score + payment_inc_ratio,
                data=loan3000)
loan_lda$scaling
                          LD1
borrower_score     7.17583880
payment_inc_ratio -0.09967559
```

In *Python*, we can use `LinearDiscriminantAnalysis` from `sklearn.discriminant_analysis`. The `scalings_` property gives the estimated weights:

```
loan3000.outcome = loan3000.outcome.astype('category')

predictors = ['borrower_score', 'payment_inc_ratio']
outcome = 'outcome'

X = loan3000[predictors]
y = loan3000[outcome]

loan_lda = LinearDiscriminantAnalysis()
loan_lda.fit(X, y)
pd.DataFrame(loan_lda.scalings_, index=X.columns)
```

Using Discriminant Analysis for Feature Selection

If the predictor variables are normalized prior to running LDA, the discriminator weights are measures of variable importance, thus providing a computationally efficient method of feature selection.

The `lda` function can predict the probability of "default" versus "paid off":

```
pred <- predict(loan_lda)
head(pred$posterior)
   paid off   default
1 0.4464563 0.5535437
2 0.4410466 0.5589534
3 0.7273038 0.2726962
4 0.4937462 0.5062538
```

```
5 0.3900475 0.6099525
6 0.5892594 0.4107406
```

The `predict_proba` method of the fitted model returns the probabilities for the "default" and "paid off" outcomes:

```
pred = pd.DataFrame(loan_lda.predict_proba(loan3000[predictors]),
                    columns=loan_lda.classes_)
pred.head()
```

A plot of the predictions helps illustrate how LDA works. Using the output from the `predict` function, a plot of the estimated probability of default is produced as follows:

```
center <- 0.5 * (loan_lda$mean[1, ] + loan_lda$mean[2, ])
slope <- -loan_lda$scaling[1] / loan_lda$scaling[2]
intercept <- center[2] - center[1] * slope

ggplot(data=lda_df, aes(x=borrower_score, y=payment_inc_ratio,
                        color=prob_default)) +
  geom_point(alpha=.6) +
  scale_color_gradientn(colors=c('#ca0020', '#f7f7f7', '#0571b0')) +
  scale_x_continuous(expand=c(0,0)) +
  scale_y_continuous(expand=c(0,0), lim=c(0, 20)) +
  geom_abline(slope=slope, intercept=intercept, color='darkgreen')
```

A similar graph is created in Python using this code:

```
# Use scalings and center of means to determine decision boundary
center = np.mean(loan_lda.means_, axis=0)
slope = - loan_lda.scalings_[0] / loan_lda.scalings_[1]
intercept = center[1] - center[0] * slope

# payment_inc_ratio for borrower_score of 0 and 20
x_0 = (0 - intercept) / slope
x_20 = (20 - intercept) / slope

lda_df = pd.concat([loan3000, pred['default']], axis=1)
lda_df.head()

fig, ax = plt.subplots(figsize=(4, 4))
g = sns.scatterplot(x='borrower_score', y='payment_inc_ratio',
                    hue='default', data=lda_df,
                    palette=sns.diverging_palette(240, 10, n=9, as_cmap=True),
                    ax=ax, legend=False)

ax.set_ylim(0, 20)
ax.set_xlim(0.15, 0.8)
ax.plot((x_0, x_20), (0, 20), linewidth=3)
ax.plot(*loan_lda.means_.transpose())
```

The resulting plot is shown in Figure 5-1. Data points on the left of the diagonal line are predicted to default (probability greater than 0.5).

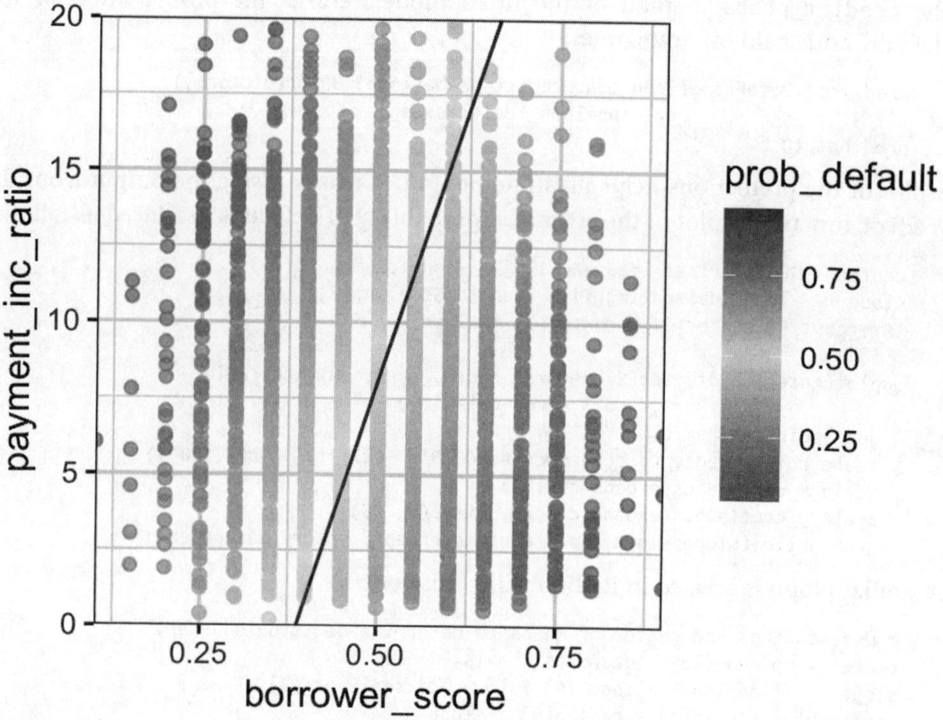

Figure 5-1. LDA prediction of loan default using two variables: a score of the borrower's creditworthiness and the payment-to-income ratio

Using the discriminant function weights, LDA splits the predictor space into two regions, as shown by the solid line. The predictions farther away from the line in both directions have a higher level of confidence (i.e., a probability further away from 0.5).

Extensions of Discriminant Analysis

More predictor variables: while the text and example in this section used just two predictor variables, LDA works just as well with more than two predictor variables. The only limiting factor is the number of records (estimating the covariance matrix requires a sufficient number of records per variable, which is typically not an issue in data science applications).

There are other variants of discriminant analysis. The best known is quadratic discriminant analysis (QDA). Despite its name, QDA is still a linear discriminant function. The main difference is that in LDA, the covariance matrix is assumed to be the same for the two groups corresponding to $Y = 0$ and $Y = 1$. In QDA, the covariance matrix is allowed to be different for the two groups. In practice, the difference in most applications is not critical.

Key Ideas

- Discriminant analysis works with continuous or categorical predictors, as well as with categorical outcomes.
- Using the covariance matrix, it calculates a *linear discriminant function*, which is used to distinguish records belonging to one class from those belonging to another.
- This function is applied to the records to derive weights, or scores, for each record (one weight for each possible class), which determines its estimated class.

Further Reading

- Both *The Elements of Statistical Learning*, 2nd ed., by Trevor Hastie, Robert Tibshirani, and Jerome Friedman (Springer, 2009), and its shorter cousin, *An Introduction to Statistical Learning* by Gareth James, Daniela Witten, Trevor Hastie, and Robert Tibshirani (Springer, 2013), have a section on discriminant analysis.
- *Data Mining for Business Analytics* by Galit Shmueli, Peter Bruce, Nitin Patel, Peter Gedeck, Inbal Yahav, and Kenneth Lichtendahl (Wiley, 2007–2020, with editions for *R*, *Python*, Excel, and JMP) has a full chapter on discriminant analysis.
- For historical interest, Fisher's original article on the topic, "The Use of Multiple Measurements in Taxonomic Problems," as published in 1936 in *Annals of Eugenics* (now called *Annals of Genetics*), can be found online (*https://oreil.ly/_TCR8*).

Logistic Regression

Logistic regression is analogous to multiple linear regression (see Chapter 4), except the outcome is binary. Various transformations are employed to convert the problem to one in which a linear model can be fit. Like discriminant analysis, and unlike *K*-Nearest Neighbor and naive Bayes, logistic regression is a structured model approach rather than a data-centric approach. Due to its fast computational speed and its output of a model that lends itself to rapid scoring of new data, it is a popular method.

> **Key Terms for Logistic Regression**
>
> ***Logit***
> The function that maps class membership probability to a range from ± ∞ (instead of 0 to 1).
>
> *Synonym*
> Log odds (see below)
>
> ***Odds***
> The ratio of "success" (1) to "not success" (0).
>
> ***Log odds***
> The response in the transformed model (now linear), which gets mapped back to a probability.

Logistic Response Function and Logit

The key ingredients for logistic regression are the *logistic response function* and the *logit*, in which we map a probability (which is on a 0–1 scale) to a more expansive scale suitable for linear modeling.

The first step is to think of the outcome variable not as a binary label but as the probability p that the label is a "1." Naively, we might be tempted to model p as a linear function of the predictor variables:

$$p = \beta_0 + \beta_1 x_1 + \beta_2 x_2 + \cdots + \beta_q x_q$$

However, fitting this model does not ensure that p will end up between 0 and 1, as a probability must.

Instead, we model p by applying a *logistic response* or *inverse logit* function to the predictors:

$$p = \frac{1}{1 + e^{-(\beta_0 + \beta_1 x_1 + \beta_2 x_2 + \cdots + \beta_q x_q)}}$$

This transform ensures that the p stays between 0 and 1.

To get the exponential expression out of the denominator, we consider *odds* instead of probabilities. Odds, familiar to bettors everywhere, are the ratio of "successes" (1) to "nonsuccesses" (0). In terms of probabilities, odds are the probability of an event divided by the probability that the event will not occur. For example, if the probability that a horse will win is 0.5, the probability of "won't win" is (1 – 0.5) = 0.5, and the odds are 1.0:

$$\text{Odds}(Y = 1) = \frac{p}{1 - p}$$

We can obtain the probability from the odds using the inverse odds function:

$$p = \frac{\text{Odds}}{1 + \text{Odds}}$$

We combine this with the logistic response function, shown earlier, to get:

$$\text{Odds}(Y = 1) = e^{\beta_0 + \beta_1 x_1 + \beta_2 x_2 + \cdots + \beta_q x_q}$$

Finally, taking the logarithm of both sides, we get an expression that involves a linear function of the predictors:

$$\log(\text{Odds}(Y = 1)) = \beta_0 + \beta_1 x_1 + \beta_2 x_2 + \cdots + \beta_q x_q$$

The *log-odds* function, also known as the *logit* function, maps the probability p from $(0, 1)$ to any value $(-\infty, +\infty)$—see Figure 5-2. The transformation circle is complete; we have used a linear model to predict a probability, which we can in turn map to a class label by applying a cutoff rule—any record with a probability greater than the cutoff is classified as a 1.

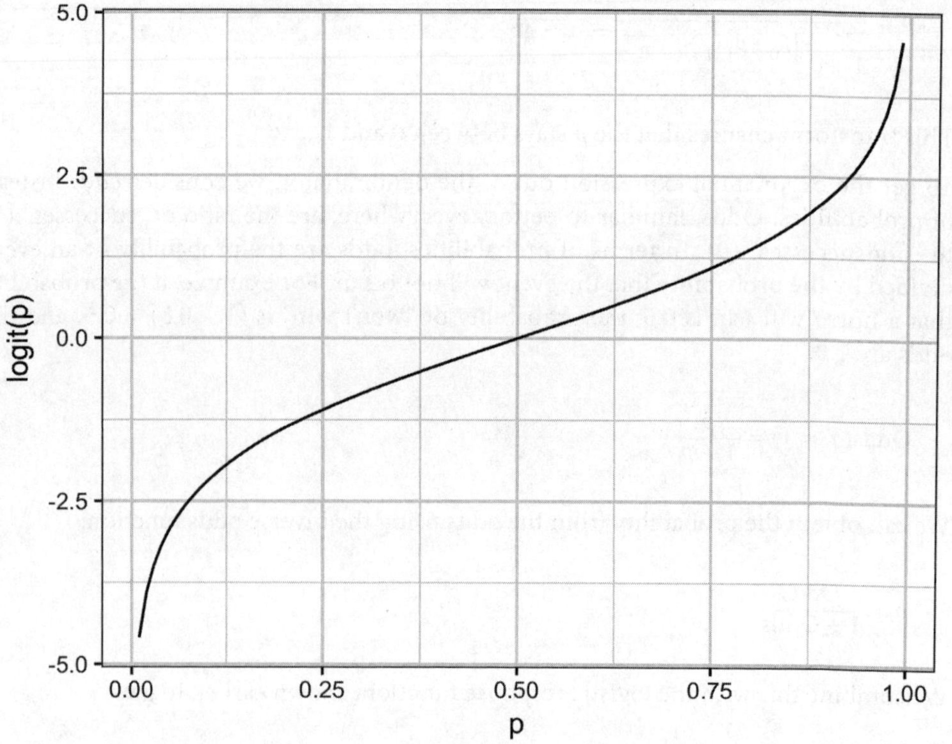

Figure 5-2. Graph of the logit function that maps a probability to a scale suitable for a linear model

Logistic Regression and the GLM

The response in the logistic regression formula is the log odds of a binary outcome of 1. We observe only the binary outcome, not the log odds, so special statistical methods are needed to fit the equation. Logistic regression is a special instance of a *generalized linear model* (GLM) developed to extend linear regression to other settings.

In *R*, to fit a logistic regression, the `glm` function is used with the `family` parameter set to `binomial`. The following code fits a logistic regression to the personal loan data introduced in "K-Nearest Neighbors" on page 238:

```
logistic_model <- glm(outcome ~ payment_inc_ratio + purpose_ +
                       home_ + emp_len_ + borrower_score,
                     data=loan_data, family='binomial')
logistic_model

Call:  glm(formula = outcome ~ payment_inc_ratio + purpose_ + home_ +
    emp_len_ + borrower_score, family = "binomial", data = loan_data)
```

```
Coefficients:
             (Intercept)            payment_inc_ratio
                 1.63809                      0.07974
purpose_debt_consolidation   purpose_home_improvement
                 0.24937                      0.40774
   purpose_major_purchase             purpose_medical
                 0.22963                      0.51048
           purpose_other       purpose_small_business
                 0.62066                      1.21526
                home_OWN                    home_RENT
                 0.04833                      0.15732
       emp_len_ > 1 Year               borrower_score
                -0.35673                     -4.61264

Degrees of Freedom: 45341 Total (i.e. Null);  45330 Residual
Null Deviance:      62860
Residual Deviance: 57510        AIC: 57540
```

The response is `outcome`, which takes a 0 if the loan is paid off and a 1 if the loan defaults. `purpose_` and `home_` are factor variables representing the purpose of the loan and the home ownership status. As in linear regression, a factor variable with *P* levels is represented with *P* – 1 columns. By default in *R*, the *reference* coding is used, and the levels are all compared to the reference level (see "Factor Variables in Regression" on page 163). The reference levels for these factors are `credit_card` and `MORTGAGE`, respectively. The variable `borrower_score` is a score from 0 to 1 representing the creditworthiness of the borrower (from poor to excellent). This variable was created from several other variables using *K*-Nearest Neighbor—see "KNN as a Feature Engine" on page 247.

In *Python*, we use the `scikit-learn` class `LogisticRegression` from `sklearn.linear_model`. The arguments `penalty` and `C` are used to prevent overfitting by L1 or L2 regularization. Regularization is switched on by default. In order to fit without regularization, we set `C` to a very large value. The `solver` argument selects the used minimizer; the method `liblinear` is the default:

```
predictors = ['payment_inc_ratio', 'purpose_', 'home_', 'emp_len_',
              'borrower_score']
outcome = 'outcome'
X = pd.get_dummies(loan_data[predictors], prefix='', prefix_sep='',
                   drop_first=True)
y = loan_data[outcome]

logit_reg = LogisticRegression(penalty='l2', C=1e42, solver='liblinear')
logit_reg.fit(X, y)
```

In contrast to *R*, `scikit-learn` derives the classes from the unique values in `y` (*paid off* and *default*). Internally, the classes are ordered alphabetically. As this is the reverse order from the factors used in *R*, you will see that the coefficients are reversed. The predict method returns the class label and predict_proba returns the probabilities in the order available from the attribute logit_reg.classes_.

Generalized Linear Models

Generalized linear models (GLMs) are characterized by two main components:

- A probability distribution or family (binomial in the case of logistic regression)
- A link function—i.e., a transformation function that maps the response to the predictors (logit in the case of logistic regression)

Logistic regression is by far the most common form of GLM. A data scientist will encounter other types of GLMs. Sometimes a log link function is used instead of the logit; in practice, use of a log link is unlikely to lead to very different results for most applications. The Poisson distribution is commonly used to model count data (e.g., the number of times a user visits a web page in a certain amount of time). Other families include negative binomial and gamma, often used to model elapsed time (e.g., time to failure). In contrast to logistic regression, application of GLMs with these models is more nuanced and involves greater care. These are best avoided unless you are familiar with and understand the utility and pitfalls of these methods.

Predicted Values from Logistic Regression

The predicted value from logistic regression is in terms of the log odds: $\hat{Y} = \log(\text{Odds}(Y = 1))$. The predicted probability is given by the logistic response function:

$$\hat{p} = \frac{1}{1 + e^{-\hat{Y}}}$$

For example, look at the predictions from the model logistic_model in *R*:

```
pred <- predict(logistic_model)
summary(pred)
     Min.   1st Qu.    Median      Mean   3rd Qu.      Max.
-2.704774 -0.518825 -0.008539  0.002564  0.505061  3.509606
```

In *Python*, we can convert the probabilities into a data frame and use the describe method to get these characteristics of the distribution:

```
pred = pd.DataFrame(logit_reg.predict_log_proba(X),
                    columns=loan_data[outcome].cat.categories)
pred.describe()
```

Converting these values to probabilities is a simple transform:

```
prob <- 1/(1 + exp(-pred))
> summary(prob)
   Min. 1st Qu.  Median    Mean 3rd Qu.    Max.
0.06269 0.37313 0.49787 0.50000 0.62365 0.97096
```

The probabilities are directly available using the `predict_proba` methods in `scikit-learn`:

```
pred = pd.DataFrame(logit_reg.predict_proba(X),
                    columns=loan_data[outcome].cat.categories)
pred.describe()
```

These are on a scale from 0 to 1 and don't yet declare whether the predicted value is default or paid off. We could declare any value greater than 0.5 as default. In practice, a lower cutoff is often appropriate if the goal is to identify members of a rare class (see "The Rare Class Problem" on page 223).

Interpreting the Coefficients and Odds Ratios

One advantage of logistic regression is that it produces a model that can be scored to new data rapidly, without recomputation. Another is the relative ease of interpretation of the model, as compared with other classification methods. The key conceptual idea is understanding an *odds ratio*. The odds ratio is easiest to understand for a binary factor variable X:

$$\text{odds ratio} = \frac{\text{Odds}(Y = 1 | X = 1)}{\text{Odds}(Y = 1 | X = 0)}$$

This is interpreted as the odds that $Y = 1$ when $X = 1$ versus the odds that $Y = 1$ when $X = 0$. If the odds ratio is 2, then the odds that $Y = 1$ are two times higher when $X = 1$ versus when $X = 0$.

Why bother with an odds ratio rather than probabilities? We work with odds because the coefficient β_j in the logistic regression is the log of the odds ratio for X_j.

An example will make this more explicit. For the model fit in "Logistic Regression and the GLM" on page 210, the regression coefficient for `purpose_small_business` is 1.21526. This means that a loan to a small business compared to a loan to pay off credit card debt reduces the odds of defaulting versus being paid off by $exp(1.21526) \approx 3.4$. Clearly, loans for the purpose of creating or expanding a small business are considerably riskier than other types of loans.

Figure 5-3 shows the relationship between the odds ratio and the log-odds ratio for odds ratios greater than 1. Because the coefficients are on the log scale, an increase of 1 in the coefficient results in an increase of $exp(1) \approx 2.72$ in the odds ratio.

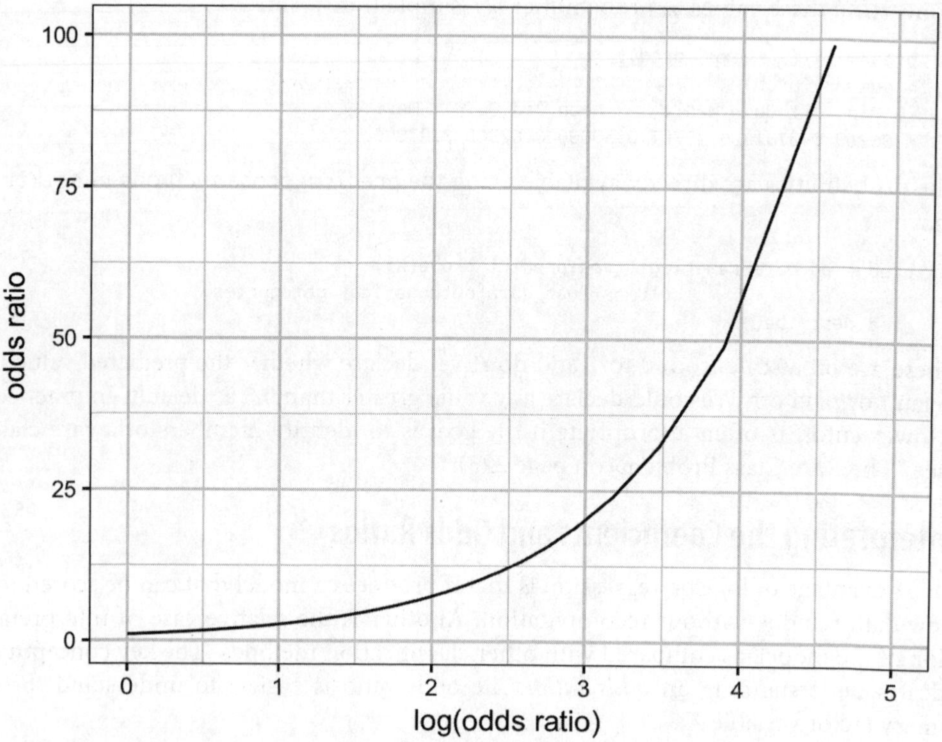

Figure 5-3. The relationship between the odds ratio and the log-odds ratio

Odds ratios for numeric variables X can be interpreted similarly: they measure the change in the odds ratio for a unit change in X. For example, the effect of increasing the payment-to-income ratio from, say, 5 to 6 increases the odds of the loan defaulting by a factor of $exp(0.08244) \approx 1.09$. The variable `borrower_score` is a score on the borrowers' creditworthiness and ranges from 0 (low) to 1 (high). The odds of the best borrowers relative to the worst borrowers defaulting on their loans is smaller by a factor of $exp(-4.61264) \approx 0.01$. In other words, the default risk from the borrowers with the poorest creditworthiness is 100 times greater than that of the best borrowers!

Linear and Logistic Regression: Similarities and Differences

Linear regression and logistic regression share many commonalities. Both assume a parametric linear form relating the predictors with the response. Exploring and finding the best model are done in very similar ways. Extensions to the linear model, like the use of a spline transform of a predictor (see "Splines" on page 189), are equally applicable in the logistic regression setting. Logistic regression differs in two fundamental ways:

- The way the model is fit (least squares is not applicable)
- The nature and analysis of the residuals from the model

Fitting the model

Linear regression is fit using least squares, and the quality of the fit is evaluated using RMSE and R-squared statistics. In logistic regression (unlike in linear regression), there is no closed-form solution, and the model must be fit using *maximum likelihood estimation* (MLE). Maximum likelihood estimation is a process that tries to find the model that is most likely to have produced the data we see. In the logistic regression equation, the response is not 0 or 1 but rather an estimate of the log odds that the response is 1. The MLE finds the solution such that the estimated log odds best describes the observed outcome. The mechanics of the algorithm involve a quasi-Newton optimization that iterates between a scoring step (*Fisher's scoring*), based on the current parameters, and an update to the parameters to improve the fit.

Maximum Likelihood Estimation

Here is a bit more detail, if you like statistical symbols: start with a set of data $(X_1, X_2, \cdots, X_n)$ and a probability model $P_\theta(X_1, X_2, \cdots, X_n)$ that depends on a set of parameters θ. The goal of MLE is to find the set of parameters $\hat{\theta}$ that maximizes the value of $P_\theta(X_1, X_2, \cdots, X_n)$; that is, it maximizes the probability of observing $(X_1, X_2, \cdots, X_n)$ given the model P. In the fitting process, the model is evaluated using a metric called *deviance*:

$$\text{deviance} = -2 \log \left(P_{\hat{\theta}}(X_1, X_2, \cdots, X_n)\right)$$

Lower deviance corresponds to a better fit.

Fortunately, most practitioners don't need to concern themselves with the details of the fitting algorithm since this is handled by the software. Most data scientists will not need to worry about the fitting method, other than understanding that it is a way to find a good model under certain assumptions.

Handling Factor Variables

In logistic regression, factor variables should be coded as in linear regression; see "Factor Variables in Regression" on page 163. In *R* and other software, this is normally handled automatically, and generally reference encoding is used. All of the other classification methods covered in this chapter typically use the one hot encoder representation (see "One Hot Encoder" on page 242). In *Python*'s `scikit-learn`, it is easiest to use one hot encoding, which means that only *n* – *1* of the resulting dummies can be used in the regression.

Assessing the Model

Like other classification methods, logistic regression is assessed by how accurately the model classifies new data (see "Evaluating Classification Models" on page 219). As with linear regression, some additional standard statistical tools are available to examine and improve the model. Along with the estimated coefficients, *R* reports the standard error of the coefficients (SE), a *z*-value, and a p-value:

```
summary(logistic_model)

Call:
glm(formula = outcome ~ payment_inc_ratio + purpose_ + home_ +
    emp_len_ + borrower_score, family = "binomial", data = loan_data)

Deviance Residuals:
     Min        1Q    Median        3Q       Max
-2.51951  -1.06908  -0.05853   1.07421   2.15528

Coefficients:
                            Estimate Std. Error z value Pr(>|z|)
(Intercept)                 1.638092   0.073708  22.224  < 2e-16 ***
payment_inc_ratio           0.079737   0.002487  32.058  < 2e-16 ***
purpose_debt_consolidation  0.249373   0.027615   9.030  < 2e-16 ***
purpose_home_improvement    0.407743   0.046615   8.747  < 2e-16 ***
purpose_major_purchase      0.229628   0.053683   4.277 1.89e-05 ***
purpose_medical             0.510479   0.086780   5.882 4.04e-09 ***
purpose_other               0.620663   0.039436  15.738  < 2e-16 ***
purpose_small_business      1.215261   0.063320  19.192  < 2e-16 ***
home_OWN                    0.048330   0.038036   1.271    0.204
home_RENT                   0.157320   0.021203   7.420 1.17e-13 ***
emp_len_ > 1 Year          -0.356731   0.052622  -6.779 1.21e-11 ***
borrower_score             -4.612638   0.083558 -55.203  < 2e-16 ***
---
Signif. codes:  0 '***' 0.001 '**' 0.01 '*' 0.05 '.' 0.1 ' ' 1

(Dispersion parameter for binomial family taken to be 1)

    Null deviance: 62857  on 45341  degrees of freedom
```

```
Residual deviance: 57515  on 45330  degrees of freedom
AIC: 57539

Number of Fisher Scoring iterations: 4
```

The package `statsmodels` has an implementation for generalized linear model (`GLM`) that provides similarly detailed information:

```
y_numbers = [1 if yi == 'default' else 0 for yi in y]
logit_reg_sm = sm.GLM(y_numbers, X.assign(const=1),
                      family=sm.families.Binomial())
logit_result = logit_reg_sm.fit()
logit_result.summary()
```

Interpretation of the p-value comes with the same caveat as in regression and should be viewed more as a relative indicator of variable importance (see "Assessing the Model" on page 153) than as a formal measure of statistical significance. A logistic regression model, which has a binary response, does not have an associated RMSE or R-squared. Instead, a logistic regression model is typically evaluated using more general metrics for classification; see "Evaluating Classification Models" on page 219.

Many other concepts for linear regression carry over to the logistic regression setting (and other GLMs). For example, you can use stepwise regression, fit interaction terms, or include spline terms. The same concerns regarding confounding and correlated variables apply to logistic regression (see "Interpreting the Regression Equation" on page 169). You can fit generalized additive models (see "Generalized Additive Models" on page 192) using the `mgcv` package in *R*:

```
logistic_gam <- gam(outcome ~ s(payment_inc_ratio) + purpose_ +
                    home_ + emp_len_ + s(borrower_score),
                    data=loan_data, family='binomial')
```

The formula interface of `statsmodels` also supports these extensions in *Python*:

```
import statsmodels.formula.api as smf
formula = ('outcome ~ bs(payment_inc_ratio, df=4) + purpose_ + ' +
           'home_ + emp_len_ + bs(borrower_score, df=4)')
model = smf.glm(formula=formula, data=loan_data, family=sm.families.Binomial())
results = model.fit()
```

Analysis of residuals

One area where logistic regression differs from linear regression is in the analysis of the residuals. As in linear regression (see Figure 4-9), it is straightforward to compute partial residuals in *R*:

```
terms <- predict(logistic_gam, type='terms')
partial_resid <- resid(logistic_model) + terms
df <- data.frame(payment_inc_ratio = loan_data[, 'payment_inc_ratio'],
                 terms = terms[, 's(payment_inc_ratio)'],
                 partial_resid = partial_resid[, 's(payment_inc_ratio)'])
```

```
ggplot(df, aes(x=payment_inc_ratio, y=partial_resid, solid = FALSE)) +
  geom_point(shape=46, alpha=0.4) +
  geom_line(aes(x=payment_inc_ratio, y=terms),
            color='red', alpha=0.5, size=1.5) +
  labs(y='Partial Residual')
```

The resulting plot is displayed in Figure 5-4. The estimated fit, shown by the line, goes between two sets of point clouds. The top cloud corresponds to a response of 1 (defaulted loans), and the bottom cloud corresponds to a response of 0 (loans paid off). This is very typical of residuals from a logistic regression since the output is binary. The prediction is measured as the logit (log of the odds ratio), which will always be some finite value. The actual value, an absolute 0 or 1, corresponds to an infinite logit, either positive or negative, so the residuals (which get added to the fitted value) will never equal 0. Hence the plotted points lie in clouds either above or below the fitted line in the partial residual plot. Partial residuals in logistic regression, while less valuable than in regression, are still useful to confirm nonlinear behavior and identify highly influential records.

There is currently no implementation of partial residuals in any of the major *Python* packages. We provide *Python* code to create the partial residual plot in the accompanying source code repository.

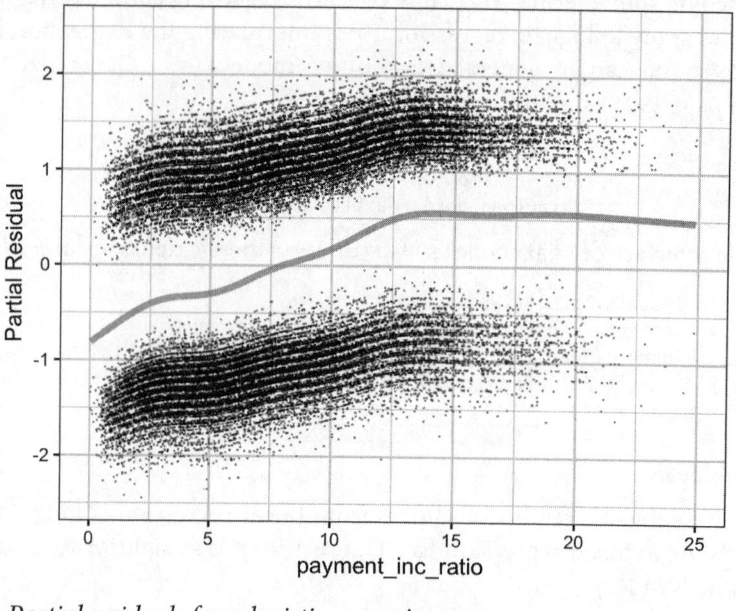

Figure 5-4. Partial residuals from logistic regression

Some of the output from the `summary` function can effectively be ignored. The dispersion parameter does not apply to logistic regression and is there for other types of GLMs. The residual deviance and the number of scoring iterations are related to the maximum likelihood fitting method; see “Maximum Likelihood Estimation” on page 215.

Key Ideas

- Logistic regression is like linear regression, except that the outcome is a binary variable.
- Several transformations are needed to get the model into a form that can be fit as a linear model, with the log of the odds ratio as the response variable.
- After the linear model is fit (by an iterative process), the log odds is mapped back to a probability.
- Logistic regression is popular because it is computationally fast and produces a model that can be scored to new data with only a few arithmetic operations.

Further Reading

- The standard reference on logistic regression is *Applied Logistic Regression*, 3rd ed., by David Hosmer, Stanley Lemeshow, and Rodney Sturdivant (Wiley, 2013).
- Also popular are two books by Joseph Hilbe: *Logistic Regression Models* (very comprehensive, 2017) and *Practical Guide to Logistic Regression* (compact, 2015), both from Chapman & Hall/CRC Press.
- Both *The Elements of Statistical Learning*, 2nd ed., by Trevor Hastie, Robert Tibshirani, and Jerome Friedman (Springer, 2009), and its shorter cousin, *An Introduction to Statistical Learning* by Gareth James, Daniela Witten, Trevor Hastie, and Robert Tibshirani (Springer, 2013), have a section on logistic regression.
- *Data Mining for Business Analytics* by Galit Shmueli, Peter Bruce, Nitin Patel, Peter Gedeck, Inbal Yahav, and Kenneth Lichtendahl (Wiley, 2007–2020, with editions for *R*, *Python*, Excel, and JMP) has a full chapter on logistic regression.

Evaluating Classification Models

It is common in predictive modeling to train a number of different models, apply each to a holdout sample, and assess their performance. Sometimes, after a number of models have been evaluated and tuned, and if there are enough data, a third holdout sample, not used previously, is used to estimate how the chosen model will perform with completely new data. Different disciplines and practitioners will also use the terms *validation* and *test* to refer to the holdout sample(s). Fundamentally, the assessment process attempts to learn which model produces the most accurate and useful predictions.

Key Terms for Evaluating Classification Models

Accuracy
The percent (or proportion) of cases classified correctly.

Confusion matrix
A tabular display (2×2 in the binary case) of the record counts by their predicted and actual classification status.

Sensitivity
The percent (or proportion) of all 1s that are correctly classified as 1s.

Synonym
Recall

Specificity
The percent (or proportion) of all 0s that are correctly classified as 0s.

Precision
The percent (proportion) of predicted 1s that are actually 1s.

ROC curve
A plot of sensitivity versus specificity.

Lift
A measure of how effective the model is at identifying (comparatively rare) 1s at different probability cutoffs.

A simple way to measure classification performance is to count the proportion of predictions that are correct, i.e., measure the *accuracy*. Accuracy is simply a measure of total error:

$$\text{accuracy} = \frac{\sum \text{TruePositive} + \sum \text{TrueNegative}}{\text{SampleSize}}$$

In most classification algorithms, each case is assigned an "estimated probability of being a 1."[3] The default decision point, or cutoff, is typically 0.50 or 50%. If the probability is above 0.5, the classification is "1"; otherwise it is "0." An alternative default cutoff is the prevalent probability of 1s in the data.

Confusion Matrix

At the heart of classification metrics is the *confusion matrix*. The confusion matrix is a table showing the number of correct and incorrect predictions categorized by type of response. Several packages are available in *R* and *Python* to compute a confusion matrix, but in the binary case, it is simple to compute one by hand.

To illustrate the confusion matrix, consider the `logistic_gam` model that was trained on a balanced data set with an equal number of defaulted and paid-off loans (see Figure 5-4). Following the usual conventions, $Y = 1$ corresponds to the event of interest (e.g., default), and $Y = 0$ corresponds to a negative (or usual) event (e.g., paid off). The following computes the confusion matrix for the `logistic_gam` model applied to the entire (unbalanced) training set in *R*:

```
pred <- predict(logistic_gam, newdata=train_set)
pred_y <- as.numeric(pred > 0)
true_y <- as.numeric(train_set$outcome=='default')
true_pos <- (true_y==1) & (pred_y==1)
true_neg <- (true_y==0) & (pred_y==0)
false_pos <- (true_y==0) & (pred_y==1)
false_neg <- (true_y==1) & (pred_y==0)
conf_mat <- matrix(c(sum(true_pos), sum(false_pos),
                     sum(false_neg), sum(true_neg)), 2, 2)
colnames(conf_mat) <- c('Yhat = 1', 'Yhat = 0')
rownames(conf_mat) <- c('Y = 1', 'Y = 0')
conf_mat
      Yhat = 1 Yhat = 0
Y = 1 14295    8376
Y = 0 8052     14619
```

In *Python*:

```
pred = logit_reg.predict(X)
pred_y = logit_reg.predict(X) == 'default'
true_y = y == 'default'
true_pos = true_y & pred_y
true_neg = ~true_y & ~pred_y
false_pos = ~true_y & pred_y
false_neg = true_y & ~pred_y
```

3 Not all methods provide unbiased estimates of probability. In most cases, it is sufficient that the method provide a ranking equivalent to the rankings that would result from an unbiased probability estimate; the cutoff method is then functionally equivalent.

```
conf_mat = pd.DataFrame([[np.sum(true_pos), np.sum(false_neg)],
                         [np.sum(false_pos), np.sum(true_neg)]],
                        index=['Y = default', 'Y = paid off'],
                        columns=['Yhat = default', 'Yhat = paid off'])
conf_mat
```

The predicted outcomes are columns and the true outcomes are the rows. The diagonal elements of the matrix show the number of correct predictions, and the off-diagonal elements show the number of incorrect predictions. For example, 14,295 defaulted loans were correctly predicted as a default, but 8,376 defaulted loans were incorrectly predicted as paid off.

Figure 5-5 shows the relationship between the confusion matrix for a binary response Y and different metrics (see "Precision, Recall, and Specificity" on page 223 for more on the metrics). As with the example for the loan data, the actual response is along the rows and the predicted response is along the columns. The diagonal boxes (upper left, lower right) show when the predictions $\hat{Y}$ correctly predict the response. One important metric not explicitly called out is the false positive *rate* (the mirror image of precision). When 1s are rare, the ratio of false positives to all predicted positives can be high, leading to the unintuitive situation in which a predicted 1 is most likely a 0. This problem plagues medical screening tests (e.g., mammograms) that are widely applied: due to the relative rarity of the condition, positive test results most likely do not mean breast cancer. This leads to much confusion in the public.

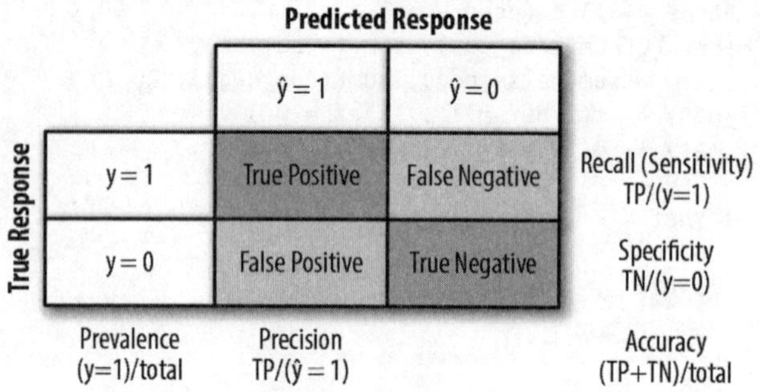

Figure 5-5. Confusion matrix for a binary response and various metrics

Here, we present the actual response along the rows and the predicted response along the columns, but it is not uncommon to see this reversed. A notable example is the popular `caret` package in *R*.

The Rare Class Problem

In many cases, there is an imbalance in the classes to be predicted, with one class much more prevalent than the other—for example, legitimate insurance claims versus fraudulent ones, or browsers versus purchasers at a website. The rare class (e.g., the fraudulent claims) is usually the class of more interest and is typically designated 1, in contrast to the more prevalent 0s. In the typical scenario, the 1s are the more important case, in the sense that misclassifying them as 0s is costlier than misclassifying 0s as 1s. For example, correctly identifying a fraudulent insurance claim may save thousands of dollars. On the other hand, correctly identifying a nonfraudulent claim merely saves you the cost and effort of going through the claim by hand with a more careful review (which is what you would do if the claim were tagged as "fraudulent").

In such cases, unless the classes are easily separable, the most accurate classification model may be one that simply classifies everything as a 0. For example, if only 0.1% of the browsers at a web store end up purchasing, a model that predicts that each browser will leave without purchasing will be 99.9% accurate. However, it will be useless. Instead, we would be happy with a model that is less accurate overall but is good at picking out the purchasers, even if it misclassifies some nonpurchasers along the way.

Precision, Recall, and Specificity

Metrics other than pure accuracy—metrics that are more nuanced—are commonly used in evaluating classification models. Several of these have a long history in statistics—especially biostatistics, where they are used to describe the expected performance of diagnostic tests. The *precision* measures the accuracy of a predicted positive outcome (see Figure 5-5):

$$\text{precision} = \frac{\sum \text{TruePositive}}{\sum \text{TruePositive} + \sum \text{FalsePositive}}$$

The *recall*, also known as *sensitivity*, measures the strength of the model to predict a positive outcome—the proportion of the 1s that it correctly identifies (see Figure 5-5). The term *sensitivity* is used a lot in biostatistics and medical diagnostics, whereas *recall* is used more in the machine learning community. The definition of recall is:

$$\text{recall} = \frac{\sum \text{TruePositive}}{\sum \text{TruePositive} + \sum \text{FalseNegative}}$$

Another metric used is *specificity*, which measures a model's ability to predict a negative outcome:

$$\text{specificity} = \frac{\sum \text{TrueNegative}}{\sum \text{TrueNegative} + \sum \text{FalsePositive}}$$

We can calculate the three metrics from `conf_mat` in *R*:

```
# precision
conf_mat[1, 1] / sum(conf_mat[,1])
# recall
conf_mat[1, 1] / sum(conf_mat[1,])
# specificity
conf_mat[2, 2] / sum(conf_mat[2,])
```

Here is the equivalent code to calculate the metrics in *Python*:

```
conf_mat = confusion_matrix(y, logit_reg.predict(X))
print('Precision', conf_mat[0, 0] / sum(conf_mat[:, 0]))
print('Recall', conf_mat[0, 0] / sum(conf_mat[0, :]))
print('Specificity', conf_mat[1, 1] / sum(conf_mat[1, :]))

precision_recall_fscore_support(y, logit_reg.predict(X),
                                labels=['default', 'paid off'])
```

`scikit-learn` has a custom method `precision_recall_fscore_support` that calculates precision and recall/specificity all at once.

ROC Curve

You can see that there is a trade-off between recall and specificity. Capturing more 1s generally means misclassifying more 0s as 1s. The ideal classifier would do an excellent job of classifying the 1s, without misclassifying more 0s as 1s.

The metric that captures this trade-off is the "Receiver Operating Characteristics" curve, usually referred to as the *ROC curve*. The ROC curve plots recall (sensitivity) on the y-axis against specificity on the x-axis.[4] The ROC curve shows the trade-off between recall and specificity as you change the cutoff to determine how to classify a record. Sensitivity (recall) is plotted on the y-axis, and you may encounter two forms in which the x-axis is labeled:

4 The ROC curve was first used during World War II to describe the performance of radar receiving stations, whose job was to correctly identify (classify) reflected radar signals and alert defense forces to incoming aircraft.

- Specificity plotted on the x-axis, with 1 on the left and 0 on the right
- 1-Specificity plotted on the x-axis, with 0 on the left and 1 on the right

The curve looks identical whichever way it is done. The process to compute the ROC curve is:

1. Sort the records by the predicted probability of being a 1, starting with the most probable and ending with the least probable.
2. Compute the cumulative specificity and recall based on the sorted records.

Computing the ROC curve in *R* is straightforward. The following code computes ROC for the loan data:

```
idx <- order(-pred)
recall <- cumsum(true_y[idx] == 1) / sum(true_y == 1)
specificity <- (sum(true_y == 0) - cumsum(true_y[idx] == 0)) / sum(true_y == 0)
roc_df <- data.frame(recall = recall, specificity = specificity)
ggplot(roc_df, aes(x=specificity, y=recall)) +
  geom_line(color='blue') +
  scale_x_reverse(expand=c(0, 0)) +
  scale_y_continuous(expand=c(0, 0)) +
  geom_line(data=data.frame(x=(0:100) / 100), aes(x=x, y=1-x),
            linetype='dotted', color='red')
```

In *Python*, we can use the `scikit-learn` function `sklearn.metrics.roc_curve` to calculate the required information for the ROC curve. You can find similar packages for *R*, e.g., ROCR:

```
fpr, tpr, thresholds = roc_curve(y, logit_reg.predict_proba(X)[:,0],
                                 pos_label='default')
roc_df = pd.DataFrame({'recall': tpr, 'specificity': 1 - fpr})

ax = roc_df.plot(x='specificity', y='recall', figsize=(4, 4), legend=False)
ax.set_ylim(0, 1)
ax.set_xlim(1, 0)
ax.plot((1, 0), (0, 1))
ax.set_xlabel('specificity')
ax.set_ylabel('recall')
```

The result is shown in Figure 5-6. The dotted diagonal line corresponds to a classifier no better than random chance. An extremely effective classifier (or, in medical situations, an extremely effective diagnostic test) will have an ROC that hugs the upper-left corner—it will correctly identify lots of 1s without misclassifying lots of 0s as 1s. For this model, if we want a classifier with a specificity of at least 50%, then the recall is about 75%.

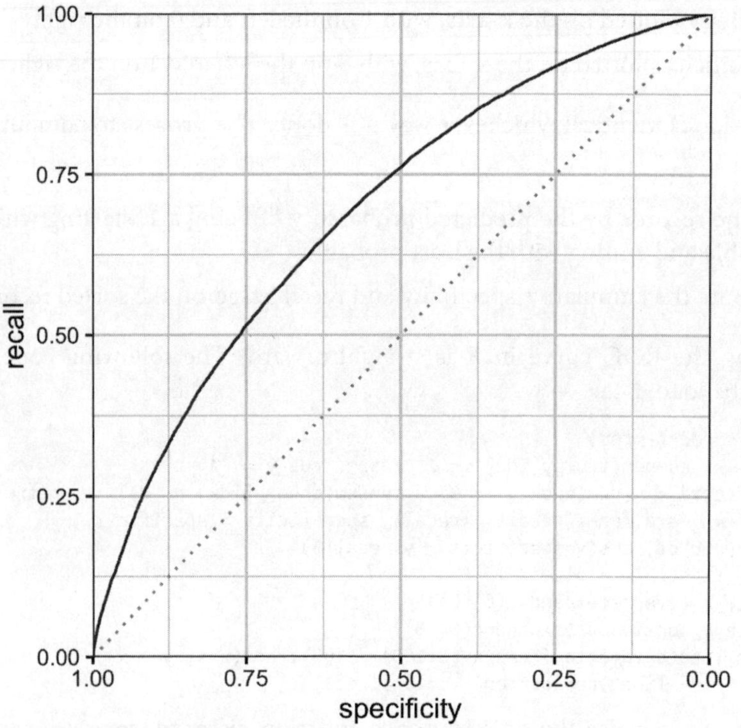

Figure 5-6. ROC curve for the loan data

Precision-Recall Curve

In addition to ROC curves, it can be illuminating to examine the precision-recall (PR) curve (*https://oreil.ly/_89Pr*). PR curves are computed in a similar way except that the data is ordered from least to most probable and cumulative precision and recall statistics are computed. PR curves are especially useful in evaluating data with highly unbalanced outcomes.

AUC

The ROC curve is a valuable graphical tool, but by itself doesn't constitute a single measure for the performance of a classifier. The ROC curve can be used, however, to produce the area underneath the curve (AUC) metric. AUC is simply the total area under the ROC curve. The larger the value of AUC, the more effective the classifier. An AUC of 1 indicates a perfect classifier: it gets all the 1s correctly classified, and it doesn't misclassify any 0s as 1s.

A completely ineffective classifier—the diagonal line—will have an AUC of 0.5.

Figure 5-7 shows the area under the ROC curve for the loan model. The value of AUC can be computed by a numerical integration in *R*:

```
sum(roc_df$recall[-1] * diff(1 - roc_df$specificity))
    [1] 0.6926172
```

In *Python*, we can either calculate the accuracy as shown for *R* or use `scikit-learn`'s function `sklearn.metrics.roc_auc_score`. You will need to provide the expected value as 0 or 1:

```
print(np.sum(roc_df.recall[:-1] * np.diff(1 - roc_df.specificity)))
print(roc_auc_score([1 if yi == 'default' else 0 for yi in y],
                    logit_reg.predict_proba(X)[:, 0]))
```

The model has an AUC of about 0.69, corresponding to a relatively weak classifier.

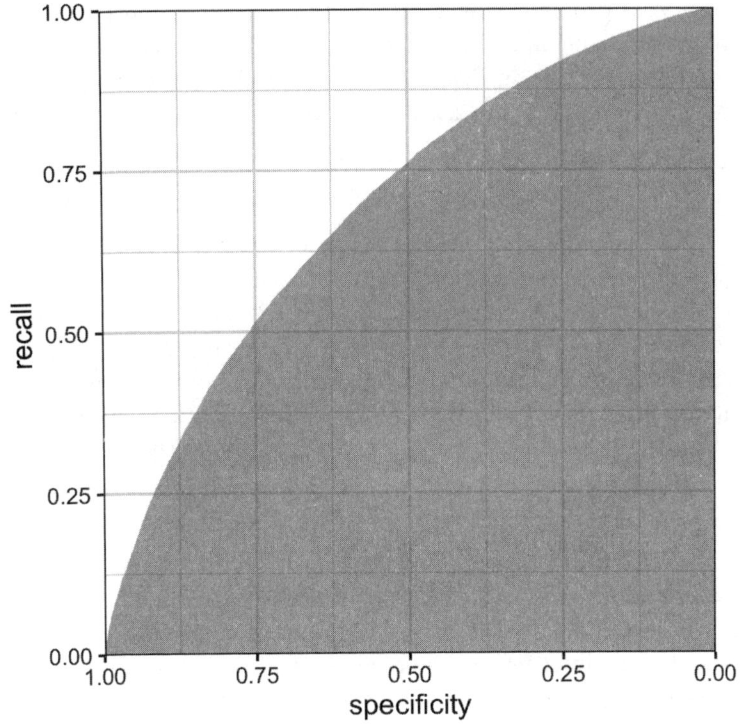

Figure 5-7. Area under the ROC curve for the loan data

False Positive Rate Confusion

False positive/negative rates are often confused or conflated with specificity or sensitivity (even in publications and software!). Sometimes the false positive rate is defined as the proportion of true negatives that test positive. In many cases (such as network intrusion detection), the term is used to refer to the proportion of positive signals that are true negatives.

Lift

Using the AUC as a metric to evaluate a model is an improvement over simple accuracy, as it can assess how well a classifier handles the trade-off between overall accuracy and the need to identify the more important 1s. But it does not completely address the rare-case problem, where you need to lower the model's probability cutoff below 0.5 to avoid having all records classified as 0. In such cases, for a record to be classified as a 1, it might be sufficient to have a probability of 0.4, 0.3, or lower. In effect, we end up overidentifying 1s, reflecting their greater importance.

Changing this cutoff will improve your chances of catching the 1s (at the cost of misclassifying more 0s as 1s). But what is the optimum cutoff?

The concept of lift lets you defer answering that question. Instead, you consider the records in order of their predicted probability of being 1s. Say, of the top 10% classified as 1s, how much better did the algorithm do, compared to the benchmark of simply picking blindly? If you can get 0.3% response in this top decile instead of the 0.1% you get overall by picking randomly, the algorithm is said to have a *lift* (also called *gains*) of 3 in the top decile. A lift chart (gains chart) quantifies this over the range of the data. It can be produced decile by decile, or continuously over the range of the data.

To compute a lift chart, you first produce a *cumulative gains chart* that shows the recall on the y-axis and the total number of records on the x-axis. The *lift curve* is the ratio of the cumulative gains to the diagonal line corresponding to random selection. *Decile gains charts* are one of the oldest techniques in predictive modeling, dating from the days before internet commerce. They were particularly popular among direct mail professionals. Direct mail is an expensive method of advertising if applied indiscriminately, and advertisers used predictive models (quite simple ones, in the early days) to identify the potential customers with the likeliest prospect of payoff.

Uplift

Sometimes the term *uplift* is used to mean the same thing as lift. An alternate meaning is used in a more restrictive setting, when an A/B test has been conducted and the treatment (A or B) is then used as a predictor variable in a predictive model. The uplift is the improvement in response predicted *for an individual case* with treatment A versus treatment B. This is determined by scoring the individual case first with the predictor set to A, and then again with the predictor toggled to B. Marketers and political campaign consultants use this method to determine which of two messaging treatments should be used with which customers or voters.

A lift curve lets you look at the consequences of setting different probability cutoffs for classifying records as 1s. It can be an intermediate step in settling on an appropriate cutoff level. For example, a tax authority might have only a certain amount of resources that it can spend on tax audits, and it wants to spend them on the likeliest tax cheats. With its resource constraint in mind, the authority would use a lift chart to estimate where to draw the line between tax returns selected for audit and those left alone.

Key Ideas

- Accuracy (the percent of predicted classifications that are correct) is but a first step in evaluating a model.
- Other metrics (recall, specificity, precision) focus on more specific performance characteristics (e.g., recall measures how good a model is at correctly identifying 1s).
- AUC (area under the ROC curve) is a common metric for the ability of a model to distinguish 1s from 0s.
- Similarly, lift measures how effective a model is in identifying the 1s, and it is often calculated decile by decile, starting with the most probable 1s.

Further Reading

Evaluation and assessment are typically covered in the context of a particular model (e.g., *K*-Nearest Neighbors or decision trees); three books that handle the subject in its own chapter are:

- *Data Mining*, 3rd ed., by Ian Whitten, Eibe Frank, and Mark Hall (Morgan Kaufmann, 2011).

- *Modern Data Science with R* by Benjamin Baumer, Daniel Kaplan, and Nicholas Horton (Chapman & Hall/CRC Press, 2017).
- *Data Mining for Business Analytics* by Galit Shmueli, Peter Bruce, Nitin Patel, Peter Gedeck, Inbal Yahav, and Kenneth Lichtendahl (Wiley, 2007–2020, with editions for *R*, *Python*, Excel, and JMP).

Strategies for Imbalanced Data

The previous section dealt with evaluation of classification models using metrics that go beyond simple accuracy and are suitable for imbalanced data—data in which the outcome of interest (purchase on a website, insurance fraud, etc.) is rare. In this section, we look at additional strategies that can improve predictive modeling performance with imbalanced data.

Key Terms for Imbalanced Data

Undersample
: Use fewer of the prevalent class records in the classification model.

  Synonym
  : Downsample

Oversample
: Use more of the rare class records in the classification model, bootstrapping if necessary.

  Synonym
  : Upsample

Up weight or down weight
: Attach more (or less) weight to the rare (or prevalent) class in the model.

Data generation
: Like bootstrapping, except each new bootstrapped record is slightly different from its source.

z-score
: The value that results after standardization.

K
: The number of neighbors considered in the nearest neighbor calculation.

Undersampling

If you have enough data, as is the case with the loan data, one solution is to *undersample* (or downsample) the prevalent class, so the data to be modeled is more balanced between 0s and 1s. The basic idea in undersampling is that the data for the dominant class has many redundant records. Dealing with a smaller, more balanced data set yields benefits in model performance, and it makes it easier to prepare the data and to explore and pilot models.

How much data is enough? It depends on the application, but in general, having tens of thousands of records for the less dominant class is enough. The more easily distinguishable the 1s are from the 0s, the less data needed.

The loan data analyzed in "Logistic Regression" on page 208 was based on a balanced training set: half of the loans were paid off, and the other half were in default. The predicted values were similar: half of the probabilities were less than 0.5, and half were greater than 0.5. In the full data set, only about 19% of the loans were in default, as shown in *R*:

```
mean(full_train_set$outcome=='default')
[1] 0.1889455
```

In *Python*:

```
print('percentage of loans in default: ',
      100 * np.mean(full_train_set.outcome == 'default'))
```

What happens if we use the full data set to train the model? Let's see what this looks like in *R*:

```
full_model <- glm(outcome ~ payment_inc_ratio + purpose_ + home_ +
                            emp_len_+ dti + revol_bal + revol_util,
                  data=full_train_set, family='binomial')
pred <- predict(full_model)
mean(pred > 0)
[1] 0.003942094
```

And in *Python*:

```
predictors = ['payment_inc_ratio', 'purpose_', 'home_', 'emp_len_',
              'dti', 'revol_bal', 'revol_util']
outcome = 'outcome'
X = pd.get_dummies(full_train_set[predictors], prefix='', prefix_sep='',
                   drop_first=True)
y = full_train_set[outcome]

full_model = LogisticRegression(penalty='l2', C=1e42, solver='liblinear')
full_model.fit(X, y)
print('percentage of loans predicted to default: ',
      100 * np.mean(full_model.predict(X) == 'default'))
```

Only 0.39% of the loans are predicted to be in default, or less than 1/47 of the expected number.[5] The loans that were paid off overwhelm the loans in default because the model is trained using all the data equally. Thinking about it intuitively, the presence of so many nondefaulting loans, coupled with the inevitable variability in predictor data, means that, even for a defaulting loan, the model is likely to find some nondefaulting loans that it is similar to, by chance. When a balanced sample was used, roughly 50% of the loans were predicted to be in default.

Oversampling and Up/Down Weighting

One criticism of the undersampling method is that it throws away data and is not using all the information at hand. If you have a relatively small data set, and the rarer class contains a few hundred or a few thousand records, then undersampling the dominant class has the risk of throwing out useful information. In this case, instead of downsampling the dominant case, you should oversample (upsample) the rarer class by drawing additional rows with replacement (bootstrapping).

You can achieve a similar effect by weighting the data. Many classification algorithms take a weight argument that will allow you to up/down weight the data. For example, apply a weight vector to the loan data using the `weight` argument to `glm` in *R*:

```
wt <- ifelse(full_train_set$outcome=='default',
             1 / mean(full_train_set$outcome == 'default'), 1)
full_model <- glm(outcome ~ payment_inc_ratio + purpose_ + home_ +
                            emp_len_+ dti + revol_bal + revol_util,
                  data=full_train_set, weight=wt, family='quasibinomial')
pred <- predict(full_model)
mean(pred > 0)
[1] 0.5767208
```

Most `scikit-learn` methods allow specifying weights in the `fit` function using the keyword argument `sample_weight`:

```
default_wt = 1 / np.mean(full_train_set.outcome == 'default')
wt = [default_wt if outcome == 'default' else 1
      for outcome in full_train_set.outcome]

full_model = LogisticRegression(penalty="l2", C=1e42, solver='liblinear')
full_model.fit(X, y, sample_weight=wt)
print('percentage of loans predicted to default (weighting): ',
      100 * np.mean(full_model.predict(X) == 'default'))
```

The weights for loans that default are set to $\frac{1}{p}$, where p is the probability of default. The nondefaulting loans have a weight of 1. The sums of the weights for the default-

5 Due to differences in implementation, results in *Python* differ slightly: 1%, or about 1/18 of the expected number.

ing loans and nondefaulting loans are roughly equal. The mean of the predicted values is now about 58% instead of 0.39%.

Note that weighting provides an alternative to both upsampling the rarer class and downsampling the dominant class.

> **Adapting the Loss Function**
>
> Many classification and regression algorithms optimize a certain criteria or *loss function*. For example, logistic regression attempts to minimize the deviance. In the literature, some propose to modify the loss function in order to avoid the problems caused by a rare class. In practice, this is hard to do: classification algorithms can be complex and difficult to modify. Weighting is an easy way to change the loss function, discounting errors for records with low weights in favor of records with higher weights.

Data Generation

A variation of upsampling via bootstrapping (see "Oversampling and Up/Down Weighting" on page 232) is *data generation* by perturbing existing records to create new records. The intuition behind this idea is that since we observe only a limited set of instances, the algorithm doesn't have a rich set of information to build classification "rules." By creating new records that are similar but not identical to existing records, the algorithm has a chance to learn a more robust set of rules. This notion is similar in spirit to ensemble statistical models such as boosting and bagging (see Chapter 6).

The idea gained traction with the publication of the *SMOTE* algorithm, which stands for "Synthetic Minority Oversampling Technique." The SMOTE algorithm finds a record that is similar to the record being upsampled (see "K-Nearest Neighbors" on page 238) and creates a synthetic record that is a randomly weighted average of the original record and the neighboring record, where the weight is generated separately for each predictor. The number of synthetic oversampled records created depends on the oversampling ratio required to bring the data set into approximate balance with respect to outcome classes.

There are several implementations of SMOTE in *R*. The most comprehensive package for handling unbalanced data is `unbalanced`. It offers a variety of techniques, including a "Racing" algorithm to select the best method. However, the SMOTE algorithm is simple enough that it can be implemented directly in *R* using the `FNN` package.

The *Python* package `imbalanced-learn` implements a variety of methods with an API that is compatible with `scikit-learn`. It provides various methods for over- and undersampling and support for using these techniques with boosting and bagging classifiers.

Cost-Based Classification

In practice, accuracy and AUC are a poor man's way to choose a classification rule. Often, an estimated cost can be assigned to false positives versus false negatives, and it is more appropriate to incorporate these costs to determine the best cutoff when classifying 1s and 0s. For example, suppose the expected cost of a default of a new loan is C and the expected return from a paid-off loan is R. Then the expected return for that loan is:

$$\text{expected return} = P(Y = 0) \times R + P(Y = 1) \times C$$

Instead of simply labeling a loan as default or paid off, or determining the probability of default, it makes more sense to determine if the loan has a positive expected return. Predicted probability of default is an intermediate step, and it must be combined with the loan's total value to determine expected profit, which is the ultimate planning metric of business. For example, a smaller value loan might be passed over in favor of a larger one with a slightly higher predicted default probability.

Exploring the Predictions

A single metric, such as AUC, cannot evaluate all aspects of the suitability of a model for a situation. Figure 5-8 displays the decision rules for four different models fit to the loan data using just two predictor variables: `borrower_score` and `payment_inc_ratio`. The models are linear discriminant analysis (LDA), logistic linear regression, logistic regression fit using a generalized additive model (GAM), and a tree model (see "Tree Models" on page 249). The region to the upper left of the lines corresponds to a predicted default. LDA and logistic linear regression give nearly identical results in this case. The tree model produces the least regular rule, with two steps. Finally, the GAM fit of the logistic regression represents a compromise between the tree model and the linear model.

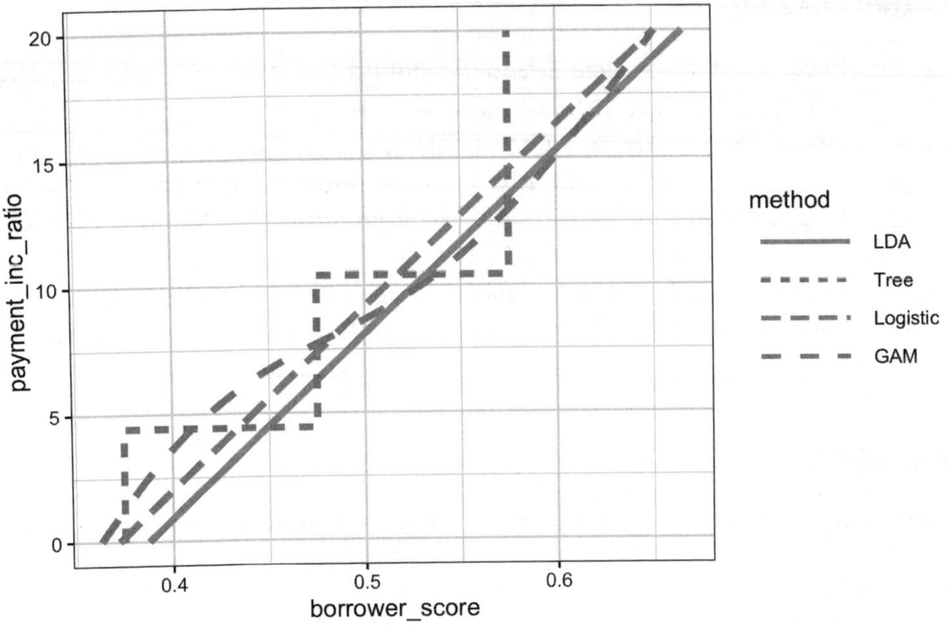

Figure 5-8. Comparison of the classification rules for four different methods

It is not easy to visualize the prediction rules in higher dimensions or, in the case of the GAM and the tree model, even to generate the regions for such rules.

In any case, exploratory analysis of predicted values is always warranted.

Key Ideas

- Highly imbalanced data (i.e., where the interesting outcomes, the 1s, are rare) are problematic for classification algorithms.
- One strategy for working with imbalanced data is to balance the training data via undersampling the abundant case (or oversampling the rare case).
- If using all the 1s still leaves you with too few 1s, you can bootstrap the rare cases, or use SMOTE to create synthetic data similar to existing rare cases.
- Imbalanced data usually indicates that correctly classifying one class (the 1s) has higher value, and that value ratio should be built into the assessment metric.

Further Reading

- Tom Fawcett, author of *Data Science for Business*, has a good article on imbalanced classes (*https://oreil.ly/us2rd*).
- For more on SMOTE, see Nitesh V. Chawla, Kevin W. Bowyer, Lawrence O. Hall, and W. Philip Kegelmeyer, "SMOTE: Synthetic Minority Over-sampling Technique," (*https://oreil.ly/bwaIQ*) *Journal of Artificial Intelligence Research* 16 (2002): 321–357.
- Also see the Analytics Vidhya Content Team's "Practical Guide to Deal with Imbalanced Classification Problems in *R*," (*https://oreil.ly/gZUDs*) March 28, 2016.

Summary

Classification, the process of predicting which of two or more categories a record belongs to, is a fundamental tool of predictive analytics. Will a loan default (yes or no)? Will it prepay? Will a web visitor click on a link? Will they purchase something? Is an insurance claim fraudulent? Often in classification problems, one class is of primary interest (e.g., the fraudulent insurance claim), and in binary classification, this class is designated as a 1, with the other, more prevalent class being a 0. Often, a key part of the process is estimating a *propensity score*, a probability of belonging to the class of interest. A common scenario is one in which the class of interest is relatively rare. When evaluating a classifier, there are a variety of model assessment metrics that go beyond simple accuracy; these are important in the rare-class situation, when classifying all records as 0s can yield high accuracy.

CHAPTER 6

Statistical Machine Learning

Recent advances in statistics have been devoted to developing more powerful automated techniques for predictive modeling—both regression and classification. These methods, like those discussed in the previous chapter, are *supervised methods*—they are trained on data where outcomes are known and learn to predict outcomes in new data. They fall under the umbrella of *statistical machine learning* and are distinguished from classical statistical methods in that they are data-driven and do not seek to impose linear or other overall structure on the data. The *K*-Nearest Neighbors method, for example, is quite simple: classify a record in accordance with how similar records are classified. The most successful and widely used techniques are based on *ensemble learning* applied to *decision trees*. The basic idea of ensemble learning is to use many models to form a prediction, as opposed to using just a single model. Decision trees are a flexible and automatic technique to learn rules about the relationships between predictor variables and outcome variables. It turns out that the combination of ensemble learning with decision trees leads to some of the best performing off-the-shelf predictive modeling techniques.

The development of many of the techniques in statistical machine learning can be traced back to the statisticians Leo Breiman (see Figure 6-1) at the University of California at Berkeley and Jerry Friedman at Stanford University. Their work, along with that of other researchers at Berkeley and Stanford, started with the development of tree models in 1984. The subsequent development of ensemble methods of bagging and boosting in the 1990s established the foundation of statistical machine learning.

Figure 6-1. Leo Breiman, who was a professor of statistics at UC Berkeley, was at the forefront of the development of many techniques in a data scientist's toolkit today

> **Machine Learning Versus Statistics**
>
> In the context of predictive modeling, what is the difference between machine learning and statistics? There is not a bright line dividing the two disciplines. Machine learning tends to be focused more on developing efficient algorithms that scale to large data in order to optimize the predictive model. Statistics generally pays more attention to the probabilistic theory and underlying structure of the model. Bagging, and the random forest (see "Bagging and the Random Forest" on page 259), grew up firmly in the statistics camp. Boosting (see "Boosting" on page 270), on the other hand, has been developed in both disciplines but receives more attention on the machine learning side of the divide. Regardless of the history, the promise of boosting ensures that it will thrive as a technique in both statistics and machine learning.

K-Nearest Neighbors

The idea behind *K*-Nearest Neighbors (KNN) is very simple.[1] For each record to be classified or predicted:

1. Find *K* records that have similar features (i.e., similar predictor values).
2. For classification, find out what the majority class is among those similar records and assign that class to the new record.
3. For prediction (also called *KNN regression*), find the average among those similar records, and predict that average for the new record.

1 This and subsequent sections in this chapter © 2020 Datastats, LLC, Peter Bruce, Andrew Bruce, and Peter Gedeck; used with permission.

Key Terms for K-Nearest Neighbors

Neighbor
A record that has similar predictor values to another record.

Distance metrics
Measures that sum up in a single number how far one record is from another.

Standardization
Subtract the mean and divide by the standard deviation.

Synonym
Normalization

z-score
The value that results after standardization.

K
The number of neighbors considered in the nearest neighbor calculation.

KNN is one of the simpler prediction/classification techniques: there is no model to be fit (as in regression). This doesn't mean that using KNN is an automatic procedure. The prediction results depend on how the features are scaled, how similarity is measured, and how big *K* is set. Also, all predictors must be in numeric form. We will illustrate how to use the KNN method with a classification example.

A Small Example: Predicting Loan Default

Table 6-1 shows a few records of personal loan data from LendingClub. LendingClub is a leader in peer-to-peer lending in which pools of investors make personal loans to individuals. The goal of an analysis would be to predict the outcome of a new potential loan: paid off versus default.

Table 6-1. A few records and columns for LendingClub loan data

Outcome	Loan amount	Income	Purpose	Years employed	Home ownership	State
Paid off	10000	79100	debt_consolidation	11	MORTGAGE	NV
Paid off	9600	48000	moving	5	MORTGAGE	TN
Paid off	18800	120036	debt_consolidation	11	MORTGAGE	MD
Default	15250	232000	small_business	9	MORTGAGE	CA
Paid off	17050	35000	debt_consolidation	4	RENT	MD
Paid off	5500	43000	debt_consolidation	4	RENT	KS

Consider a very simple model with just two predictor variables: dti, which is the ratio of debt payments (excluding mortgage) to income, and payment_inc_ratio, which is the ratio of the loan payment to income. Both ratios are multiplied by 100. Using a small set of 200 loans, loan200, with known binary outcomes (default or no-default, specified in the predictor outcome200), and with *K* set to 20, the KNN estimate for a new loan to be predicted, newloan, with dti=22.5 and payment_inc_ratio=9 can be calculated in *R* as follows:[2]

```
newloan <- loan200[1, 2:3, drop=FALSE]
knn_pred <- knn(train=loan200[-1, 2:3], test=newloan, cl=loan200[-1, 1], k=20)
knn_pred == 'paid off'
[1] TRUE
```

The KNN prediction is for the loan to default.

While *R* has a native knn function, the contributed *R* package FNN, for Fast Nearest Neighbor (*https://oreil.ly/RMQFG*), scales more effectively to big data and provides more flexibility.

The scikit-learn package provides a fast and efficient implementation of KNN in *Python*:

```
predictors = ['payment_inc_ratio', 'dti']
outcome = 'outcome'

newloan = loan200.loc[0:0, predictors]
X = loan200.loc[1:, predictors]
y = loan200.loc[1:, outcome]

knn = KNeighborsClassifier(n_neighbors=20)
knn.fit(X, y)
knn.predict(newloan)
```

Figure 6-2 gives a visual display of this example. The new loan to be predicted is the cross in the middle. The squares (paid off) and circles (default) are the training data. The large black circle shows the boundary of the nearest 20 points. In this case, 9 defaulted loans lie within the circle, as compared with 11 paid-off loans. Hence the predicted outcome of the loan is paid off. Note that if we consider only three nearest neighbors, the prediction would be that the loan defaults.

2 For this example, we take the first row in the loan200 data set as the newloan and exclude it from the data set for training.

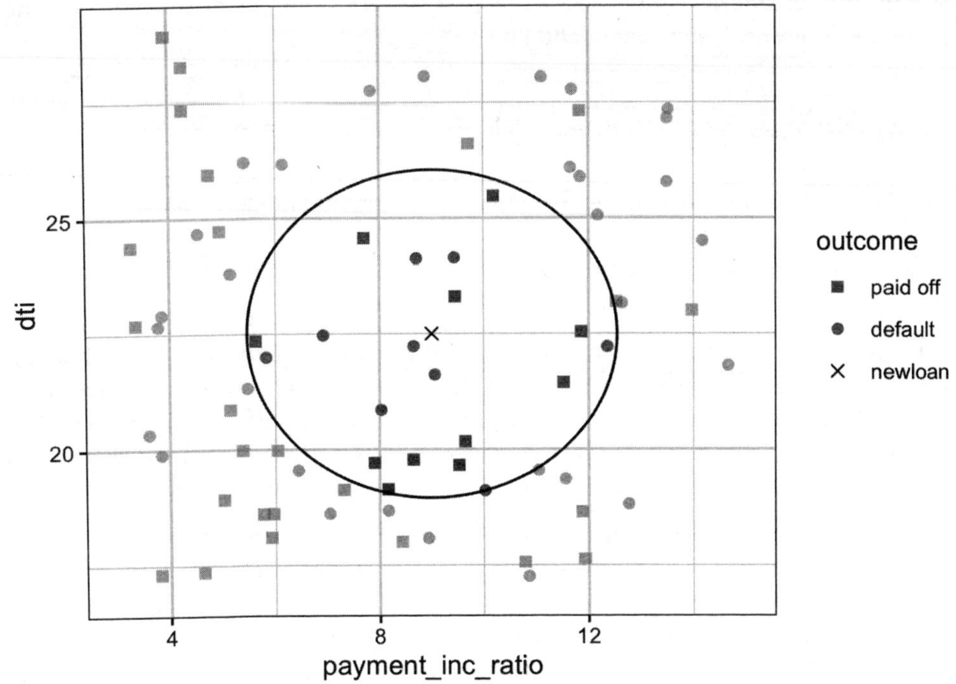

Figure 6-2. KNN prediction of loan default using two variables: debt-to-income ratio and loan-payment-to-income ratio

While the output of KNN for classification is typically a binary decision, such as default or paid off in the loan data, KNN routines usually offer the opportunity to output a probability (propensity) between 0 and 1. The probability is based on the fraction of one class in the *K* nearest neighbors. In the preceding example, this probability of default would have been estimated at $\frac{9}{20}$, or 0.45. Using a probability score lets you use classification rules other than simple majority votes (probability of 0.5). This is especially important in problems with imbalanced classes; see "Strategies for Imbalanced Data" on page 230. For example, if the goal is to identify members of a rare class, the cutoff would typically be set below 50%. One common approach is to set the cutoff at the probability of the rare event.

Distance Metrics

Similarity (nearness) is determined using a *distance metric*, which is a function that measures how far two records ($x_1, x_2, \ldots, x_p$) and ($u_1, u_2, \ldots, u_p$) are from one another. The most popular distance metric between two vectors is *Euclidean distance*. To measure the Euclidean distance between two vectors, subtract one from the other, square the differences, sum them, and take the square root:

$$\sqrt{(x_1 - u_1)^2 + (x_2 - u_2)^2 + \cdots + \left(x_p - u_p\right)^2}.$$

Another common distance metric for numeric data is *Manhattan distance*:

$$|x_1 - u_1| + |x_2 - u_2| + \cdots + |x_p - u_p|$$

Euclidean distance corresponds to the straight-line distance between two points (e.g., as the crow flies). Manhattan distance is the distance between two points traversed in a single direction at a time (e.g., traveling along rectangular city blocks). For this reason, Manhattan distance is a useful approximation if similarity is defined as point-to-point travel time.

In measuring distance between two vectors, variables (features) that are measured with comparatively large scale will dominate the measure. For example, for the loan data, the distance would be almost solely a function of the income and loan amount variables, which are measured in tens or hundreds of thousands. Ratio variables would count for practically nothing in comparison. We address this problem by standardizing the data; see "Standardization (Normalization, z-Scores)" on page 243.

Other Distance Metrics

There are numerous other metrics for measuring distance between vectors. For numeric data, *Mahalanobis distance* is attractive since it accounts for the correlation between two variables. This is useful since if two variables are highly correlated, Mahalanobis will essentially treat these as a single variable in terms of distance. Euclidean and Manhattan distance do not account for the correlation, effectively placing greater weight on the attribute that underlies those features. Mahalanobis distance is the Euclidean distance between the principal components (see "Principal Components Analysis" on page 284). The downside of using Mahalanobis distance is increased computational effort and complexity; it is computed using the *covariance matrix* (see "Covariance Matrix" on page 202).

One Hot Encoder

The loan data in Table 6-1 includes several factor (string) variables. Most statistical and machine learning models require this type of variable to be converted to a series of binary dummy variables conveying the same information, as in Table 6-2. Instead of a single variable denoting the home occupant status as "owns with a mortgage," "owns with no mortgage," "rents," or "other," we end up with four binary variables. The first would be "owns with a mortgage—Y/N," the second would be "owns with no mortgage—Y/N," and so on. This one predictor, home occupant status, thus yields a vector with one 1 and three 0s that can be used in statistical and machine learning algorithms. The phrase *one hot encoding* comes from digital circuit terminology, where it describes circuit settings in which only one bit is allowed to be positive (hot).

Table 6-2. Representing home ownership factor data in Table 6-1 as a numeric dummy variable

OWNS_WITH_MORTGAGE	OWNS_WITHOUT_MORTGAGE	OTHER	RENT
1	0	0	0
1	0	0	0
1	0	0	0
1	0	0	0
0	0	0	1
0	0	0	1

In linear and logistic regression, one hot encoding causes problems with multicollinearity; see "Multicollinearity" on page 172. In such cases, one dummy is omitted (its value can be inferred from the other values). This is not an issue with KNN and other methods discussed in this book.

Standardization (Normalization, z-Scores)

In measurement, we are often not so much interested in "how much" but in "how different from the average." Standardization, also called *normalization*, puts all variables on similar scales by subtracting the mean and dividing by the standard deviation; in this way, we ensure that a variable does not overly influence a model simply due to the scale of its original measurement:

$$z = \frac{x - \bar{x}}{s}$$

The result of this transformation is commonly referred to as a *z-score*. Measurements are then stated in terms of "standard deviations away from the mean."

Normalization in this statistical context is not to be confused with *database normalization*, which is the removal of redundant data and the verification of data dependencies.

For KNN and a few other procedures (e.g., principal components analysis and clustering), it is essential to consider standardizing the data prior to applying the procedure. To illustrate this idea, KNN is applied to the loan data using `dti` and `payment_inc_ratio` (see "A Small Example: Predicting Loan Default" on page 239) plus two other variables: `revol_bal`, the total revolving credit available to the applicant in dollars, and `revol_util`, the percent of the credit being used. The new record to be predicted is shown here:

```
newloan
  payment_inc_ratio dti revol_bal revol_util
1            2.3932   1      1687        9.4
```

The magnitude of `revol_bal`, which is in dollars, is much bigger than that of the other variables. The `knn` function returns the index of the nearest neighbors as an attribute `nn.index`, and this can be used to show the top-five closest rows in `loan_df`:

```
loan_df <- model.matrix(~ -1 + payment_inc_ratio + dti + revol_bal +
                          revol_util, data=loan_data)
newloan <- loan_df[1, , drop=FALSE]
loan_df <- loan_df[-1,]
outcome <- loan_data[-1, 1]
knn_pred <- knn(train=loan_df, test=newloan, cl=outcome, k=5)
loan_df[attr(knn_pred, "nn.index"),]

        payment_inc_ratio  dti revol_bal revol_util
35537             1.47212 1.46      1686       10.0
33652             3.38178 6.37      1688        8.4
25864             2.36303 1.39      1691        3.5
42954             1.28160 7.14      1684        3.9
43600             4.12244 8.98      1684        7.2
```

Following the model fit, we can use the `kneighbors` method to identify the five closest rows in the training set with `scikit-learn`:

```
predictors = ['payment_inc_ratio', 'dti', 'revol_bal', 'revol_util']
outcome = 'outcome'

newloan = loan_data.loc[0:0, predictors]
X = loan_data.loc[1:, predictors]
y = loan_data.loc[1:, outcome]

knn = KNeighborsClassifier(n_neighbors=5)
knn.fit(X, y)

nbrs = knn.kneighbors(newloan)
X.iloc[nbrs[1][0], :]
```

The value of `revol_bal` in these neighbors is very close to its value in the new record, but the other predictor variables are all over the map and essentially play no role in determining neighbors.

Compare this to KNN applied to the standardized data using the *R* function `scale`, which computes the *z*-score for each variable:

```
loan_df <- model.matrix(~ -1 + payment_inc_ratio + dti + revol_bal +
                          revol_util, data=loan_data)
loan_std <- scale(loan_df)
newloan_std <- loan_std[1, , drop=FALSE]
loan_std <- loan_std[-1,]
loan_df <- loan_df[-1,]  ❶
outcome <- loan_data[-1, 1]
knn_pred <- knn(train=loan_std, test=newloan_std, cl=outcome, k=5)
loan_df[attr(knn_pred, "nn.index"),]
        payment_inc_ratio   dti  revol_bal  revol_util
2081              2.61091  1.03       1218         9.7
1439              2.34343  0.51        278         9.9
30216             2.71200  1.34       1075         8.5
28543             2.39760  0.74       2917         7.4
44738             2.34309  1.37        488         7.2
```

❶ We need to remove the first row from `loan_df` as well, so that the row numbers correspond to each other.

The `sklearn.preprocessing.StandardScaler` method is first trained with the predictors and is subsequently used to transform the data set prior to training the KNN model:

```
newloan = loan_data.loc[0:0, predictors]
X = loan_data.loc[1:, predictors]
y = loan_data.loc[1:, outcome]

scaler = preprocessing.StandardScaler()
scaler.fit(X * 1.0)

X_std = scaler.transform(X * 1.0)
newloan_std = scaler.transform(newloan * 1.0)

knn = KNeighborsClassifier(n_neighbors=5)
knn.fit(X_std, y)

nbrs = knn.kneighbors(newloan_std)
X.iloc[nbrs[1][0], :]
```

The five nearest neighbors are much more alike in all the variables, providing a more sensible result. Note that the results are displayed on the original scale, but KNN was applied to the scaled data and the new loan to be predicted.

Using the *z*-score is just one way to rescale variables. Instead of the mean, a more robust estimate of location could be used, such as the median. Likewise, a different estimate of scale such as the interquartile range could be used instead of the standard deviation. Sometimes, variables are "squashed" into the 0–1 range. It's also important to realize that scaling each variable to have unit variance is somewhat arbitrary. This implies that each variable is thought to have the same importance in predictive power. If you have subjective knowledge that some variables are more important than others, then these could be scaled up. For example, with the loan data, it is reasonable to expect that the payment-to-income ratio is very important.

Normalization (standardization) does not change the distributional shape of the data; it does not make it normally shaped if it was not already normally shaped (see "Normal Distribution" on page 69).

Choosing K

The choice of *K* is very important to the performance of KNN. The simplest choice is to set $K = 1$, known as the 1-nearest neighbor classifier. The prediction is intuitive: it is based on finding the data record in the training set most similar to the new record to be predicted. Setting $K = 1$ is rarely the best choice; you'll almost always obtain superior performance by using $K > 1$-nearest neighbors.

Generally speaking, if *K* is too low, we may be overfitting: including the noise in the data. Higher values of *K* provide smoothing that reduces the risk of overfitting in the training data. On the other hand, if *K* is too high, we may oversmooth the data and miss out on KNN's ability to capture the local structure in the data, one of its main advantages.

The *K* that best balances between overfitting and oversmoothing is typically determined by accuracy metrics and, in particular, accuracy with holdout or validation data. There is no general rule about the best *K*—it depends greatly on the nature of the data. For highly structured data with little noise, smaller values of *K* work best. Borrowing a term from the signal processing community, this type of data is sometimes referred to as having a high *signal-to-noise ratio* (*SNR*). Examples of data with a typically high SNR are data sets for handwriting and speech recognition. For noisy data with less structure (data with a low SNR), such as the loan data, larger values of *K* are appropriate. Typically, values of *K* fall in the range 1 to 20. Often, an odd number is chosen to avoid ties.

Bias-Variance Trade-off

The tension between oversmoothing and overfitting is an instance of the *bias-variance trade-off*, a ubiquitous problem in statistical model fitting. Variance refers to the modeling error that occurs because of the choice of training data; that is, if you were to choose a different set of training data, the resulting model would be different. Bias refers to the modeling error that occurs because you have not properly identified the underlying real-world scenario; this error would not disappear if you simply added more training data. When a flexible model is overfit, the variance increases. You can reduce this by using a simpler model, but the bias may increase due to the loss of flexibility in modeling the real underlying situation. A general approach to handling this trade-off is through *cross-validation*. See "Cross-Validation" on page 155 for more details.

KNN as a Feature Engine

KNN gained its popularity due to its simplicity and intuitive nature. In terms of performance, KNN by itself is usually not competitive with more sophisticated classification techniques. In practical model fitting, however, KNN can be used to add "local knowledge" in a staged process with other classification techniques:

1. KNN is run on the data, and for each record, a classification (or quasi-probability of a class) is derived.
2. That result is added as a new feature to the record, and another classification method is then run on the data. The original predictor variables are thus used twice.

At first you might wonder whether this process, since it uses some predictors twice, causes a problem with multicollinearity (see "Multicollinearity" on page 172). This is not an issue, since the information being incorporated into the second-stage model is highly local, derived only from a few nearby records, and is therefore additional information and not redundant.

You can think of this staged use of KNN as a form of ensemble learning, in which multiple predictive modeling methods are used in conjunction with one another. It can also be considered as a form of feature engineering in which the aim is to derive features (predictor variables) that have predictive power. Often this involves some manual review of the data; KNN gives a fairly automatic way to do this.

For example, consider the King County housing data. In pricing a home for sale, a realtor will base the price on similar homes recently sold, known as "comps." In essence, realtors are doing a manual version of KNN: by looking at the sale prices of similar homes, they can estimate what a home will sell for. We can create a new feature for a statistical model to mimic the real estate professional by applying KNN to recent sales. The predicted value is the sales price, and the existing predictor variables could include location, total square feet, type of structure, lot size, and number of bedrooms and bathrooms. The new predictor variable (feature) that we add via KNN is the KNN predictor for each record (analogous to the realtors' comps). Since we are predicting a numerical value, the average of the *K*-Nearest Neighbors is used instead of a majority vote (known as *KNN regression*).

Similarly, for the loan data, we can create features that represent different aspects of the loan process. For example, the following *R* code would build a feature that represents a borrower's creditworthiness:

```
borrow_df <- model.matrix(~ -1 + dti + revol_bal + revol_util + open_acc +
                          delinq_2yrs_zero + pub_rec_zero, data=loan_data)
borrow_knn <- knn(borrow_df, test=borrow_df, cl=loan_data[, 'outcome'],
              prob=TRUE, k=20)
prob <- attr(borrow_knn, "prob")
borrow_feature <- ifelse(borrow_knn == 'default', prob, 1 - prob)
summary(borrow_feature)
   Min. 1st Qu.  Median    Mean 3rd Qu.    Max.
  0.000   0.400   0.500   0.501   0.600   0.950
```

With `scikit-learn`, we use the `predict_proba` method of the trained model to get the probabilities:

```
predictors = ['dti', 'revol_bal', 'revol_util', 'open_acc',
              'delinq_2yrs_zero', 'pub_rec_zero']
outcome = 'outcome'

X = loan_data[predictors]
y = loan_data[outcome]

knn = KNeighborsClassifier(n_neighbors=20)
knn.fit(X, y)

loan_data['borrower_score'] = knn.predict_proba(X)[:, 1]
loan_data['borrower_score'].describe()
```

The result is a feature that predicts the likelihood a borrower will default based on his credit history.

Key Ideas

- *K*-Nearest Neighbors (KNN) classifies a record by assigning it to the class that similar records belong to.
- Similarity (distance) is determined by Euclidian distance or other related metrics.
- The number of nearest neighbors to compare a record to, *K*, is determined by how well the algorithm performs on training data, using different values for *K*.
- Typically, the predictor variables are standardized so that variables of large scale do not dominate the distance metric.
- KNN is often used as a first stage in predictive modeling, and the predicted value is added back into the data as a *predictor* for second-stage (non-KNN) modeling.

Tree Models

Tree models, also called *Classification and Regression Trees* (*CART*),[3] *decision trees*, or just *trees*, are an effective and popular classification (and regression) method initially developed by Leo Breiman and others in 1984. Tree models, and their more powerful descendants *random forests* and *boosted trees* (see "Bagging and the Random Forest" on page 259 and "Boosting" on page 270), form the basis for the most widely used and powerful predictive modeling tools in data science for regression and classification.

Key Terms for Trees

Recursive partitioning
Repeatedly dividing and subdividing the data with the goal of making the outcomes in each final subdivision as homogeneous as possible.

Split value
A predictor value that divides the records into those where that predictor is less than the split value, and those where it is more.

Node
In the decision tree, or in the set of corresponding branching rules, a node is the graphical or rule representation of a split value.

3 The term CART is a registered trademark of Salford Systems related to their specific implementation of tree models.

Leaf
: The end of a set of if-then rules, or branches of a tree—the rules that bring you to that leaf provide one of the classification rules for any record in a tree.

Loss
: The number of misclassifications at a stage in the splitting process; the more losses, the more impurity.

Impurity
: The extent to which a mix of classes is found in a subpartition of the data (the more mixed, the more impure).

  Synonym
  : Heterogeneity

  Antonyms
  : Homogeneity, purity

Pruning
: The process of taking a fully grown tree and progressively cutting its branches back to reduce overfitting.

A tree model is a set of "if-then-else" rules that are easy to understand and to implement. In contrast to linear and logistic regression, trees have the ability to discover hidden patterns corresponding to complex interactions in the data. However, unlike KNN or naive Bayes, simple tree models can be expressed in terms of predictor relationships that are easily interpretable.

Decision Trees in Operations Research

The term *decision trees* has a different (and older) meaning in decision science and operations research, where it refers to a human decision analysis process. In this meaning, decision points, possible outcomes, and their estimated probabilities are laid out in a branching diagram, and the decision path with the maximum expected value is chosen.

A Simple Example

The two main packages to fit tree models in *R* are `rpart` and `tree`. Using the `rpart` package, a model is fit to a sample of 3,000 records of the loan data using the variables `payment_inc_ratio` and `borrower_score` (see "K-Nearest Neighbors" on page 238 for a description of the data):

```
library(rpart)
loan_tree <- rpart(outcome ~ borrower_score + payment_inc_ratio,
                   data=loan3000, control=rpart.control(cp=0.005))
```

```
plot(loan_tree, uniform=TRUE, margin=0.05)
text(loan_tree)
```

The `sklearn.tree.DecisionTreeClassifier` provides an implementation of a decision tree. The `dmba` package provides a convenience function to create a visualization inside a Jupyter notebook:

```
predictors = ['borrower_score', 'payment_inc_ratio']
outcome = 'outcome'

X = loan3000[predictors]
y = loan3000[outcome]

loan_tree = DecisionTreeClassifier(random_state=1, criterion='entropy',
                                   min_impurity_decrease=0.003)
loan_tree.fit(X, y)
plotDecisionTree(loan_tree, feature_names=predictors,
                 class_names=loan_tree.classes_)
```

The resulting tree is shown in Figure 6-3. Due to the different implementations, you will find that the results from *R* and *Python* are not identical; this is expected. These classification rules are determined by traversing through a hierarchical tree, starting at the root and moving left if the node is true and right if not, until a leaf is reached.

Typically, the tree is plotted upside-down, so the root is at the top and the leaves are at the bottom. For example, if we get a loan with `borrower_score` of 0.6 and a `payment_inc_ratio` of 8.0, we end up at the leftmost leaf and predict the loan will be paid off.

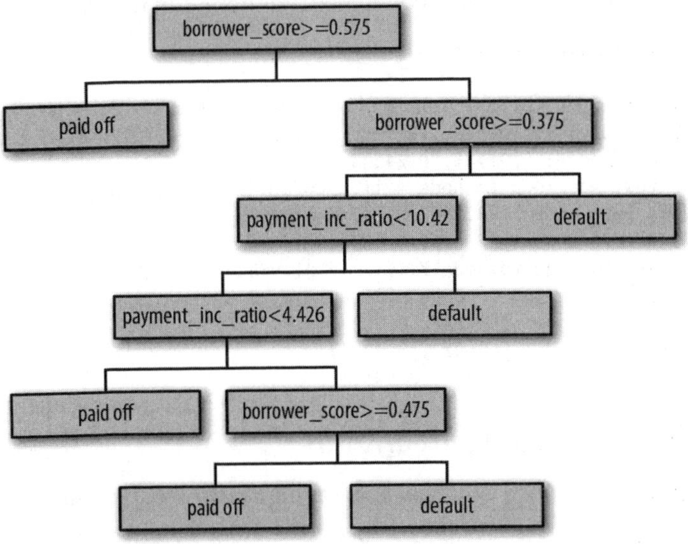

Figure 6-3. The rules for a simple tree model fit to the loan data

A nicely printed version of the tree is also easily produced in *R*:

```
loan_tree
n= 3000

node), split, n, loss, yval, (yprob)
    * denotes terminal node

1) root 3000 1445 paid off (0.5183333 0.4816667)
  2) borrower_score>=0.575 878  261 paid off (0.7027335 0.2972665) *
  3) borrower_score< 0.575 2122  938 default (0.4420358 0.5579642)
    6) borrower_score>=0.375 1639  802 default (0.4893228 0.5106772)
      12) payment_inc_ratio< 10.42265 1157  547 paid off (0.5272256 0.4727744)
        24) payment_inc_ratio< 4.42601 334  139 paid off (0.5838323 0.4161677) *
        25) payment_inc_ratio>=4.42601 823  408 paid off (0.5042527 0.4957473)
          50) borrower_score>=0.475 418  190 paid off (0.5454545 0.4545455) *
          51) borrower_score< 0.475 405  187 default (0.4617284 0.5382716) *
      13) payment_inc_ratio>=10.42265 482  192 default (0.3983402 0.6016598) *
    7) borrower_score< 0.375 483  136 default (0.2815735 0.7184265) *
```

The depth of the tree is shown by the indent. Each node corresponds to a provisional classification determined by the prevalent outcome in that partition. The "loss" is the number of misclassifications yielded by the provisional classification in a partition. For example, in node 2, there were 261 misclassifications out of a total of 878 total records. The values in the parentheses correspond to the proportion of records that are paid off or in default, respectively. For example, in node 13, which predicts default, over 60 percent of the records are loans that are in default.

The `scikit-learn` documentation describes how to create a text representation of a decision tree model. We included a convenience function in our `dmba` package:

```
print(textDecisionTree(loan_tree))
--
node=0 test node: go to node 1 if 0 <= 0.5750000178813934 else to node 6
  node=1 test node: go to node 2 if 0 <= 0.32500000298023224 else to node 3
    node=2 leaf node: [[0.785, 0.215]]
    node=3 test node: go to node 4 if 1 <= 10.42264986038208 else to node 5
      node=4 leaf node: [[0.488, 0.512]]
      node=5 leaf node: [[0.613, 0.387]]
  node=6 test node: go to node 7 if 1 <= 9.19082498550415 else to node 10
    node=7 test node: go to node 8 if 0 <= 0.7249999940395355 else to node 9
      node=8 leaf node: [[0.247, 0.753]]
      node=9 leaf node: [[0.073, 0.927]]
    node=10 leaf node: [[0.457, 0.543]]
```

The Recursive Partitioning Algorithm

The algorithm to construct a decision tree, called *recursive partitioning*, is straightforward and intuitive. The data is repeatedly partitioned using predictor values that do the best job of separating the data into relatively homogeneous partitions. Figure 6-4 shows the partitions created for the tree in Figure 6-3. The first rule, depicted by rule 1, is `borrower_score >= 0.575` and segments the right portion of the plot. The second rule is `borrower_score < 0.375` and segments the left portion.

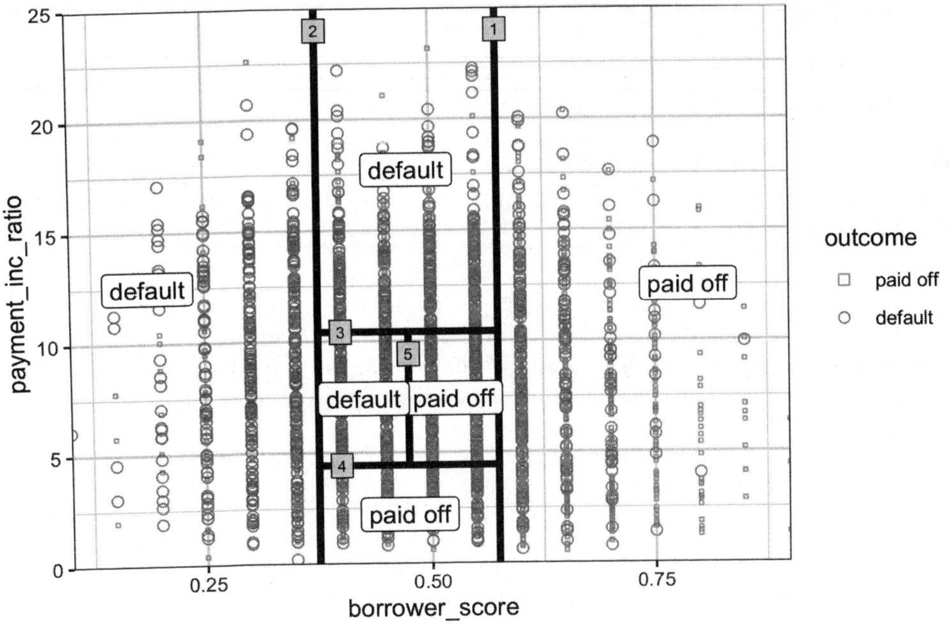

Figure 6-4. The first three rules for a simple tree model fit to the loan data

Suppose we have a response variable Y and a set of P predictor variables X_j for $j = 1, \cdots, P$. For a partition A of records, recursive partitioning will find the best way to partition A into two subpartitions:

1. For each predictor variable X_j:
   a. For each value s_j of X_j:
      i. Split the records in A with X_j values $< s_j$ as one partition, and the remaining records where $X_j \geq s_j$ as another partition.
      ii. Measure the homogeneity of classes within each subpartition of A.
   b. Select the value of s_j that produces maximum within-partition homogeneity of class.
2. Select the variable X_j and the split value s_j that produces maximum within-partition homogeneity of class.

Now comes the recursive part:

1. Initialize A with the entire data set.
2. Apply the partitioning algorithm to split A into two subpartitions, A_1 and A_2.
3. Repeat step 2 on subpartitions A_1 and A_2.
4. The algorithm terminates when no further partition can be made that sufficiently improves the homogeneity of the partitions.

The end result is a partitioning of the data, as in Figure 6-4, except in P-dimensions, with each partition predicting an outcome of 0 or 1 depending on the majority vote of the response in that partition.

> In addition to a binary 0/1 prediction, tree models can produce a probability estimate based on the number of 0s and 1s in the partition. The estimate is simply the sum of 0s or 1s in the partition divided by the number of observations in the partition:
>
> $$\text{Prob}(Y = 1) = \frac{\text{Number of 1s in the partition}}{\text{Size of the partition}}$$
>
> The estimated $\text{Prob}(Y = 1)$ can then be converted to a binary decision; for example, set the estimate to 1 if $\text{Prob}(Y = 1) > 0.5$.

Measuring Homogeneity or Impurity

Tree models recursively create partitions (sets of records), A, that predict an outcome of $Y = 0$ or $Y = 1$. You can see from the preceding algorithm that we need a way to measure homogeneity, also called *class purity*, within a partition. Or equivalently, we need to measure the impurity of a partition. The accuracy of the predictions is the proportion p of misclassified records within that partition, which ranges from 0 (perfect) to 0.5 (purely random guessing).

It turns out that accuracy is not a good measure for impurity. Instead, two common measures for impurity are the *Gini impurity* and *entropy* of *information*. While these (and other) impurity measures apply to classification problems with more than two classes, we focus on the binary case. The Gini impurity for a set of records A is:

$$I(A) = p(1 - p)$$

The entropy measure is given by:

$$I(A) = -p \log_2(p) - (1 - p) \log_2(1 - p)$$

Figure 6-5 shows that Gini impurity (rescaled) and entropy measures are similar, with entropy giving higher impurity scores for moderate and high accuracy rates.

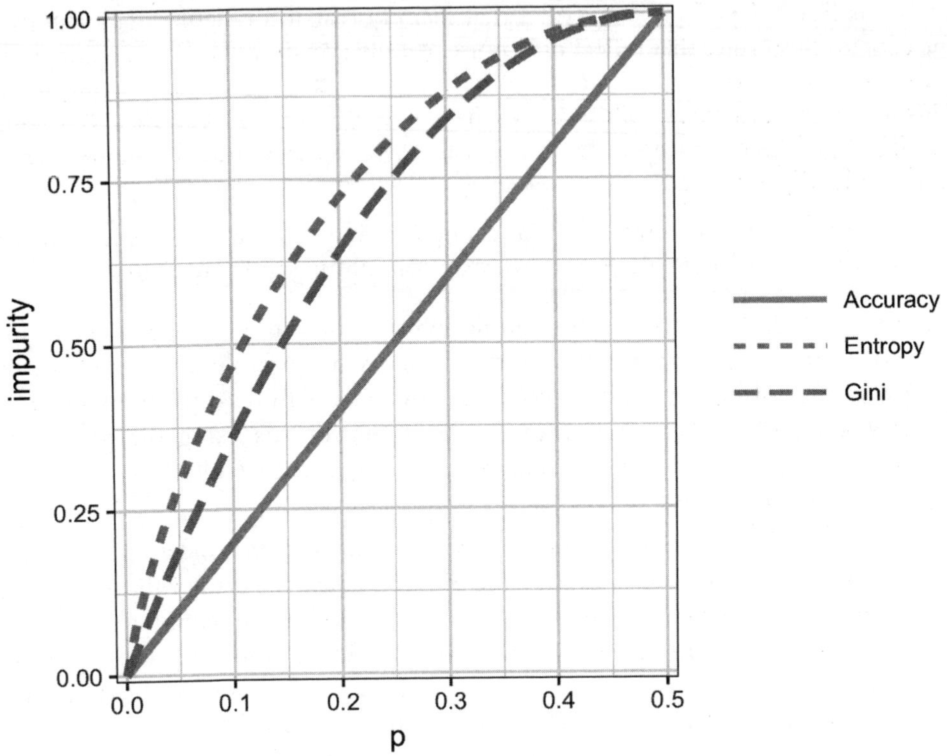

Figure 6-5. Gini impurity and entropy measures

Gini Coefficient

Gini impurity is not to be confused with the *Gini coefficient*. They represent similar concepts, but the Gini coefficient is limited to the binary classification problem and is related to the AUC metric (see "AUC" on page 226).

The impurity metric is used in the splitting algorithm described earlier. For each proposed partition of the data, impurity is measured for each of the partitions that result from the split. A weighted average is then calculated, and whichever partition (at each stage) yields the lowest weighted average is selected.

Stopping the Tree from Growing

As the tree grows bigger, the splitting rules become more detailed, and the tree gradually shifts from identifying "big" rules that identify real and reliable relationships in the data to "tiny" rules that reflect only noise. A fully grown tree results in completely pure leaves and, hence, 100% accuracy in classifying the data that it is trained on. This accuracy is, of course, illusory—we have overfit (see "Bias-Variance Trade-off" on page 247) the data, fitting the noise in the training data, not the signal that we want to identify in new data.

We need some way to determine when to stop growing a tree at a stage that will generalize to new data. There are various ways to stop splitting in *R* and *Python*:

- Avoid splitting a partition if a resulting subpartition is too small, or if a terminal leaf is too small. In `rpart` (*R*), these constraints are controlled separately by the parameters `minsplit` and `minbucket`, respectively, with defaults of `20` and `7`. In *Python*'s `DecisionTreeClassifier`, we can control this using the parameters `min_samples_split` (default 2) and `min_samples_leaf` (default `1`).
- Don't split a partition if the new partition does not "significantly" reduce the impurity. In `rpart`, this is controlled by the *complexity parameter* `cp`, which is a measure of how complex a tree is—the more complex, the greater the value of `cp`. In practice, `cp` is used to limit tree growth by attaching a penalty to additional complexity (splits) in a tree. `DecisionTreeClassifier` (*Python*) has the parameter `min_impurity_decrease`, which limits splitting based on a weighted impurity decrease value. Here, smaller values will lead to more complex trees.

These methods involve arbitrary rules and can be useful for exploratory work, but we can't easily determine optimum values (i.e., values that maximize predictive accuracy with new data). We need to combine cross-validation with either systematically changing the model parameters or modifying the tree through pruning.

Controlling tree complexity in *R*

With the complexity parameter, `cp`, we can estimate what size tree will perform best with new data. If `cp` is too small, then the tree will overfit the data, fitting noise and not signal. On the other hand, if `cp` is too large, then the tree will be too small and have little predictive power. The default in `rpart` is 0.01, although for larger data sets, you are likely to find this is too large. In the previous example, `cp` was set to `0.005` since the default led to a tree with a single split. In exploratory analysis, it is sufficient to simply try a few values.

Determining the optimum `cp` is an instance of the bias-variance trade-off. The most common way to estimate a good value of `cp` is via cross-validation (see "Cross-Validation" on page 155):

1. Partition the data into training and validation (holdout) sets.
2. Grow the tree with the training data.
3. Prune it successively, step by step, recording `cp` (using the *training* data) at each step.
4. Note the `cp` that corresponds to the minimum error (loss) on the *validation* data.
5. Repartition the data into training and validation, and repeat the growing, pruning, and `cp` recording process.
6. Do this again and again, and average the `cp`s that reflect minimum error for each tree.
7. Go back to the original data, or future data, and grow a tree, stopping at this optimum `cp` value.

In `rpart`, you can use the argument `cptable` to produce a table of the `cp` values and their associated cross-validation error (`xerror` in *R*), from which you can determine the `cp` value that has the lowest cross-validation error.

Controlling tree complexity in *Python*

Neither the complexity parameter nor pruning is available in `scikit-learn`'s decision tree implementation. The solution is to use grid search over combinations of different parameter values. For example, we can vary `max_depth` in the range 5 to 30 and `min_samples_split` between 20 and 100. The `GridSearchCV` method in `scikit-learn` is a convenient way to combine the exhaustive search through all combinations with cross-validation. An optimal parameter set is then selected using the cross-validated model performance.

Predicting a Continuous Value

Predicting a continuous value (also termed *regression*) with a tree follows the same logic and procedure, except that impurity is measured by squared deviations from the mean (squared errors) in each subpartition, and predictive performance is judged by the square root of the mean squared error (RMSE) (see "Assessing the Model" on page 153) in each partition.

`scikit-learn` has the `sklearn.tree.DecisionTreeRegressor` method to train a decision tree regression model.

How Trees Are Used

One of the big obstacles faced by predictive modelers in organizations is the perceived "black box" nature of the methods they use, which gives rise to opposition from other elements of the organization. In this regard, the tree model has two appealing aspects:

- Tree models provide a visual tool for exploring the data, to gain an idea of what variables are important and how they relate to one another. Trees can capture nonlinear relationships among predictor variables.
- Tree models provide a set of rules that can be effectively communicated to nonspecialists, either for implementation or to "sell" a data mining project.

When it comes to prediction, however, harnessing the results from multiple trees is typically more powerful than using just a single tree. In particular, the random forest and boosted tree algorithms almost always provide superior predictive accuracy and performance (see "Bagging and the Random Forest" on page 259 and "Boosting" on page 270), but the aforementioned advantages of a single tree are lost.

Key Ideas

- Decision trees produce a set of rules to classify or predict an outcome.
- The rules correspond to successive partitioning of the data into subpartitions.
- Each partition, or split, references a specific value of a predictor variable and divides the data into records where that predictor value is above or below that split value.
- At each stage, the tree algorithm chooses the split that minimizes the outcome impurity within each subpartition.
- When no further splits can be made, the tree is fully grown and each terminal node, or leaf, has records of a single class; new cases following that rule (split) path would be assigned that class.
- A fully grown tree overfits the data and must be pruned back so that it captures signal and not noise.
- Multiple-tree algorithms like random forests and boosted trees yield better predictive performance, but they lose the rule-based communicative power of single trees.

Further Reading

- Analytics Vidhya Content Team, "Tree Based Algorithms: A Complete Tutorial from Scratch (in *R* & *Python*)" (*https://oreil.ly/zOr4B*), April 12, 2016.
- Terry M. Therneau, Elizabeth J. Atkinson, and the Mayo Foundation, "An Introduction to Recursive Partitioning Using the RPART Routines" (*https://oreil.ly/6rLGk*), April 11, 2019.

Bagging and the Random Forest

In 1906, the statistician Sir Francis Galton was visiting a county fair in England, at which a contest was being held to guess the dressed weight of an ox that was on exhibit. There were 800 guesses, and while the individual guesses varied widely, both the mean and the median came out within 1% of the ox's true weight. James Surowiecki has explored this phenomenon in his book *The Wisdom of Crowds* (Doubleday, 2004). This principle applies to predictive models as well: averaging (or taking majority votes) of multiple models—an *ensemble* of models—turns out to be more accurate than just selecting one model.

Key Terms for Bagging and the Random Forest

Ensemble
Forming a prediction by using a collection of models.

Synonym
Model averaging

Bagging
A general technique to form a collection of models by bootstrapping the data.

Synonym
Bootstrap aggregation

Random forest
A type of bagged estimate based on decision tree models.

Synonym
Bagged decision trees

Variable importance
A measure of the importance of a predictor variable in the performance of the model.

The ensemble approach has been applied to and across many different modeling methods, most publicly in the Netflix Prize, in which Netflix offered a \$1 million prize to any contestant who came up with a model that produced a 10% improvement in predicting the rating that a Netflix customer would award a movie. The simple version of ensembles is as follows:

1. Develop a predictive model and record the predictions for a given data set.
2. Repeat for multiple models on the same data.
3. For each record to be predicted, take an average (or a weighted average, or a majority vote) of the predictions.

Ensemble methods have been applied most systematically and effectively to decision trees. Ensemble tree models are so powerful that they provide a way to build good predictive models with relatively little effort.

Going beyond the simple ensemble algorithm, there are two main variants of ensemble models: *bagging* and *boosting*. In the case of ensemble tree models, these are referred to as *random forest* models and *boosted tree* models. This section focuses on bagging; boosting is covered in "Boosting" on page 270.

Bagging

Bagging, which stands for "bootstrap aggregating," was introduced by Leo Breiman in 1994. Suppose we have a response Y and P predictor variables $\mathbf{X} = X_1, X_2, \cdots, X_P$ with N records.

Bagging is like the basic algorithm for ensembles, except that, instead of fitting the various models to the same data, each new model is fitted to a bootstrap resample. Here is the algorithm presented more formally:

1. Initialize M, the number of models to be fit, and n, the number of records to choose ($n < N$). Set the iteration $m = 1$.
2. Take a bootstrap resample (i.e., with replacement) of n records from the training data to form a subsample Y_m and $\mathbf{X}_m$ (the bag).
3. Train a model using Y_m and $\mathbf{X}_m$ to create a set of decision rules $\hat{f}_m(\mathbf{X})$.
4. Increment the model counter $m = m + 1$. If $m <= M$, go to step 2.

In the case where $\hat{f}_m$ predicts the probability $Y = 1$, the bagged estimate is given by:

$$\hat{f} = \frac{1}{M}\left(\hat{f}_1(\mathbf{X}) + \hat{f}_2(\mathbf{X}) + \cdots + \hat{f}_M(\mathbf{X})\right)$$

Random Forest

The *random forest* is based on applying bagging to decision trees, with one important extension: in addition to sampling the records, the algorithm also samples the variables.[4] In traditional decision trees, to determine how to create a subpartition of a partition A, the algorithm makes the choice of variable and split point by minimizing a criterion such as Gini impurity (see "Measuring Homogeneity or Impurity" on page 254). With random forests, at each stage of the algorithm, the choice of variable is limited to a *random subset of variables*. Compared to the basic tree algorithm (see "The Recursive Partitioning Algorithm" on page 252), the random forest algorithm adds two more steps: the bagging discussed earlier (see "Bagging and the Random Forest" on page 259), and the bootstrap sampling of variables at each split:

1. Take a bootstrap (with replacement) subsample from the *records*.
2. For the first split, sample $p < P$ *variables* at random without replacement.
3. For each of the sampled variables $X_{j(1)}, X_{j(2)}, ..., X_{j(p)}$, apply the splitting algorithm:
   a. For each value $s_{j(k)}$ of $X_{j(k)}$:
      i. Split the records in partition A, with $X_{j(k)} < s_{j(k)}$ as one partition and the remaining records where $X_{j(k)} \geq s_{j(k)}$ as another partition.
      ii. Measure the homogeneity of classes within each subpartition of A.
   b. Select the value of $s_{j(k)}$ that produces maximum within-partition homogeneity of class.
4. Select the variable $X_{j(k)}$ and the split value $s_{j(k)}$ that produces maximum within-partition homogeneity of class.
5. Proceed to the next split and repeat the previous steps, starting with step 2.
6. Continue with additional splits, following the same procedure until the tree is grown.
7. Go back to step 1, take another bootstrap subsample, and start the process over again.

How many variables to sample at each step? A rule of thumb is to choose $\sqrt{P}$ where P is the number of predictor variables. The package `randomForest` implements the random forest in *R*. The following applies this package to the loan data (see "K-Nearest Neighbors" on page 238 for a description of the data):

4 The term *random forest* is a trademark of Leo Breiman and Adele Cutler and licensed to Salford Systems. There is no standard nontrademark name, and the term random forest is as synonymous with the algorithm as Kleenex is with facial tissues.

```
rf <- randomForest(outcome ~ borrower_score + payment_inc_ratio,
                   data=loan3000)
rf

Call:
 randomForest(formula = outcome ~ borrower_score + payment_inc_ratio,
    data = loan3000)
               Type of random forest: classification
                     Number of trees: 500
No. of variables tried at each split: 1

    OOB estimate of error rate: 39.17%
Confusion matrix:
        default paid off  class.error
default     873      572   0.39584775
paid off    603      952   0.38778135
```

In *Python*, we use the method `sklearn.ensemble.RandomForestClassifier`:

```
predictors = ['borrower_score', 'payment_inc_ratio']
outcome = 'outcome'

X = loan3000[predictors]
y = loan3000[outcome]

rf = RandomForestClassifier(n_estimators=500, random_state=1, oob_score=True)
rf.fit(X, y)
```

By default, 500 trees are trained. Since there are only two variables in the predictor set, the algorithm randomly selects the variable on which to split at each stage (i.e., a bootstrap subsample of size 1).

The *out-of-bag* (*OOB*) estimate of error is the error rate for the trained models, applied to the data left out of the training set for that tree. Using the output from the model, the OOB error can be plotted versus the number of trees in the random forest in *R*:

```
error_df = data.frame(error_rate=rf$err.rate[,'OOB'],
                      num_trees=1:rf$ntree)
ggplot(error_df, aes(x=num_trees, y=error_rate)) +
  geom_line()
```

The `RandomForestClassifier` implementation has no easy way to get out-of-bag estimates as a function of number of trees in the random forest. We can train a sequence of classifiers with an increasing number of trees and keep track of the `oob_score_` values. This method is, however, not efficient:

```
n_estimator = list(range(20, 510, 5))
oobScores = []
for n in n_estimator:
    rf = RandomForestClassifier(n_estimators=n, criterion='entropy',
                                max_depth=5, random_state=1, oob_score=True)
    rf.fit(X, y)
    oobScores.append(rf.oob_score_)
df = pd.DataFrame({ 'n': n_estimator, 'oobScore': oobScores })
df.plot(x='n', y='oobScore')
```

The result is shown in Figure 6-6. The error rate rapidly decreases from over 0.44 before stabilizing around 0.385. The predicted values can be obtained from the `predict` function and plotted as follows in *R*:

```
pred <- predict(rf, prob=TRUE)
rf_df <- cbind(loan3000, pred = pred)
ggplot(data=rf_df, aes(x=borrower_score, y=payment_inc_ratio,
                       shape=pred, color=pred, size=pred)) +
    geom_point(alpha=.8) +
    scale_color_manual(values = c('paid off'='#b8e186', 'default'='#d95f02')) +
    scale_shape_manual(values = c('paid off'=0, 'default'=1)) +
    scale_size_manual(values = c('paid off'=0.5, 'default'=2))
```

In *Python*, we can create a similar plot as follows:

```
predictions = X.copy()
predictions['prediction'] = rf.predict(X)
predictions.head()

fig, ax = plt.subplots(figsize=(4, 4))

predictions.loc[predictions.prediction=='paid off'].plot(
    x='borrower_score', y='payment_inc_ratio', style='.',
    markerfacecolor='none', markeredgecolor='C1', ax=ax)
predictions.loc[predictions.prediction=='default'].plot(
    x='borrower_score', y='payment_inc_ratio', style='o',
    markerfacecolor='none', markeredgecolor='C0', ax=ax)
ax.legend(['paid off', 'default']);
ax.set_xlim(0, 1)
ax.set_ylim(0, 25)
ax.set_xlabel('borrower_score')
ax.set_ylabel('payment_inc_ratio')
```

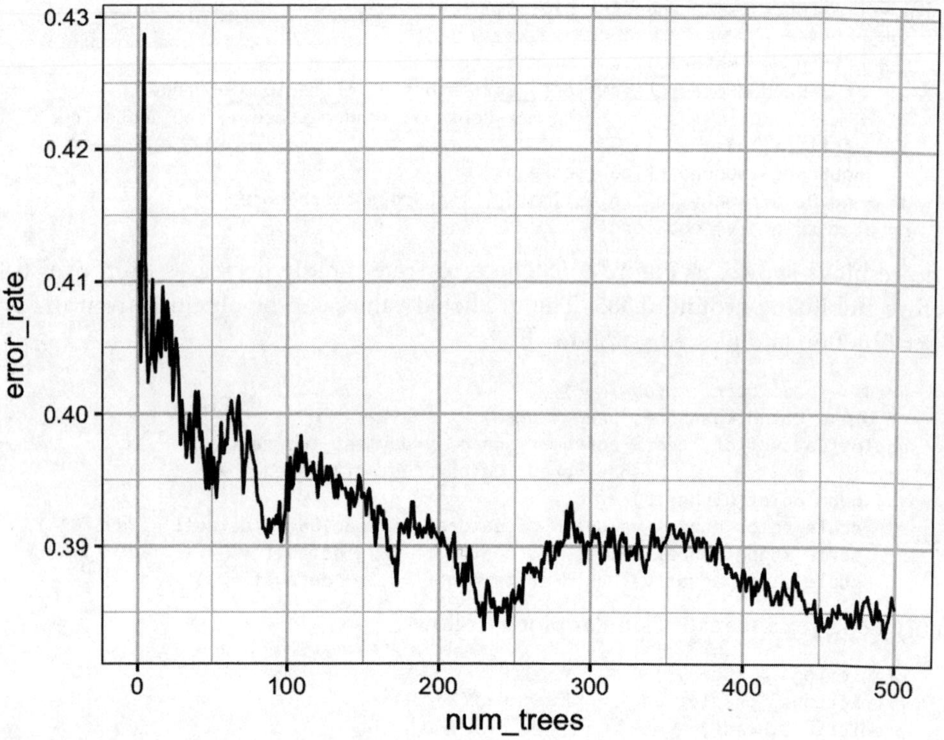

Figure 6-6. An example of the improvement in accuracy of the random forest with the addition of more trees

The plot, shown in Figure 6-7, is quite revealing about the nature of the random forest.

The random forest method is a "black box" method. It produces more accurate predictions than a simple tree, but the simple tree's intuitive decision rules are lost. The random forest predictions are also somewhat noisy: note that some borrowers with a very high score, indicating high creditworthiness, still end up with a prediction of default. This is a result of some unusual records in the data and demonstrates the danger of overfitting by the random forest (see "Bias-Variance Trade-off" on page 247).

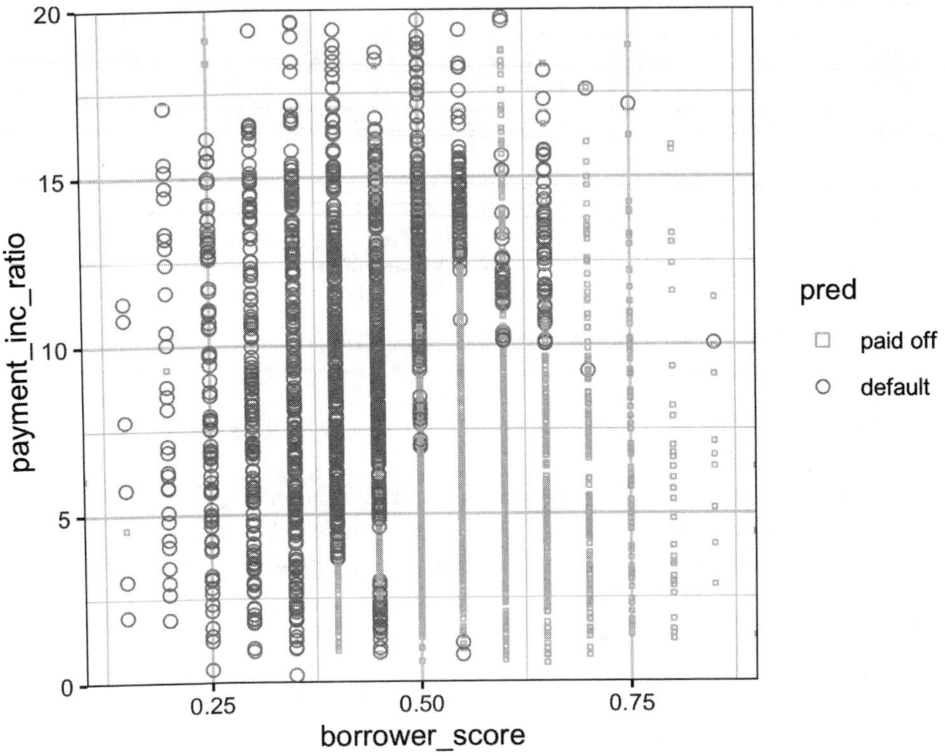

Figure 6-7. The predicted outcomes from the random forest applied to the loan default data

Variable Importance

The power of the random forest algorithm shows itself when you build predictive models for data with many features and records. It has the ability to automatically determine which predictors are important and discover complex relationships between predictors corresponding to interaction terms (see "Interactions and Main Effects" on page 174). For example, fit a model to the loan default data with all columns included. The following shows this in *R*:

```
rf_all <- randomForest(outcome ~ ., data=loan_data, importance=TRUE)
rf_all
Call:
 randomForest(formula = outcome ~ ., data = loan_data, importance = TRUE)
               Type of random forest: classification
                     Number of trees: 500
No. of variables tried at each split: 4

        OOB estimate of  error rate: 33.79%
```

```
Confusion matrix:
         paid off default class.error
paid off    14676    7995   0.3526532
default      7325   15346   0.3231000
```

And in *Python*:

```
predictors = ['loan_amnt', 'term', 'annual_inc', 'dti', 'payment_inc_ratio',
              'revol_bal', 'revol_util', 'purpose', 'delinq_2yrs_zero',
              'pub_rec_zero', 'open_acc', 'grade', 'emp_length', 'purpose_',
              'home_', 'emp_len_', 'borrower_score']
outcome = 'outcome'

X = pd.get_dummies(loan_data[predictors], drop_first=True)
y = loan_data[outcome]

rf_all = RandomForestClassifier(n_estimators=500, random_state=1)
rf_all.fit(X, y)
```

The argument `importance=TRUE` requests that the `randomForest` store additional information about the importance of different variables. The function `varImpPlot` will plot the relative performance of the variables (relative to permuting that variable):

```
varImpPlot(rf_all, type=1) ❶
varImpPlot(rf_all, type=2) ❷
```

❶ mean decrease in accuracy

❷ mean decrease in node impurity

In *Python*, the `RandomForestClassifier` collects information about feature importance during training and makes it available with the field `feature_importances_`:

```
importances = rf_all.feature_importances_
```

The "Gini decrease" is available as the `feature_importance_` property of the fitted classifier. Accuracy decrease, however, is not available out of the box for *Python*. We can calculate it (`scores`) using the following code:

```
rf = RandomForestClassifier(n_estimators=500)
scores = defaultdict(list)

# cross-validate the scores on a number of different random splits of the data
for _ in range(3):
    train_X, valid_X, train_y, valid_y = train_test_split(X, y, test_size=0.3)
    rf.fit(train_X, train_y)
    acc = metrics.accuracy_score(valid_y, rf.predict(valid_X))
    for column in X.columns:
        X_t = valid_X.copy()
        X_t[column] = np.random.permutation(X_t[column].values)
```

```
        shuff_acc = metrics.accuracy_score(valid_y, rf.predict(X_t))
        scores[column].append((acc-shuff_acc)/acc)
```

The result is shown in Figure 6-8. A similar graph can be created with this *Python* code:

```
df = pd.DataFrame({
    'feature': X.columns,
    'Accuracy decrease': [np.mean(scores[column]) for column in X.columns],
    'Gini decrease': rf_all.feature_importances_,
})
df = df.sort_values('Accuracy decrease')

fig, axes = plt.subplots(ncols=2, figsize=(8, 4.5))
ax = df.plot(kind='barh', x='feature', y='Accuracy decrease',
             legend=False, ax=axes[0])
ax.set_ylabel('')

ax = df.plot(kind='barh', x='feature', y='Gini decrease',
             legend=False, ax=axes[1])
ax.set_ylabel('')
ax.get_yaxis().set_visible(False)
```

There are two ways to measure variable importance:

- By the decrease in accuracy of the model if the values of a variable are randomly permuted (`type=1`). Randomly permuting the values has the effect of removing all predictive power for that variable. The accuracy is computed from the out-of-bag data (so this measure is effectively a cross-validated estimate).
- By the mean decrease in the Gini impurity score (see "Measuring Homogeneity or Impurity" on page 254) for all of the nodes that were split on a variable (`type=2`). This measures how much including that variable improves the purity of the nodes. This measure is based on the training set and is therefore less reliable than a measure calculated on out-of-bag data.

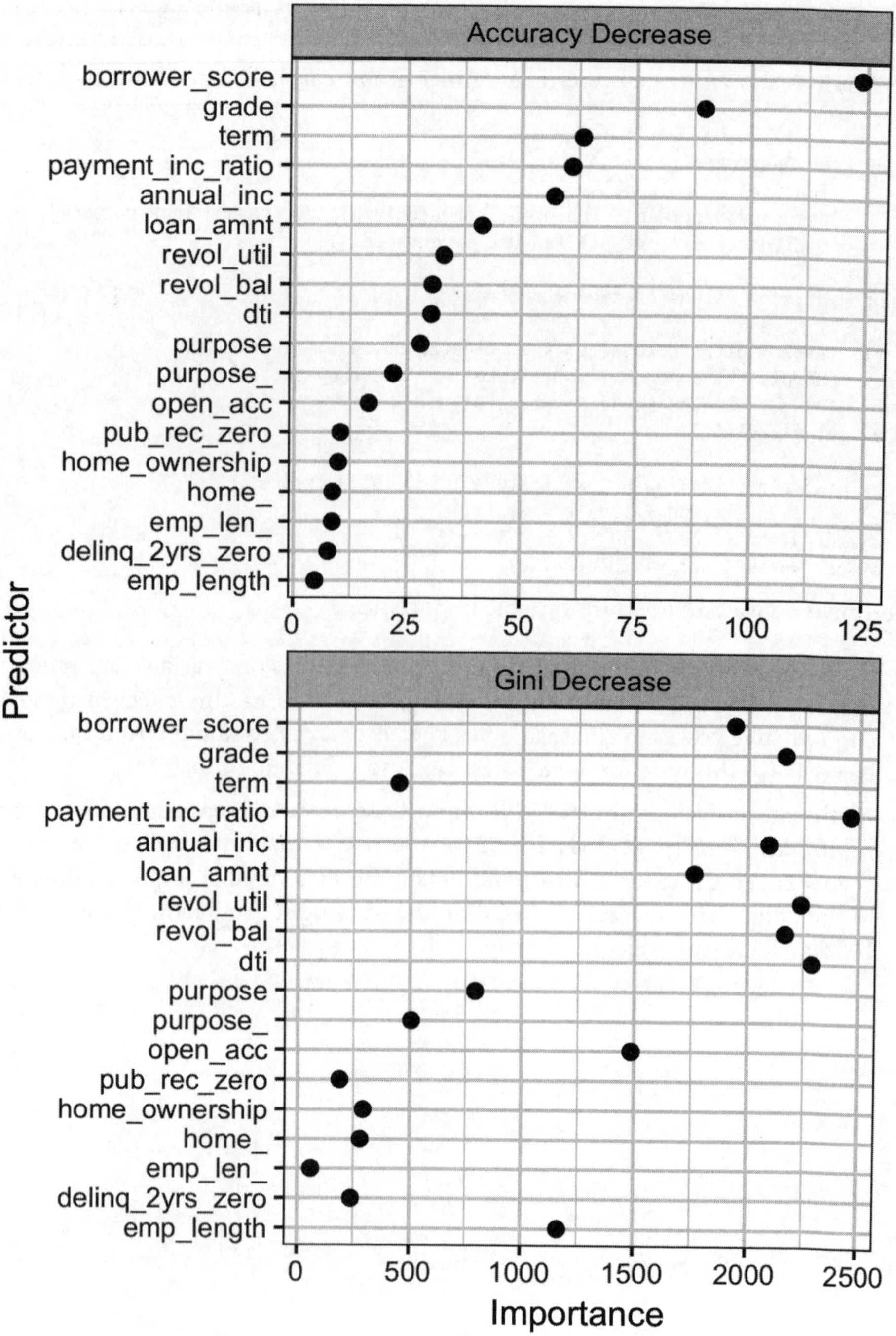

Figure 6-8. The importance of variables for the full model fit to the loan data

The top and bottom panels of Figure 6-8 show variable importance according to the decrease in accuracy and in Gini impurity, respectively. The variables in both panels are ranked by the decrease in accuracy. The variable importance scores produced by these two measures are quite different.

Since the accuracy decrease is a more reliable metric, why should we use the Gini impurity decrease measure? By default, `randomForest` computes only this Gini impurity: Gini impurity is a byproduct of the algorithm, whereas model accuracy by variable requires extra computations (randomly permuting the data and predicting this data). In cases where computational complexity is important, such as in a production setting where thousands of models are being fit, it may not be worth the extra computational effort. In addition, the Gini decrease sheds light on which variables the random forest is using to make its splitting rules (recall that this information, readily visible in a simple tree, is effectively lost in a random forest).

Hyperparameters

The random forest, as with many statistical machine learning algorithms, can be considered a black-box algorithm with knobs to adjust how the box works. These knobs are called *hyperparameters*, which are parameters that you need to set before fitting a model; they are not optimized as part of the training process. While traditional statistical models require choices (e.g., the choice of predictors to use in a regression model), the hyperparameters for random forest are more critical, especially to avoid overfitting. In particular, the two most important hyperparameters for the random forest are:

`nodesize`/`min_samples_leaf`
: The minimum size for terminal nodes (leaves in the tree). The default is 1 for classification and 5 for regression in *R*. The `scikit-learn` implementation in *Python* uses a default of 1 for both.

`maxnodes`/`max_leaf_nodes`
: The maximum number of nodes in each decision tree. By default, there is no limit and the largest tree will be fit subject to the constraints of `nodesize`. Note that in *Python*, you specify the maximum number of terminal nodes. The two parameters are related:

$$\text{maxnodes} = 2\text{max\_leaf\_nodes} - 1$$

It may be tempting to ignore these parameters and simply go with the default values. However, using the defaults may lead to overfitting when you apply the random forest to noisy data. When you increase `nodesize`/`min_samples_leaf` or set `maxnodes`/`max_leaf_nodes`, the algorithm will fit smaller trees and is less likely to create spurious predictive rules. Cross-validation (see "Cross-Validation" on page 155) can be used to test the effects of setting different values for hyperparameters.

> ### Key Ideas
>
> - Ensemble models improve model accuracy by combining the results from many models.
> - Bagging is a particular type of ensemble model based on fitting many models to bootstrapped samples of the data and averaging the models.
> - Random forest is a special type of bagging applied to decision trees. In addition to resampling the data, the random forest algorithm samples the predictor variables when splitting the trees.
> - A useful output from the random forest is a measure of variable importance that ranks the predictors in terms of their contribution to model accuracy.
> - The random forest has a set of hyperparameters that should be tuned using cross-validation to avoid overfitting.

Boosting

Ensemble models have become a standard tool for predictive modeling. *Boosting* is a general technique to create an ensemble of models. It was developed around the same time as *bagging* (see "Bagging and the Random Forest" on page 259). Like bagging, boosting is most commonly used with decision trees. Despite their similarities, boosting takes a very different approach—one that comes with many more bells and whistles. As a result, while bagging can be done with relatively little tuning, boosting requires much greater care in its application. If these two methods were cars, bagging could be considered a Honda Accord (reliable and steady), whereas boosting could be considered a Porsche (powerful but requires more care).

In linear regression models, the residuals are often examined to see if the fit can be improved (see "Partial Residual Plots and Nonlinearity" on page 185). Boosting takes this concept much further and fits a series of models, in which each successive model seeks to minimize the error of the previous model. Several variants of the algorithm are commonly used: *Adaboost*, *gradient boosting*, and *stochastic gradient boosting*. The latter, stochastic gradient boosting, is the most general and widely used. Indeed, with the right choice of parameters, the algorithm can emulate the random forest.

Key Terms for Boosting

Ensemble
Forming a prediction by using a collection of models.

Synonym
Model averaging

Boosting
A general technique to fit a sequence of models by giving more weight to the records with large residuals for each successive round.

Adaboost
An early version of boosting that reweights the data based on the residuals.

Gradient boosting
A more general form of boosting that is cast in terms of minimizing a cost function.

Stochastic gradient boosting
The most general algorithm for boosting that incorporates resampling of records and columns in each round.

Regularization
A technique to avoid overfitting by adding a penalty term to the cost function on the number of parameters in the model.

Hyperparameters
Parameters that need to be set before fitting the algorithm.

The Boosting Algorithm

There are various boosting algorithms, and the basic idea behind all of them is essentially the same. The easiest to understand is Adaboost, which proceeds as follows:

1. Initialize M, the maximum number of models to be fit, and set the iteration counter $m = 1$. Initialize the observation weights $w_i = 1/N$ for $i = 1, 2, ..., N$. Initialize the ensemble model $\hat{F}_0 = 0$.
2. Using the observation weights $w_1, w_2, ..., w_N$, train a model $\hat{f}_m$ that minimizes the weighted error e_m defined by summing the weights for the misclassified observations.
3. Add the model to the ensemble: $\hat{F}_m = \hat{F}_{m-1} + \alpha_m \hat{f}_m$ where $\alpha_m = \frac{\log 1 - e_m}{e_m}$.

4. Update the weights $w_1, w_2, ..., w_N$ so that the weights are increased for the observations that were misclassified. The size of the increase depends on α_m, with larger values of α_m leading to bigger weights.
5. Increment the model counter $m = m + 1$. If $m \leq M$, go to step 2.

The boosted estimate is given by:

$$\hat{F} = \alpha_1 \hat{f}_1 + \alpha_2 \hat{f}_2 + \cdots + \alpha_M \hat{f}_M$$

By increasing the weights for the observations that were misclassified, the algorithm forces the models to train more heavily on the data for which it performed poorly. The factor α_m ensures that models with lower error have a bigger weight.

Gradient boosting is similar to Adaboost but casts the problem as an optimization of a cost function. Instead of adjusting weights, gradient boosting fits models to a *pseudo-residual*, which has the effect of training more heavily on the larger residuals. In the spirit of the random forest, stochastic gradient boosting adds randomness to the algorithm by sampling observations and predictor variables at each stage.

XGBoost

The most widely used public domain software for boosting is XGBoost, an implementation of stochastic gradient boosting originally developed by Tianqi Chen and Carlos Guestrin at the University of Washington. A computationally efficient implementation with many options, it is available as a package for most major data science software languages. In *R*, XGBoost is available as the package `xgboost` (*https://xgboost.readthedocs.io*) and with the same name also for *Python*.

The method `xgboost` has many parameters that can, and should, be adjusted (see "Hyperparameters and Cross-Validation" on page 279). Two very important parameters are `subsample`, which controls the fraction of observations that should be sampled at each iteration, and `eta`, a shrinkage factor applied to α_m in the boosting algorithm (see "The Boosting Algorithm" on page 271). Using `subsample` makes boosting act like the random forest except that the sampling is done without replacement. The shrinkage parameter `eta` is helpful to prevent overfitting by reducing the change in the weights (a smaller change in the weights means the algorithm is less likely to overfit to the training set). The following applies `xgboost` in *R* to the loan data with just two predictor variables:

```
predictors <- data.matrix(loan3000[, c('borrower_score', 'payment_inc_ratio')])
label <- as.numeric(loan3000[,'outcome']) - 1
xgb <- xgboost(data=predictors, label=label, objective="binary:logistic",
               params=list(subsample=0.63, eta=0.1), nrounds=100)
```

```
[1]     train-error:0.358333
[2]     train-error:0.346333
[3]     train-error:0.347333
...
[99]    train-error:0.239333
[100]   train-error:0.241000
```

Note that `xgboost` does not support the formula syntax, so the predictors need to be converted to a `data.matrix` and the response needs to be converted to 0/1 variables. The `objective` argument tells `xgboost` what type of problem this is; based on this, `xgboost` will choose a metric to optimize.

In *Python*, `xgboost` has two different interfaces: a `scikit-learn` API and a more functional interface like in *R*. To be consistent with other `scikit-learn` methods, some parameters were renamed. For example, `eta` is renamed to `learning_rate`; using `eta` will not fail, but it will not have the desired effect:

```
predictors = ['borrower_score', 'payment_inc_ratio']
outcome = 'outcome'

X = loan3000[predictors]
y = loan3000[outcome]

xgb = XGBClassifier(objective='binary:logistic', subsample=0.63)
xgb.fit(X, y)
--
XGBClassifier(base_score=0.5, booster='gbtree', colsample_bylevel=1,
       colsample_bynode=1, colsample_bytree=1, gamma=0, learning_rate=0.1,
       max_delta_step=0, max_depth=3, min_child_weight=1, missing=None,
       n_estimators=100, n_jobs=1, nthread=None, objective='binary:logistic',
       random_state=0, reg_alpha=0, reg_lambda=1, scale_pos_weight=1, seed=None,
       silent=None, subsample=0.63, verbosity=1)
```

The predicted values can be obtained from the `predict` function in *R* and, since there are only two variables, plotted versus the predictors:

```
pred <- predict(xgb, newdata=predictors)
xgb_df <- cbind(loan3000, pred_default = pred > 0.5, prob_default = pred)
ggplot(data=xgb_df, aes(x=borrower_score, y=payment_inc_ratio,
                  color=pred_default, shape=pred_default, size=pred_default)) +
         geom_point(alpha=.8) +
         scale_color_manual(values = c('FALSE'='#b8e186', 'TRUE'='#d95f02')) +
         scale_shape_manual(values = c('FALSE'=0, 'TRUE'=1)) +
         scale_size_manual(values = c('FALSE'=0.5, 'TRUE'=2))
```

The same figure can be created in *Python* using the following code:

```
fig, ax = plt.subplots(figsize=(6, 4))

xgb_df.loc[xgb_df.prediction=='paid off'].plot(
    x='borrower_score', y='payment_inc_ratio', style='.',
    markerfacecolor='none', markeredgecolor='C1', ax=ax)
```

```
xgb_df.loc[xgb_df.prediction=='default'].plot(
    x='borrower_score', y='payment_inc_ratio', style='o',
    markerfacecolor='none', markeredgecolor='C0', ax=ax)
ax.legend(['paid off', 'default']);
ax.set_xlim(0, 1)
ax.set_ylim(0, 25)
ax.set_xlabel('borrower_score')
ax.set_ylabel('payment_inc_ratio')
```

The result is shown in Figure 6-9. Qualitatively, this is similar to the predictions from the random forest; see Figure 6-7. The predictions are somewhat noisy in that some borrowers with a very high borrower score still end up with a prediction of default.

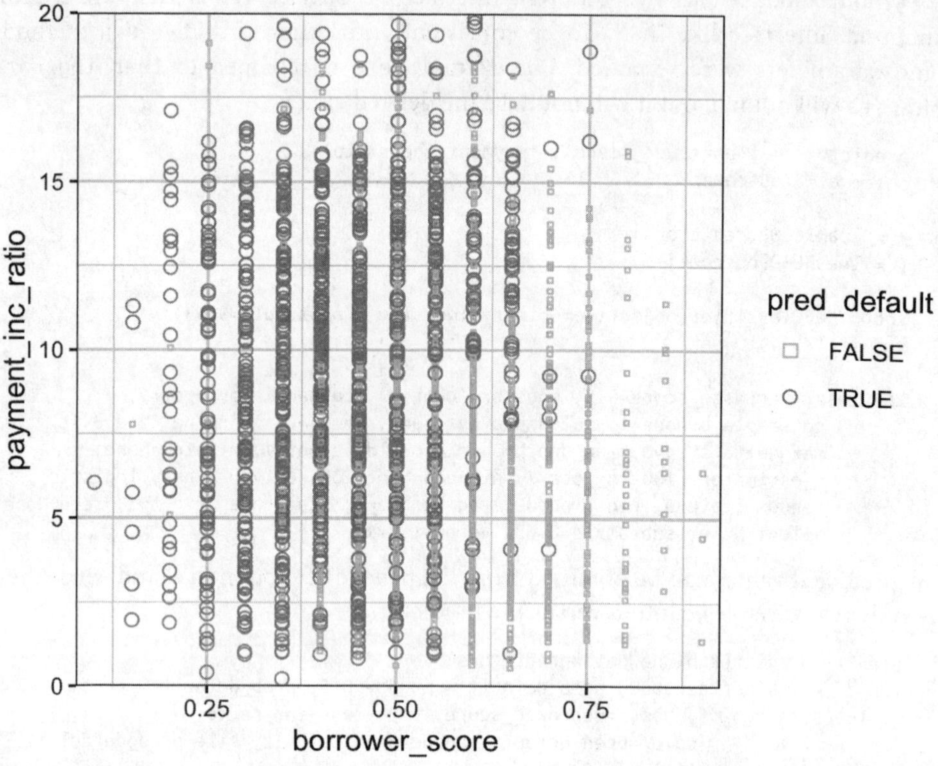

Figure 6-9. The predicted outcomes from XGBoost applied to the loan default data

Regularization: Avoiding Overfitting

Blind application of `xgboost` can lead to unstable models as a result of *overfitting* to the training data. The problem with overfitting is twofold:

- The accuracy of the model on new data not in the training set will be degraded.
- The predictions from the model are highly variable, leading to unstable results.

Any modeling technique is potentially prone to overfitting. For example, if too many variables are included in a regression equation, the model may end up with spurious predictions. However, for most statistical techniques, overfitting can be avoided by a judicious selection of predictor variables. Even the random forest generally produces a reasonable model without tuning the parameters.

This, however, is not the case for `xgboost`. Fit `xgboost` to the loan data for a training set with all of the variables included in the model. In *R*, you can do this as follows:

```
seed <- 400820
predictors <- data.matrix(loan_data[, -which(names(loan_data) %in%
                                        'outcome')])
label <- as.numeric(loan_data$outcome) - 1
test_idx <- sample(nrow(loan_data), 10000)

xgb_default <- xgboost(data=predictors[-test_idx,], label=label[-test_idx],
                       objective='binary:logistic', nrounds=250, verbose=0)
pred_default <- predict(xgb_default, predictors[test_idx,])
error_default <- abs(label[test_idx] - pred_default) > 0.5
xgb_default$evaluation_log[250,]
mean(error_default)
-
iter train_error
1:  250    0.133043

[1] 0.3529
```

We use the function `train_test_split` in *Python* to split the data set into training and test sets:

```
predictors = ['loan_amnt', 'term', 'annual_inc', 'dti', 'payment_inc_ratio',
              'revol_bal', 'revol_util', 'purpose', 'delinq_2yrs_zero',
              'pub_rec_zero', 'open_acc', 'grade', 'emp_length', 'purpose_',
              'home_', 'emp_len_', 'borrower_score']
outcome = 'outcome'

X = pd.get_dummies(loan_data[predictors], drop_first=True)
y = pd.Series([1 if o == 'default' else 0 for o in loan_data[outcome]])

train_X, valid_X, train_y, valid_y = train_test_split(X, y, test_size=10000)

xgb_default = XGBClassifier(objective='binary:logistic', n_estimators=250,
                            max_depth=6, reg_lambda=0, learning_rate=0.3,
                            subsample=1)
xgb_default.fit(train_X, train_y)

pred_default = xgb_default.predict_proba(valid_X)[:, 1]
```

```
error_default = abs(valid_y - pred_default) > 0.5
print('default: ', np.mean(error_default))
```

The test set consists of 10,000 randomly sampled records from the full data, and the training set consists of the remaining records. Boosting leads to an error rate of only 13.3% for the training set. The test set, however, has a much higher error rate of 35.3%. This is a result of overfitting: while boosting can explain the variability in the training set very well, the prediction rules do not apply to new data.

Boosting provides several parameters to avoid overfitting, including the parameters `eta` (or `learning_rate`) and `subsample` (see "XGBoost" on page 272). Another approach is *regularization*, a technique that modifies the cost function in order to *penalize* the complexity of the model. Decision trees are fit by minimizing cost criteria such as Gini's impurity score (see "Measuring Homogeneity or Impurity" on page 254). In `xgboost`, it is possible to modify the cost function by adding a term that measures the complexity of the model.

There are two parameters in `xgboost` to regularize the model: `alpha` and `lambda`, which correspond to Manhattan distance (L1-regularization) and squared Euclidean distance (L2-regularization), respectively (see "Distance Metrics" on page 241). Increasing these parameters will penalize more complex models and reduce the size of the trees that are fit. For example, see what happens if we set `lambda` to 1,000 in *R*:

```
xgb_penalty <- xgboost(data=predictors[-test_idx,], label=label[-test_idx],
                       params=list(eta=.1, subsample=.63, lambda=1000),
                       objective='binary:logistic', nrounds=250, verbose=0)
pred_penalty <- predict(xgb_penalty, predictors[test_idx,])
error_penalty <- abs(label[test_idx] - pred_penalty) > 0.5
xgb_penalty$evaluation_log[250,]
mean(error_penalty)
-
iter train_error
1:  250     0.30966

[1] 0.3286
```

In the `scikit-learn` API, the parameters are called `reg_alpha` and `reg_lambda`:

```
xgb_penalty = XGBClassifier(objective='binary:logistic', n_estimators=250,
                            max_depth=6, reg_lambda=1000, learning_rate=0.1,
                            subsample=0.63)
xgb_penalty.fit(train_X, train_y)
pred_penalty = xgb_penalty.predict_proba(valid_X)[:, 1]
error_penalty = abs(valid_y - pred_penalty) > 0.5
print('penalty: ', np.mean(error_penalty))
```

Now the training error is only slightly lower than the error on the test set.

The `predict` method in *R* offers a convenient argument, `ntreelimit`, that forces only the first *i* trees to be used in the prediction. This lets us directly compare the in-sample versus out-of-sample error rates as more models are included:

```
error_default <- rep(0, 250)
error_penalty <- rep(0, 250)
for(i in 1:250){
  pred_def <- predict(xgb_default, predictors[test_idx,], ntreelimit=i)
  error_default[i] <- mean(abs(label[test_idx] - pred_def) >= 0.5)
  pred_pen <- predict(xgb_penalty, predictors[test_idx,], ntreelimit=i)
  error_penalty[i] <- mean(abs(label[test_idx] - pred_pen) >= 0.5)
}
```

In *Python*, we can call the `predict_proba` method with the `ntree_limit` argument:

```
results = []
for i in range(1, 250):
    train_default = xgb_default.predict_proba(train_X, ntree_limit=i)[:, 1]
    train_penalty = xgb_penalty.predict_proba(train_X, ntree_limit=i)[:, 1]
    pred_default = xgb_default.predict_proba(valid_X, ntree_limit=i)[:, 1]
    pred_penalty = xgb_penalty.predict_proba(valid_X, ntree_limit=i)[:, 1]
    results.append({
        'iterations': i,
        'default train': np.mean(abs(train_y - train_default) > 0.5),
        'penalty train': np.mean(abs(train_y - train_penalty) > 0.5),
        'default test': np.mean(abs(valid_y - pred_default) > 0.5),
        'penalty test': np.mean(abs(valid_y - pred_penalty) > 0.5),
    })

results = pd.DataFrame(results)
results.head()
```

The output from the model returns the error for the training set in the component `xgb_default$evaluation_log`. By combining this with the out-of-sample errors, we can plot the errors versus the number of iterations:

```
errors <- rbind(xgb_default$evaluation_log,
                xgb_penalty$evaluation_log,
                ata.frame(iter=1:250, train_error=error_default),
                data.frame(iter=1:250, train_error=error_penalty))
errors$type <- rep(c('default train', 'penalty train',
                     'default test', 'penalty test'), rep(250, 4))
ggplot(errors, aes(x=iter, y=train_error, group=type)) +
  geom_line(aes(linetype=type, color=type))
```

We can use the `pandas` plot method to create the line graph. The axis returned from the first plot allows us to overlay additional lines onto the same graph. This is a pattern that many of *Python*'s graph packages support:

```
ax = results.plot(x='iterations', y='default test')
results.plot(x='iterations', y='penalty test', ax=ax)
results.plot(x='iterations', y='default train', ax=ax)
results.plot(x='iterations', y='penalty train', ax=ax)
```

The result, displayed in Figure 6-10, shows how the default model steadily improves the accuracy for the training set but actually gets worse for the test set. The penalized model does not exhibit this behavior.

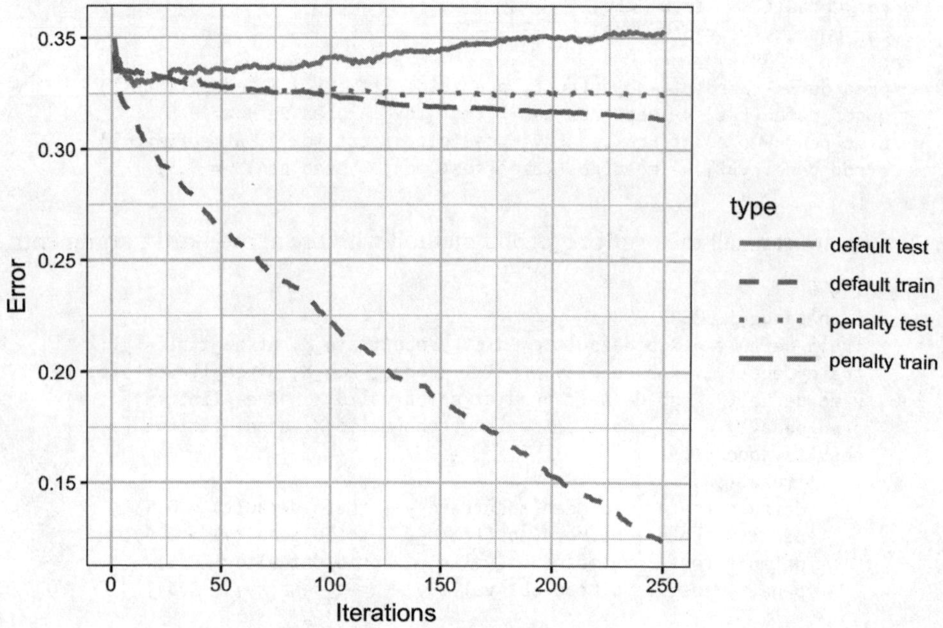

Figure 6-10. The error rate of the default XGBoost versus a penalized version of XGBoost

Ridge Regression and the Lasso

Adding a penalty on the complexity of a model to help avoid overfitting dates back to the 1970s. Least squares regression minimizes the residual sum of squares (RSS); see "Least Squares" on page 148. *Ridge regression* minimizes the sum of squared residuals plus a penalty term that is a function of the number and size of the coefficients:

$$\sum_{i=1}^{n} \left(Y_i - \hat{b}_0 - \hat{b}_1 X_i - \cdots \hat{b} X_p\right)^2 + \lambda\left(\hat{b}_1^2 + \cdots + \hat{b}_p^2\right)$$

The value of λ determines how much the coefficients are penalized; larger values produce models that are less likely to overfit the data. The *Lasso* is similar, except that it uses Manhattan distance instead of Euclidean distance as a penalty term:

$$\sum_{i=1}^{n} \left(Y_i - \hat{b}_0 - \hat{b}_1 X_i - \cdots \hat{b} X_p\right)^2 + \alpha\left(\left|\hat{b}_1\right| + \cdots + \left|\hat{b}_p\right|\right)$$

The xgboost parameters lambda (reg_lambda) and alpha (reg_alpha) are acting in a similar manner.

Using Euclidean distance is also known as L2 regularization, and using Manhattan distance as L1 regularization. The xgboost parameters lambda (reg_lambda) and alpha (reg_alpha) are acting in a similar manner.

Hyperparameters and Cross-Validation

xgboost has a daunting array of hyperparameters; see "XGBoost Hyperparameters" on page 281 for a discussion. As seen in "Regularization: Avoiding Overfitting" on page 274, the specific choice can dramatically change the model fit. Given a huge combination of hyperparameters to choose from, how should we be guided in our choice? A standard solution to this problem is to use *cross-validation*; see "Cross-Validation" on page 155. Cross-validation randomly splits up the data into *K* different groups, also called *folds*. For each fold, a model is trained on the data not in the fold and then evaluated on the data in the fold. This yields a measure of accuracy of the model on out-of-sample data. The best set of hyperparameters is the one given by the model with the lowest overall error as computed by averaging the errors from each of the folds.

To illustrate the technique, we apply it to parameter selection for xgboost. In this example, we explore two parameters: the shrinkage parameter eta (learning_rate—see "XGBoost" on page 272) and the maximum depth of trees max_depth. The parameter max_depth is the maximum depth of a leaf node to the root of the tree with a default value of six. This gives us another way to control overfitting: deep trees tend to be more complex and may overfit the data. First we set up the folds and parameter list. In *R*, this is done as follows:

```
N <- nrow(loan_data)
fold_number <- sample(1:5, N, replace=TRUE)
params <- data.frame(eta = rep(c(.1, .5, .9), 3),
                     max_depth = rep(c(3, 6, 12), rep(3,3)))
```

Now we apply the preceding algorithm to compute the error for each model and each fold using five folds:

```
error <- matrix(0, nrow=9, ncol=5)
for(i in 1:nrow(params)){
  for(k in 1:5){
    fold_idx <- (1:N)[fold_number == k]
    xgb <- xgboost(data=predictors[-fold_idx,], label=label[-fold_idx],
                   params=list(eta=params[i, 'eta'],
                               max_depth=params[i, 'max_depth']),
                   objective='binary:logistic', nrounds=100, verbose=0)
    pred <- predict(xgb, predictors[fold_idx,])
    error[i, k] <- mean(abs(label[fold_idx] - pred) >= 0.5)
```

```
    }
}
```

In the following *Python* code, we create all possible combinations of hyperparameters and fit and evaluate models with each combination:

```
idx = np.random.choice(range(5), size=len(X), replace=True)
error = []
for eta, max_depth in product([0.1, 0.5, 0.9], [3, 6, 9]):  ❶
    xgb = XGBClassifier(objective='binary:logistic', n_estimators=250,
                        max_depth=max_depth, learning_rate=eta)
    cv_error = []
    for k in range(5):
        fold_idx = idx == k
        train_X = X.loc[~fold_idx]; train_y = y[~fold_idx]
        valid_X = X.loc[fold_idx]; valid_y = y[fold_idx]

        xgb.fit(train_X, train_y)
        pred = xgb.predict_proba(valid_X)[:, 1]
        cv_error.append(np.mean(abs(valid_y - pred) > 0.5))
    error.append({
        'eta': eta,
        'max_depth': max_depth,
        'avg_error': np.mean(cv_error)
    })
    print(error[-1])
errors = pd.DataFrame(error)
```

❶ We use the function `itertools.product` from the *Python* standard library to create all possible combinations of the two hyperparameters.

Since we are fitting 45 total models, this can take a while. The errors are stored as a matrix with the models along the rows and folds along the columns. Using the function `rowMeans`, we can compare the error rate for the different parameter sets:

```
avg_error <- 100 * round(rowMeans(error), 4)
cbind(params, avg_error)
  eta max_depth avg_error
1 0.1         3     32.90
2 0.5         3     33.43
3 0.9         3     34.36
4 0.1         6     33.08
5 0.5         6     35.60
6 0.9         6     37.82
7 0.1        12     34.56
8 0.5        12     36.83
9 0.9        12     38.18
```

Cross-validation suggests that using shallower trees with a smaller value of `eta`/`learning_rate` yields more accurate results. Since these models are also more stable, the best parameters to use are `eta=0.1` and `max_depth=3` (or possibly `max_depth=6`).

XGBoost Hyperparameters

The hyperparameters for `xgboost` are primarily used to balance overfitting with the accuracy and computational complexity. For a complete discussion of the parameters, refer to the `xgboost` documentation (*https://oreil.ly/xC_OY*).

`eta/learning_rate`
: The shrinkage factor between 0 and 1 applied to α in the boosting algorithm. The default is 0.3, but for noisy data, smaller values are recommended (e.g., 0.1). In *Python*, the default value is 0.1.

`nrounds/n_estimators`
: The number of boosting rounds. If `eta` is set to a small value, it is important to increase the number of rounds since the algorithm learns more slowly. As long as some parameters are included to prevent overfitting, having more rounds doesn't hurt.

`max_depth`
: The maximum depth of the tree (the default is 6). In contrast to the random forest, which fits very deep trees, boosting usually fits shallow trees. This has the advantage of avoiding spurious complex interactions in the model that can arise from noisy data. In *Python*, the default is 3.

`subsample` *and* `colsample_bytree`
: Fraction of the records to sample without replacement and the fraction of predictors to sample for use in fitting the trees. These parameters, which are similar to those in random forests, help avoid overfitting. The default is 1.0.

`lambda/reg_lambda` *and* `alpha/reg_alpha`
: The regularization parameters to help control overfitting (see "Regularization: Avoiding Overfitting" on page 274). Default values for *Python* are `reg_lambda=1` and `reg_alpha=0`. In *R*, both values have default of 0.

Key Ideas

- Boosting is a class of ensemble models based on fitting a sequence of models, with more weight given to records with large errors in successive rounds.
- Stochastic gradient boosting is the most general type of boosting and offers the best performance. The most common form of stochastic gradient boosting uses tree models.
- XGBoost is a popular and computationally efficient software package for stochastic gradient boosting; it is available in all common languages used in data science.
- Boosting is prone to overfitting the data, and the hyperparameters need to be tuned to avoid this.
- Regularization is one way to avoid overfitting by including a penalty term on the number of parameters (e.g., tree size) in a model.
- Cross-validation is especially important for boosting due to the large number of hyperparameters that need to be set.

Summary

This chapter has described two classification and prediction methods that "learn" flexibly and locally from data, rather than starting with a structural model (e.g., a linear regression) that is fit to the entire data set. *K*-Nearest Neighbors is a simple process that looks around at similar records and assigns their majority class (or average value) to the record being predicted. Trying various cutoff (split) values of predictor variables, tree models iteratively divide the data into sections and subsections that are increasingly homogeneous with respect to class. The most effective split values form a path, and also a "rule," to a classification or prediction. Tree models are a very powerful and popular predictive tool, often outperforming other methods. They have given rise to various ensemble methods (random forests, boosting, bagging) that sharpen the predictive power of trees.

CHAPTER 7

Unsupervised Learning

The term *unsupervised learning* refers to statistical methods that extract meaning from data without training a model on labeled data (data where an outcome of interest is known). In Chapters 4 to 6, the goal is to build a model (set of rules) to predict a response variable from a set of predictor variables. This is supervised learning. In contrast, unsupervised learning also constructs a model of the data, but it does not distinguish between a response variable and predictor variables.

Unsupervised learning can be used to achieve different goals. In some cases, it can be used to create a predictive rule in the absence of a labeled response. *Clustering* methods can be used to identify meaningful groups of data. For example, using the web clicks and demographic data of a user on a website, we may be able to group together different types of users. The website could then be personalized to these different types.

In other cases, the goal may be to *reduce the dimension* of the data to a more manageable set of variables. This reduced set could then be used as input into a predictive model, such as regression or classification. For example, we may have thousands of sensors to monitor an industrial process. By reducing the data to a smaller set of features, we may be able to build a more powerful and interpretable model to predict process failure than could be built by including data streams from thousands of sensors.

Finally, unsupervised learning can be viewed as an extension of the exploratory data analysis (see Chapter 1) to situations in which you are confronted with a large number of variables and records. The aim is to gain insight into a set of data and how the different variables relate to each other. Unsupervised techniques allow you to sift through and analyze these variables and discover relationships.

Unsupervised Learning and Prediction

Unsupervised learning can play an important role in prediction, both for regression and classification problems. In some cases, we want to predict a category in the absence of any labeled data. For example, we might want to predict the type of vegetation in an area from a set of satellite sensory data. Since we don't have a response variable to train a model, clustering gives us a way to identify common patterns and categorize the regions.

Clustering is an especially important tool for the "cold-start problem." In this type of problem, such as launching a new marketing campaign or identifying potential new types of fraud or spam, we initially may not have any response to train a model. Over time, as data is collected, we can learn more about the system and build a traditional predictive model. But clustering helps us start the learning process more quickly by identifying population segments.

Unsupervised learning is also important as a building block for regression and classification techniques. With big data, if a small subpopulation is not well represented in the overall population, the trained model may not perform well for that subpopulation. With clustering, it is possible to identify and label subpopulations. Separate models can then be fit to the different subpopulations. Alternatively, the subpopulation can be represented with its own feature, forcing the overall model to explicitly consider subpopulation identity as a predictor.

Principal Components Analysis

Often, variables will vary together (covary), and some of the variation in one is actually duplicated by variation in another (e.g., restaurant checks and tips). Principal components analysis (PCA) is a technique to discover the way in which numeric variables covary.[1]

1 This and subsequent sections in this chapter © 2020 Datastats, LLC, Peter Bruce, Andrew Bruce, and Peter Gedeck; used with permission.

Key Terms for Principal Components Analysis

Principal component
: A linear combination of the predictor variables.

Loadings
: The weights that transform the predictors into the components.

  Synonym
  : Weights

Screeplot
: A plot of the variances of the components, showing the relative importance of the components, either as explained variance or as proportion of explained variance.

The idea in PCA is to combine multiple numeric predictor variables into a smaller set of variables, which are weighted linear combinations of the original set. The smaller set of variables, the *principal components*, "explains" most of the variability of the full set of variables, reducing the dimension of the data. The weights used to form the principal components reveal the relative contributions of the original variables to the new principal components.

PCA was first proposed by Karl Pearson (*https://oreil.ly/o4EeC*). In what was perhaps the first paper on unsupervised learning, Pearson recognized that in many problems there is variability in the predictor variables, so he developed PCA as a technique to model this variability. PCA can be viewed as the unsupervised version of linear discriminant analysis; see"Discriminant Analysis" on page 201.

A Simple Example

For two variables, X_1 and X_2, there are two principal components Z_i ($i = 1$ or 2):

$$Z_i = w_{i,1}X_1 + w_{i,2}X_2$$

The weights $\left(w_{i,1}, w_{i,2}\right)$ are known as the component *loadings*. These transform the original variables into the principal components. The first principal component, Z_1, is the linear combination that best explains the total variation. The second principal component, Z_2, is orthogonal to the first and explains as much of the remaining variation as it can. (If there were additional components, each additional one would be orthogonal to the others.)

> It is also common to compute principal components on deviations from the means of the predictor variables, rather than on the values themselves.

You can compute principal components in *R* using the `princomp` function. The following performs a PCA on the stock price returns for Chevron (CVX) and ExxonMobil (XOM):

```
oil_px <- sp500_px[, c('CVX', 'XOM')]
pca <- princomp(oil_px)
pca$loadings

Loadings:
    Comp.1 Comp.2
CVX -0.747  0.665
XOM -0.665 -0.747

               Comp.1 Comp.2
SS loadings       1.0    1.0
Proportion Var    0.5    0.5
Cumulative Var    0.5    1.0
```

In *Python*, we can use the `scikit-learn` implementation `sklearn.decomposition.PCA`:

```
pcs = PCA(n_components=2)
pcs.fit(oil_px)
loadings = pd.DataFrame(pcs.components_, columns=oil_px.columns)
loadings
```

The weights for CVX and XOM for the first principal component are –0.747 and –0.665, and for the second principal component they are 0.665 and –0.747. How to interpret this? The first principal component is essentially an average of CVX and XOM, reflecting the correlation between the two energy companies. The second principal component measures when the stock prices of CVX and XOM diverge.

It is instructive to plot the principal components with the data. Here we create a visualization in *R*:

```
loadings <- pca$loadings
ggplot(data=oil_px, aes(x=CVX, y=XOM)) +
  geom_point(alpha=.3) +
  stat_ellipse(type='norm', level=.99) +
  geom_abline(intercept = 0, slope = loadings[2,1]/loadings[1,1]) +
  geom_abline(intercept = 0, slope = loadings[2,2]/loadings[1,2])
```

The following code creates a similar visualization in *Python*:

```
def abline(slope, intercept, ax):
    """Calculate coordinates of a line based on slope and intercept"""
    x_vals = np.array(ax.get_xlim())
    return (x_vals, intercept + slope * x_vals)

ax = oil_px.plot.scatter(x='XOM', y='CVX', alpha=0.3, figsize=(4, 4))
ax.set_xlim(-3, 3)
ax.set_ylim(-3, 3)
ax.plot(*abline(loadings.loc[0, 'CVX'] / loadings.loc[0, 'XOM'], 0, ax),
        '--', color='C1')
ax.plot(*abline(loadings.loc[1, 'CVX'] / loadings.loc[1, 'XOM'], 0, ax),
        '--', color='C1')
```

The result is shown in Figure 7-1.

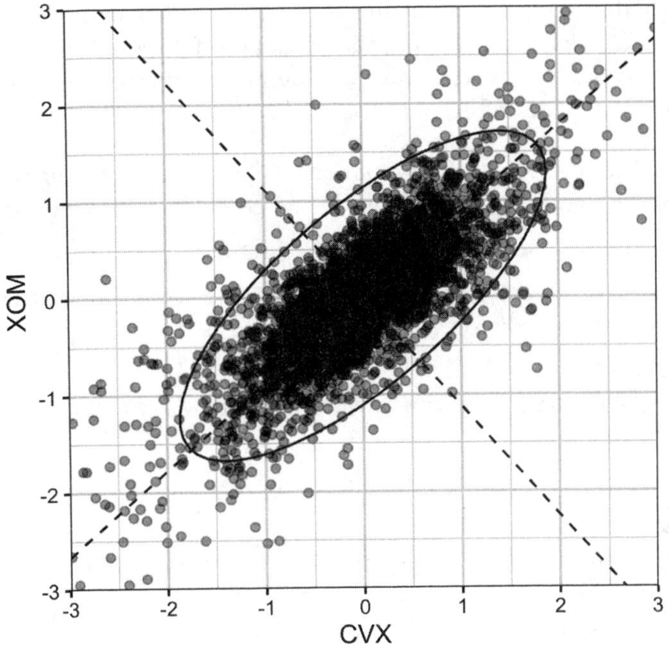

Figure 7-1. The principal components for the stock returns for Chevron (CVX) and ExxonMobil (XOM)

The dashed lines show the direction of the two principal components: the first one is along the long axis of the ellipse, and the second one is along the short axis. You can see that a majority of the variability in the two stock returns is explained by the first principal component. This makes sense since energy stock prices tend to move as a group.

> The weights for the first principal component are both negative, but reversing the sign of all the weights does not change the principal component. For example, using weights of 0.747 and 0.665 for the first principal component is equivalent to the negative weights, just as an infinite line defined by the origin and 1,1 is the same as one defined by the origin and –1, –1.

Computing the Principal Components

Going from two variables to more variables is straightforward. For the first component, simply include the additional predictor variables in the linear combination, assigning weights that optimize the collection of the covariation from all the predictor variables into this first principal component (*covariance* is the statistical term; see "Covariance Matrix" on page 202). Calculation of principal components is a classic statistical method, relying on either the correlation matrix of the data or the covariance matrix, and it executes rapidly, not relying on iteration. As noted earlier, principal components analysis works only with numeric variables, not categorical ones. The full process can be described as follows:

1. In creating the first principal component, PCA arrives at the linear combination of predictor variables that maximizes the percent of total variance explained.
2. This linear combination then becomes the first "new" predictor, Z_1.
3. PCA repeats this process, using the same variables with different weights, to create a second new predictor, Z_2. The weighting is done such that Z_1 and Z_2 are uncorrelated.
4. The process continues until you have as many new variables, or components, Z_i as original variables X_i.
5. Choose to retain as many components as are needed to account for most of the variance.
6. The result so far is a set of weights for each component. The final step is to convert the original data into new principal component scores by applying the weights to the original values. These new scores can then be used as the reduced set of predictor variables.

Interpreting Principal Components

The nature of the principal components often reveals information about the structure of the data. There are a couple of standard visualization displays to help you glean insight about the principal components. One such method is a *screeplot* to visualize the relative importance of principal components (the name derives from the resemblance of the plot to a scree slope; here, the y-axis is the eigenvalue). The following *R* code shows an example for a few top companies in the S&P 500:

```
syms <- c( 'AAPL', 'MSFT', 'CSCO', 'INTC', 'CVX', 'XOM',
   'SLB', 'COP', 'JPM', 'WFC', 'USB', 'AXP', 'WMT', 'TGT', 'HD', 'COST')
top_sp <- sp500_px[row.names(sp500_px)>='2005-01-01', syms]
sp_pca <- princomp(top_sp)
screeplot(sp_pca)
```

The information to create a loading plot from the `scikit-learn` result is available in `explained_variance_`. Here, we convert it into a `pandas` data frame and use it to make a bar chart:

```
syms = sorted(['AAPL', 'MSFT', 'CSCO', 'INTC', 'CVX', 'XOM', 'SLB', 'COP',
               'JPM', 'WFC', 'USB', 'AXP', 'WMT', 'TGT', 'HD', 'COST'])
top_sp = sp500_px.loc[sp500_px.index >= '2011-01-01', syms]

sp_pca = PCA()
sp_pca.fit(top_sp)

explained_variance = pd.DataFrame(sp_pca.explained_variance_)
ax = explained_variance.head(10).plot.bar(legend=False, figsize=(4, 4))
ax.set_xlabel('Component')
```

As seen in Figure 7-2, the variance of the first principal component is quite large (as is often the case), but the other top principal components are significant.

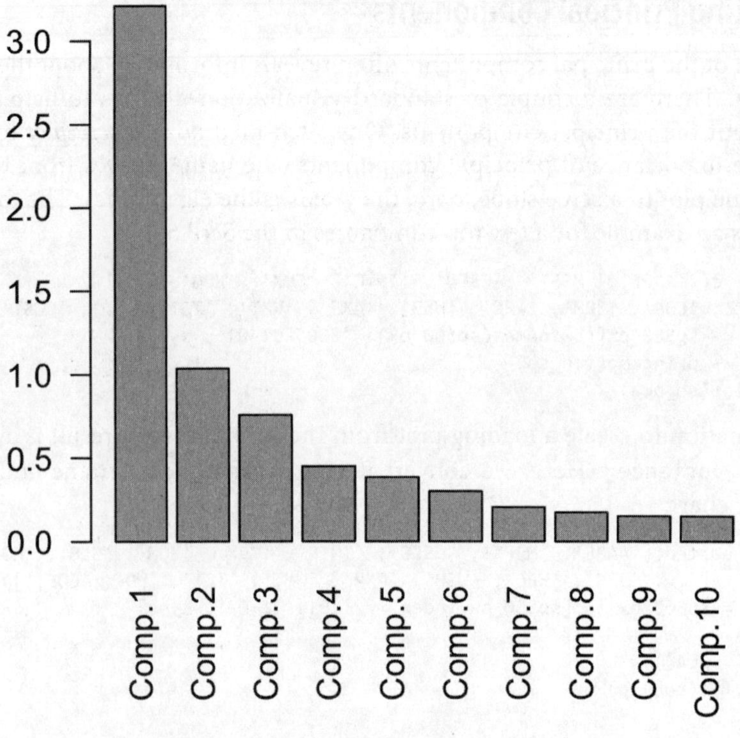

Figure 7-2. A screeplot for a PCA of top stocks from the S&P 500

It can be especially revealing to plot the weights of the top principal components. One way to do this in *R* is to use the `gather` function from the `tidyr` package in conjunction with `ggplot`:

```
library(tidyr)
loadings <- sp_pca$loadings[,1:5]
loadings$Symbol <- row.names(loadings)
loadings <- gather(loadings, 'Component', 'Weight', -Symbol)
ggplot(loadings, aes(x=Symbol, y=Weight)) +
  geom_bar(stat='identity') +
  facet_grid(Component ~ ., scales='free_y')
```

Here is the code to create the same visualization in *Python*:

```
loadings = pd.DataFrame(sp_pca.components_[0:5, :], columns=top_sp.columns)
maxPC = 1.01 * np.max(np.max(np.abs(loadings.loc[0:5, :])))

f, axes = plt.subplots(5, 1, figsize=(5, 5), sharex=True)
for i, ax in enumerate(axes):
    pc_loadings = loadings.loc[i, :]
    colors = ['C0' if l > 0 else 'C1' for l in pc_loadings]
    ax.axhline(color='#888888')
```

```
pc_loadings.plot.bar(ax=ax, color=colors)
ax.set_ylabel(f'PC{i+1}')
ax.set_ylim(-maxPC, maxPC)
```

The loadings for the top five components are shown in Figure 7-3. The loadings for the first principal component have the same sign: this is typical for data in which all the columns share a common factor (in this case, the overall stock market trend). The second component captures the price changes of energy stocks as compared to the other stocks. The third component is primarily a contrast in the movements of Apple and CostCo. The fourth component contrasts the movements of Schlumberger (SLB) to the other energy stocks. Finally, the fifth component is mostly dominated by financial companies.

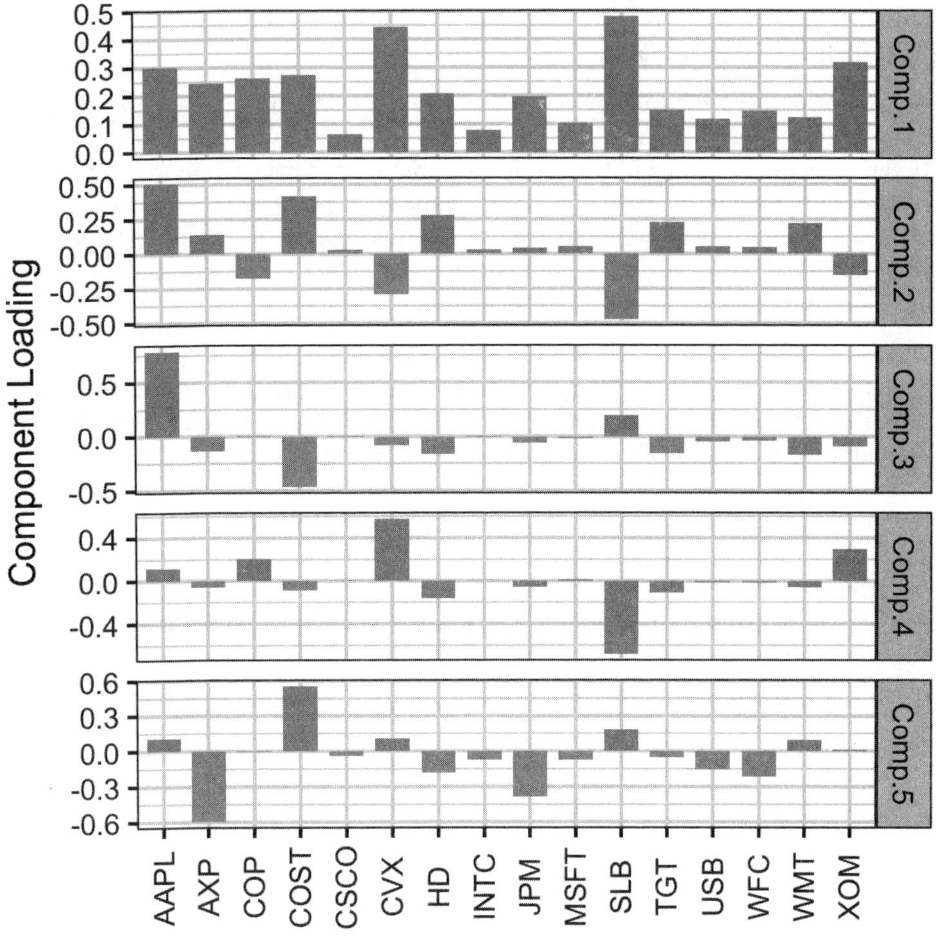

Figure 7-3. The loadings for the top five principal components of stock price returns

How Many Components to Choose?

If your goal is to reduce the dimension of the data, you must decide how many principal components to select. The most common approach is to use an ad hoc rule to select the components that explain "most" of the variance. You can do this visually through the screeplot, as, for example, in Figure 7-2. Alternatively, you could select the top components such that the cumulative variance exceeds a threshold, such as 80%. Also, you can inspect the loadings to determine if the component has an intuitive interpretation. Cross-validation provides a more formal method to select the number of significant components (see "Cross-Validation" on page 155 for more).

Correspondence Analysis

PCA cannot be used for categorical data; however, a somewhat related technique is *correspondence analysis*. The goal is to recognize associations between categories, or between categorical features. The similarities between correspondence analysis and principal components analysis are mainly under the hood—the matrix algebra for dimension scaling. Correspondence analysis is used mainly for graphical analysis of low-dimensional categorical data and is not used in the same way that PCA is for dimension reduction as a preparatory step with big data.

The input can be seen as a table, with rows representing one variable and columns another, and the cells representing record counts. The output (after some matrix algebra) is a *biplot*—a scatterplot with axes scaled (and with percentages indicating how much variance is explained by that dimension). The meaning of the units on the axes is not intuitively connected to the original data, and the main value of the scatterplot is to illustrate graphically variables that are associated with one another (by proximity on the plot). See for example, Figure 7-4, in which household tasks are arrayed according to whether they are done jointly or solo (vertical axis), and whether wife or husband has primary responsibility (horizontal axis). Correspondence analysis is many decades old, as is the spirit of this example, judging by the assignment of tasks.

There are a variety of packages for correspondence analysis in *R*. Here, we use the package `ca`:

```
ca_analysis <- ca(housetasks)
plot(ca_analysis)
```

In *Python*, we can use the `prince` package, which implements correspondence analysis using the `scikit-learn` API:

```
ca = prince.CA(n_components=2)
ca = ca.fit(housetasks)

ca.plot_coordinates(housetasks, figsize=(6, 6))
```

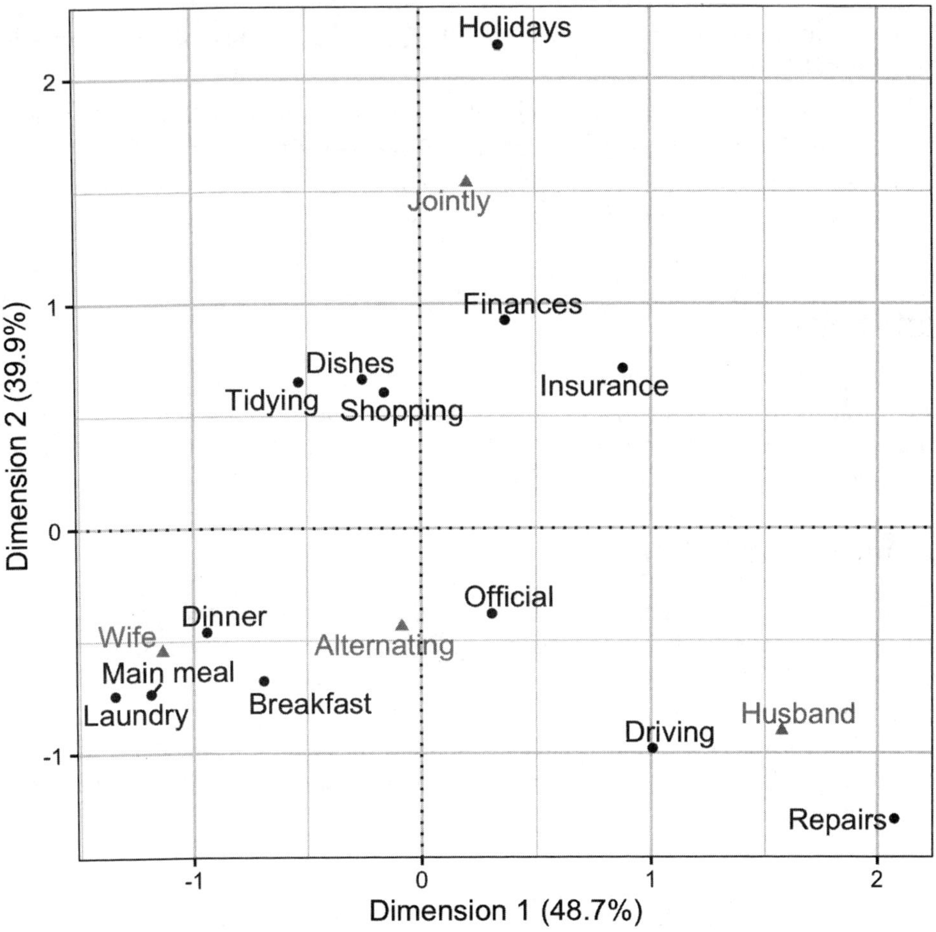

Figure 7-4. Graphical representation of a correspondence analysis of house task data

Key Ideas

- Principal components are linear combinations of the predictor variables (numeric data only).
- Principal components are calculated so as to minimize correlation between components, reducing redundancy.
- A limited number of components will typically explain most of the variance in the outcome variable.
- The limited set of principal components can then be used in place of the (more numerous) original predictors, reducing dimensionality.
- A superficially similar technique for categorical data is correspondence analysis, but it is not useful in a big data context.

Further Reading

For a detailed look at the use of cross-validation in principal components, see Rasmus Bro, K. Kjeldahl, A.K. Smilde, and Henk A. L. Kiers, "Cross-Validation of Component Models: A Critical Look at Current Methods" (*https://oreil.ly/yVryf*), *Analytical and Bioanalytical Chemistry* 390, no. 5 (2008).

K-Means Clustering

Clustering is a technique to divide data into different groups, where the records in each group are similar to one another. A goal of clustering is to identify significant and meaningful groups of data. The groups can be used directly, analyzed in more depth, or passed as a feature or an outcome to a predictive regression or classification model. *K-means* was the first clustering method to be developed; it is still widely used, owing its popularity to the relative simplicity of the algorithm and its ability to scale to large data sets.

Key Terms for K-Means Clustering

Cluster
A group of records that are similar.

Cluster mean
The vector of variable means for the records in a cluster.

K
The number of clusters.

K-means divides the data into *K* clusters by minimizing the sum of the squared distances of each record to the *mean* of its assigned cluster. This is referred to as the *within-cluster sum of squares* or *within-cluster SS*. *K*-means does not ensure the clusters will have the same size but finds the clusters that are the best separated.

Normalization

It is typical to normalize (standardize) continuous variables by subtracting the mean and dividing by the standard deviation. Otherwise, variables with large scale will dominate the clustering process (see "Standardization (Normalization, z-Scores)" on page 243).

A Simple Example

Start by considering a data set with n records and just two variables, x and y. Suppose we want to split the data into $K = 4$ clusters. This means assigning each record (x_i, y_i) to a cluster k. Given an assignment of n_k records to cluster k, the center of the cluster $(\bar{x}_k, \bar{y}_k)$ is the mean of the points in the cluster:

$$\bar{x}_k = \frac{1}{n_k} \sum_{\substack{i \in \\ \text{Cluster } k}} x_i$$

$$\bar{y}_k = \frac{1}{n_k} \sum_{\substack{i \in \\ \text{Cluster } k}} y_i$$

Cluster Mean

In clustering records with multiple variables (the typical case), the term *cluster mean* refers not to a single number but to the vector of means of the variables.

The sum of squares within a cluster is given by:

$$\text{SS}_k = \sum_{i \in \text{Cluster } k} \left(x_i - \bar{x}_k\right)^2 + \left(y_i - \bar{y}_k\right)^2$$

K-means finds the assignment of records that minimizes within-cluster sum of squares across all four clusters $\text{SS}_1 + \text{SS}_2 + \text{SS}_3 + \text{SS}_4$:

$$\sum_{k=1}^{4} \text{SS}_k$$

A typical use of clustering is to locate natural, separate clusters in the data. Another application is to divide the data into a predetermined number of separate groups, where clustering is used to ensure the groups are as different as possible from one another.

For example, suppose we want to divide daily stock returns into four groups. *K*-means clustering can be used to separate the data into the best groupings. Note that daily stock returns are reported in a fashion that is, in effect, standardized, so we do not need to normalize the data. In *R*, *K*-means clustering can be performed using the `kmeans` function. For example, the following finds four clusters based on two variables—the daily stock returns for ExxonMobil (`XOM`) and Chevron (`CVX`):

```
df <- sp500_px[row.names(sp500_px)>='2011-01-01', c('XOM', 'CVX')]
km <- kmeans(df, centers=4)
```

We use the `sklearn.cluster.KMeans` method from `scikit-learn` in *Python*:

```
df = sp500_px.loc[sp500_px.index >= '2011-01-01', ['XOM', 'CVX']]
kmeans = KMeans(n_clusters=4).fit(df)
```

The cluster assignment for each record is returned as the `cluster` component (*R*):

```
> df$cluster <- factor(km$cluster)
> head(df)
                  XOM        CVX cluster
2011-01-03 0.73680496  0.2406809       2
2011-01-04 0.16866845 -0.5845157       1
2011-01-05 0.02663055  0.4469854       2
2011-01-06 0.24855834 -0.9197513       1
2011-01-07 0.33732892  0.1805111       2
2011-01-10 0.00000000 -0.4641675       1
```

In `scikit-learn`, the cluster labels are available in the `labels_` field:

```
df['cluster'] = kmeans.labels_
df.head()
```

The first six records are assigned to either cluster 1 or cluster 2. The means of the clusters are also returned (*R*):

```
> centers <- data.frame(cluster=factor(1:4), km$centers)
> centers
  cluster        XOM        CVX
1       1 -0.3284864 -0.5669135
2       2  0.2410159  0.3342130
3       3 -1.1439800 -1.7502975
4       4  0.9568628  1.3708892
```

In `scikit-learn`, the cluster centers are available in the `cluster_centers_` field:

```
centers = pd.DataFrame(kmeans.cluster_centers_, columns=['XOM', 'CVX'])
centers
```

Clusters 1 and 3 represent "down" markets, while clusters 2 and 4 represent "up markets."

As the *K*-means algorithm uses randomized starting points, the results may differ between subsequent runs and different implementations of the method. In general, you should check that the fluctuations aren't too large.

In this example, with just two variables, it is straightforward to visualize the clusters and their means:

```
ggplot(data=df, aes(x=XOM, y=CVX, color=cluster, shape=cluster)) +
  geom_point(alpha=.3) +
  geom_point(data=centers,  aes(x=XOM, y=CVX), size=3, stroke=2)
```

The `seaborn` `scatterplot` function makes it easy to color (`hue`) and style (`style`) the points by a property:

```
fig, ax = plt.subplots(figsize=(4, 4))
ax = sns.scatterplot(x='XOM', y='CVX', hue='cluster', style='cluster',
                     ax=ax, data=df)
ax.set_xlim(-3, 3)
ax.set_ylim(-3, 3)
centers.plot.scatter(x='XOM', y='CVX', ax=ax, s=50, color='black')
```

The resulting plot, shown in Figure 7-5, shows the cluster assignments and the cluster means. Note that *K*-means will assign records to clusters, even if those clusters are not well separated (which can be useful if you need to optimally divide records into groups).

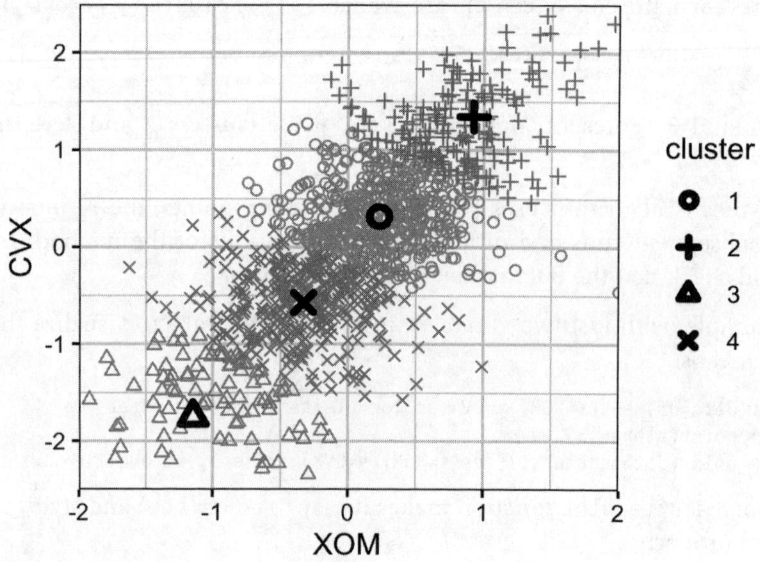

Figure 7-5. The clusters of K-means applied to daily stock returns for ExxonMobil and Chevron (the cluster centers are highlighted with black symbols)

K-Means Algorithm

In general, *K*-means can be applied to a data set with *p* variables $X_1, ..., X_p$. While the exact solution to *K*-means is computationally very difficult, heuristic algorithms provide an efficient way to compute a locally optimal solution.

The algorithm starts with a user-specified *K* and an initial set of cluster means and then iterates the following steps:

1. Assign each record to the nearest cluster mean as measured by squared distance.
2. Compute the new cluster means based on the assignment of records.

The algorithm converges when the assignment of records to clusters does not change.

For the first iteration, you need to specify an initial set of cluster means. Usually you do this by randomly assigning each record to one of the *K* clusters and then finding the means of those clusters.

Since this algorithm isn't guaranteed to find the best possible solution, it is recommended to run the algorithm several times using different random samples to initialize the algorithm. When more than one set of iterations is used, the *K*-means result is given by the iteration that has the lowest within-cluster sum of squares.

The `nstart` parameter to the *R* function `kmeans` allows you to specify the number of random starts to try. For example, the following code runs *K*-means to find 5 clusters using 10 different starting cluster means:

```
syms <- c( 'AAPL', 'MSFT', 'CSCO', 'INTC', 'CVX', 'XOM', 'SLB', 'COP',
           'JPM', 'WFC', 'USB', 'AXP', 'WMT', 'TGT', 'HD', 'COST')
df <- sp500_px[row.names(sp500_px) >= '2011-01-01', syms]
km <- kmeans(df, centers=5, nstart=10)
```

The function automatically returns the best solution out of the 10 different starting points. You can use the argument `iter.max` to set the maximum number of iterations the algorithm is allowed for each random start.

The `scikit-learn` algorithm is repeated 10 times by default (`n_init`). The argument `max_iter` (default 300) can be used to control the number of iterations:

```
syms = sorted(['AAPL', 'MSFT', 'CSCO', 'INTC', 'CVX', 'XOM', 'SLB', 'COP',
               'JPM', 'WFC', 'USB', 'AXP', 'WMT', 'TGT', 'HD', 'COST'])
top_sp = sp500_px.loc[sp500_px.index >= '2011-01-01', syms]
kmeans = KMeans(n_clusters=5).fit(top_sp)
```

Interpreting the Clusters

An important part of cluster analysis can involve the interpretation of the clusters. The two most important outputs from `kmeans` are the sizes of the clusters and the cluster means. For the example in the previous subsection, the sizes of resulting clusters are given by this *R* command:

```
km$size
[1] 106 186 285 288 266
```

In *Python*, we can use the `collections.Counter` class from the standard library to get this information. Due to differences in the implementation and the inherent randomness of the algorithm, results will vary:

```
from collections import Counter
Counter(kmeans.labels_)

Counter({4: 302, 2: 272, 0: 288, 3: 158, 1: 111})
```

The cluster sizes are relatively balanced. Imbalanced clusters can result from distant outliers, or from groups of records very distinct from the rest of the data—both may warrant further inspection.

You can plot the centers of the clusters using the `gather` function in conjunction with `ggplot`:

```
centers <- as.data.frame(t(centers))
names(centers) <- paste("Cluster", 1:5)
centers$Symbol <- row.names(centers)
centers <- gather(centers, 'Cluster', 'Mean', -Symbol)
centers$Color = centers$Mean > 0
ggplot(centers, aes(x=Symbol, y=Mean, fill=Color)) +
  geom_bar(stat='identity', position='identity', width=.75) +
  facet_grid(Cluster ~ ., scales='free_y')
```

The code to create this visualization in *Python* is similar to what we used for PCA:

```
centers = pd.DataFrame(kmeans.cluster_centers_, columns=syms)

f, axes = plt.subplots(5, 1, figsize=(5, 5), sharex=True)
for i, ax in enumerate(axes):
    center = centers.loc[i, :]
    maxPC = 1.01 * np.max(np.max(np.abs(center)))
    colors = ['C0' if l > 0 else 'C1' for l in center]
    ax.axhline(color='#888888')
    center.plot.bar(ax=ax, color=colors)
    ax.set_ylabel(f'Cluster {i + 1}')
    ax.set_ylim(-maxPC, maxPC)
```

The resulting plot is shown in Figure 7-6 and reveals the nature of each cluster. For example, clusters 4 and 5 correspond to days on which the market is down and up, respectively. Clusters 2 and 3 are characterized by up-market days for consumer stocks and down-market days for energy stocks, respectively. Finally, cluster 1 captures the days in which energy stocks were up and consumer stocks were down.

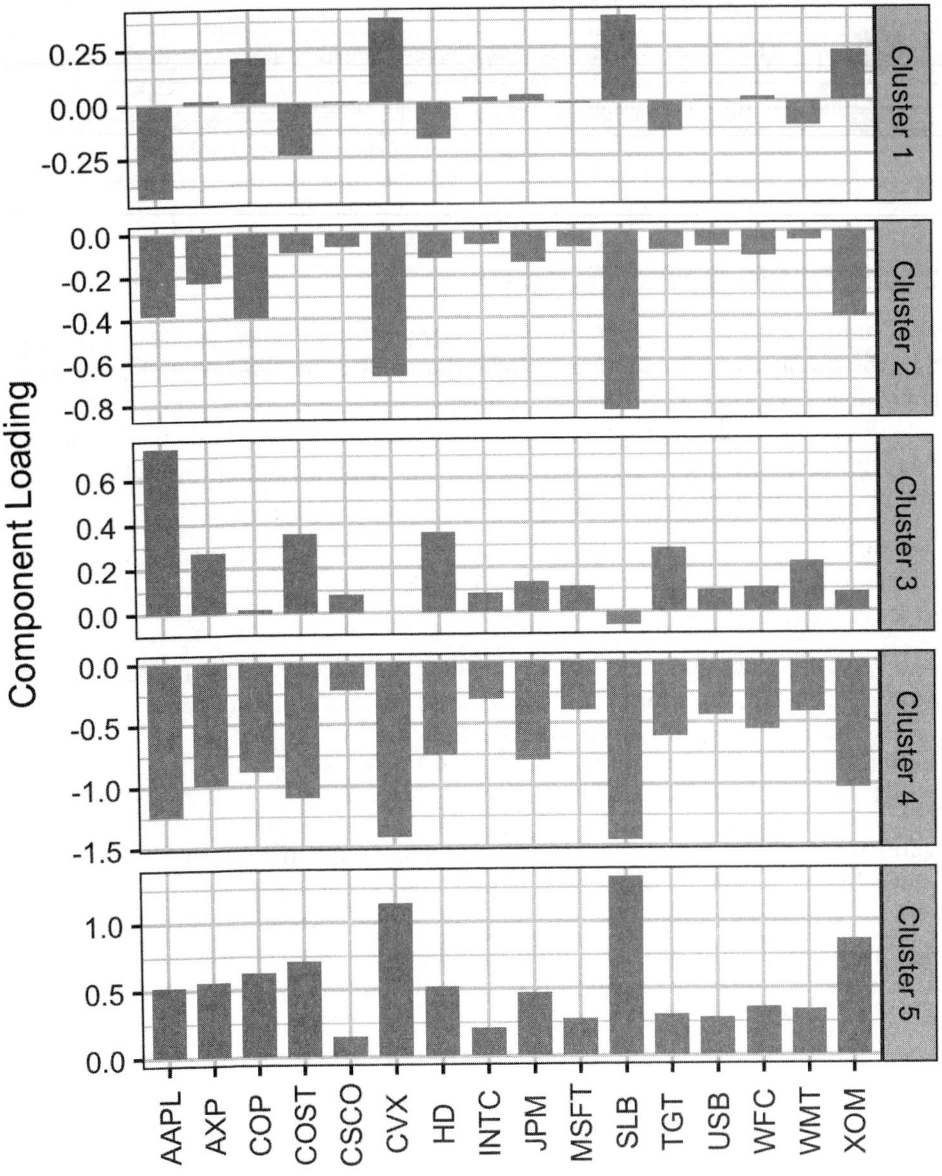

Figure 7-6. The means of the variables in each cluster ("cluster means")

Cluster Analysis Versus PCA

The plot of cluster means is similar in spirit to looking at the loadings for principal components analysis (PCA); see “Interpreting Principal Components” on page 289. A major distinction is that unlike with PCA, the sign of the cluster means is meaningful. PCA identifies principal directions of variation, whereas cluster analysis finds groups of records located near one another.

Selecting the Number of Clusters

The *K*-means algorithm requires that you specify the number of clusters *K*. Sometimes the number of clusters is driven by the application. For example, a company managing a sales force might want to cluster customers into “personas” to focus and guide sales calls. In such a case, managerial considerations would dictate the number of desired customer segments—for example, two might not yield useful differentiation of customers, while eight might be too many to manage.

In the absence of a cluster number dictated by practical or managerial considerations, a statistical approach could be used. There is no single standard method to find the “best” number of clusters.

A common approach, called the *elbow method*, is to identify when the set of clusters explains “most” of the variance in the data. Adding new clusters beyond this set contributes relatively little in the variance explained. The elbow is the point where the cumulative variance explained flattens out after rising steeply, hence the name of the method.

Figure 7-7 shows the cumulative percent of variance explained for the default data for the number of clusters ranging from 2 to 15. Where is the elbow in this example? There is no obvious candidate, since the incremental increase in variance explained drops gradually. This is fairly typical in data that does not have well-defined clusters. This is perhaps a drawback of the elbow method, but it does reveal the nature of the data.

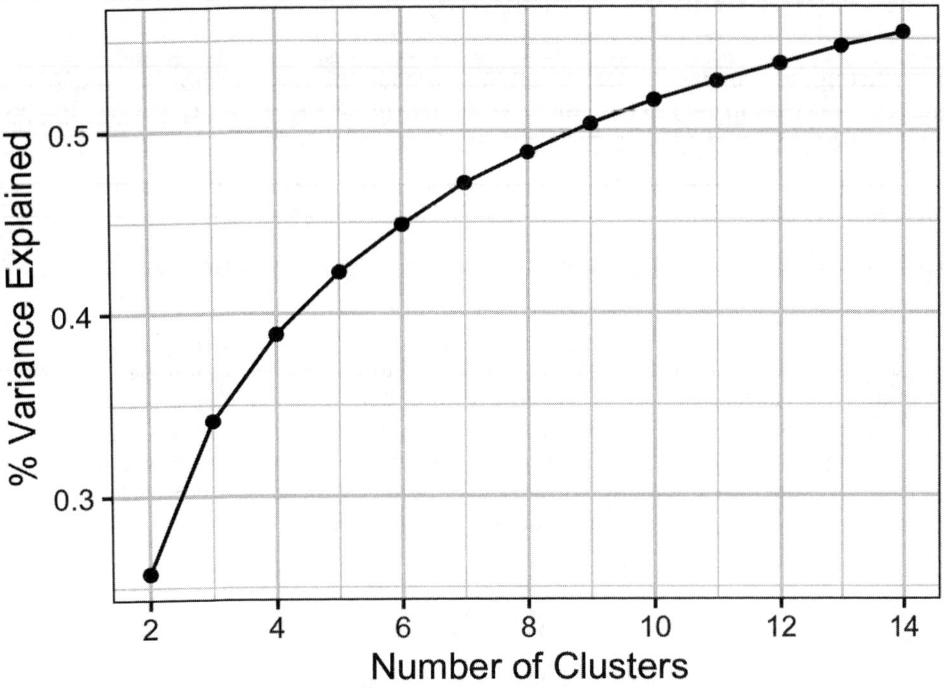

Figure 7-7. The elbow method applied to the stock data

In *R*, the kmeans function doesn't provide a single command for applying the elbow method, but it can be readily applied from the output of kmeans as shown here:

```
pct_var <- data.frame(pct_var = 0,
                      num_clusters = 2:14)
totalss <- kmeans(df, centers=14, nstart=50, iter.max=100)$totss
for (i in 2:14) {
  kmCluster <- kmeans(df, centers=i, nstart=50, iter.max=100)
  pct_var[i-1, 'pct_var'] <- kmCluster$betweenss / totalss
}
```

For the KMeans result, we get this information from the property inertia_. After conversion into a pandas data frame, we can use its plot method to create the graph:

```
inertia = []
for n_clusters in range(2, 14):
    kmeans = KMeans(n_clusters=n_clusters, random_state=0).fit(top_sp)
    inertia.append(kmeans.inertia_ / n_clusters)

inertias = pd.DataFrame({'n_clusters': range(2, 14), 'inertia': inertia})
ax = inertias.plot(x='n_clusters', y='inertia')
plt.xlabel('Number of clusters(k)')
plt.ylabel('Average Within-Cluster Squared Distances')
```

```
plt.ylim((0, 1.1 * inertias.inertia.max()))
ax.legend().set_visible(False)
```

In evaluating how many clusters to retain, perhaps the most important test is this: how likely are the clusters to be replicated on new data? Are the clusters interpretable, and do they relate to a general characteristic of the data, or do they just reflect a specific instance? You can assess this, in part, using cross-validation; see "Cross-Validation" on page 155.

In general, there is no single rule that will reliably guide how many clusters to produce.

> There are several more formal ways to determine the number of clusters based on statistical or information theory. For example, Robert Tibshirani, Guenther Walther, and Trevor Hastie propose a "gap" statistic (*https://oreil.ly/d-N3_*) based on statistical theory to identify the elbow. For most applications, a theoretical approach is probably not necessary, or even appropriate.

Key Ideas

- The number of desired clusters, *K*, is chosen by the user.
- The algorithm develops clusters by iteratively assigning records to the nearest cluster mean until cluster assignments do not change.
- Practical considerations usually dominate the choice of *K*; there is no statistically determined optimal number of clusters.

Hierarchical Clustering

Hierarchical clustering is an alternative to *K*-means that can yield very different clusters. Hierarchical clustering allows the user to visualize the effect of specifying different numbers of clusters. It is more sensitive in discovering outlying or aberrant groups or records. Hierarchical clustering also lends itself to an intuitive graphical display, leading to easier interpretation of the clusters.

> **Key Terms for Hierarchical Clustering**
>
> *Dendrogram*
> A visual representation of the records and the hierarchy of clusters to which they belong.
>
> *Distance*
> A measure of how close one *record* is to another.
>
> *Dissimilarity*
> A measure of how close one *cluster* is to another.

Hierarchical clustering's flexibility comes with a cost, and hierarchical clustering does not scale well to large data sets with millions of records. For even modest-sized data with just tens of thousands of records, hierarchical clustering can require intensive computing resources. Indeed, most of the applications of hierarchical clustering are focused on relatively small data sets.

A Simple Example

Hierarchical clustering works on a data set with n records and p variables and is based on two basic building blocks:

- A distance metric $d_{i,j}$ to measure the distance between two records i and j.
- A dissimilarity metric $D_{A,B}$ to measure the difference between two clusters A and B based on the distances $d_{i,j}$ between the members of each cluster.

For applications involving numeric data, the most importance choice is the dissimilarity metric. Hierarchical clustering starts by setting each record as its own cluster and iterates to combine the least dissimilar clusters.

In *R*, the `hclust` function can be used to perform hierarchical clustering. One big difference with `hclust` versus `kmeans` is that it operates on the pairwise distances $d_{i,j}$ rather than the data itself. You can compute these using the `dist` function. For example, the following applies hierarchical clustering to the stock returns for a set of companies:

```
syms1 <- c('GOOGL', 'AMZN', 'AAPL', 'MSFT', 'CSCO', 'INTC', 'CVX', 'XOM', 'SLB',
           'COP', 'JPM', 'WFC', 'USB', 'AXP', 'WMT', 'TGT', 'HD', 'COST')
# take transpose: to cluster companies, we need the stocks along the rows
df <- t(sp500_px[row.names(sp500_px) >= '2011-01-01', syms1])
d <- dist(df)
hcl <- hclust(d)
```

Clustering algorithms will cluster the records (rows) of a data frame. Since we want to cluster the companies, we need to *transpose* (t) the data frame and put the stocks along the rows and the dates along the columns.

The scipy package offers a number of different methods for hierarchical clustering in the scipy.cluster.hierarchy module. Here we use the linkage function with the "complete" method:

```
syms1 = ['AAPL', 'AMZN', 'AXP', 'COP', 'COST', 'CSCO', 'CVX', 'GOOGL', 'HD',
         'INTC', 'JPM', 'MSFT', 'SLB', 'TGT', 'USB', 'WFC', 'WMT', 'XOM']
df = sp500_px.loc[sp500_px.index >= '2011-01-01', syms1].transpose()

Z = linkage(df, method='complete')
```

The Dendrogram

Hierarchical clustering lends itself to a natural graphical display as a tree, referred to as a *dendrogram*. The name comes from the Greek words *dendro* (tree) and *gramma* (drawing). In *R*, you can easily produce this using the plot command:

```
plot(hcl)
```

We can use the dendrogram method to plot the result of the linkage function in *Python*:

```
fig, ax = plt.subplots(figsize=(5, 5))
dendrogram(Z, labels=df.index, ax=ax, color_threshold=0)
plt.xticks(rotation=90)
ax.set_ylabel('distance')
```

The result is shown in Figure 7-8 (note that we are now plotting companies that are similar to one another, not days). The leaves of the tree correspond to the records. The length of the branch in the tree indicates the degree of dissimilarity between corresponding clusters. The returns for Google and Amazon are quite dissimilar to one another and to the returns for the other stocks. The oil stocks (SLB, CVX, XOM, COP) are in their own cluster, Apple (AAPL) is by itself, and the rest are similar to one another.

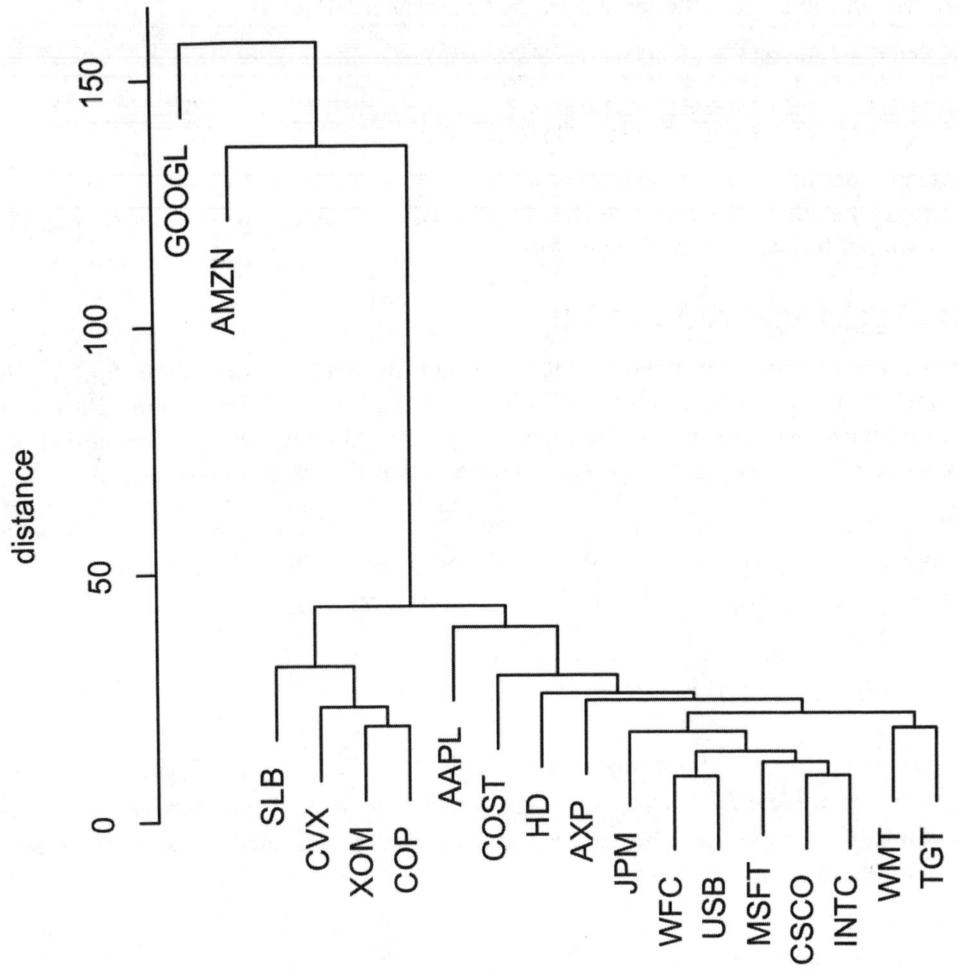

Figure 7-8. A dendrogram of stocks

In contrast to *K*-means, it is not necessary to prespecify the number of clusters. Graphically, you can identify different numbers of clusters with a horizontal line that slides up or down; a cluster is defined wherever the horizontal line intersects the vertical lines. To extract a specific number of clusters, you can use the `cutree` function:

```
cutree(hcl, k=4)
GOOGL  AMZN  AAPL  MSFT  CSCO  INTC   CVX   XOM   SLB   COP   JPM   WFC
    1     2     3     3     3     3     4     4     4     4     3     3
  USB   AXP   WMT   TGT    HD  COST
    3     3     3     3     3     3
```

In *Python*, you achieve the same with the `fcluster` method:

```
memb = fcluster(Z, 4, criterion='maxclust')
memb = pd.Series(memb, index=df.index)
for key, item in memb.groupby(memb):
    print(f"{key} : {', '.join(item.index)}")
```

The number of clusters to extract is set to 4, and you can see that Google and Amazon each belong to their own cluster. The oil stocks all belong to another cluster. The remaining stocks are in the fourth cluster.

The Agglomerative Algorithm

The main algorithm for hierarchical clustering is the *agglomerative* algorithm, which iteratively merges similar clusters. The agglomerative algorithm begins with each record constituting its own single-record cluster and then builds up larger and larger clusters. The first step is to calculate distances between all pairs of records.

For each pair of records $\left(x_1, x_2, ..., x_p\right)$ and $\left(y_1, y_2, ..., y_p\right)$, we measure the distance between the two records, $d_{x, y}$, using a distance metric (see "Distance Metrics" on page 241). For example, we can use Euclidian distance:

$$d(x, y) = \sqrt{(x_1 - y_1)^2 + (x_2 - y_2)^2 + \cdots + \left(x_p - y_p\right)^2}$$

We now turn to inter-cluster distance. Consider two clusters A and B, each with a distinctive set of records, $A = \left(a_1, a_2, ..., a_m\right)$ and $B = \left(b_1, b_2, ..., b_q\right)$. We can measure the dissimilarity between the clusters $D(A, B)$ by using the distances between the members of A and the members of B.

One measure of dissimilarity is the *complete-linkage* method, which is the maximum distance across all pairs of records between A and B:

$$D(A, B) = \max d\left(a_i, b_j\right) \text{ for all pairs } i, j$$

This defines the dissimilarity as the biggest difference between all pairs.

The main steps of the agglomerative algorithm are:

1. Create an initial set of clusters with each cluster consisting of a single record for all records in the data.
2. Compute the dissimilarity $D(C_k, C_\ell)$ between all pairs of clusters k, ℓ.
3. Merge the two clusters C_k and C_ℓ that are least dissimilar as measured by $D(C_k, C_\ell)$.
4. If we have more than one cluster remaining, return to step 2. Otherwise, we are done.

Measures of Dissimilarity

There are four common measures of dissimilarity: *complete linkage*, *single linkage*, *average linkage*, and *minimum variance*. These (plus other measures) are all supported by most hierarchical clustering software, including `hclust` and `linkage`. The complete linkage method defined earlier tends to produce clusters with members that are similar. The single linkage method is the minimum distance between the records in two clusters:

$$D(A, B) = \min d(a_i, b_j) \text{ for all pairs } i, j$$

This is a "greedy" method and produces clusters that can contain quite disparate elements. The average linkage method is the average of all distance pairs and represents a compromise between the single and complete linkage methods. Finally, the minimum variance method, also referred to as *Ward's* method, is similar to *K*-means since it minimizes the within-cluster sum of squares (see "K-Means Clustering" on page 294).

Figure 7-9 applies hierarchical clustering using the four measures to the ExxonMobil and Chevron stock returns. For each measure, four clusters are retained.

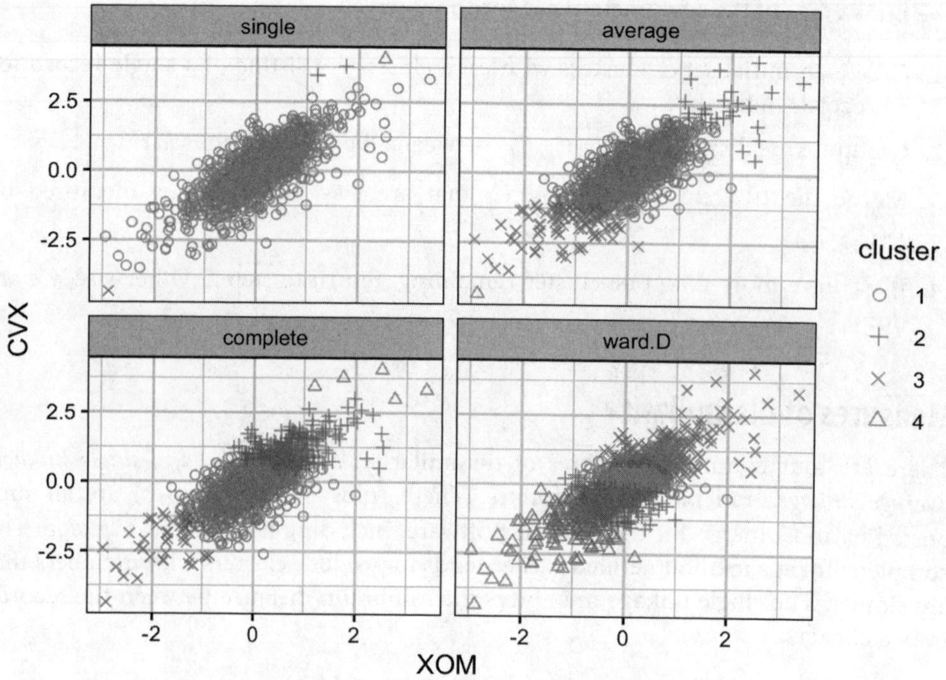

Figure 7-9. A comparison of measures of dissimilarity applied to stock data

The results are strikingly different: the single linkage measure assigns almost all of the points to a single cluster. Except for the minimum variance method (*R*: `Ward.D`; *Python*: `ward`), all measures end up with at least one cluster with just a few outlying points. The minimum variance method is most similar to the *K*-means cluster; compare with Figure 7-5.

Key Ideas

- Hierarchical clustering starts with every record in its own cluster.
- Progressively, clusters are joined to nearby clusters until all records belong to a single cluster (the agglomerative algorithm).
- The agglomeration history is retained and plotted, and the user (without specifying the number of clusters beforehand) can visualize the number and structure of clusters at different stages.
- Inter-cluster distances are computed in different ways, all relying on the set of all inter-record distances.

Model-Based Clustering

Clustering methods such as hierarchical clustering and *K*-means are based on heuristics and rely primarily on finding clusters whose members are close to one another, as measured directly with the data (no probability model involved). In the past 20 years, significant effort has been devoted to developing *model-based clustering* methods. Adrian Raftery and other researchers at the University of Washington made critical contributions to model-based clustering, including both theory and software. The techniques are grounded in statistical theory and provide more rigorous ways to determine the nature and number of clusters. They could be used, for example, in cases where there might be one group of records that are similar to one another but not necessarily close to one another (e.g., tech stocks with high variance of returns), and another group of records that are similar and also close (e.g., utility stocks with low variance).

Multivariate Normal Distribution

The most widely used model-based clustering methods rest on the *multivariate normal* distribution. The multivariate normal distribution is a generalization of the normal distribution to a set of p variables $X_1, X_2, ..., X_p$. The distribution is defined by a set of means $\mu = \mu_1, \mu_2, ..., \mu_{\mathbf{p}}$ and a covariance matrix Σ. The covariance matrix is a measure of how the variables correlate with each other (see "Covariance Matrix" on page 202 for details on the covariance). The covariance matrix Σ consists of p variances $\sigma_1^2, \sigma_2^2, ..., \sigma_p^2$ and covariances $\sigma_{i,j}$ for all pairs of variables $i \neq j$. With the variables put along the rows and duplicated along the columns, the matrix looks like this:

$$\Sigma = \begin{bmatrix} \sigma_1^2 & \sigma_{1,2} & \cdots & \sigma_{1,p} \\ \sigma_{2,1} & \sigma_2^2 & \cdots & \sigma_{2,p} \\ \vdots & \vdots & \ddots & \vdots \\ \sigma_{p,1} & \sigma_{p,2}^2 & \cdots & \sigma_p^2 \end{bmatrix}$$

Note that the covariance matrix is symmetric around the diagonal from upper left to lower right. Since $\sigma_{i,j} = \sigma_{j,i}$, there are only $(p \times (p-1))/2$ covariance terms. In total, the covariance matrix has $(p \times (p-1))/2 + p$ parameters. The distribution is denoted by:

$$\left(X_1, X_2, ..., X_p\right) \sim N_p(\mu, \Sigma)$$

This is a symbolic way of saying that the variables are all normally distributed, and the overall distribution is fully described by the vector of variable means and the covariance matrix.

Figure 7-10 shows the probability contours for a multivariate normal distribution for two variables X and Y (the 0.5 probability contour, for example, contains 50% of the distribution).

The means are $\mu_x = 0.5$ and $\mu_y = -0.5$, and the covariance matrix is:

$$\Sigma = \begin{bmatrix} 1 & 1 \\ 1 & 2 \end{bmatrix}$$

Since the covariance σ_{xy} is positive, X and Y are positively correlated.

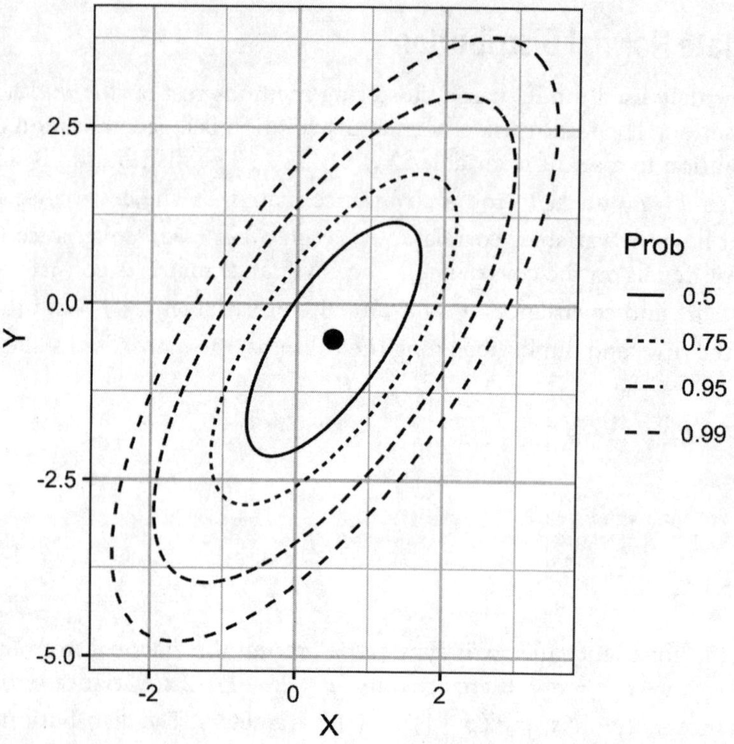

Figure 7-10. Probability contours for a two-dimensional normal distribution

Mixtures of Normals

The key idea behind model-based clustering is that each record is assumed to be distributed as one of K multivariate normal distributions, where K is the number of clusters. Each distribution has a different mean μ and covariance matrix Σ. For example, if you have two variables, X and Y, then each row (X_i, Y_i) is modeled as having been sampled from one of K multivariate normal distributions $N(\mu_1, \Sigma_1), N(\mu_2, \Sigma_2), ..., N(\mu_K, \Sigma_K)$.

R has a very rich package for model-based clustering called `mclust`, originally developed by Chris Fraley and Adrian Raftery. With this package, we can apply model-based clustering to the stock return data we previously analyzed using *K*-means and hierarchical clustering:

```
> library(mclust)
> df <- sp500_px[row.names(sp500_px) >= '2011-01-01', c('XOM', 'CVX')]
> mcl <- Mclust(df)
> summary(mcl)
Mclust VEE (ellipsoidal, equal shape and orientation) model with 2 components:


 log.likelihood    n df       BIC       ICL
      -2255.134 1131  9 -4573.546 -5076.856

Clustering table:
  1   2
963 168
```

`scikit-learn` has the `sklearn.mixture.GaussianMixture` class for model-based clustering:

```
df = sp500_px.loc[sp500_px.index >= '2011-01-01', ['XOM', 'CVX']]
mclust = GaussianMixture(n_components=2).fit(df)
mclust.bic(df)
```

If you execute this code, you will notice that the computation takes significantly longer than other procedures. Extracting the cluster assignments using the `predict` function, we can visualize the clusters:

```
cluster <- factor(predict(mcl)$classification)
ggplot(data=df, aes(x=XOM, y=CVX, color=cluster, shape=cluster)) +
  geom_point(alpha=.8)
```

Here is the *Python* code to create a similar figure:

```
fig, ax = plt.subplots(figsize=(4, 4))
colors = [f'C{c}' for c in mclust.predict(df)]
df.plot.scatter(x='XOM', y='CVX', c=colors, alpha=0.5, ax=ax)
ax.set_xlim(-3, 3)
ax.set_ylim(-3, 3)
```

The resulting plot is shown in Figure 7-11. There are two clusters: one cluster in the middle of the data, and a second cluster in the outer edge of the data. This is very different from the clusters obtained using *K*-means (Figure 7-5) and hierarchical clustering (Figure 7-9), which find clusters that are compact.

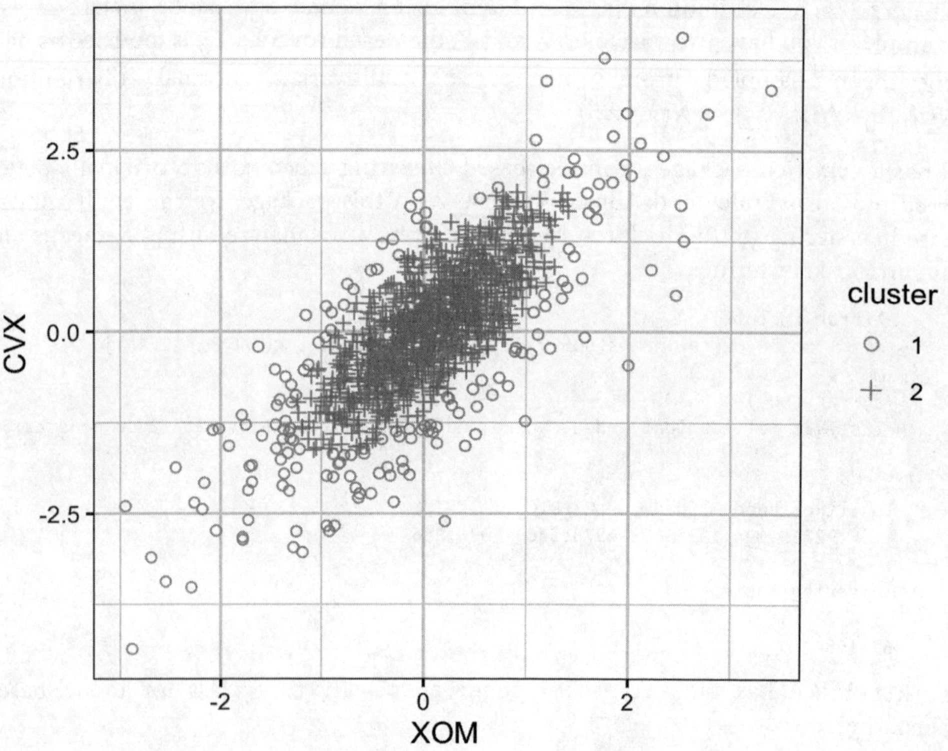

Figure 7-11. Two clusters are obtained for stock return data using `mclust`

You can extract the parameters to the normal distributions using the `summary` function:

```
> summary(mcl, parameters=TRUE)$mean
          [,1]        [,2]
XOM 0.05783847 -0.04374944
CVX 0.07363239 -0.21175715
> summary(mcl, parameters=TRUE)$variance
, , 1
          XOM       CVX
XOM 0.3002049 0.3060989
CVX 0.3060989 0.5496727
, , 2

         XOM      CVX
XOM 1.046318 1.066860
CVX 1.066860 1.915799
```

In *Python*, you get this information from the `means_` and `covariances_` properties of the result:

```
print('Mean')
print(mclust.means_)
print('Covariances')
print(mclust.covariances_)
```

The distributions have similar means and correlations, but the second distribution has much larger variances and covariances. Due to the randomness of the algorithm, results can vary slightly between different runs.

The clusters from `mclust` may seem surprising, but in fact, they illustrate the statistical nature of the method. The goal of model-based clustering is to find the best-fitting set of multivariate normal distributions. The stock data appears to have a normal-looking shape: see the contours of Figure 7-10. In fact, though, stock returns have a longer-tailed distribution than a normal distribution. To handle this, `mclust` fits a distribution to the bulk of the data but then fits a second distribution with a bigger variance.

Selecting the Number of Clusters

Unlike *K*-means and hierarchical clustering, `mclust` automatically selects the number of clusters in *R* (in this case, two). It does this by choosing the number of clusters for which the *Bayesian Information Criteria* (*BIC*) has the largest value (BIC is similar to AIC; see "Model Selection and Stepwise Regression" on page 156). BIC works by selecting the best-fitting model with a penalty for the number of parameters in the model. In the case of model-based clustering, adding more clusters will always improve the fit at the expense of introducing additional parameters in the model.

> Note that in most cases BIC is usually minimized. The authors of the `mclust` package decided to define BIC to have the opposite sign to make interpretation of plots easier.

`mclust` fits 14 different models with increasing number of components and chooses an optimal model automatically. You can plot the BIC values of these models using a function in `mclust`:

```
plot(mcl, what='BIC', ask=FALSE)
```

The number of clusters—or number of different multivariate normal models (components)—is shown on the x-axis (see Figure 7-12).

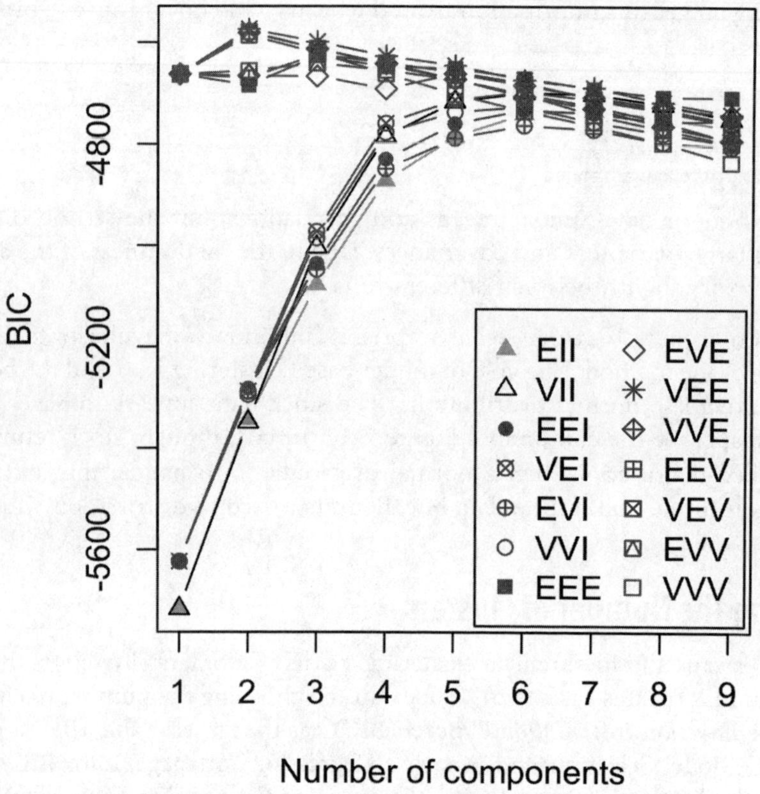

Figure 7-12. BIC values for 14 models of the stock return data with increasing numbers of components

The `GaussianMixture` implementation on the other hand will not try out various combinations. As shown here, it is straightforward to run multiple combinations using *Python*. This implementation defines BIC as usual. Therefore, the calculated BIC value will be positive, and we need to minimize it.

```
results = []
covariance_types = ['full', 'tied', 'diag', 'spherical']
for n_components in range(1, 9):
    for covariance_type in covariance_types:
        mclust = GaussianMixture(n_components=n_components, warm_start=True,
                                 covariance_type=covariance_type) ❶
        mclust.fit(df)
        results.append({
            'bic': mclust.bic(df),
            'n_components': n_components,
            'covariance_type': covariance_type,
        })
```

```
results = pd.DataFrame(results)

colors = ['C0', 'C1', 'C2', 'C3']
styles = ['C0-','C1:','C0-.', 'C1--']

fig, ax = plt.subplots(figsize=(4, 4))
for i, covariance_type in enumerate(covariance_types):
    subset = results.loc[results.covariance_type == covariance_type, :]
    subset.plot(x='n_components', y='bic', ax=ax, label=covariance_type,
                kind='line', style=styles[i])
```

❶ With the `warm_start` argument, the calculation will reuse information from the previous fit. This will speed up the convergence of subsequent calculations.

This plot is similar to the elbow plot used to identify the number of clusters to choose for *K*-means, except the value being plotted is BIC instead of percent of variance explained (see Figure 7-7). One big difference is that instead of one line, `mclust` shows 14 different lines! This is because `mclust` is actually fitting 14 different models for each cluster size, and ultimately it chooses the best-fitting model. `GaussianMixture` implements fewer approaches, so the number of lines will be only four.

Why does `mclust` fit so many models to determine the best set of multivariate normals? It's because there are different ways to parameterize the covariance matrix Σ for fitting a model. For the most part, you do not need to worry about the details of the models and can simply use the model chosen by `mclust`. In this example, according to BIC, three different models (called VEE, VEV, and VVE) give the best fit using two components.

> Model-based clustering is a rich and rapidly developing area of study, and the coverage in this text spans only a small part of the field. Indeed, the `mclust` help file is currently 154 pages long. Navigating the nuances of model-based clustering is probably more effort than is needed for most problems encountered by data scientists.

Model-based clustering techniques do have some limitations. The methods require an underlying assumption of a model for the data, and the cluster results are very dependent on that assumption. The computations requirements are higher than even hierarchical clustering, making it difficult to scale to large data. Finally, the algorithm is more sophisticated and less accessible than that of other methods.

Key Ideas

- Clusters are assumed to derive from different data-generating processes with different probability distributions.
- Different models are fit, assuming different numbers of (typically normal) distributions.
- The method chooses the model (and the associated number of clusters) that fits the data well without using too many parameters (i.e., overfitting).

Further Reading

For more detail on model-based clustering, see the `mclust` (*https://oreil.ly/bHDvR*) and `GaussianMixture` (*https://oreil.ly/GaVVv*) documentation.

Scaling and Categorical Variables

Unsupervised learning techniques generally require that the data be appropriately scaled. This is different from many of the techniques for regression and classification in which scaling is not important (an exception is *K*-Nearest Neighbors; see "K-Nearest Neighbors" on page 238).

Key Terms for Scaling Data

Scaling
: Squashing or expanding data, usually to bring multiple variables to the same scale.

Normalization
: One method of scaling—subtracting the mean and dividing by the standard deviation.

  Synonym
  : Standardization

Gower's distance
: A scaling algorithm applied to mixed numeric and categorical data to bring all variables to a 0–1 range.

For example, with the personal loan data, the variables have widely different units and magnitude. Some variables have relatively small values (e.g., number of years employed), while others have very large values (e.g., loan amount in dollars). If the data is not scaled, then the PCA, *K*-means, and other clustering methods will be dominated by the variables with large values and ignore the variables with small values.

Categorical data can pose a special problem for some clustering procedures. As with *K*-Nearest Neighbors, unordered factor variables are generally converted to a set of binary (0/1) variables using one hot encoding (see "One Hot Encoder" on page 242). Not only are the binary variables likely on a different scale from other data, but the fact that binary variables have only two values can prove problematic with techniques such as PCA and *K*-means.

Scaling the Variables

Variables with very different scale and units need to be normalized appropriately before you apply a clustering procedure. For example, let's apply `kmeans` to a set of data of loan defaults without normalizing:

```
defaults <- loan_data[loan_data$outcome=='default',]
df <- defaults[, c('loan_amnt', 'annual_inc', 'revol_bal', 'open_acc',
                   'dti', 'revol_util')]
km <- kmeans(df, centers=4, nstart=10)
centers <- data.frame(size=km$size, km$centers)
round(centers, digits=2)

   size loan_amnt annual_inc revol_bal open_acc   dti revol_util
1    52  22570.19  489783.40  85161.35    13.33  6.91      59.65
2  1192  21856.38  165473.54  38935.88    12.61 13.48      63.67
3 13902  10606.48   42500.30  10280.52     9.59 17.71      58.11
4  7525  18282.25   83458.11  19653.82    11.66 16.77      62.27
```

Here is the corresponding *Python* code:

```
defaults = loan_data.loc[loan_data['outcome'] == 'default',]
columns = ['loan_amnt', 'annual_inc', 'revol_bal', 'open_acc',
           'dti', 'revol_util']

df = defaults[columns]
kmeans = KMeans(n_clusters=4, random_state=1).fit(df)
counts = Counter(kmeans.labels_)

centers = pd.DataFrame(kmeans.cluster_centers_, columns=columns)
centers['size'] = [counts[i] for i in range(4)]
centers
```

The variables `annual_inc` and `revol_bal` dominate the clusters, and the clusters have very different sizes. Cluster 1 has only 52 members with comparatively high income and revolving credit balance.

A common approach to scaling the variables is to convert them to *z*-scores by subtracting the mean and dividing by the standard deviation. This is termed *standardization* or *normalization* (see "Standardization (Normalization, z-Scores)" on page 243 for more discussion about using *z*-scores):

$$z = \frac{x - \bar{x}}{s}$$

See what happens to the clusters when `kmeans` is applied to the normalized data:

```
df0 <- scale(df)
km0 <- kmeans(df0, centers=4, nstart=10)
centers0 <- scale(km0$centers, center=FALSE,
                  scale=1 / attr(df0, 'scaled:scale'))
centers0 <- scale(centers0, center=-attr(df0, 'scaled:center'), scale=FALSE)
centers0 <- data.frame(size=km0$size, centers0)
round(centers0, digits=2)

  size loan_amnt annual_inc revol_bal open_acc   dti revol_util
1 7355  10467.65   51134.87  11523.31     7.48 15.78      77.73
2 5309  10363.43   53523.09   6038.26     8.68 11.32      30.70
3 3713  25894.07  116185.91  32797.67    12.41 16.22      66.14
4 6294  13361.61   55596.65  16375.27    14.25 24.23      59.61
```

In *Python*, we can use `scikit-learn`'s `StandardScaler`. The `inverse_transform` method allows converting the cluster centers back to the original scale:

```
scaler = preprocessing.StandardScaler()
df0 = scaler.fit_transform(df * 1.0)

kmeans = KMeans(n_clusters=4, random_state=1).fit(df0)
counts = Counter(kmeans.labels_)

centers = pd.DataFrame(scaler.inverse_transform(kmeans.cluster_centers_),
                       columns=columns)
centers['size'] = [counts[i] for i in range(4)]
centers
```

The cluster sizes are more balanced, and the clusters are not dominated by `annual_inc` and `revol_bal`, revealing more interesting structure in the data. Note that the centers are rescaled to the original units in the preceding code. If we had left them unscaled, the resulting values would be in terms of *z*-scores and would therefore be less interpretable.

> Scaling is also important for PCA. Using the *z*-scores is equivalent to using the correlation matrix (see "Correlation" on page 30) instead of the covariance matrix in computing the principal components. Software to compute PCA usually has an option to use the correlation matrix (in *R*, the `princomp` function has the argument `cor`).

Dominant Variables

Even in cases where the variables are measured on the same scale and accurately reflect relative importance (e.g., movement to stock prices), it can sometimes be useful to rescale the variables.

Suppose we add Google (GOOGL) and Amazon (AMZN) to the analysis in "Interpreting Principal Components" on page 289. We see how this is done in *R* below:

```
syms <- c('GOOGL', 'AMZN', 'AAPL', 'MSFT', 'CSCO', 'INTC', 'CVX', 'XOM',
          'SLB', 'COP', 'JPM', 'WFC', 'USB', 'AXP', 'WMT', 'TGT', 'HD', 'COST')
top_sp1 <- sp500_px[row.names(sp500_px) >= '2005-01-01', syms]
sp_pca1 <- princomp(top_sp1)
screeplot(sp_pca1)
```

In *Python*, we get the screeplot as follows:

```
syms = ['GOOGL', 'AMZN', 'AAPL', 'MSFT', 'CSCO', 'INTC', 'CVX', 'XOM',
        'SLB', 'COP', 'JPM', 'WFC', 'USB', 'AXP', 'WMT', 'TGT', 'HD', 'COST']
top_sp1 = sp500_px.loc[sp500_px.index >= '2005-01-01', syms]

sp_pca1 = PCA()
sp_pca1.fit(top_sp1)

explained_variance = pd.DataFrame(sp_pca1.explained_variance_)
ax = explained_variance.head(10).plot.bar(legend=False, figsize=(4, 4))
ax.set_xlabel('Component')
```

The screeplot displays the variances for the top principal components. In this case, the screeplot in Figure 7-13 reveals that the variances of the first and second components are much larger than the others. This often indicates that one or two variables dominate the loadings. This is, indeed, the case in this example:

```
round(sp_pca1$loadings[,1:2], 3)
      Comp.1 Comp.2
GOOGL  0.781  0.609
AMZN   0.593 -0.792
AAPL   0.078  0.004
MSFT   0.029  0.002
CSCO   0.017 -0.001
INTC   0.020 -0.001
CVX    0.068 -0.021
XOM    0.053 -0.005
...
```

In *Python*, we use the following:

```
loadings = pd.DataFrame(sp_pca1.components_[0:2, :], columns=top_sp1.columns)
loadings.transpose()
```

The first two principal components are almost completely dominated by GOOGL and AMZN. This is because the stock price movements of GOOGL and AMZN dominate the variability.

To handle this situation, you can either include them as is, rescale the variables (see "Scaling the Variables" on page 319), or exclude the dominant variables from the analysis and handle them separately. There is no "correct" approach, and the treatment depends on the application.

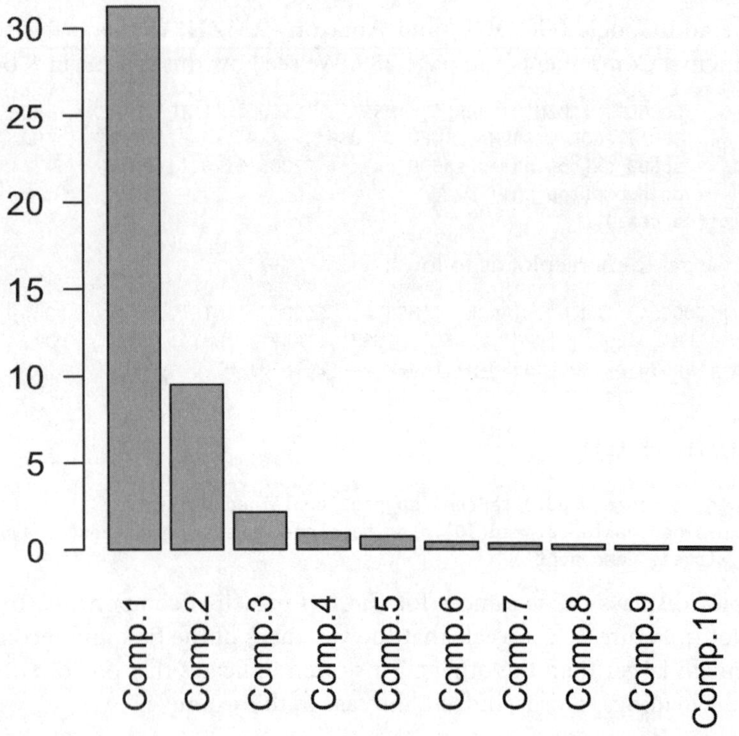

Figure 7-13. A screeplot for a PCA of top stocks from the S&P 500, including GOOGL and AMZN

Categorical Data and Gower's Distance

In the case of categorical data, you must convert it to numeric data, either by ranking (for an ordered factor) or by encoding as a set of binary (dummy) variables. If the data consists of mixed continuous and binary variables, you will usually want to scale the variables so that the ranges are similar; see "Scaling the Variables" on page 319. One popular method is to use *Gower's distance*.

The basic idea behind Gower's distance is to apply a different distance metric to each variable depending on the type of data:

- For numeric variables and ordered factors, distance is calculated as the absolute value of the difference between two records (*Manhattan distance*).

- For categorical variables, the distance is 1 if the categories between two records are different, and the distance is 0 if the categories are the same.

Gower's distance is computed as follows:

1. Compute the distance $d_{i, j}$ for all pairs of variables i and j for each record.
2. Scale each pair $d_{i, j}$ so the minimum is 0 and the maximum is 1.
3. Add the pairwise scaled distances between variables together, using either a simple or a weighted mean, to create the distance matrix.

To illustrate Gower's distance, take a few rows from the loan data in *R*:

```
> x <- loan_data[1:5, c('dti', 'payment_inc_ratio', 'home_', 'purpose_')]
> x
# A tibble: 5 × 4
    dti payment_inc_ratio   home            purpose
  <dbl>             <dbl> <fctr>             <fctr>
1  1.00           2.39320   RENT                car
2  5.55           4.57170    OWN     small_business
3 18.08           9.71600   RENT              other
4 10.08          12.21520   RENT debt_consolidation
5  7.06           3.90888   RENT              other
```

The function `daisy` in the `cluster` package in *R* can be used to compute Gower's distance:

```
library(cluster)
daisy(x, metric='gower')
Dissimilarities :
          1         2         3         4
2 0.6220479
3 0.6863877 0.8143398
4 0.6329040 0.7608561 0.4307083
5 0.3772789 0.5389727 0.3091088 0.5056250

Metric :  mixed ;  Types = I, I, N, N
Number of objects : 5
```

At the moment of this writing, Gower's distance is not available in any of the popular Python packages. However, activities are ongoing to include it in `scikit-learn`. We will update the accompanying source code once the implementation is released.

All distances are between 0 and 1. The pair of records with the biggest distance is 2 and 3: neither has the same values for `home` and `purpose`, and they have very different levels of `dti` (debt-to-income) and `payment_inc_ratio`. Records 3 and 5 have the smallest distance because they share the same values for `home` and `purpose`.

You can pass the Gower's distance matrix calculated from `daisy` to `hclust` for hierarchical clustering (see "Hierarchical Clustering" on page 304):

```
df <- defaults[sample(nrow(defaults), 250),
                c('dti', 'payment_inc_ratio', 'home', 'purpose')]
d = daisy(df, metric='gower')
hcl <- hclust(d)
dnd <- as.dendrogram(hcl)
plot(dnd, leaflab='none')
```

The resulting dendrogram is shown in Figure 7-14. The individual records are not distinguishable on the x-axis, but we can cut the dendrogram horizontally at 0.5 and examine the records in one of the subtrees with this code:

```
dnd_cut <- cut(dnd, h=0.5)
df[labels(dnd_cut$lower[[1]]),]
        dti payment_inc_ratio home_           purpose_
44532 21.22           8.37694   OWN debt_consolidation
39826 22.59           6.22827   OWN debt_consolidation
13282 31.00           9.64200   OWN debt_consolidation
31510 26.21          11.94380   OWN debt_consolidation
6693  26.96           9.45600   OWN debt_consolidation
7356  25.81           9.39257   OWN debt_consolidation
9278  21.00          14.71850   OWN debt_consolidation
13520 29.00          18.86670   OWN debt_consolidation
14668 25.75          17.53440   OWN debt_consolidation
19975 22.70          17.12170   OWN debt_consolidation
23492 22.68          18.50250   OWN debt_consolidation
```

This subtree consists entirely of owners with a loan purpose labeled as "debt_consolidation." While strict separation is not true of all subtrees, this illustrates that the categorical variables tend to be grouped together in the clusters.

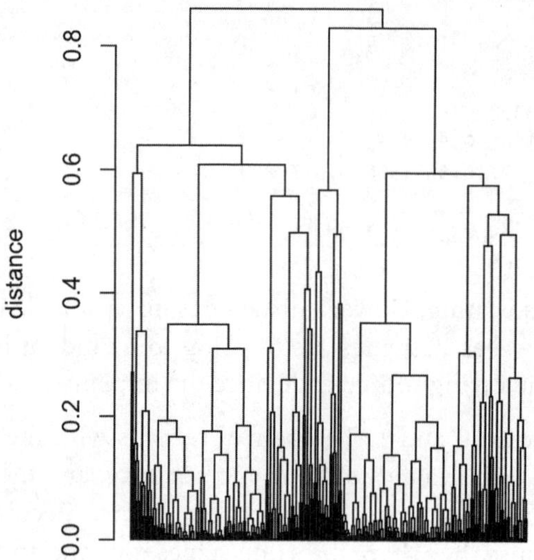

Figure 7-14. A dendrogram of `hclust` applied to a sample of loan default data with mixed variable types

Problems with Clustering Mixed Data

K-means and PCA are most appropriate for continuous variables. For smaller data sets, it is better to use hierarchical clustering with Gower's distance. In principle, there is no reason why *K*-means can't be applied to binary or categorical data. You would usually use the "one hot encoder" representation (see "One Hot Encoder" on page 242) to convert the categorical data to numeric values. In practice, however, using *K*-means and PCA with binary data can be difficult.

If the standard *z*-scores are used, the binary variables will dominate the definition of the clusters. This is because 0/1 variables take on only two values, and *K*-means can obtain a small within-cluster sum-of-squares by assigning all the records with a 0 or 1 to a single cluster. For example, apply `kmeans` to loan default data including factor variables `home` and `pub_rec_zero`, shown here in *R*:

```
df <- model.matrix(~ -1 + dti + payment_inc_ratio + home_ + pub_rec_zero,
                   data=defaults)
df0 <- scale(df)
km0 <- kmeans(df0, centers=4, nstart=10)
centers0 <- scale(km0$centers, center=FALSE,
                 scale=1/attr(df0, 'scaled:scale'))
round(scale(centers0, center=-attr(df0, 'scaled:center'), scale=FALSE), 2)

    dti payment_inc_ratio home_MORTGAGE home_OWN home_RENT pub_rec_zero
1 17.20              9.27          0.00        1      0.00         0.92
2 16.99              9.11          0.00        0      1.00         1.00
3 16.50              8.06          0.52        0      0.48         0.00
4 17.46              8.42          1.00        0      0.00         1.00
```

In *Python*:

```
columns = ['dti', 'payment_inc_ratio', 'home_', 'pub_rec_zero']
df = pd.get_dummies(defaults[columns])

scaler = preprocessing.StandardScaler()
df0 = scaler.fit_transform(df * 1.0)
kmeans = KMeans(n_clusters=4, random_state=1).fit(df0)
centers = pd.DataFrame(scaler.inverse_transform(kmeans.cluster_centers_),
                       columns=df.columns)
centers
```

The top four clusters are essentially proxies for the different levels of the factor variables. To avoid this behavior, you could scale the binary variables to have a smaller variance than other variables. Alternatively, for very large data sets, you could apply clustering to different subsets of data taking on specific categorical values. For example, you could apply clustering separately to those loans made to someone who has a mortgage, owns a home outright, or rents.

Key Ideas

- Variables measured on different scales need to be transformed to similar scales so that their impact on algorithms is not determined mainly by their scale.
- A common scaling method is normalization (standardization)—subtracting the mean and dividing by the standard deviation.
- Another method is Gower's distance, which scales all variables to the 0–1 range (it is often used with mixed numeric and categorical data).

Summary

For dimension reduction of numeric data, the main tools are either principal components analysis or *K*-means clustering. Both require attention to proper scaling of the data to ensure meaningful data reduction.

For clustering with highly structured data in which the clusters are well separated, all methods will likely produce a similar result. Each method offers its own advantage. *K*-means scales to very large data and is easily understood. Hierarchical clustering can be applied to mixed data types—numeric and categorical—and lends itself to an intuitive display (the dendrogram). Model-based clustering is founded on statistical theory and provides a more rigorous approach, as opposed to the heuristic methods. For very large data, however, *K*-means is the main method used.

With noisy data, such as the loan and stock data (and much of the data that a data scientist will face), the choice is more stark. *K*-means, hierarchical clustering, and especially model-based clustering all produce very different solutions. How should a data scientist proceed? Unfortunately, there is no simple rule of thumb to guide the choice. Ultimately, the method used will depend on the data size and the goal of the application.

Bibliography

[Baumer-2017] Baumer, Benjamin, Daniel Kaplan, and Nicholas Horton. *Modern Data Science with R*. Boca Raton, Fla.: Chapman & Hall/CRC Press, 2017.

[bokeh] Bokeh Development Team. "Bokeh: Python library for interactive visualization" (2014). *https://bokeh.pydata.org*.

[Deng-Wickham-2011] Deng, Henry, and Hadley Wickham. "Density Estimation in R." September 2011. *https://oreil.ly/-Ny_6*.

[Donoho-2015] Donoho, David. "50 Years of Data Science." September 18, 2015. *https://oreil.ly/kqFb0*.

[Duong-2001] Duong, Tarn. "An Introduction to Kernel Density Estimation." 2001. *https://oreil.ly/Z5A7W*.

[Few-2007] Few, Stephen. "Save the Pies for Dessert." *Visual Business Intelligence Newsletter*. Perceptual Edge. August 2007. *https://oreil.ly/_iGAL*.

[Freedman-2007] Freedman, David, Robert Pisani, and Roger Purves. *Statistics*. 4th ed. New York: W. W. Norton, 2007.

[Hintze-Nelson-1998] Hintze, Jerry L., and Ray D. Nelson. "Violin Plots: A Box Plot–Density Trace Synergism." *The American Statistician* 52, no. 2 (May 1998): 181–84.

[Galton-1886] Galton, Francis. "Regression Towards Mediocrity in Hereditary Stature." *The Journal of the Anthropological Institute of Great Britain and Ireland* 15 (1886): 246–63. *https://oreil.ly/DqoAk*.

[ggplot2] Wickham, Hadley. *ggplot2: Elegant Graphics for Data Analysis*. New York: Springer-Verlag New York, 2009. *https://oreil.ly/O92vC*.

[Hyndman-Fan-1996] Hyndman, Rob J., and Yanan Fan. "Sample Quantiles in Statistical Packages." *American Statistician* 50, no. 4 (1996): 361–65.

[lattice] Sarkar, Deepayan. *Lattice: Multivariate Data Visualization with R*. New York: Springer, 2008. *http://lmdvr.r-forge.r-project.org*.

[Legendre] Legendre, Adrien-Marie. *Nouvelle méthodes pour la détermination des orbites des comètes*. Paris: F. Didot, 1805. *https://oreil.ly/8FITJ*.

[NIST-Handbook-2012] "Measures of Skewness and Kurtosis." In *NIST/SEMATECH e-Handbook of Statistical Methods*. 2012. *https://oreil.ly/IAdHA*.

[R-base-2015] R Core Team. "R: A Language and Environment for Statistical Computing." R Foundation for Statistical Computing. 2015. *https://www.r-project.org*.

[Salsburg-2001] Salsburg, David. *The Lady Tasting Tea: How Statistics Revolutionized Science in the Twentieth Century*. New York: W. H. Freeman, 2001.

[seaborn] Waskom, Michael. "Seaborn: Statistical Data Visualization." 2015. *https://seaborn.pydata.org*.

[Trellis-Graphics] Becker, Richard A., William S.Cleveland, Ming-Jen Shyu, and Stephen P. Kaluzny. "A Tour of Trellis Graphics." April 15, 1996. *https://oreil.ly/LVnOV*.

[Tukey-1962] Tukey, John W. "The Future of Data Analysis." *The Annals of Mathematical Statistics* 33, no. 1 (1962): 1–67. *https://oreil.ly/qrYNW*.

[Tukey-1977] Tukey, John W. *Exploratory Data Analysis*. Reading, Mass.: Addison-Wesley, 1977.

[Tukey-1987] Tukey, John W. *The Collected Works of John W. Tukey*. Vol. 4, *Philosophy and Principles of Data Analysis: 1965–1986*, edited by Lyle V. Jones. Boca Raton, Fla.: Chapman & Hall/CRC Press, 1987.

[Zhang-Wang-2007] Zhang, Qi, and Wei Wang. "A Fast Algorithm for Approximate Quantiles in High Speed Data Streams." *19th International Conference on Scientific and Statistical Database Management (SSDBM 2007)*. Piscataway, NJ: IEEE, 2007. Also available at *https://oreil.ly/qShjk*.

Index

A

B

C

D

E

M

N

O

P

Q

R

S

T

U

V

W

X

Z

About the Authors

Peter Bruce founded and grew the Institute for Statistics Education at Statistics.com, which now offers about one hundred courses in statistics, roughly a third of which are aimed at the data scientist. In recruiting top authors as instructors and forging a marketing strategy to reach professional data scientists, Peter has developed both a broad view of the target market and his own expertise to reach it.

Andrew Bruce has over 30 years of experience in statistics and data science in academia, government, and business. He has a PhD in statistics from the University of Washington and has published numerous papers in refereed journals. He has developed statistical-based solutions to a wide range of problems faced by a variety of industries, from established financial firms to internet startups, and offers a deep understanding of the practice of data science.

Peter Gedeck has over 30 years of experience in scientific computing and data science. After 20 years as a computational chemist at Novartis, he now works as a senior data scientist at Collaborative Drug Discovery. He specializes in the development of machine learning algorithms to predict biological and physicochemical properties of drug candidates. Coauthor of *Data Mining for Business Analytics*, he earned a PhD in chemistry from the University of Erlangen-Nürnberg in Germany and studied mathematics at the Fernuniversität Hagen, Germany.

Colophon

The animal on the cover of *Practical Statistics for Data Scientists* is a lined shore crab (*Pachygrapsus crassipes*), also known as a striped shore crab. It is found along the coasts and beaches of the Pacific Ocean in North America, Central America, Korea, and Japan. These crustaceans live under rocks, in tidepools, and within crevices. They spend about half their time on land, and periodically return to the water to wet their gills.

The lined shore crab is named for the green stripes on its brown-black carapace. It has red claws and purple legs, which also have a striped or mottled pattern. The crab generally grows to be 3–5 centimeters in size; females are slightly smaller. Their eyes are on flexible stalks that can rotate to give them a full field of vision as they walk.

Crabs are omnivores, feeding primarily on algae but also on mollusks, worms, fungi, dead animals, and other crustaceans (depending on what is available). They moult many times as they grow to adulthood, taking in water to expand and crack open their old shell. Once this is achieved, they spend several difficult hours getting free, and then must hide until the new shell hardens.

Many of the animals on O'Reilly covers are endangered; all of them are important to the world.

The cover illustration is by Karen Montgomery, based on a black-and-white engraving from *Pictorial Museum of Animated Nature*. The cover fonts are Gilroy Semibold and Guardian Sans. The text font is Adobe Minion Pro; the heading font is Adobe Myriad Condensed; and the code font is Dalton Maag's Ubuntu Mono.

O'Reilly Media, Inc.介绍

O'Reilly以"分享创新知识、改变世界"为己任。40多年来我们一直向企业、个人提供成功必需之技能及思想，激励他们创新并做得更好。

O'Reilly业务的核心是独特的专家及创新者网络，他们通过我们分享知识。我们的在线学习（Online Learning）平台提供独家的直播培训、图书及视频，使客户更容易获取业务成功所需的专业知识。几十年来O'Reilly图书一直被视为学习开创未来之技术的权威资料。我们全年举办的诸多会议是活跃的技术聚会场所，来自各领域的专业人士在此建立联系，讨论最佳实践并发现可能影响技术行业未来的新趋势。

我们的客户渴望作出推动世界前进的创新，我们能祝您一臂之力。

业界评论

"O'Reilly Radar博客有口皆碑。"

——Wired

"O'Reilly凭借一系列（真希望当初我也想到了）非凡想法建立了数百万美元的业务。"

——Business 2.0

"O'Reilly Conference是聚集关键思想领袖的绝对典范。"

——CRN

"一本O'Reilly的书就代表一个有用、有前途、需要学习的主题。"

——Irish Times

"Tim是位特立独行的商人，他不光放眼于最长远、最广阔的视野并且切实地按照Yogi Berra的建议去做了：'如果你在路上遇到岔路口，走小路（岔路）。'回顾过去Tim似乎每一次都选择了小路，而且有几次都是一闪即逝的机会，尽管大路也不错。"

——Linux Journal